Out of the
Shadow of War

To Margaret, David, and Richard

Out of the Shadow of War

The German Connection with New Zealand in the Twentieth Century

Edited by
JAMES N. BADE

With the assistance of
JAMES BRAUND

Melbourne
OXFORD UNIVERSITY PRESS
Oxford Auckland New York

OXFORD UNIVERSITY PRESS NEW ZEALAND

Oxford New York
Athens Auckland Bangkok Bogotá
Buenos Aires Calcutta Cape Town Chennai
Dar es Salaam Delhi Florence Hong Kong Istanbul
Karachi Kuala Lumpur Madrid Melbourne
Mexico City Mumbai Nairobi Paris Port Moresby
São Paulo Singapore Taipei Tokyo Toronto Warsaw
and associated companies in
Berlin Ibadan

OXFORD is a trade mark of Oxford University Press

ISBN 019 558363 9

Copy-edited by Cathryn Game
Indexed by James Braund
Text designed by Derrick I. Stone Design
Cover designed by Anitra Blackford
Typeset by Derrick I. Stone Design
Printed through Bookpac Production Services, Singapore
Published by Oxford University Press
540 Great South Road, Greenlane, PO Box 11-149, Auckland,
New Zealand

Contents

Preface   vii
  James N. Bade

Part 1 In the shadow of war   1
  Introduction *James N. Bade*   3
  1   Germany and New Zealand at war *Ian McGibbon*   5
  2   Anti-German hysteria during World War I *Jean King*   19
  3   Refugees from Nazi Germany and Austria 1933–45   25
       Ann Beaglehole
  4   Count Felix von Luckner *James N. Bade*   37
  5   Major Geoffrey Bedding *Graeme Horne*   50

Part 2 The German connection in the arts   57
  Introduction *James N. Bade*   59
  6   Art, photography, the crafts, and
       German-speaking immigrants *Leonard Bell*   61
  7   Literary points of contact *James Braund*   77
  8   German influences on New Zealand music   90
       J.M. Thomson
  9   The film connection *Lauren Jackson*   95
  10   Karl Wolfskehl *Friedrich Voit*   106
  11   Maria Dronke *Peter Vere-Jones*   113
  12   Marie Vandewart Blaschke   118
       Maja Beutler and Kathryn Smits
  13   Margot Philips *Margaret Sutherland*   123
  14   Friedensreich Hundertwasser *Hansgerd Delbrück*   128

Part 3 The academic world   133
  Introduction *James N. Bade*   135
  15   George von Zedlitz *Nelson Wattie*   137
  16   Paul Hoffmann *Hansgerd Delbrück*   142
  17   Gerda Bell *Renate Koch*   147
  18   Werner Droescher *Norman Franke*   153
  19   Sir Karl Popper *Nelson Wattie*   157
  20   Wolfgang Rosenberg *Gerhard Träbing*   162
  21   Peter Munz *David Venables*   169

Part 4   ***The business and professional world***   175
    Introduction *James N. Bade*   177
    22   Joseph Kühtze *Axel Laurs*   180
    23   Willi Fels *James Braund*   186
    24   Ernst Plischke *Janet Paul*   192
    25   Georg Lemchen *David Schnellenberg*   199
    26   Peter Jacoby *Peter Russell*   204
    27   Erich Geiringer *Bevan Burgess*   208
    28   Arthur and Lisl Hilton *Margaret Sutherland*   214
    29   Gregory Riethmaier *James N. Bade*   218
    30   Denis Adam *Peter Russell*   224
    31   Sir Thomas Eichelbaum *Bill Sewell*   229

Part 5   ***The present-day German connection***   235
    Introduction *James N. Bade*   237
    32   Political and economic links since World War II   239
        Michael McBryde
    33   The image of New Zealand in German-speaking   245
        Europe *Gisela Holfter*
    34   The German winemakers *Rod Fisher*   251
    35   German immigrants and New Zealand politics   256
        Ray Miller
    36   German studies in New Zealand *Peter Oettli*   264

Contributors   275
Index   279

Preface

This volume is intended as a companion volume to *The German Connection: New Zealand and German-speaking Europe in the Nineteenth Century*, first published by Oxford University Press in 1993. From the beginning, it was evident that a volume on Germany and New Zealand in the twentieth century would be a complex undertaking, for there were three main areas to be covered, and each represented a challenge in itself: the two world wars, the huge contribution of the refugees from Nazi Europe, and the distinctive impact of the wave of German immigration since the 1970s. The most difficult area to cover proved to be the last. The fifth section of this book covers some aspects of recent German immigration, but the motivation of the new German arrivals and their impact on this country deserve more comprehensive evaluation. It is to be hoped that this present volume will serve as an impetus to further research.

The title 'Out of the Shadow of War' was chosen because it characterises the German–New Zealand relationship so well—whereas the two world wars dominated relations between the two countries in the first half of this century, relations in the second half of the twentieth century have moved steadily out of the shadow of war into the sunlight.

I would like to thank a number of people who have helped bring this volume to fruition: my research assistant, Dr James Braund, for so cheerfully taking on editorial assignments when the need arose and for the assiduous attention to detail with which he approached both his own and others' work; my 'Editorial Board' (students taking my 1997 MA and Stage III papers on the German connection with New Zealand in the twentieth century)—Rochelle Gebbie, Maria Lukanow, Rowena Baines, Brigitte Grant, Sabine Huth, Lauren Jackson, Edwina King, Callan Mantell, Natasha Prohl, and Caroline Schweder—for their eagerness to assist with research and verification of sources; the University of Auckland Research Committee, for funding research assistance in relation to this project; Janet Kelsey and Nes Ogden, of the Department of Germanic Languages and Literature of the University of Auckland, for valued secretarial assistance; Rex Brown, Honorary German Consul in Auckland, and Dr Ole Diehl, of the German Embassy in Wellington, for their support; Dr Linda Cassells, of Oxford University Press, for the enthusiasm with which she followed this project from its inception to its completion; and, not least, the contributors, for making this such an interesting volume.

I wish to acknowledge the generosity of the following in their support of this publication: Bayer New Zealand, Agfa New Zealand, Hamburg-Süd/Columbus Shipping Line, Lufthansa German Airlines, and the embassy of the Federal Republic of Germany, Wellington.

James N. Bade

Part 1

In the shadow of war

Introduction

JAMES N. BADE

New Zealand and Germany were at war for more than ten years of the twentieth century, but the lead-up to and the aftermath of the wars with Germany were such that relations between the two countries have until relatively recently remained in the shadow of these hostilities. As Ian McGibbon writes in his chapter on Germany and New Zealand at war, for a generation of New Zealanders, war and Germans were almost synonymous. No volume on the German connection with New Zealand can overlook the catastrophic effect that the world wars had on New Zealand. During World War I, whole communities were practically wiped out as the young men on whom the future of these communities depended were killed or injured in action. The atmosphere of distrust towards all things German that pervaded New Zealand at that time, as described in Jean King's chapter on anti-German hysteria, is in some ways understandable given the circumstances, although its more extreme forms must have been worrying to the wider community. It is difficult for us now to imagine the devastating effect that the regular lists of hundreds of New Zealand sons and husbands killed or injured had on their families. Someone had to take the blame, and New Zealand newspapers had no choice but to toe the patriotic British line. During World War II, as Ann Beaglehole ably demonstrates in her chapter, it was often the refugees from Nazi Germany, many of them Jewish, who settled in New Zealand in the 1930s and 1940s, who had to bear the brunt of anti-German sentiment.

The bitterness of the relationship between Germans and New Zealanders on the battlefield is well brought out by Ian McGibbon, and it would be irresponsible to maintain that the relationship between the two countries during the two world wars was ever other than acrimonious. But there were occasions when individuals transcended the barriers of hostility and were able to command the respect and indeed the affection of the citizens of the 'enemy' country. Two such cases, one from each war, and one from each side, are documented in this section. Count Felix von Luckner's story is a remarkable one considering the intensity of anti-German sentiment at that stage of World War I, but his daring escape from Motuihe Island, together with his gentlemanly treatment of those whom he took prisoner during his raiding activities in the Pacific, earned him the respect of many New Zealanders, and his return in 1938, at a time when Germany was once more in serious trouble on the international stage, did not seem to affect his folk hero status.

Major Geoffrey Bedding's intervention at the closing stages of World War II to save two German towns from destruction by invading American forces is no less astonishing, particularly when one bears in mind the very real risks that this entailed on all sides. His attitude of reconciliation at the end of the war somehow encapsulates the desire for positive cooperation that has characterised post-war German–New Zealand relations.

1

Germany and New Zealand at war

IAN McGIBBON

'Why are you New Zealanders here?' New Zealand Brigadier George Clifton was asked by Afrika Korps commander General Erwin Rommel shortly after being captured in 1942. 'This is a European war, not yours! Are you in it for the sport?'[1] Rommel's questions reflected a common perplexity among German troops who found themselves fighting against New Zealanders during two world wars in the first half of the twentieth century. Two countries, situated on opposite sides of the globe and with no apparent grievances against each other, spent more than ten years at war. Indeed, for a generation of New Zealanders, war and Germans were almost synonymous. More than three quarters of New Zealand's 28,000 dead in all foreign wars have fallen in combat with Germans on battlefields ranging from Belgium to Egypt. The Somme, Passchendaele, Crete, El Alamein, Cassino—all became bloody symbols of the German–New Zealand relationship during this troubled period.

New Zealand–German enmity was essentially a New Zealand initiative. To be sure, New Zealand found itself at war with Germany for the first time through no action of its own, but rather because of its international position as part of the British Empire. When King George V declared war on Germany on 4 August 1914, he did so on behalf of all his territories and dominions. But the conflict helped to precipitate constitutional changes within the British Empire, reflected in New Zealand's signature of the Treaty of Peace with Germany at Versailles on 28 June 1919 and its membership in its own right of the League of Nations. Twenty years later, when a new crisis arose between Germany and its former foes, New Zealand again acted in its own right, taking the deliberate step of declaring war on Germany and backdating its decision to the same moment as that of Britain.[2] New Zealand was therefore one of the first countries to be involved in World War II.

Whether formally declaring war or not, however, New Zealand determined the extent of the conflict between the two countries. On both occasions, it wholeheartedly supported the stand taken by the British Government and promised all possible material assistance to the imperial or Commonwealth coalition. Strategic considerations ensured that such assistance would entail the despatch of New Zealand personnel to the main theatres of the conflict, for there was no possibility of serious or sustained German attack on New Zealand itself in either 1914 or 1939. New Zealand, then, took the steps necessary to bring German and New Zealander into violent confrontation on battlefields far away from the South Pacific.

The alacrity with which New Zealand responded to these two crises was in part a reflection of imperial or Commonwealth solidarity. 'Where she goes, we go. Where she stands, we stand,' Prime Minister Michael Savage might have declared on 5 September 1939 in reference to New Zealand's decision to follow Britain into World War II.[3] But New Zealand's own interests were recognised to be at stake, and Germany was seen as a potential threat to them. Even before World War I New Zealand had viewed with unease Germany's penetration of the South Pacific and acquisition of colonies. Indeed, Germany had in the late nineteenth century been seen as thwarting New Zealand's ambitions in Samoa. But general defence considerations were of even more significance. Far distant from the centre of imperial power, New Zealand was increasingly conscious of the potential threat posed by Japan in its region. Anything that threatened Britain's capacity to project its power into the Pacific indirectly threatened New Zealand. Moreover, any threat to Britain itself or to the long sea routes between it and the South Pacific immediately brought into question New Zealand's economic viability, so heavily was New Zealand dependent on the British market for the sale of its produce. New Zealanders recognised that a British defeat would open the way to possible incorporation of their country in the German Empire—just as much of the British Empire had been acquired during peace settlements.

Early in the twentieth century, New Zealand concern was aroused by the challenge to the supremacy of the Royal Navy represented by Germany's decision to build a powerful battle fleet. When in 1909 it seemed that the Royal Navy was slipping behind in the naval arms race, New Zealand offered to pay for the construction of a battle-cruiser, HMS *New Zealand*. Partly because of these developments, and partly because of the alliance structure that emerged in the early years of the twentieth century, Germany was perceived as the British Empire's most likely enemy. As early as 1912, the commander of the New Zealand military forces, Major-General A.J. Godley, proposed that in the event of war New Zealand should despatch an expeditionary force to the main theatres of war in Europe.[4]

Similar impulses underlay New Zealand's approach in the 1930s, when a resurgent Germany again appeared to threaten British, and thereby indirectly New Zealand's, security. As Carl Berendsen, the influential head of the Prime Minister's Department, warned in 1938, the front line of New Zealand defence lay in Europe.[5] No less than in 1914, defeat for Britain, which was the linchpin of the British Commonwealth defence system, would leave New Zealand and Australia vulnerable to the increasingly aggressive Japanese, especially with the United States' isolationist stance offering little prospect of support from that quarter. Trade and economic questions were no less compelling than in 1914.

If self-interest provided a solid foundation for New Zealand's stance in both world wars, it was reinforced by emotion. In both instances, Germany, in New Zealand eyes, had embarked on an aggressive course by invading its neighbours: little Belgium in 1914 and hapless Poland in 1939. For New

Zealanders, whose newspapers were dominated by British news and comment, these events might have been in their own neighbourhood, so strongly did they abhor the German actions. Such feelings were enhanced by reports of German atrocities. In 1914, for example, Berendsen, then a junior civil servant, was appalled by Germany's apparent 'relapse into barbarism' demonstrated by its 'ruthless rape of Belgium'.[6] While some of the atrocity reports were undoubtedly inspired by Allied propaganda, all too many were true, as the number of Belgian and Polish victims testify. In the 1930s many New Zealanders watched with mounting anxiety the re-emergence of militarism in Germany and the excesses perpetrated by the Nazis. The government called for a strong stance to be adopted against Germany as Adolf Hitler set it off down the path to war once more. New Zealanders needed no convincing of Germany's culpability on 1 September 1939, and were unimpressed by German claims to be responding to a Polish attack. They were horrified by the ruthlessness with which Poland was subjugated.

Although well removed from the centre of conflict, the South Pacific was not exempt from German action in either world war. In World War I the existence of German colonies within the region provided an immediate focus of concern. One of New Zealand's first actions in 1914 was to raise and despatch, on 15 August, an expeditionary force to capture the wireless station in German Samoa. This was accomplished without any fighting on 29 August—the second German territory, after Togoland, to be taken by the Allies. New Zealand fulfilled a longstanding aspiration and after the war would retain control of the territory as a mandated territory under the League of Nations. German New Guinea was also rapidly occupied by the Australians in 1914, while Japan dealt with German colonies north of the equator. For a time New Zealand authorities were concerned by the possibility of the German Asiatic Squadron making a descent on the South Pacific, and the Territorials were called up to man the guns at the main ports. In the event, the German squadron stayed well to the north, although making a brief appearance at Apia in September. After crossing the Pacific and rounding Cape Horn, it was destroyed near the Falkland Islands by a British squadron in December 1914.

Route march of Samoa Expeditionary Force members at Noumea, 20 August 1914, *en route* to Samoa. *(Auckland War Memorial Museum)*

Not until 1917 did the German Navy make its presence felt in New Zealand waters. Under the command of the intrepid Captain Karl August Nerger, the armed merchant raider *Wolf* surreptitiously laid mines off North Cape on the night of 25–26 June 1917 and off Cape Farewell two nights later. These mines accounted for two ships. One was the passenger liner *Wimmera*, which went down off North Cape on 26 June 1918 with the loss of twenty-six lives. The *Wolf* also captured a ship outward bound from Auckland in the Kermadec Islands.[7] The public was occasionally reminded of the incursion when mines washed up on beaches along the coast. In August 1917 another German raider, the *Seeadler*, commanded by Commander Felix von Luckner, was wrecked on Mopelia Atoll in the Society Islands. After being captured in the Fijian Islands, her crew were imprisoned in New Zealand. Ten of them, including von Luckner, and an interned German civilian made a daring escape from Motuihe Island in December 1917. Seizing a scow in the Bay of Plenty, they made off to the north-east but were recaptured in the Kermadecs within a week.

While there were no German colonies in the Pacific at the outset of World War II, the German Navy again sent raiders into the South Pacific. The first to make its mark was the *Orion*. Commanded by Captain Kurt Weyher, she spent seven hours on the night of 13–14 June 1940 laying 228 mines in the Hauraki Gulf, one of which accounted for the cargo ship *Niagara* on 19 June.[8] Although no lives were lost in this incident, the minesweeper HMS *Puriri* fared less well when it hit another mine later (on 14 May 1941) in the same area, losing five of her crew. On 20 August 1940, the *Orion* intercepted the steamer *Turakina* some 400 kilometres from Cape Egmont and opened fire when she attempted to use her radio. The *Turakina* fired back, wounding some Germans, but thirty-four members of her crew were killed in this one-sided fight, the closest to take place to New Zealand in both world wars, and twenty were made prisoners. The *Orion* escaped into the vastness of the ocean.[9] Joined by the *Komet*, she returned to the vicinity of New Zealand later in the year. On 25 November 1940 she intercepted the small steamer *Holmwood en route* from the Chatham Islands to Lyttelton and two days later the motor liner *Rangitane* about 450 kilometres from East Cape. Again New Zealanders died when the raider opened fire to prevent the *Rangitane* using her radio. Six passengers, including four women, and five crew members were killed or mortally wounded. The *Rangitane* was sunk after the survivors had been taken off her.[10] Another German raider, the *Adjutant*, laid small minefields in the entrances to both Wellington and Lyttelton harbours in 1941, although without effect: the existence of the fields was only revealed by captured German documents after the war.[11] During 1945, the German submarine *U862* made a cruise along the North Island's east coast, although without sinking any New Zealand vessels.[12]

While the enemy without made its presence felt intermittently, there was more sustained concern among New Zealanders about the possibility of an enemy within. Anti-German feeling in New Zealand quickly emerged during World War I, with a female-dominated Anti-German League leading the charge.[13] All sectors of society were affected. Seamen, for example, refused to work with Germans (and later even men of German extraction).[14] German goods were boycotted, and individuals found themselves being hounded because of their German origins, perhaps the most prominent example being the dismissal of university professor George von Zedlitz from Victoria University College.[15] Some men who served with distinction in the New Zealand armed forces also fell victim to prejudice.[16] Aliens were interned, and after the war several hundred of them were deported.[17] While feelings did not run so high during World War II,[18] there was nevertheless some anti-German agitation, and the 1,500 Germans in New Zealand at the outbreak of war, some of them Jewish refugees, were the focus of hostility.[19] The activities of Germans in New Zealand had long been of concern to the authorities. The Auckland German Club had been under surveillance as early as 1934 because of the presence of an active Nazi group within it.[20] When hostilities began, all aliens were required to register, even if naturalised, and once again a number were interned: by June 1940, sixteen were being held, plus fifteen from Samoa.[21] The German victories in Europe in 1940 and a British round-up of aliens 'caused some near-panic ripples of hostility towards aliens' in New Zealand, which were heightened by the sinking of the *Niagara* in June of that year.[22] Fears of a 'Fifth Column'—a clandestine network of enemy agents or sympathisers working to subvert the nation's security—became exaggerated. All enemy aliens, of whom there were 1,241 Germans in a total 2,341, were examined by a tribunal.[23] The peak number of internees was 185 in December 1942. About half were German, and half of them were from outside New Zealand (for example, from Samoa). They were held on Somes Island until 1943, then at a camp near Pahiatua, but were transferred back to Somes Island in September 1944.[24] Not until November 1945 were restrictions on aliens lifted.

Although war between New Zealand and Germany had its manifestations in the South Pacific, for New Zealanders it was essentially a contest waged at a distance. They were involved in all dimensions of both world wars: land, sea, and air. In the first, several hundred served in the Royal Navy. New Zealanders were present at all the major engagements between the battle fleets, including the Battle of Jutland in 1916, some aboard HMS *New Zealand*, which went into action with a Maori piupiu hanging in the bridge as a talisman. Others served in the small ships that sought to prevent German submarines from cutting the vital sea lanes. New Zealand fighter pilots duelled with German airmen on the Western Front while serving in the Royal Flying Corps or, from 1918, the Royal Air Force.

The same pattern was repeated in World War II, albeit on a much greater scale. New Zealand naval personnel made an early impact. One of New Zealand's two cruisers, HMS *Achilles*, took part in the destruction of the German commerce raider *Admiral Graf Spee* at the Battle of the River Plate on 13 December 1939. Seconded to the Royal Navy, New Zealanders were to be found in all the theatres of the naval struggle: manning escort ships in the Battle of the Atlantic, on the Murmansk convoys, in the English Channel, at the Normandy landings. Altogether 7,000 spent varying periods in British ships or naval establishments during the conflict.[25]

Even before the war, New Zealanders had gone to Britain to take up short service commissions in the RAF. Many of these men were in action from the outset of the war. There were 103 New Zealanders among the pilots of Fighter Command who fought the Luftwaffe in British skies in 1940—the third largest national component after Britons and Poles. Sixteen of them were killed.[26] Other New Zealanders took part in the air war as members of Coastal Command or Bomber Command, many in the seven New Zealand squadrons that were formed in the RAF to emphasise the national identity of New Zealand's contribution. By 1945, 11,000 New Zealanders in all had served in the RAF. More than 4,000 lost their lives, many during bombing raids over Germany. Some 500 became prisoners of war.[27]

While New Zealanders and Germans clashed repeatedly on sea and in the air, it was on land that the most direct confrontation took place. In both world wars, expeditionary forces were despatched from New Zealand as its main contribution to the war effort against Germany. A high proportion of New Zealand's manpower of military age was mobilised. Conscription was used after voluntary enlistment proved insufficient in both wars.

The 8,444-strong main body of New Zealand's World War I Expeditionary Force sailed from Wellington on 16 October 1914. Although the initial intention was to deploy it against Germany in France, Turkey's entry to the war as a German ally led to its being retained in Egypt. The passage across the Indian Ocean had been safely accomplished despite the proximity of the German raider *Emden*, which was destroyed by one of the convoy's escorts, HMAS *Sydney*, at the Cocos Islands on 9 November 1914. From April to December 1915 the New Zealanders fought in the ill-fated Gallipoli campaign as part of a composite Australian–New Zealand division, after which most of them, now reinforced and formed as a separate New Zealand division, were transferred to France.

During the next two and a half years New Zealand troops were locked in struggle with Germans on the Western Front. The division, after a period

Volunteers at Wellington waiting to board troop-ship no. 10, September 1914. *(Auckland Public Library)*

in a relatively quiet sector, was thrown into the Battle of the Somme in September 1916. During the twenty-three days that it was engaged, more than 7,000 casualties were suffered. Fifteen hundred New Zealanders were killed or mortally wounded. During 1917 the division was deployed in Flanders. It took the town of Messines in June but later in the year was sucked into the third battle of Ypres. At Passchendaele the worst disaster in New Zealand history was inflicted by Germans on 12 October 1917 when a New Zealand attack failed. More than 600 New Zealanders were killed in a few hours. In 1918 the New Zealand Division was one of the divisions thrown into the yawning gap torn in the Allied line by the mighty German offensive launched in March. After this onslaught had faltered, and the Allied position had been consolidated, the New Zealanders took part in the successful Allied counter-offensive. Their advance culminated in the dramatic seizure of the walled fortress town of Le Quesnoy on 4 November, just a week before the Armistice.

Burying the dead during a truce on 24 May 1917. *(Auckland War Memorial Museum)*

The Allies had won the war, although at a huge cost. The number of British troops killed on the Western Front exceeded 740,000, of which New Zealand's toll was 13,250. Some 35,000 New Zealanders were wounded. More than half those who had been engaged became casualties.[28] Many of the dead were lost without trace and are commemorated only by name on the various memorials to the missing; the rest lie in the many immaculately kept cemeteries that dot the fields of northern France and Belgium.

In the midst of this carnage both New Zealanders and Germans formed impressions of each other that were conditioned by the circumstances. 'Fritz', the New Zealanders found, was an entirely different proposition from 'Johnny Turk'. Relentless, methodical, and determined, German soldiery proved much more adept at killing their enemies on the battlefield. Men under constant shellfire or exposed to the insidious poison gas soon began to hate their tormentors, and they killed them without compunction, often giving no quarter. The Germans reciprocated. There was, nevertheless, respect on both sides for the others' fighting qualities. In July 1918 a German view of the New Zealanders was provided in a captured intelligence document. It spoke of a 'particularly good assault Division' whose characteristics

were 'a very strongly developed individual self-confidence or enterprise …
and a specially pronounced hatred of the Germans'.[29]

The bitterness of the relationship was occasionally offset by acts of
humanity on both sides. A notable example occurred early in 1917, when a
number of New Zealand wounded were left lying between the lines following a fierce German response to a New Zealand raid.

A man crossed at the risk of his life to one of these [wounded]. Two or three others followed with nerves tautened, knowing that the Mauser rifles were levelled at heart and
brain. But no shot came! A German stood up on his parapet with his hands held high.
Up beside him came another and another, and another, until a whole line stood there.
Quickly now the stretchers went over and our wounded were brought in. An enemy
machine-gun commenced to fire from some distance in the rear. A tall German waved
back to the gunners and they ceased firing. When all was clear, a shot was fired in the air.
Both sides took cover and the war went on. But the action of those chivalrous Germans
is not forgotten in New Zealand. It was a very fine and splendid thing for men to come
back into a broken line in which lay two hundred of their dead and then, still in hot
blood, to show mercy to those who had slain their friends.[30]

However strongly an impersonal enemy at a distance might be hated, close
contact often alleviated such feelings. Encounters with German prisoners of
war sometimes led New Zealanders to a realisation of common humanity
and of a shared sense of victimisation—a phenomenon that was no doubt
evident on the other side of the line as well.

The New Zealand Division crossed the frontier into Germany on 20
December 1918. With the 1st Canterbury Battalion in the vanguard, the
troops passed through 'silent expressionless crowds' as they marched into
Cologne, and were quartered in various of its suburbs.[31] Demobilisation soon
began, however, and the Division, by now concentrated at Mülheim, was
finally disbanded on 25 March 1919. Fraternisation had been strictly forbidden, but the rules were soon openly flouted as the men rapidly became
popular with the local womenfolk, not least because of their courtesy. 'If
demobilization had not commenced rapidly and proceeded apace', it was
noted later, 'there might well have been German war brides in New Zealand
to-day.'[32]

Volunteers lined up in
the Rutland Street Drill
Hall to register with
their chosen unit,
September 1939.
(Auckland Public Library)

When the war to end all wars proved to be merely the first round of a contest that was resumed in 1939, New Zealand once again raised an infantry division to fight in the main theatres against the Germans. It was commanded by a man with family roots in Germany, Major-General Bernard Freyberg, while several other senior officers, such as Howard Kippenberger and George Dittmer, were also of German descent. As in 1914, the 2nd New Zealand Expeditionary Force proceeded initially to Egypt, where it completed training and prepared for action. However, its Second Echelon was diverted to Britain and became part of the anti-invasion forces. With Hitler's decision to call off Operation Sea Lion, the possibility of New Zealander and German fighting each other on British soil was removed, and the New Zealand troops were eventually redeployed to Egypt to join their compatriots.

As in World War I, the New Zealand force went into action initially against not Germany but rather one of its allies—in this case Italy, which had entered the war on 10 June 1940. Not until April 1941 did the New Zealanders have their first encounter with the Germans, after the 2nd New Zealand Division had been deployed, like its predecessor, to a Mediterranean peninsula as part of an ill-fated Allied campaign—this time in Greece. Several sharp actions were fought as the Germans swept south, and evacuation quickly became the primary objective. Most of the troops were rescued and some 7,700 of them landed in Crete,[33] which itself soon came under attack.

Although the New Zealanders comprised only a sixth of the Allied troops on Crete, the battle for the island has become a highly symbolic New Zealand action. This is partly because Freyberg was, as Commander Creforce, responsible for the defence of the island and partly because New Zealand troops were involved in the crucial operations, around Maleme airfield, that decided the fate of the island. Things did not go well at first for

Sandstorm at Khartoum.
(R. Warnock Collection)

the German paratroops of Fliegerdivision 7 who descended on the island as part of Operation Merkur on 20 May 1940, supported by the aircraft of Fliegerkorps 11. By nightfall they were still well short of capturing one of the three vital airfields at which they had aimed, and had virtually no airborne reserves. However, misjudgements and lethargy on the part of certain New Zealand senior officers opened the way for the paratroops to take and hold Maleme, and from this point the fate of the island was sealed. Once again, the Allied troops were forced into retreat and eventual evacuation. New Zealand's dead numbered 671, while nearly a thousand were wounded and 2,180 taken prisoner. The Germans suffered 6,700 casualties, of whom more than 3,300 were killed, out of 23,000 who landed—a toll which led the commander of Fliegerkorps 11, General Kurt Student, to proclaim Crete 'the grave of the German parachutist'.[34]

During the next two years, New Zealander and German fought each other in the deserts of North Africa. The campaign seesawed as the Axis forces, led by Rommel, fought a dashing but ultimately unsuccessful campaign. At the climactic battle, at El Alamein in October–November 1942, the New Zealanders played an important role in the eventual break-out. A long pursuit followed before the campaign ended with the capitulation of the German–Italian forces in Tunisia in May 1943. Many men of the German 90th Light Division were glad to surrender to the New Zealanders, against whom they had fought so many hard battles.[35] This was the prelude to the last land campaign between New Zealander and German, which was fought in Italy from 1943 to 1945. The troops on both sides contended with difficult terrain and bitterly cold conditions in winter. Nowhere was the fighting more ferocious than at Cassino. In February–March 1944, more than 600 New Zealanders were killed amid the ruins of this town in battle once again with German paratroopers, now fighting as infantry.

An air raid over Alexandria, July 1941. A cotton factory is ablaze at right. *(R. Warnock Collection)*

As in World War I, both sides sized each other up as adversaries. Between New Zealanders and Germans there was renewed mutual respect. Among the former, the Afrika Korps assumed the mantle of a worthy opponent, an attitude encouraged by the untrammelled nature of the desert war. With no civilians present, it was essentially a purely military contest. As Walter Murphy later noted, 'many New Zealanders concluded from the conduct of the desert war that, as they often put it, "Jerry" was a "good joker"'.[36] They shared the privations, the searing heat by day, the flies, the thirst, even the songs, as New Zealanders took to the lilting tones of 'Lili Marlene' broadcast on German radio. Dan Davin, a 2nd New Zealand Expeditionary Force veteran, caught the mood in his novel of the Desert War, *For the Rest of Our Lives*: 'Fight long enough and you shared even your sorrows with your enemies. For theirs had come in the same battlefields and they knew the same language.'[37]

General Erwin Rommel. *(C. Jackson Collection)*

Lieutenant Pat Kane, who fought in the infantry in both North Africa and Italy, no doubt spoke for many of his compatriots when he recalled that 'the war was an impersonal one'. It was not Germans but their system that New Zealanders were aiming to destroy. 'They were fighting against Nazism and Fascism and a police state rather than people.' Very few, in Kane's opinion, 'conjured up that hatred towards the enemy which is alleged to be necessary in a good soldier'.[38] Shocked and horrified by later accounts of the concentration camps and the persecution of the Jews, he found it difficult to equate such barbarism with the men of the Afrika Korps whom he fought in North Africa and was 'sure that they would have experienced the same horror and revulsion as we did'.[39] The paratroopers tended to be regarded in a different light, however. Geoffrey Cox, a junior staff officer, dismissed them as 'typical products of Hitler schools and the Hitler Youth, physically fine and yet degenerate and repugnant to a degree, with brutality and their warped minds'.[40] His commander, Freyberg, thought they represented 'all that is worst in the Nazi system'.[41]

Rommel's own photograph of his headquarters near Tobruk, taken from his *Storch*. *(Auckland War Memorial Museum)*

Members of a group of drivers and firemen from 16th Railway Operating Company, Middle East Forces, in Alexandria, June–July 1941 (left to right): Alf Fiveash, Jim Thompson, Ross Warnock, George Squire, Stan Baker. *(R. Warnock Collection)*

For their part, the Germans recognised a redoubtable adversary in the New Zealand Division. Rommel regarded it as 'among the élite of the British Army',[42] and was impressed by New Zealand officers whom he encountered. For example, the courage and demeanour of Brigadier Clifton—he briefly escaped and spent a number of trying days in the desert before being retaken—appealed to Rommel, as did his request to be a prisoner of the Germans rather than the despised Italians.[43] But Germans also had room for complaint at the conduct of the New Zealanders, who on occasions acted contrary to the rules of war themselves. German feeling ran high after a night bayonet attack by the New Zealanders during the desperate break-out of the New Zealand Division at Minqar Qaim in June 1942.[44] It might have been this incident that prompted Rommel to complain to Clifton about repeated cases 'of prisoners and wounded being massacred by this particular division'.[45] There was at least one unfortunate incident involving the killing of German prisoners in Italy.

Many New Zealanders developed a close acquaintance with Germans and Germany. Although fewer than 500 men were captured during World War I, largely because of the stalemated nature of the Western Front, some 9,000 fell into German hands during the more mobile fighting in the later conflict, many in Greece and Crete. Ninety per cent of New Zealand army prisoners were captured before the battle of El Alamein in October 1942. Most of the rest were air force personnel, taken throughout the conflict, including one unfortunate officer who was shot down and captured two days after the declaration of war.[46] A high proportion of these men ended up in Germany, where they remained until liberated in 1945. A minority found themselves in concentration camps, but most were in work camps or stalags. There were in addition about a hundred interned New Zealanders, mostly merchant seamen and passengers captured at sea by raiders. With the Germans generally adhering to the Geneva Conventions in regard to Western prisoners, most could have little complaint about their treatment, apart from the general deprivation associated with their status.[47] But there were instances of brutality, as when escaping prisoners were shot or on the marches away from the front that prisoners were forced to undergo in the closing months of the war. A New Zealander was, for example, shot by a guard as he received food from a bystander during one march through occupied Czechoslovakia in February 1945.[48] Nevertheless, almost all of the prisoners were safely recovered in 1945, some after interesting experiences in the post-capitulation chaos. Several New Zealanders, for example, found themselves briefly in charge of towns in Austria or Germany.[49] For one prisoner, the end of the war had less favourable consequences: he was sentenced to fifteen years' imprisonment by a New Zealand court martial for consorting with the enemy by joining the British Free Corps and later serving in Waffen-SS uniform.[50]

For New Zealanders and Germans, the era of warfare ended on 8 May 1945. Despite individual atrocities and horror at what was uncovered in defeated Germany, there was generally mutual respect between fighting men at least—a feeling that has been reflected in meetings between the two countries' veterans in subsequent years.[51] However much they loathed the Nazi regime, New Zealanders usually found ordinary Germans easy to get along with. The fact that they did not share the sense of grievance held by many in Europe whose homes had been destroyed or families killed by Germans meant that for them the war remained essentially a contest, rather than a crusade. Once the fighting ended and the men returned to their homes in New Zealand, distance further encouraged this dispassionate stance—as did the state of Germany. Far from being a threat to future peace, it became a pawn in the Cold War between the Soviet Union and the Western democracies, which came to dominate international relations in the next four decades. The rift between the former allies prevented the conclusion of a peace treaty, and Germany remained divided until 1990. As nuclear weapons changed the strategic balance of power and made war between great powers a suicidal prospect, the likelihood of New Zealander and German resuming their contest on the battlefield quickly faded.

Original cemetery of New Zealand and enemy near Point 175, not far from Sidi Resegh, after the 1941 campaign. *(Auckland War Memorial Museum)*

1 Brigadier George Clifton, *The Happy Hunted* (London, 1952), p. 5.
2 See F.L.W. Wood, *The New Zealand People at War: Political and External Affairs* (Wellington, 1958), chap. 1.

3 Wood [note 2], p. 11.

4 Ian McGibbon, *The Path to Gallipoli: Defending New Zealand 1840–1915* (Wellington, 1991), pp. 239–40.

5 Ian McGibbon, *Blue-water Rationale: The Naval Defence of New Zealand 1914–42* (Wellington, 1981), p. 394.

6 Carl Berendsen, 'Reminiscences of an ambassador' (unpublished manuscript held by Ministry of Foreign Affairs and Trade, Wellington), n. d. (1955?), vol. 1, p. 220.

7 Ian McGibbon, 'Victims of the "Wolf"', *New Zealand's Heritage* (1973), vol. 6, pp. 2101–4.

8 S.D. Waters, *The Royal New Zealand Navy* (Wellington, 1956), pp. 119–20.

9 Waters [note 8], pp. 125–9.

10 Waters [note 8], pp. 137–41.

11 Waters [note 8], p. 157.

12 'The last cruise of *U862*', *New Zealand Herald*, 29 December 1994.

13 See Paul Baker, *King and Country Call: New Zealand, Conscription and the Great War* (Auckland, 1988), p. 27.

14 Baker [note 13], p. 65.

15 *Dictionary of New Zealand Biography*, vol. 3, 1901–20 (Auckland, 1996), pp. 580f.

16 See Baker [note 13], p. 223.

17 Nan Taylor, *The New Zealand People at War, The Home Front* (Wellington, 1986), vol. 2, p. 851.

18 Taylor [note 17], p. 853.

19 Taylor [note 17], p. 851.

20 W. Wynne Mason, *Prisoners of War* (Wellington, 1954), p. 16.

21 Taylor [note 17], p. 857.

22 Taylor [note 17], p. 859.

23 Taylor [note 17], p. 866, n. 83; cf. Mason [note 20], p. 444.

24 Taylor [note 17], pp. 883f.

25 Waters [note 8], p. 467.

26 See Francis K. Mason, *Battle Over Britain* (London, 1969).

27 'Statement of strengths and losses in the armed services and mercantile marine in the 1939–45 war', *Appendices to the Journals of the House of Representatives* 1948, H–19B, pp. 13, 19.

28 A.H. McLintock (ed.), *An Encyclopaedia of New Zealand* (Wellington, 1966), vol. 3, p. 566.

29 Colonel H. Stewart, *The New Zealand Division 1916–1919* (Auckland, 1921), p. 617.

30 O.E. Burton, *The Silent Division* (Sydney, 1935), p. 187.

31 Stewart [note 29], p. 606.

32 Burton [note 30], p. 314.

33 Dan Davin, *Crete* (Wellington, 1953), p. 480.

34 Davin [note 33], p. 464.

35 W.G. Stevens, *Bardia to Enfidaville* (Wellington, 1962), p. 366.

36 W.E. Murphy, *The Relief of Tobruk* (Wellington, 1961), p. 521.

37 Dan Davin, *For the Rest of Our Lives* (London, 1947), p. 379.

38 Pat Kane, *A Soldier's Story: A Mediterranean Odyssey* (Wellington, 1995), pp. 144f.

39 Kane [note 38], p. 141.

40 Geoffrey Cox, *The Road to Trieste* (London, 1947), p. 158.

41 Peter Singleton-Gates, *General Lord Freyberg VC* (London, 1963), p. 299.

42 B.H. Liddell Hart (ed.), *The Rommel Papers* (London, 1953), p. 240.

43 Liddell Hart [note 42], p. 281.

44 Mason [note 20], p. 192.

45 Liddell Hart [note 42], p. 281.

46 Mason [note 20], p. 1.

47 D.O.W. Hall, *Prisoners of Germany* (Wellington, 1949), p. 32.

48 Mason [note 20], p. 453.

49 See Hall [note 47], p. 31.

50 See Hank Schouten, 'A Nazi traitor in Godzone', *Evening Post*, 25 May 1990.

51 See e.g. Noel 'Wig' Gardiner, *Bringing up the Rear: The Sequel to Freyberg's Circus: Further Reminiscences of a Kiwi Soldier* (Auckland, 1983), pp. 126–30.

2

Anti-German hysteria during World War I

JEAN KING

When the first German migrants came to live in the Nelson area in the 1840s, they were warmly welcomed by the British settlers. Their first attempts at building homes and establishing small farm holdings were fraught with problems, as their land was prone to flooding. There was sympathy and support from the other pioneers, and as the Germans were willing to be naturalised as British subjects, there was little, if any, friction between the two groups. The Germans' customs and of course their language might have been considered strange, but on the whole New Zealanders of British origin were more tolerant of the Germans than, for instance, of the French or Russians, long considered enemies of Britain.

However, by the time of the Boer War (1899–1902), a number of people in New Zealand had begun to have some misgivings about Germany because of the growing race between Germany and Britain for naval supremacy. There was also a German colony in Samoa, uncomfortably close should Germany decide to continue its aggressive colonial expansion policy. To quote Simon Johnson: 'This notion of a territorial threat to the Dominion became a powerful one, and a very necessary ingredient in the arousal of hostility towards Germany.'[1] Reports in German newspapers accusing Britain of committing atrocities in South Africa were indignantly denied. New Zealanders were beginning to see the need for a defence force that would be able to defend the country in case of invasion. It is no wonder, then, that when war was declared in August 1914, the public was already mentally prepared. The anti-German propaganda machine could have full reign.

Tales of German 'frightfulness' began pouring in, specifically with regard to the invasion of Belgium, with lurid reports of the killing of civilians, child refugees with fingers and hands cut off, and the destruction of ancient cities. The belief that Germany was wholly to blame was stressed at every opportunity. The Allied nations, as Simon Johnson writes, 'rapidly became paragons of virtue. In many cases history was rewritten to preserve this illusion'.[2] New Zealand's principal source of news was the British press, and it painted Germany very black. The Germans, it was claimed, were a race of barbarians, as was apparent from the bombing of coastal towns, the use of poison gas, and the submarine warfare that was Germany's answer to Britain's naval blockade. France, Russia, and Japan, once feared enemies, were now regarded as brethren.

Cartoon of Kaiser Wilhelm as 'the modern pirate' in response to the sinking of the *Lusitania*. (New Zealand Listener Library)

The situation gave New Zealanders a common cause, not only increasing their hatred of Germans but also renewing their loyalty to the Empire and reducing dissent at home.[3] The call to intern all Germans in New Zealand came as soon as war was declared. About a hundred people, some of whom were reservists and not yet naturalised, were arrested and detained as prisoners of war on Somes Island. Among them were a dozen members of the German administration staff in Samoa, accompanied by their wives, who had been taken prisoner by New Zealand forces after Britain had requested that Samoa be placed under military control on 29 August 1914.[4] Some Germans who had lived here for many years brought British friends to vouch for their character. They were exempted from arrest, but were required to report to the police daily.

German internees on Somes Island during World War I. Note the fiddler near the front of the group. *(Alexander Turnbull Library, Ref. no. F-75448-1/2)*

An outpost of German *Kultur*? Some of the German internees formed an orchestra, seen here performing on Somes Island. *(R. Harte Collection, Alexander Turnbull Library, Ref. no. F-112230-1/2)*

Public meetings and organisations of all kinds passed resolutions demanding better control of all enemy aliens, with some even wanting confiscation of all land belonging to Germans. With 6,000 German or Austrian people in New Zealand, it was impossible to place them all in internment camps, as Somes and Motuihe Islands held only 450. Even then, there were protests that the internees had better conditions than civilians.[5] The little settlement of German-speaking Bohemians in Puhoi was saved from the demand for mass internment. Insults were traded and loyalties were questioned. Prime Minister Massey saved them by attesting to 'the settlers' industriousness and patriotism' in a stirring speech.[6]

'In Remembrance of War Captivity, Somes Island, New Zealand.' Among the papers of Johann Anton Bock, interned on Somes Island during World War I. *(Errol Bock Collection)*

The secretary to the German Consul, Mr Heinsen, along with six German reservists, was arrested and placed on Somes Island. The windows of the office of Mr E. Focke, the German consular agent and agent for the Norddeutscher Lloyd Company, were smashed. Mr Focke was a well-known and respected citizen of Wellington and his son a keen member of the New Zealand Territorial Force. A number of local residents asked to be allowed to repair the damage. Mr Focke explained he would need to wait for instructions from the German consular service before he could close the office.[7]

Widespread feeling against employing Germans meant that even skilled tradesmen were dismissed. A specialist technician in the Telegraph Department in Wellington was dismissed when it was found he was not naturalised. His services were much in demand, however, so he was re-employed. Protests from the mechanicians branch ensued, so he was given work 'by the day'.[8] The captain of the steamer *Pakeha* took his twenty-three greasers and firemen to court when they refused to work beside several Germans in the crew who were found to be reservists. The case was thrown out because 'No loyal British community and no loyal colonial government would expect a crew to work with Germans'.[9]

The fear generated by the belief that German influence was everywhere, in the form of spies and wireless and signalling stations, gave rise to some fairly bizarre acts. It was suggested that any German lighthouse keepers be removed from their post, as they could easily signal to an enemy ship. A young German, Hugh Sewald, was charged 'with establishing in a house in Taranaki Street a wireless installation capable of receiving and transmitting messages, without first obtaining the permission of the Government-in-

Council'. Sewald had been naturalised in Australia. He was fined £20 and was to be detained after his sentence expired. The apparatus was very weak, but 'an expert witness said it only required more cells to enable a message to be sent several miles'.[10]

Probably one of the most notable examples of 'the massive and hysterical antagonism towards everything German'[11] was that of G.W. von Zedlitz, who was dismissed from his post as Professor of Modern Languages at Victoria University by an act of Parliament, the Alien Enemies Teachers Act (1915). In spite of the university's protests at losing one of its most capable and popular staff members, public pressure groups were adamant that the nation's youth was at risk from his teaching.

The changing of German street and place names had been called for when the first wave of anti-German hysteria swept the country. Many people of German descent, although born in New Zealand, anglicised their names. Mr Max Thorn of Hamilton remembers two spinster aunts who kept a sweets and cake shop in Taihape. Their name was Behrendt, which they changed to Brent, although no official record was made. The family had spoken German at home, but at the start of World War I they had made a decision never to speak German again. The grandchildren were expressly forbidden to mention their German ancestry to anyone.

The presence of German products in New Zealand shops was a particularly emotional issue and seems to have led to the formation of the Women's Anti-German League. Although women had quickly rallied to provide support for the men fighting overseas with fundraising, knitting, and other activities, the league offered even more active support. One of its aims was to try to persuade women to boycott any remaining German goods in shops and to buy only British. Another objective was to seek information about any Germans, or sons of Germans, naturalised or not, who had joined the army. It was thought that these men, especially those who had received commissions, could pass on vital information of use to the enemy.

Police, members of parliament, and government departments were continually plagued with allegations of German subversive activity, all of which proved groundless when investigated. The police protested eventually that this kept them from doing their real work. The league wanted the naturalisation law changed, and promised to assist in returning to parliament any candidates who pledged themselves to support its objectives.[12]

On New Year's Eve 1914, a Gisborne butcher's shop was the target of anti-German sentiment. The recently formed British Protection League[13] had organised pickets outside Wohnsiedler's butchery on Christmas Eve, but the pickets were dispersed by the police. When a crowd of about a thousand gathered on New Year's Eve, many no doubt animated by festive cheer, they came prepared to hurl stones and broke the windows of the butcher's shop.

The sinking by a German submarine of the ocean liner *Lusitania* with the loss of 1,200 lives on 7 May 1915 seems to have triggered a wave of horror and disgust across New Zealand. It was presented by the press as the worst atrocity to date. 'It was murder, murder so foul and monstrous that words fail to deal with it, murder that will never be forgiven as long as German "kultur" remains a menace to mankind.'[14] Little wonder that the sinking led to

The Gisborne butcher's shop that was attacked on New Year's Eve 1914. (New Zealand Listener Library)

violent outbursts of anti-German activity, such as the attacking of German tradespeople in shops and the passing of resolutions demanding the internment of all enemy aliens of German or Austrian descent.

In German settlements such as Marton and Upper Moutere, the Lutheran churches ceased holding services in the German language—a practice that had been continued until then for the benefit of the older members of the congregation. After an episode in Christchurch when the bells of a church were destroyed in the mistaken belief that they had been made from German cannon, the same suspicions were levelled at the bells of a church in Marton. Two churches in Rongotea and Halcombe were burnt down,[15] and Marton parishioners worked a roster to keep a watch against a similar fate for their church.[16] The Lutheran Synod was advised by the government not to hold their annual convention because of the anti-German feeling.

Former Prime Minister David Lange recalls that his grandfather's tailor's shop in Thames was destroyed by a 'misguidedly patriotic mob' concerned about the German name, although his grandfather had been born in New Zealand.[17] Wanganui township experienced even worse problems. There was little doubt that feelings about the sinking of the *Lusitania* were the basis for the build-up of emotions culminating in the rioting that took place on the Avenue on the night of 15 May 1915. All week long, rumours of an attack on a butcher's shop owned by a Mr C. Heinold were circulating, and he had, in fact, received a number of letters and threats warning him of trouble. An unruly crowd gathered outside the shop; and despite attempts by the police to stop the agitators, as well as pleas for calm from the mayor, Mr McKay, who for his efforts suffered a blow to the head from a stone hurled at the store, soon all the windows were broken. The same fate befell other shops in the vicinity. Mr Heinold's shop, recently stocked with hams and pickles as well as meat, was too great a temptation for some of the rioters, who gained many prizes from wholesale looting. The mob moved on to Hallensteins' shop where all but one of the windows was broken; the Bristol Piano Company, formerly the Dresden Piano Company, was also attacked. Many reasons were given for the hostile demonstration against Mr Heinold, among them the claim that he would not permit his children to sing the National Anthem at the local school. The allegations were totally without foundation.[18]

Destruction of the Lutheran Church bells, Christchurch 1918. (New Zealand Listener Library)

A serious fire in New Plymouth, which started in the Theatre Royal in Devon Street and later destroyed the whole block, was regarded by many as 'an act of defiance (and retaliation against the theatre's owners) by "the enemy"'.[19] It might not have had anything to do with the anger displayed, but that night the film *The Martyrdom of Nurse Cavell*—about Edith Cavell, an English nurse who had been executed by the Germans in Belgium in 1914 for helping wanted people to evade capture—had been screened. After the fire, feelings ran high, and scapegoats were immediately found in the persons of two brothers by the name of Nippert. They had been staying the night at the hotel across the road. No matter that they were third-generation New Zealanders from a well-known Taranaki family who had emigrated in the 1870s and had for many years run a paint shop, which also sold wallpaper and hardware. One brother in fact had spent ten minutes trying to alert the authorities about the fire. The Nippert brothers came close to a beating, if not a lynching, until a person of 'unquestionable character and racial origin' vouched for the fact that the pair had never left the room which they all shared.[20]

Fear of the enemy is natural in wartime, but the vindictiveness displayed by many people was undoubtedly fed by the propagandists, who knew well how to inflame hatred with repeated stories of atrocities, until even myths and legends achieved the status of truth. Newspapers performed the important function of spreading war news quickly and effectively. The loss of relatives and friends added to emotional pressures, and the need to blame someone guaranteed that anti-German hysteria was kept at a high level.

1 Simon Johnson, 'The home front: Aspects of civilian patriotism in New Zealand during the First World War', MA thesis, Massey University, 1975, p. 17.
2 Johnson [note 1], p. 43.
3 Johnson [note 1], p. 23.
4 A.H. McLintock (ed.), *An Encyclopaedia of New Zealand* (Wellington, 1966), vol. 3, p. 168.
5 See e.g. *New Zealand Herald*, 21 October 1914.
6 Jennifer Haworth, 'Faith and brotherhood', *New Zealand Geographic*, 21 (January–March 1994), pp. 86–8.
7 *New Zealand Herald*, 10 August 1914.
8 *New Zealand Herald*, 9 September 1914.
9 Cf. *New Zealand Herald*, 26 September 1914.
10 *New Zealand Herald*, 8 October 1914.
11 E.J. Haughey, *Evening Post*, 22 January 1976.
12 Johnson [note 1], p. 113 (appendix 1).
13 A local organisation set up in Gisborne by tradesmen to boycott foreign-owned shops.
14 *Auckland Weekly News*, 13 May 1915, p. 51, quoted in Johnson [note 1], p. 76.
15 Reports of the arson of the Lutheran churches in Rongotea and Halcombe can be found in the *Manawatu Daily Times* of 3 July 1917 and the *Feilding Star* of 16 July 1917 respectively. (Additional information kindly supplied at this point by Val Burr of Palmerston North.)
16 A. Gudopp and D. Strauch, *St Martin's Lutheran Church, Marton: 1877–1977 Centennial* (Marton, 1977), p. 17.
17 *New Zealand Listener*, 23 October 1993 (book review).
18 *Wanganui Chronicle*, 17 May 1915.
19 Murray Moorhead, 'Burned by the beastly Hun?', *North Taranaki Weekender*, July 1989.
20 Moorhead [note 19].

3

Refugees from Nazi Germany and Austria 1933–45

ANN BEAGLEHOLE

In the late 1930s, Jewish refugees from Nazi Europe, inquiring about migration to New Zealand, were informed by the New Zealand High Commissioner's Office in London:

The New Zealand Government is not at present encouraging immigration … In the case of persons not of British birth and parentage, it is necessary for such persons to obtain permits from the Minister of Customs at Wellington before they may proceed to the Dominion. The High Commissioner has received advice from his Government that it has recently been found necessary to discontinue the issuing of such permits except in very special cases. It is considered, therefore, that it would probably be hardly worth your while making application.[1]

The key act determining New Zealand's immigration policy in the years 1933–39 was the Immigration Restriction Amendment Act of 1920. This Act allowed free entry to immigrants of British birth or descent, while persons of any other origin had to obtain entry permits. In particular, the Act aimed to restrict the entry of 'race aliens'—Chinese, Indians—and Jews.[2]

It is uncertain how many refugees from Nazi Europe, many of whom were Jewish or had a Jewish background, were declined entry to New Zealand or were discouraged from even applying for a permit.[3] Unlike the United States or Australia, New Zealand did not have a quota for refugees. Nor did it have a set of rules that applied in every case; each application was 'treated on its merits'.[4] The guidelines adopted for processing applications and the way they were interpreted ensured that most refugees were prevented from entering New Zealand. One of the most important considerations was 'the suitability of the immigrant for absorption into the Dominion's population'.[5] E.D. Good, Comptroller of Customs during this period, was quite explicit in his interpretation of this guideline: 'Non-Jewish applicants are regarded as a more suitable type of immigrant.'[6] Walter Nash, who was Minister of Customs, held the same view.[7]

Despite the restrictions, about 1,100 refugees from Central and Eastern Europe, 900 of them from Germany and Austria,[8] settled in New Zealand in the years between the rise of Hitler and the outbreak of World War II. This chapter focuses on their early settlement experiences, including aspects of their life during the war years when most were classified 'enemy aliens'. The chapter is based on interviews with former refugees and on official papers.[9]

The refugees who came to New Zealand were mainly middle-class, well-educated professional or business people. Although the majority had some connection with Judaism,[10] their self-identification was diverse and complicated. Some identified strongly as Jews, others were connected to Judaism only by reason of birth, the origin of a grandparent or by marriage. The refugees were almost all city people, accustomed to a culturally heterogeneous environment and the cultural and social amenities of Central European cities. New Zealand cities, and the cultural life that existed in them, reminded the newcomers of small provincial towns in Europe. Most experienced severe cultural dislocation. The refugees' common reaction to this dislocation and to other difficulties arising from cultural differences was to try very hard to put the past behind them. Wanting above all to settle down again, they worked hard at fitting in and adapting to New Zealand.

Refugees' knowledge of New Zealand was based mainly on hearsay and a little reading. New Zealand's distance from the wars and upheavals of Europe appealed to many. They hoped for a haven for Jews, a place free from anti-Semitism. Some imagined life would be easier in a small country. Supporters of Weimar and left-wing political ideologies were excited by the prospect of going to a country with one of the first Labour governments in the western world, a government that was introducing important social legislation. New Zealand's reputation for beautiful scenery—forests, mountains, beaches—attracted others. There were also expectations of a country with a moderate, benevolent climate, a sub-tropical island or a 'land of eternal spring'. 'I felt very lucky to have got to New Zealand' was a frequently repeated statement, stressing that New Zealand offered what was most important for the refugees, a home at last, somewhere in the world.

Some hopes and expectations were met during those first weeks and months in New Zealand while others were abandoned. Wellington's harbour and the views from the hills, for example, met the expectations of some refugees of finding beautiful landscape. Its bare hills, when first sighted, were enthusiastically admired by some as 'marvellous for skiing'. Later the hills impressed as bleak, sparse, raw, rough, overwhelming, and enclosing. Other early visual impressions concerned the poor, dilapidated appearance of the cities and of the countryside. There was no obvious poverty as in Europe, but everything seemed unkempt and unpainted. One man was especially struck by the corrugated iron roofs predominating in cities and suburbs. (In Europe, corrugated iron was usually used for housing animals.)

Encounters with New Zealanders featured prominently in the early impressions of some refugees. They were struck by the kindness of people, which provided a great contrast to the rudeness and arrogance of the officials they had encountered in Nazi Europe. Arriving in New Zealand, the passport officials greeted one new arrival with a friendly 'How are you?' and 'Are you all right?' 'It was such a relief; it was as though a great burden like a stone, dropped from your heart …,' she recalled. Some refugees' early contact with New Zealanders was not so agreeable, however. They recalled mutterings of 'bloody reffos' and other derogatory references.

Newcomers mentioned different foods, peculiar smells, strange colours, old-fashioned clothes, the early closing of shops, drunken people in the streets, and much else. The cumulative effect of all that was different must have been overwhelming for some. As one pointed out: '… it is not the important things that actually seem to get you down in the so-called culture shock, but the small things which make you feel completely strange.'

Finding somewhere suitable to live was the first urgent task the new-comers faced. They encountered a shortage of housing, particularly of rental accommodation. The appearance and lack of variety of New Zealand houses was unappealing to many refugees. Features that were particularly disliked included 'fire places with glazed tiles', 'ugly furniture', 'naked bulbs', 'horrible colours, kitchens always green, the other rooms beige'. 'Primitive' was how some refugees described the houses they first lived in or visited in New Zealand. They were referring not only to the absence of objects and comforts to which they had been accustomed—Persian carpets, orna-ments, pictures on the wall—but also to the lack of warmth and comfort. As one interviewee recollected, in the family's first flat, there was only one power point, namely in the kitchen. There were two fireplaces but nowhere to plug in heaters or lamps by which to read in bed. For many refugees, accustomed to central heating, the worst aspect of the houses was their unsuitability for the climate. 'We were used to Central European housing which had double-glazed windows and proper heating,' one explained. Another remembered sitting in front of a little bar-heater and freezing: 'The outside temperature and wind came right into the house.'

Some of the women found that life in these 'primitive' houses meant hav-ing to do housework and cooking for the first time in their lives. Many had been accustomed to some help in the house. Others had employed maids, chauffeurs, cooks, gardeners, someone to do the washing, and someone else to assist with the children. In New Zealand, not many of the refugees were straight away able to afford servants had they been available, but in any case, the demand for domestic workers was always greater than the supply. Some young refugee women themselves filled this gap in the supply of servants and earned a living as maids in their early years in New Zealand. Not all the women had been sheltered from the drudgery of 'women's work'. For them the transition to doing domestic work in New Zealand was easier.

Adjustments in domestic life were also required of men. To their surprise, New Zealand men of all walks of life took a pride in jobs done with their own hands. One interviewee recalled that 'the first time' he 'touched a ham-mer' was in New Zealand. The New Zealand wife of another observed that one of the differences between a Central European husband and a New Zealand one was that if, for example, a fuse needed fixing, the Central European was inclined to say immediately: 'There are men to do those things.'

Compared to the intensely active cultural life of their cities of origin, what was available in the New Zealand cities of the 1930s was for many refugees, at best, disappointing. Some missed professional theatre, ballet, symphony orchestra, chamber music; others missed cafés and restaurants. Several refugees singled out lack of music as the most significant gap in their new lives. However, as one observed, these losses had to be regarded in the context of what the refugees had escaped from. 'Not to be able to go to the opera in the evening was a small price to pay for being safe.' Many refugees repeatedly stressed how lucky they believed themselves to be because they were in New Zealand. Most tried to appreciate the forms of cultural life and entertainment that were available. Books, plays, dance classes, the cinema, learning to play the piano, involvement in amateur theatre, and generally making one's own entertainment were rewarding experiences.

The absence of a place to meet friends was a serious drawback, however. Some refugees tried the milk bars, 'so funny' for people 'accustomed to coffee houses', when they wanted somewhere to go after the cinema. Eventually, a coffee house, the French Maid, opened in Wellington. Refugees thankfully gathered there to meet friends and drink good coffee, the availability of which coincided with the arrival of United States servicemen.[11] Another meeting place in Wellington was the Czech Club, known to refugees as the 'Coffee House'. Here people played cards. There was music. Sometimes picnics were organised. Social occasions such as weddings were celebrated. Members helped each other trace relatives and shared information about matters of mutual concern. Especially in wartime, the Czech Club was a great refuge for people who were not Czechs at all but Jewish refugees of German or Austrian nationality.

While many refugees relied on each other for their social life and social support, others were determined not to. Becoming integrated meant having New Zealand friends. The first friends many refugees made in New Zealand were often their sponsors or guarantors and later their colleagues, fellow students, and neighbours. Valuable contacts and sometimes friendships were made through involvement with the Plunket Society, play groups, and other voluntary associations, especially those related to children and their diverse activities. Shared interest in the arts also provided a common ground for friendships between refugees and some New Zealanders. As one interviewee observed: '… as a foreigner, you became wanted. You were somebody who had been to the theatre and to the opera, who had done different things,

French Maid Coffee Bar, Lambton Quay, Wellington, in the 1940s. *(A.D. Singleton Collection, Alexander Turnbull Library, Ref. no. F-96756-1/2)*

Dorothy Davies Trio. Left to right: Marie Vandewart (cello), Erika Schorss (violin), Dorothy Davies (piano). *(Dorothy Davies Collection, Alexander Turnbull Library, Ref. no. F-152668-1/2)*

who came from a different place.' Some New Zealand writers, musicians, and scholars eagerly sought out the newcomers from Europe. In this way, refugees found congenial New Zealand friends, and the New Zealanders found support, encouragement, and an audience.

In some respects, however, the refugees and New Zealanders coming into contact was, as one interviewee observed, a situation of 'two worlds coming together, absolutely, grotesquely alien to each other'. Although few in number, the refugees seemed to attract attention. With their different clothes, their bowing and their hand-shaking, their foreign accents, they stood out in the monocultural New Zealand cities of the 1930s and 1940s. The smaller the town, the more the newcomers stood out as curiosities. People stared at them in the bus and on the streets. Neighbours commented when they hung out washing that was different. Shopkeepers made remarks when refugees sought to buy food different from that usually eaten by New Zealanders. This invited curiosity and questions about how it was cooked.

Being regarded as a curiosity, although irritating, was not necessarily unpleasant. However, the insularity and ignorance of some New Zealanders led to a dislike of people who looked different or who behaved differently. For one woman, hanging out her washing on her first Good Friday in New Zealand resulted in her neighbour yelling over the fence: 'These foreigners, they don't know our customs, hanging out the washing on our holiest day.' Differences in manners could also be regarded as offensive. 'The refuges lack discretion and tact. They revel in displays of emotionalism and self-pity and fail to realize how we despise such lack of self-control. On social occasions, and other occasions too, they talk loudly and untiringly about their own affairs. Being bad listeners they cannot take a hint, nor sense an attitude from what we prefer to leave unsaid,' wrote Reuel Lochore,[12] voicing his own and prevailing prejudices.

The variety of ways in which New Zealanders reacted to the new-comers needs to be emphasised. There was friendliness, helpfulness, and admiration. There was curiosity about differences as well as intolerance of them. There was suspicion and hostility, particularly during the war years. There was also the expectation that the newcomers would assimilate, and the more rapidly they did so, the more positively they were regarded by New Zealanders.

The refugees had been forced to resign from professions, abandon businesses, or interrupt studies. In New Zealand they eagerly sought opportunities to begin again, to resume interrupted careers, to compensate for lost years of professional development, and above all to earn a living to support themselves and their families. Although the aftermath of the Depression meant that there was still unemployment in New Zealand in the years 1933–40, most refugees were able to obtain some employment. The jobs were frequently not in the refugees' former occupations, but they provided an income and a start in the new country.

Sewing, cleaning, cooking, child care, shop work—whatever their previous background, many of the jobs women did when they first arrived fell into one or other of these categories. For men who were young and healthy, there were more opportunities and a greater variety of jobs, particularly of the labouring type, to choose from. Experiences varied. Some refugees encountered tolerant bosses and goodwill towards them among fellow workers. Others met with resentment when refugees worked harder and more quickly than New Zealanders. As the wife of one observed bitterly: '… my husband did over-time so that we could *live* and the other workers were jealous.'

Although most refugees started their New Zealand working lives in occupations unrelated to their former training or work experience, there were opportunities to retrain and undertake part-time study. Refugees were quick to take advantage of these opportunities, which enabled them to move into professional occupations in the years ahead.[13] There were also business opportunities in New Zealand for refugees with entrepreneurial skills, ingenuity, and a willingness to work hard.

The move by refugees into the professions took place in the face of considerable opposition from professional bodies,[14] particularly from the British Medical Association (BMA). At every step, from entering New Zealand to gaining full professional acceptance, the doctors who came as refugees were opposed by the BMA.[15] As a result, the number of doctors who had come as refugees and who were actually practising medicine in 1945 was only thirty-four[16]—hardly the 'influx' repeatedly claimed by those opposed to refugee doctors practising in New Zealand.

Despite the benefits to New Zealand, refugees' business activities also took place in the face of considerable opposition. As was the case with refugee doctors, claims were frequently made that New Zealand had suffered an 'influx of alien businessmen'.[17] In fact, 123 businesses, employing 300 people, had been started by refugees by 1945. A number of these ventures led to 'valuable, if minor, diversification of the New Zealand economy'.[18] Seven of the industries were believed to be new ones for New Zealand.[19] Several of the new ventures were declared to be essential war industries.[20]

Tensions aroused by the settlement of the refugees increased when war began. There were calls on the government to set up an administrative system to sort out potential fifth columnists from the rest of the resident aliens in New Zealand. Refugees from Nazi Europe were among those regarded as potential fifth columnists. The Aliens Emergency Regulations under which the government could deport, intern, and set up authorities and tribunals to investigate and classify aliens came into being in October 1940, and the administrative machinery accompanying the regulations was set to work in the following months. Most refugees from Germany and Austria were classified as 'enemy aliens', which meant that they escaped internment but were subject to certain regulations. These included restrictions on the possession of articles such as arms, maps, radios with short wave reception, cameras, and X-ray equipment. Certain places of residence were forbidden to enemy aliens. The necessity to register with the police was imposed, and permits had to be obtained if an alien in a restricted category was moving more than twenty-four miles from his or her usual residence or expected to be absent from there for more than twenty-four hours. Refugees were also restricted from certain occupations and, most significantly, were excluded from service in the armed forces.[21]

The system of classification set up did not generally inflict great hardship on the refugees, partly because, coming from Germany and Austria, they were accustomed to registering and reporting to the police. The requirement to do so in New Zealand was not at all unexpected. It also seemed understandable to them that refugees who had been living in enemy territory a short time before should now come under some sort of scrutiny.

The hardship that refugees did suffer during the war years was more likely to be brought about by their encounter with the hostile and suspicious attitudes of employers, colleagues, and neighbours. Reports attacking refugees in newspapers, and particularly in the tabloid *Truth,* also caused considerable grief and anxiety. These attitudes were prevalent in part because, despite the system of alien control set in place, refugees continued to be regarded as potential fifth columnists. Furthermore, by preventing refugees from participating in the war effort, the authorities themselves fuelled the suspicion and hostility the refugees already faced from some New Zealanders.

An editorial in the *Dominion* in 1940 summarised the dilemma, as some New Zealanders saw it, caused by the presence of aliens, regarded as possible enemies: 'How is equality of sacrifice to be achieved and at the same time the community protected from refugees who may be fifth columnists?' The writer commented on the dangers of the situation in which 'aliens remained in civilian security or in the indolence of internment' while New Zealanders made every kind of sacrifice.[22] Partly as a response to comments of this kind and partly because of the threat of invasion by Japan, the government took steps in 1942 to involve refugees in the war effort. However, the damage had been done. Some continued to regard refugees as defaulters from the war by their own choice, who were sheltering in New Zealand, unwilling to serve their adopted country and, worst of all, were 'prospering while our boys fight'.[23]

While some refugees escaped the hostility and ensuing harassment almost entirely, the climate of opinion affected other refugees in every aspect of their wartime lives. Some had difficulty obtaining work; others were dismissed from jobs they already had. A refugee working as a cleaner in a Wellington boarding house was asked by one of the residents why she had chosen to emigrate to New Zealand. To her answer that there had been no choice and that New Zealand was the first country to give her an entry permit, her questioner remarked sarcastically: 'Poor New Zealand.' The owner of a dairy was advised to take out glass insurance in case her being an enemy alien aroused the wrath of neighbours.

The attitude of neighbours was particularly distressing. 'My son was only a small child,' recalled one interviewee. 'One day my neighbour with a threatening face said to him: "You, scum of the earth."' The neighbours of a refugee family expressed their dislike of hearing the German language spoken by throwing dead fish over the fence into their garden. A refugee out shopping protested on one occasion when sold bad merchandise. The shopkeeper turned on her with the words: 'You be satisfied with what you get. Lucky you're not in a concentration camp.' Such encounters with hostile New Zealanders featured prominently in the recollections of some refugees, not because such incidents occurred constantly but because of their devastating effect at the time.

Refugees with homes overlooking the harbour were sometimes accused of using their views to obtain information for the enemy concerning shipping movements. Public alarm about such a possibility continued in spite of the fact that the Minister of Justice had the power to restrict where aliens lived[24] and could prevent aliens buying property in view of shipping or other places of military significance if investigation of the aliens concerned showed that there were any suspicious circumstances.[25]

A refugee family, living in a suburb from where it was possible to see the harbour, had ostensibly a most amicable relationship with their neighbours.

The neighbours were very friendly, but suspicious. One weekend, I was on the roof doing some soldering. The next day, the police came enquiring if I was looking at the shipping movements in the harbour. On another day, a friend, another refugee, came in New Zealand army uniform to visit me. The next day the police came asking: 'Who was that soldier?' On a third occasion, I was at the beach near my home with my small daughter and I took her photograph. Again the police came, asking about my camera. In each case, it was my friendly neighbours reporting my activities. It was unpleasant.[26]

In the climate of suspicion and watchfulness, innocent gestures and comments were given a sinister interpretation by neighbours and others. An elderly foreign man's parting wave each day to his wife was observed by neighbours to be the Hitler salute. A refugee was reported to the police because he was speaking German in a public telephone box. A man was denounced as a spy by his landlady because every evening when he took out the milk bottles he smoked a cigarette. (In the far, far distance the harbour was visible and he was thought to be signalling to the enemy.) Many more examples could be given.

Refugees entering the professions or becoming established in business were particularly affected during the war years. 'Evidence is accumulating to show the extraordinary inroads that aliens are making into New Zealand's industrial and commercial life,' began a *Truth* columnist in 1942, and then went on to list by name a few refugees who had started businesses.[27] The writer juxtaposed the stories of successful refugees with the plight of New Zealand servicemen, a connection made repeatedly to demonstrate that the commercial 'infiltration' by the refugees was to the detriment of the men who were away fighting: 'Should the ex-servicemen enter the same line of business with these aliens, they will find themselves handicapped in competing with people who have been free to use the war years to establish them solidly in the Dominion's economic life. The fur, the clothing and the manufacturing trades are already experiencing the results of this foreign invasion.'

In particular the prospect of alien businessmen being the employers of returning servicemen aroused much angry comment and led to demands that the commercial activities of aliens be controlled by the government. The Returned Servicemen's Association (RSA) wished the government to introduce a system of control 'whereby no alien would be entitled to commence in any business or profession without first having obtained a licence to do so from the appropriate government department'.[28] The BMA and the New Zealand Manufacturers Federation made the same demand.[29] The possibility of licensing refugees wishing to start businesses was discussed by the Federation of Labour National Executive and supported by some members.[30] Concern over this issue also occasioned questions in the House of Representatives.[31] Regulations to prohibit 'any alien from entering or remaining in any business or profession unless he was the holder of a certificate and complied with conditions imposed by the Minister of Justice' were drawn up in 1942,[32] in 1944, and finally in 1945,[33] but were not enacted.[34]

Refugees were also believed to be acquiring excessive amounts of property. One example used to highlight this 'problem' was that of a German Jewish refugee who had arrived in New Zealand in 1938 and by 1942 had acquired 'no less than thirteen house properties in Auckland'.[35] Housing was already in short supply, and returned servicemen would suffer if deprived by aliens of access to suitable dwellings.[36] On this issue, the government acted. The Aliens Land Purchase Regulations of March 1942 prohibited land or property transfers to aliens without the consent of the Minister of Justice. The regulations applied both to all unnaturalised aliens and to those aliens of enemy origin who had become naturalised since 1914. Before consent was given to a purchase by an alien, inquiries were made into the security aspects of the sale, whether the property was required for the rehabilitation of servicemen, and whether the need of New Zealanders was greater than that of the applicant. The extent of the alien's previous purchases was also examined and the alien's contribution to the war effort investigated. The measures were justified in the interests of security and public morale.[37]

The resentment against refugees became particularly marked in the last two years of the war. The BMA (Otago division) moved that a resolution be passed requesting all refugee doctors in New Zealand to be returned to their own countries to help in reconstruction now that the war was over.[38] The RSA at its annual conference in July 1945 passed a similar resolution:

Any person or persons who arrived in New Zealand from Germany, Austria, Hungary, or Italy since 1939 must return to their own countries within two years after hostilities with Germany have ceased and they should be allowed to take out of New Zealand the same amount of money or property or both that they declared to the Customs Department on entering New Zealand; any further money or property that they possess to be realised and the proceeds handed to the New Zealand Government for distribution among needy wives and dependants of those who fought while the enemy aliens enjoyed peace and plenty in New Zealand.[39]

While editorial backing for this resolution came from some newspapers,[40] others condemned such extreme expressions of racism and intolerance. Some clergy and academics spoke out against prejudice and intolerance. The Prime Minister, Peter Fraser, also raised these issues on a number of occasions in 1945:

If in this country, a spirit of animosity and hatred against any race raised its head, that would be a triumph of Nazism or fascism, though they have been stamped out in Germany ... I say that because it is easy to stir the feelings which ended in cruelties and concentration camps in Germany. I speak that as a word of warning. ... I hope that nowhere will any section of the community or any individual make any attack upon any of our people and particularly on strangers in our midst to whom we have given refuge.[41]

The experiences of refugees from Nazi Germany and Austria in New Zealand were largely determined by their relatively high level of education and mainly middle-class and urban origin. Perhaps because the refugees were not numerous and because they possessed the material and personal resources which ensured that they were not dependent on public assistance,

Karl Wolfskehl's house, Coronation Road, Epsom. *(Rochelle Gebbie)*

conflicts and tension between them and New Zealanders before the war were not significant. However, the relative ease of their integration was interrupted by the antagonisms that surfaced during the war years. At that time, for some refugees, New Zealand became an uneasy haven with echoes of the Nazism they had sought to escape.

This chapter has focused on the early settlement and wartime experiences of the approximately 900 refugees from Nazi Germany and Austria who, despite extremely restrictive immigration policies, succeeded in gaining entrance to New Zealand. In the years to come, this small group, which included some men and women particularly eminent in their field—poet Karl Wolfskehl, philosopher Karl Popper, architect Ernst Plischke, and actor Maria Dronke—went on to make a significant contribution in the fields of music, theatre, architecture, medicine, engineering, and business, among others. Most importantly perhaps, the refugees, along with other immigrants from Central and Eastern Europe, played a big part in enlivening the social and cultural climate of their adopted country.

1 Letter to Dr S. Rothmann of 9 September 1938 (in possession of the writer).

2 For further discussion, see Ann Beaglehole, *A Small Price to Pay: Refugees from Hitler in New Zealand, 1936–1946* (Wellington, 1988), pp. 8–34.

3 According to one estimate, 50,000 refugees applied for permits to enter New Zealand; see R.A. Lochore, *From Europe to New Zealand: An Account of Our Continental European Settlers* (Wellington, 1951), p. 81. According to another estimate, 1,731 applications were declined and 727 were granted in the period 1936–38; see F.A. Ponton, 'Immigration restriction in New Zealand: A study of policy from 1908 to 1939', MA thesis, University of New Zealand, 1946, p. 114 (quoting from C 33/253, memo of Comptroller to Minister, 30 November 1938). There are gaps in the evidence relating to pressure applied to New Zealand to accept refugees. The Customs Department files dealing with this issue have not survived.

4 National Archives, Nash 1311/0593, F.A. de la Mare, 'The refugee problem'; IC 20/86 part 1, memo for New Zealand Trade and Tourist Commissioner, Brussels, on the admission to New Zealand of foreign European nationals, from E.D. Good, Comptroller of Customs, 3 March 1939.

5 National Archives, IC 20/86 part 1, memo for New Zealand Trade and Tourist Commissioner from Good.

6 National Archives, IC 20/86 part 1, memo for New Zealand Trade and Tourist Commissioner from Good.

7 Nash's views are expressed in a number of letters. For example, in National Archives, Nash 1311/0607, letter from Nash to Mrs J. Hall of 21 March 1939.

8 German and Austrian figures are shown together in the records after 1938. There are some problems with stating exactly how many refugees from Central and Eastern Europe came to New Zealand, partly because accurate figures that distinguished between refugee immigrants and ordinary immigrants were not kept. Additionally, a number of difficulties arose when officials attempted to classify according to nationality people left stateless by Hitler's persecution. Some of these people had fled from one temporary home to another, and their passports and travel documents reflected not their nationalities but their escape routes from Europe. Problems also occurred in classifying by nationality people who did not easily fit into such a category, for example, those of Czech nationality who had lived all their lives in Austria or Germany. The figures (by nationality) of the refugees who came to New Zealand given here are the 'private calculations based on official data, published and unpublished' of Lochore (see [note 3], pp. 72f). Different figures were presented to the High Commissioner's office in London. For the years 1933–42, it was stated that 27 Austrians, 126 Czechs, 874 Germans and 85 Hungarians arrived in New Zealand; see National Archives, EA 108/4/1 1B, letter from the Secretary of External Affairs, A.D. McIntosh, to the Official Secretary, High Commissioner for the United Kingdom,

8 September 1944. This letter includes a table showing the number of refugees who arrived in New Zealand from 1933 to 1942 (inclusive). It is clear that both these sets of figures and others that are available were estimates only and that the interpretation of nationality varied.

9 For a full discussion of sources, including details about the interviews, see Beaglehole [note 2], pp. 1–7 and 134–40.

10 Lochore [note 3], p. 75.

11 No exact date for the opening of the French Maid was established.

12 Lochore [note 3], p. 87.

13 In 1945, 166 refugees, a quarter of all those 'gainfully employed', were working in one of the professions, about eighty of them in one of the health professions (Lochore [note 3], p. 78).

14 Only nurses were welcomed; see *Kai Tiaki: The New Zealand Nursing Journal*, vol. 32, no. 9 (15 September 1939), p. 310. Physiotherapists placed restrictions on the numbers of refugees accepted for requalification. Dentists met considerable opposition from the New Zealand Dental Association; see Ponton [note 3], p. 114.

15 Beaglehole [note 2], pp. 79ff.

16 Lochore [note 3], p. 78.

17 See for example *New Zealand Truth*, 29 September 1942.

18 National Archives, CAB 66/1/1, part 1, Individual Immigration of Aliens, 14 August 1950.

19 *New Zealand Jewish Chronicle*, August 1945, p. 233 (text of an address by Howard Wadham to the Optimists Club, Wellington, 26 July 1945).

20 Alexander Turnbull Library, Arthur Hilton folder 174; Lochore [note 3], p. 79.

21 National Archives, AD MO 16/15, 'Control of aliens during World War II', volumes 1 and 2. Some details concerning the restrictions on enemy aliens may be found in a report in the *Evening Post*, 10 April 1947.

22 *Dominion*, 10 June 1940 (editorial).

23 *New Zealand Truth*, 29 September 1942.

24 National Archives, Aliens and Naturalization, Notes, p. 17, refers to Regulation 50 of the Aliens Emergency Regulations 1940.

25 Aliens Land Purchase Regulations, March 1942.

26 Beaglehole [note 2], pp. 110f.

27 *New Zealand Truth*, 29 September 1942.

28 National Archives, EA 89/2/1, report entitled 'Aliens', 24 August 1944, refers to resolution at the annual general meeting of the RSA, 30 May 1941.

29 *Dominion*, 29 May 1944.

30 Federation of Labour Archives, NZFOL Minutes of National Executive, 20 August 1940.

31 For example, *New Zealand Parliamentary Debates*, vol. 265, 7 August 1944, p. 148.

32 National Archives, EA 89/2/9, part 1A. Approved by Cabinet on 22 July 1942.

33 National Archives EA 89/2/9, part 1A. This file contains correspondence and discussion papers on the proposed Aliens in Business Regulations 1944, including a paper, 'The employment of aliens'. National Archives, PM 89/2/4, part 2, contains the draft of Aliens in Business Regulations 1945.

34 National Archives, War History Narrative, Series 10, 114, p. 46.

35 National Archives, War History Narrative, Series 10, 114, p. 47.

36 National Archives, War History Narrative, Series 10, 114, p. 48.

37 National Archives, War History Narrative, Series 10, 114, p. 48. The Aliens Land Purchase Regulations 1942 are found in *Statutory Regulations* 1942, pp. 168–71.

38 L.M. Goldman, *The History of the Jews in New Zealand* (Wellington, 1958), p. 233. The resolution was in fact defeated.

39 The resolution is printed in Goldman [note 38], p. 232.

40 For example from the *Dominion*, 2 July 1945.

41 *Dominion*, 6 July 1945. This was a speech given by Peter Fraser at a civic reception in Auckland on his return from the San Francisco conference.

4

Count Felix von Luckner

JAMES N. BADE

Count Felix von Luckner remains one of the most controversial figures in twentieth-century New Zealand history. When he first arrived in New Zealand in October 1917 as a German prisoner of war, he had to be protected from outraged members of the public, who were demanding that he be hanged.[1] Yet when he returned in 1938 he was treated like a national hero.[2] He is a legend in his own right. But, as with all legends, it is sometimes difficult to separate fact from fiction, both in what he writes about himself and in what is written about him. Did he really beat the British blockade in 1916 by dressing up a 17-year-old crew member as a woman and passing him off as his Norwegian wife, unfortunately unable to speak because 'she' had bad toothache?[3] Were his plans to escape from Ripapa Island in early 1918 in a wooden barrel really delayed by his desire not to offend Major Leeming, the camp commandant, and then thwarted by his transfer to Motuihe Island, or were they just fanciful ideas?[4] Similarly, were his plans to escape from Motuihe for a second time really so far advanced that the escape, set down for 18 November 1918, was frustrated only by the armistice declaration a week earlier?[5] After all, von Luckner says himself that a search by hundreds of New Zealanders failed to locate their dug-out.[6] Did he really once save himself from drowning by grabbing hold of a low-flying albatross?[7] Was that really a severed thumb that he spied in the boudoir of the old gentleman in Hawaii who was helping him out of his clothes for the hula-hula dance?[8] Did Countess von Luckner really lock herself into a bathroom with a communist?[9] When assessing Count von Luckner's exploits it is necessary to maintain a modicum of healthy scepticism. Exciting though these accounts might be, we need to lay the myths aside; only those aspects that can be corroborated by outside sources can be regarded as historical fact.

Count Felix von Luckner was born in June 1881 into a family that, according to his own account, had a distinguished military history.[10] His great-grandfather, Count Nikolaus von Luckner, was a general in the Hanoverian army and at the time of his death in 1794 was Marshall of France.[11] Nikolaus von Luckner had acquired land in Holstein through marriage, and it was in Holstein that Felix von Luckner's father was born. The family later moved to Dresden, where his cousin lived.[12] Felix von Luckner attended grammar school (*Gymnasium*) in Dresden. His academic progress, he says, did not match his parents' expectations, and at the age of 13 he ran

Felix von Luckner on Motuihe Island, 1917. (*G. Riethmaier Collection*)

away from home, determined to go to sea.[13] Assuming the name of Phylax Lüdicke, he joined a Russian ship, the *Niobe*, as a cabin boy and jumped ship when it arrived in Fremantle, Australia.[14] For a while, he writes, he joined the Salvation Army, selling the *War Cry*. There followed a series of occupations as he worked his way across Australia and then, being rather disappointed with Australia, which he had expected to be much more interesting—'full of palms and Negroes with bows and arrows'[15]—he left Brisbane on board the *Golden Shore*, bound for Hawaii and Seattle. He spent some time in North America, returning to Hamburg via Vancouver and Liverpool.[16] After further adventures on the high seas, he returned to Germany and entered the navy. Eight years after leaving home he returned to his parents as Naval Lieutenant Felix von Luckner.[17] His years of wandering—'Wanderjahre'—were over.[18]

When World War I broke out, von Luckner was determined to help the German war effort by harassing Allied shipping, but the British blockade of German ports was a formidable obstacle to this objective.[19] On 23 December 1916, however, he managed to break through the British blockade in an American clipper that the Germans had captured and converted for the purpose. Von Luckner and his crew pretended that they were Norwegians carrying timber to Australia. Once through the blockade, the clipper, now named the *Seeadler*, proceeded into the Atlantic and the Pacific in pursuit of Allied merchant shipping. Between 9 January and 8 July 1917 the *Seeadler* sank fourteen Allied ships, including the *Pinmore*, the British vessel on which von Luckner had himself sailed to Liverpool.[20] In all these operations, there was only one fatality.[21] Those who were taken captive by von Luckner unanimously spoke well of him.[22]

Because of his concern for the health of his crew, von Luckner decided to head for an uninhabited island in the Society Islands group, which might afford fresh water and provisions. The scene was now set for the extraordinary train of events that would make von Luckner a living legend in this part of the world. On 29 July 1917 the *Seeadler* approached Mopelia Island, which appeared like Paradise before them.[23] The island lived up to their expectations. There were fish, birds, coconut palms, tortoises, and wild pigs in abundance. On the morning of 2 August, however, a wave dashed the *Seeadler* against a coral reef.[24] The crew salvaged what they could and made tents out of the *Seeadler*'s sails. A little tent village was set up, which they called 'Seeadlerdorf', 'the last German colony'.[25] On 26 August von Luckner, his navigating officer Lieutenant Kircheiss, two petty officers, and two leading seamen set off in a six-metre-long open boat for the Cook Islands, leaving fifty-eight crew and prisoners of war on Mopelia Island under the command of his First Officer, Lieutenant Kling.[26]

On 30 August they arrived at Aitutaki, telling the Resident Agent that they were Dutch Americans. The Resident Agent did not seem altogether satisfied with this explanation, and others on the island were convinced that they were Germans. Nevertheless, they were allowed to continue after replenishing supplies, and they set sail for Fiji.[27] After taking on provisions at Niue, where, von Luckner says, they were given a grand welcome as the enemy of the much-hated English, they arrived, exhausted, at Wakaya Island,

Fiji, on 23 September. This time von Luckner pretended to be a Dane whose launch had broken down. He writes that his talent for lying at this point exceeded even that of New Zealand newspapers. He was told to await the arrival of a vessel, the *Amra*, carrying the owner of a boat that could tow him. Much to von Luckner's surprise, a boat lowered from the *Amra* pulled alongside, and an officer called on him to surrender.[28] That officer was Sub-Inspector Hill of the Fiji Police, who had four armed policemen with him. In his account, Sub-Inspector Hill, stationed in Levuka, says that on 23 September a boy from Wakaya Island named McPherson arrived in a cutter and stated that there was a strange launch there with a crew of six. The crew, the boy reported, 'talked English in a peculiar way—very much like Mr Straub, the ex-German Consul at Levuka, and asked many questions'. Hill was convinced that the crew must in some way be associated with the launch that called at the Cook Islands in August. With the Governor's blessing, Hill took the *Amra* to Wakaya and intercepted the German boat.[29] Kircheiss stepped on board first, followed by von Luckner and the others. The Germans' launch was taken to Suva, where it was later sold.[30]

After a brief imprisonment in Suva, von Luckner and his crew were brought to New Zealand, arriving in Auckland on 7 October. At this stage of the war, newspapers were carrying daily lists, often numbering hundreds at a time, of New Zealand soldiers killed or wounded, and the whole nation was in a state of grief. It was only natural that this sorrow was likely to be expressed in anger and hostility towards the German captives. In order to protect the Germans from outraged members of the public, von Luckner and Kircheiss were first hidden in the detention barracks at Devonport before being sent to the internment camp at Motuihe Island. The other four were sent to the internment camp at Somes Island in Wellington Harbour, but one of them, Leading Seaman Erdmann, was transferred to Motuihe in November at von Luckner's request to act as his orderly and valet.[31] A number of Germans were already interned at Motuihe, including the former German Governor of Samoa, Dr Schulz, and his officials.[32]

Von Luckner and Kircheiss on Motuihe Island, 1917.
(G. Riethmaier Collection)

Group on Motuihe Island; von Luckner centre, von Zatorski in uniform to the right of von Luckner.
(G. Riethmaier Collection)

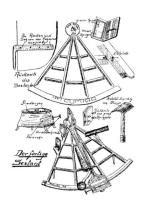

Sketch of von Zatorski's sextant indicating where the various parts came from. (*W. von Zatorski, Es kämpfen Männer und nicht Schiffe, Bremen, 1930*)

The German internees were permitted full freedom of movement over most of the island, and von Luckner appreciated the natural beauty of the surroundings. The fact remained, however, that it was an internment camp, and from their very first days on Motuihe Island, von Luckner and Kircheiss were formulating plans for escape.[33] This seemed best achieved by seizing the camp commandant's launch, the *Pearl*. Von Luckner selected a potential crew from among the German contingent at Motuihe who had been captured in Samoa, and these, some of whom were cadets from Norddeutscher Lloyd, were to accompany Kircheiss, Erdmann, and himself on this mission.

Over the next few weeks, using preparations for a camp variety concert as a front, makeshift nautical instruments were made by metal workers in the workshop, including a sextant constructed by Walther von Zatorski from odds and ends he found lying around the island;[34] old explosives were found and made into bombs by the metalworkers; provisions were set aside; and Kircheiss worked out a nautical map based on information in the camp library. Some of the internees were instructed as to how to distract the guards should the appropriate moment come for capturing the launch. That moment arrived at 6 p.m. on 13 December, when the Commandant of Motuihe Island, Lieutenant-Colonel C.H. Turner, returned from Auckland with the *Pearl*.[35] As soon as the Commandant was safely in the barracks, the signal was given, the telephone line to Auckland was earthed, and all crew members converged separately on the arranged spot. By 6.15 they had departed: the *Pearl* was plying her way north towards Cape Colville.[36]

One might well ask what the point of the escape was. In von Luckner's German narrative,[37] he says the aim was to seize a sailing ship and head for Samoa, where they would entice the New Zealand Governor, Logan, on board by pretending that they were a New Zealand vessel carrying a message from the New Zealand Minister of Defence. The plan then was to arrest the Governor and intern him and the other New Zealanders on Samoa. A fanciful plan, but one that would have appealed to those involved.[38] In the meantime, however, the immediate objective was to get as far away from

Motuihe Island, 1997. The area previously occupied by the internment camp is now a popular picnic area. (*James N. Bade*)

Auckland as was reasonably possible given the circumstances and the craft involved, and then to lie in wait for a suitable vessel to commandeer, heading initially for the Kermadec Islands, where they could raid the New Zealand Government's depot on Curtis Island to obtain provisions. They passed Cape Colville during the course of the night and next morning sheltered at Red Mercury Island. Two days later, two scows, the *Rangi* and the *Moa*, were spied coming up from the south. Von Luckner decided to capture the *Moa* first, threatening the crew with hand grenades and demanding their surrender. He was unable to capture the *Rangi*, however, as she was moving too fast.[39] Captain Bourke, of the *Moa*, was ordered to sail to the Kermadecs, and, sporting a German ensign that the internees had made out of an old sheet at Motuihe, the *Moa* arrived at Curtis Island on 21 December.[40]

In the meantime, the news of the escape had broken in Auckland, and Aucklanders responded *en masse* to the appeal from the Minister of Defence, Sir James Allen, which appeared in the *New Zealand Herald* of Saturday 15 December, to be on the lookout for the escapees: 'It is not known in what direction they have gone. Steps have been taken to search for them, and the public are invited to be on the watch, and to report at once to the police any information which may aid in the discovery of those who escaped.' Recreational craft of all descriptions helped with the search. The official patrol comprised twenty-nine craft: eight Defence, Harbour Board, and Police steamers, nine Defence motorboats, ten privately owned launches, and two private yachts.[41]

The public's readiness to help was matched only by the public outrage at the lax security arrangements that had allowed the internees to escape in the first place. The *Herald* reported three days later: 'No local news which has been published in Auckland or in New Zealand since the war commenced has aroused such an indignant storm of protest as the escape of the Germans from Motuihi.'[42] Even the Prime Minister, Mr Massey, was quoted as saying that the escape from Motuihe was 'the most regrettable thing that has occurred since the war has begun'.[43] Such public indignation was no doubt fuelled further by responses from the Commandant of Motuihe Island, Lieutenant-Colonel Turner, to questions addressed to him at the Motuihe enquiry. For instance, asked by Colonel C.R. Macdonald, presiding over the inquiry, whether he had any misgivings at not reporting what he saw as the increased possibility of an escape attempt with the arrival of the *Seeadler* officers on Motuihe Island, Lieutenant-Colonel Turner replied: 'No, as I could not see what the *Seeadler* officers could do if they did get away.'[44]

As it turned out, Captain Francis of the *Rangi* reported the *Moa* incident to the New Zealand Government cable ship, the *Iris*, which was rounding Cape Colville on the afternoon of 16 December, having been despatched from Auckland at midday at the request of the Minister of Defence.[45] Correctly surmising that the German party would be replenishing stores at the Curtis Island depot, Captain Holmes, captain of the *Iris*, headed for the Kermadecs. He sighted the *Moa* on the afternoon of 21 December and pursued and intercepted her. The *Moa* stopped after a shot was fired across her bows, whereupon von Luckner came on board the *Iris* and formally surrendered.[46] In spite of his somewhat harrowing experience, Captain Bourke of

GERMANS CAPTURED

VON LUCKNER AND WHOLE PARTY

SURRENDER AT KERMADECS

NOW ON BOARD THE IRIS

CREW OF SCOW MOA SAFE

Official advice was received in Auckland last evening that the eleven German prisoners who escaped from the Motuihi Internment Camp on the evening of December 13 were recaptured by the Pacific Cable Board's steamer Iris about mid-day yesterday at the Kermadecs Islands. This group is 600 miles from Auckland.

Few details were available last evening as to the exact nature of the recapture, but it is fairly certain that it was effected without bloodshed. All the Germans were secured. They were on board the scow Moa, which they seized off Mercury Bay last Sunday.

The crew of the Moa, consisting of five men and a boy, were found safe on board and all well.

The Moa was flying the German flag.

The intention of the escaped men in proceeding to the Kermadecs was apparently to secure food, it being well-known that there is a provision depot on the islands for castaways.

The Iris left Auckland last Sunday about noon. She had mounted two six-pounder guns, one forward and one aft. Besides the ordinary crew two gun crews were sent, consisting of men from the Garrison Artillery under the command of Captain Mellows, A.S.C. The Iris is capable of steaming about 11 knots an hour. Her first call was at Great Mercury Island, where there is a small resident population. She also visited the islets in the vicinity of Mercury Bay, on the eastern side of the Coromandel Peninsula. An armed party was landed on most of the islands and a thorough search made for the fugitives or the members of the Moa's crew, it having become fairly certain by this time that the Germans had captured the scow. The Alderman Islands, which lie, roughly, 17 miles east-south-east of Mercury Bay and 11 miles off the nearest land, were also visited, but the search was unsuccessful.

By instructions from the Auckland military authorities the Iris then steamed to the Kermadec group, it being considered extremely likely that the escaped men would make for the provision depot in order to secure a supply of food. The Iris arrived at the Kermadecs at noon on Wednesday and cruised about in the vicinity. Anticipations were realized yesterday when the Moa was sighted and the whole party captured. Considering her speed and the weather conditions, it is judged that the scow must have sailed direct for the Kermadecs.

Late last night a wireless message was received to the effect that the Iris was on her way back to Auckland with the German prisoners of war on board.

As far as is known, the Moa will be brought back to port by her own crew.

The leader and senior officer of the escaped Germans was Lieutenant-Commander Count Felix von Luckner, whose exploits as commander of the raider Seeadler in the Pacific will be keenly remembered. Next in seniority was Second-Lieutenant Carl Theodore Frederich Kirscheiss, who was second in command of the Seeadler. Hermann Erdmann was a leading seaman on the raider and an expert signaler. There were five naval cadets—Walter von Zatorski, Walter Schmidt, Fritz Mellert, Albert Paulsen, and Ernest Klohs. Otto Freund was a wireless engineer, and Carl Grunn a morse operator. The remaining member of the party was Albrecht von Egidy, a plantation owner, formerly of Samoa.

Banner headlines in the *New Zealand Herald* of Saturday, 22 December 1917 announce the capture of von Luckner and his crew.

the *Moa* described von Luckner as being 'a good sport'. He reported that the Germans had 'treated the crew of the "Moa" well'.[47]

The capture of the German escapees was given banner headlines in the *New Zealand Herald* of 22 December, a wireless message having been received on the preceding evening that the *Iris* was 'on her way back to Auckland with the German prisoners of war on board'.[48] On their return to Auckland, the Germans were placed in Mount Eden Jail. Here the prison inmates gave von Luckner a hero's welcome—he described them as practically without exception 'extraordinarily pro-German'. He put this down to a belief (which he may or may not have encouraged) that, if Germany won the war, von Luckner would be appointed German governor of New Zealand and that he would be able to pardon them all.[49] Sympathy for the underdog and a healthy disrespect for those in authority, however, are two typical New Zealand traits, and von Luckner's escape from Motuihe Island—described by Titchener as 'one of the most audacious escape attempts in the history of war'[50]—held a tremendous appeal for New Zealanders both inside and outside Mount Eden Jail. To this equation one must add von Luckner's remarkable capacity to adjust to new situations and his ability to relate to people of all social and ethnic backgrounds.

After three weeks in Mount Eden Jail, the conspirators were split up and sent to various camps throughout New Zealand. Von Luckner and Kircheiss were sent to Ripapa Island in Lyttelton Harbour. Von Luckner had a particularly good rapport with the camp commandant there, Major Leeming—'a gentleman from head to toe'[51]—who joined him and Kircheiss in evening card games. Von Luckner writes that he did not want to betray Major Leeming's trust by carrying out another escape bid and therefore waited for his temporary replacement, Lieutenant Gilmore, before any further attempt. Lieutenant Gilmore, however, turned out to be 'quite a nice chap'[52] also. After four months, von Luckner and Kircheiss were returned to Motuihe.

During the weeks that followed, von Luckner writes, various schemes were mooted for possible attempts to escape. The most daring involved the construction of a hidden dug-out, which would house five escapees (including the former German governor of Samoa, Dr Schulz) for six weeks, the idea being that by that time the New Zealand authorities, thinking they had escaped by sea, would have given up looking for them. They could then escape surreptitiously in a small collapsible raft and commandeer a yacht or steal a boat from Auckland. A second plan involved setting fire to the barracks, taking possession of the guards' quarters, and capturing the first vessel that berthed at the wharf. In a third plan, the crew of the government steamer *Lady Roberts*, a regular visitor to the island, were to be overpowered. The war ended before any of these plans could be realised.[53] Von Luckner claims that the preparations for the dug-out escape were well advanced by the time the armistice was announced on 11 November 1918, but it would be an exaggeration to refer to this scheme, as has been done in the past, as 'von Luckner's second attempt to escape'.[54]

Some four months later, von Luckner and his fellow prisoners were released. They were returned to Germany on board the *Willochra* in July 1919. The rest of the *Seeadler* crew, who had been taken to Chile after sail-

Ripapa Island (upper left) in Lyttelton Harbour is today a historical reserve. *(James N. Bade)*

Von Luckner and his crew on board the *Seeteufel* at Tahiti in 1937. Left to right: Paul Kunert (Engineer), Paul Krause (First Officer), Frederick Thiele (Able Seaman), Otto Katschke (Able Seaman), Holm Winter (Cook), Gregory Riethmaier (Wireless Operator), Countess Ingeborg von Luckner, Count von Luckner, Karl Müller (Boatswain). *(G. Riethmaier Collection)*

ing to Easter Island on the Tahitian schooner *Lutece* (which they had captured when it visited Mopelia Island), arrived back in Germany in January 1920.[55]

Von Luckner returned to New Zealand in 1938 as part of a world tour on the windjammer *Seeteufel*—the name he had given his German memoirs, and the name by which he liked to refer to himself.[56] This time he was again a controversial figure but of a different kind. The Germany to which he returned in 1919 was no longer the old fatherland of which he had been so fond. His background and his experiences led him, like many others of his ilk, to oppose the new German republic. His apparent refusal to fly the flag of the Weimar Republic on the naval training ship he was commanding might attest to the intensity of his anti-republic feelings.[57] These sentiments, combined with statements that appeared to be sympathetic to the National

Socialist Party, led to suspicions that von Luckner was a Nazi emissary.[58] There is no doubt that a world cruise by von Luckner would have been of tremendous propaganda value for the Nazis. Von Luckner was not, however, a member of the Nazi Party.

Nevertheless, there was a great deal of opposition to his visit here, particularly among the organised labour movement. As early as August 1937 the Auckland District Council of the New Zealand Federation of Labour passed a resolution condemning 'Count von Luckner as a self-declared agent of Hitler, and of a social order that has destroyed legal trade unionism in Germany'.[59] In March 1938, when Count von Luckner, together with his wife, Countess Ingeborg, arrived in Wellington, the National Council of the New Zealand Federation of Labour, which was meeting there at that time, challenged him to a public debate on fascism and democracy. Von Luckner declined, but commented:

I can tell you, it is in the working people that the strength of Hitler is placed. I am not a member of the Nazi Party. I am an officer and can belong to no political party. I tell you frankly, at first many of us were not in favour of the Nazi movement, but today we have come to think otherwise. But I do not want to argue with these people. If Wellington does not want me, why, I will go elsewhere. I have come only to spread the gospel of good will. In wartime, for the service of my God, I sank the nitrate carriers whose cargoes would have been converted into munitions to kill thousands of people. I never deprived a mother of her son. I loved the New Zealand people because they were sportsmen when I was imprisoned here, and escaped, captured the *Moa*, and afterwards was caught again. … What have I done to deserve this? It hurts me.[60]

The Federation of Labour offered this rejoinder:

We regret that an invitation to publicly debate his ideas should have so hurt Count von Luckner, but it is only just to remind him that the Nazis have never considered the feelings of other people whose ideas differed from theirs. Even today the feelings of some people are being so outraged by the Nazis that they prefer suicide to the prospect of continued existence under Nazi domination.[61]

Count and Countess von Luckner, March 1938. *(Alexander Turnbull Library, Ref. no. C-1243)*

Von Luckner revisiting Motuihe Island in 1938 with Countess Ingeborg, surrounded by the crew of the *Seeteufel* and officials of the Auckland Harbour Board.
(G. Riethmaier Collection)

The fact that von Luckner's visit coincided with the Nazi invasion of Austria did not help matters. Newspaper headlines highlighted the declaration of Austria as 'a state of the Reich'[62] as she was 'swiftly invaded' and her independence 'swept away';[63] they pointed to the lengthening of the 'Nazi shadow',[64] the suffering of the Jews in Vienna at the 'seizure by the Nazis' of Jewish cafés, shops, and hotels,[65] and a 'crisis in Europe' said to be 'as serious as in 1914'.[66] Von Luckner's interpretation of the invasion of Austria as a 'powerful factor towards the peace of Europe' and for the 'ultimate good of Austria'[67] was dismissed by Professor A.B. Fitt of Auckland University College, who had himself studied in Germany, as 'nothing but Nazi propaganda'. Professor Fitt asked, with considerable insight: 'Does he assure us that what happened and still happens to the Jews in Germany will not happen to the Jews in Austria? That persecution of the German Jews will make unpleasant reading in history.'[68]

In spite of such controversy, or perhaps partly because of it, people flocked to von Luckner's public lectures, which were given throughout the length and breadth of New Zealand.[69] A warm welcome was afforded him at the Eden-Roskill Returned Soldiers' Club in Auckland. 'You will attend no meeting in New Zealand', Sir George Richardson is quoted as saying in his vote of thanks, 'where there will be more sincere feelings and warmer regard extended to you than you have received from the returned men in Auckland tonight.'[70] A large audience gave him an enthusiastic reception at the Wellington Opera House on 19 March, and subsequent lectures in Wellington, Lower Hutt, Masterton, and Palmerston North seem to have been equally successful.[71] In Auckland he revisited Mount Eden Jail and his old quarters on Motuihe Island, even claiming to find the remains of the 'cave' where supplies had been hidden in preparation for his 1917 escape bid,[72] but in Christchurch he was not allowed to visit Ripapa Island because it housed a military establishment.[73]

Finally, on 3 May 1938, the time had come for him to leave. He told a crowd of well-wishers who had gathered in Auckland to farewell him and the *Seeteufel* that he was leaving his heart in New Zealand. He thanked the people of New Zealand 'for their wonderful hospitality' and added: 'I will long to come back again; indeed, I must, for I am leaving my heart here.'[74] He was not destined to return, however. He spent the war years in his home town of Halle and in the final stages of the war is said to have saved Halle from destruction by persuading the general in charge of the American forces to spare it.[75] After the war, he moved to Countess Ingeborg's home town, Malmö, in southern Sweden, where he died in 1966.[76]

Apart from his irritation at New Zealanders' politeness (he stated that he preferred an honest German refusal to the polite New Zealand phrase 'We will see what we can do for you'[77]) and the constant impression he gives that New Zealanders were easy to dupe, von Luckner wrote positively about New Zealand and its people in the German version of his memoirs. Even taking into account his propensity for exaggeration, there is no doubt that he regarded New Zealand with some fondness. He was later to refer to New Zealand as 'this country of my dreams'[78] and 'the most wonderful country I know'.[79] New Zealanders respected the fact that, in all his raiding and commandeering activities, he did everything he could to avoid any loss of life. Although it is clear from his memoirs that he often contemplated the option of using armed force to get his way, in reality he only used force as a last resort. An arrogant braggart he might have been, and who knows whether half of his stories are to be believed?[80] But, in his raiding activities at least, he played the game strictly by the rules. He treated his victims with respect and received their respect in return. In the official British naval war history, Henry Newbolt, full of 'admiration' for the 'seamanlike chivalry' with which he carried out his operations, wrote of von Luckner:

In all the testimonies of his English and French prisoners there is no word of complaint against him; some even go out of their way to say that he treated them kindly; we can therefore conclude, with certainty, that he was a bold, calculating and adventurous leader; and we have every reason to believe that he was a kindly and courteous gentleman as well.[81]

Shirley Maddock writes that her sister once asked von Luckner whether he had ever worried about the risks and danger he incurred in the course of his wartime exploits. 'Risks? Danger?' he replied. 'Ah my dear, those days were different. We were all gentlemen then.'[82] And New Zealand, he told an assembly of well-wishers gathered to farewell him from Auckland in May 1938, 'is indeed a country of gentlemen'.[83]

1 Paul Titchener, *The Von Luckner Incident* (Auckland, 1978), p. 11.
2 Matthew Wright, 'Von Luckner—the gentleman warrior', *Dominion Sunday Times*, 17 March 1991.
3 'Von Luckner's narrative', in *Pirate von Luckner and the Cruise of the 'Seeadler'* (Auckland, 1919), p. 5.
4 Graf Felix von Luckner, *Seeteufel: Abenteuer aus meinem Leben* (Berlin and Leipzig, 1926), pp. 297–9.
5 Von Luckner [note 4], p. 303.
6 Von Luckner [note 4], p. 303. Count von Luckner claims that he found 'our hole in the ground' on his return to Motuihe in 1938. See Felix Count von Luckner, *Out of an Old Sea Chest*, translated by Edward Fitzgerald (London, 1958), p. 141.
7 See Lowell Thomas, *Count Luckner, the Sea Devil* (New York 1928), pp. 23f. As Thomas's English

rendering of von Luckner's exploits is not as detailed as von Luckner's German original, most of the references in this chapter will be to von Luckner's *Seeteufel* [note 4].

8 Von Luckner [note 4], pp. 27–9.

9 See Carl Rühen, *The Sea Devil: The Controversial Cruise of the Nazi Emissary von Luckner to Australia and New Zealand in 1938* (Kenthurst, 1988), p. 93.

10 Rühen [note 9], p. 9. Walther von Zatorski, in his book *Es kämpfen Männer und nicht Schiffe: Südseeabenteuer mit Graf Luckner* (Bremen, 1930), prefers to call Luckner 'Graf Luckner', raising the possibility that von Luckner's aristocratic 'von' may have been an affectation. As he was known in New Zealand as 'von Luckner', I have retained the 'von' in this chapter.

11 Von Luckner [note 4], pp. 81f.

12 Von Luckner [note 4], pp. 82f.

13 Von Luckner [note 4], pp. 1–5.

14 Von Luckner [note 4], pp. 9–19.

15 Von Luckner [note 4], p. 19.

16 Von Luckner [note 4], pp. 19–33.

17 Von Luckner [note 4], pp. 69–80. Cf. Thomas [note 7], pp. 78–84.

18 Von Luckner [note 4], p. 80.

19 Titchener [note 1], p. 3.

20 Von Luckner [note 4], pp. 147–98, Thomas [note 7], pp. 110–222, Titchener [note 1], p. 4. In 'Von Luckner's narrative' [note 3], pp. 11–22, von Luckner claimed that he commandeered the *Pinmore* and took her to Rio de Janeiro in March 1917 to obtain provisions before sinking her, but there is no mention of this in *Seeteufel* [note 4] or in Thomas [note 7]. Henry Newbolt, in *History of the Great War Based on Official Documents: Naval Operations*, Vol. 4 (London, 1928), p. 200, says of this version: 'The story is not, in itself, impossible; but it is more likely that Count von Luckner could not resist the temptation to score off his captors by making them believe that they had been more careless and stupid than was really the case.'

21 Von Luckner was fond of saying that not a single life was lost during his raiding operations. In *Out of an Old Sea Chest* [note 6], for example, he writes: 'The enemy certainly lost a good few ships at our hands, but he didn't lose a single life, and before I gave the order to sink any of the many ships we accounted for I took care to see that even the ship's cat was safe' (p. 15). However, in his narrative in *Pirate von Luckner* [note 3], von Luckner writes that the steamer *Hongarth* was fired on after ignoring a signal from the *Seeadler* and that during the firing one of the crew of the *Hongarth* was 'badly injured by a shell splinter'. As soon as possible, he continues, the injured crewman was brought aboard the *Seeadler* and treated by the ship's surgeon, who operated and removed the splinter from the man's forehead, 'but at 10 p.m. he died' (pp. 13f). This incident is corroborated by the account of a sailor among the captives on board the *Seeadler* who witnessed the capture of the *Hongarth*. He writes: 'And now happened our one and only tragedy. An apprentice aboard the *Hongarth* had been wounded, and in spite of the skill of the German doctor he died. He was buried next day with all honors, the raider was stopped, the British flag covering his canvas shroud, and the band playing the Dead March. The burial service was held and he was committed to the deep. The Count himself performed the ceremony, and all could see that he was genuinely grieved' ('The man who met von Luckner: True story of an encounter with the Seeadler', in *World's News*, 25 June 1938, p. 41). This incident is not mentioned in *Seeteufel* [note 4], *Count Luckner, the Sea Devil* [note 7], nor in *Out of an Old Sea Chest* [note 6].

22 Robin Bromby, *German Raiders of the South Seas* (Sydney and Auckland 1985), p. 172.

23 Von Luckner [note 4], p. 203. 'Von Luckner's narrative' [note 3] gives the date as 26 August, but as that same date is also given in this account for his departure from Mopelia for the Cook Islands, it is obviously false.

24 The *New Zealand Herald* carried two reports on the stranding of the *Seeadler*. The first, on 23 October, described the event thus: 'One day, before the cleaning was completed, a gale swung the ship on to the reef. There the heavy seas caught her. Several big rollers lifted her and dashed her down on to the sharp coral reef, and her back was broken.' In a further report in the *Herald* two days later, Captain Holder Smith, of the American schooner *R.C. Slade*, who had been captured by the *Seeadler* and marooned with the other captives on Mopelia Island, described the incident as follows: 'On August 2, in the morning at half-past nine o'clock, there was a little puff

of wind from the westward, and the ship went ashore, and there she stuck. She started to pound to pieces, and about noon time she was half-full of water. The officers were away on a picnic, and left the vessel. They left one officer on board. Half the crew was ashore, too. Before they could get up steam she struck.'

25 Von Luckner [note 4], pp. 200–12.

26 Von Luckner [note 4], pp. 217–19, 'Von Luckner's narrative' [note 3], p. 17.

27 Von Luckner [note 4], pp. 225–8, 'Von Luckner's narrative' [note 3], pp. 17–19.

28 Von Luckner [note 4], pp. 233–6, 'Von Luckner's narrative' [note 3], p. 19. The latter does not mention the Niue incident, but it is included in Thomas [note 7], pp. 262–4.

29 A report from the Suva correspondent of the *New Zealand Herald* dated 2 October, which appeared in the *New Zealand Herald* of 11 October, states that the steamer *Amra* was expected to arrive in Suva 'with a detachment of German prisoners' on the evening of Friday 21 September. As the report contains other inaccuracies (in the spelling of names, for example), this date is presumably erroneous.

30 'Sub-Inspector Hill's account' in *Pirate von Luckner* [note 3], pp. 21–2.

31 'Von Luckner's narrative' [note 3], p. 20; cf. Titchener [note 1], p. 11.

32 Von Luckner [note 4], pp. 252f.

33 According to Walther von Zatorski ([note 10], pp. 170, 173, 177f), plans for escape were well advanced before von Luckner's arrival. Von Zatorski had helped to build a boat for the canteen manager in 1916, but the boat was sold before it could be used for an escape. When the camp commandant got his own boat the following year, Freund, Paulsen, and von Zatorski offered their services again with the same end in mind. Von Luckner's arrival, von Zatorski writes, intensified the plans for escape in that his presence meant that the Germans were less likely to come to harm during an escape bid as von Luckner would be their commandant and they could be sworn in as German soldiers.

34 Von Zatorski ([note 10], pp. 174–6) describes in some detail how he made the sextant. He noted that New Zealand authorities concluded that someone on land must have helped him, but in fact, he writes, only one screw was provided from outside (via Grün in Devonport).

35 Von Luckner [note 4], pp. 252–81; 'Von Luckner's narrative: Planning escape', in *Pirate von Luckner* [note 3], pp. 22–7.

36 Thomas's version ([note 7], p. 299)—that barracks were set on fire to distract attention from the escape—is not mentioned in other accounts. It appears to have been based on a scheme von Luckner devised on his second internment at Motuihe. See 'Von Luckner's narrative' [note 3], p. 41. In an interview with J. Wadham on 2 September 1982 (Auckland Institute and Museum Reference File No. 849), Frederick Stunzner, who was also interned on Motuihe, commented: 'The barracks were never set on fire as is reported in Lowell Thomas' book.'

37 Von Luckner [note 4], pp. 273f.

38 Von Zatorski ([note 10], pp. 223–5), on the other hand, indicates that the escapees had hopes of returning to Germany. In a passage which is highly critical of von Luckner's handling of the escape bid, von Zatorski claims that, in deciding not to capture a vessel they had sighted on the evening of 15 December, they had missed the opportunity to commandeer a newer, more seaworthy vessel with plenty of supplies, which could have taken them back to 'home waters' and conceivably, despite the blockade, back to Germany. Titchener ([note 1], p. 20) suggests that they intended sailing back to Mopelia Island to rescue the stranded crew, but the news that the *Seeadler*'s crew had left Mopelia on the *Lutece* on 9 September and that the rest of the marooned victims of the *Seeadler* had been rescued by an expedition which left Papeete on 10 October had been widely reported. (See *New Zealand Herald*, 19 October 1917.)

39 'Von Luckner's narrative' [note 3], pp. 27–9.

40 Von Luckner [note 4], p. 286.

41 'Hunting the escapees' in *Pirate von Luckner* [note 3], p. 43.

42 *New Zealand Herald*, 18 December 1917.

43 *New Zealand Herald*, 19 December 1917.

44 *New Zealand Herald*, 22 December 1917.

45 'Captain Francis' story' and 'Hunting the escapees' in *Pirate von Luckner* [note 3], pp. 33f and 44.

46 'Report by the captain of the "Iris"' in *Pirate von Luckner* [note 3], p. 37.

47 'Capt. Bourke's experiences' in *Pirate von Luckner* [note 3], p. 36.
48 *New Zealand Herald*, 22 December 1917.
49 Von Luckner [note 4], pp. 294f.
50 Titchener [note 1], p. 11.
51 Von Luckner [note 4], pp. 296f.
52 Von Luckner [note 4], p. 299.
53 'Von Luckner's narrative' [note 3], pp. 38–42; von Luckner [note 4], pp. 301–3.
54 See, for example, 'Von Luckner's second attempt to escape' in *Pirate von Luckner* [note 3], p. 38.
55 'Fate of the "Lutece"' in *Pirate von Luckner* [note 3], p. 48. The only crew member who did not
    return was the ship's doctor, Dr Pietsch, who died of a heart attack in Chile in 1918. See von
    Luckner [note 4], p. 307.
56 'Sea Devil'. Cf. note 4.
57 Carl Rühen [note 9], p. 9.
58 See Rühen [note 9], pp. 23–60.
59 Rühen [note 9], p. 40.
60 *Evening Post*, 19 March 1938.
61 *Evening Post*, 19 March 1938.
62 *Evening Post*, 14 March 1938.
63 *New Zealand Herald*, 14 March 1938.
64 *New Zealand Herald*, 15 March 1938.
65 *New Zealand Herald*, 17 March 1938.
66 *Evening Post*, 17 March 1938.
67 *New Zealand Herald*, 16 March 1938.
68 *New Zealand Herald*, 16 March 1938. Nazi files indicate that von Luckner's voyage was in fact
    conceived by the authorities as a propaganda exercise. Relations between von Luckner and the
    Nazi authorities deteriorated rapidly after his return, however, partly because there was some
    doubt as to whether he had attached sufficient importance to the propaganda aspect of his voy-
    age. See Norbert von Frankenstein, *'Seeteufel' Felix Graf Luckner: Wahrheit und Legende* (Hamburg,
    1997), pp. 173–237.
69 Rühen [note 9], pp. 49–60.
70 *New Zealand Herald*, 17 March 1938.
71 *Evening Post*, 21 March 1938.
72 *New Zealand Herald*, 15 March 1938.
73 Rühen [note 9], pp. 47–50 and 56f.
74 *New Zealand Herald*, 4 May 1938.
75 Von Luckner [note 6], pp. 193–200.
76 'Flag story revives memories of sea raider', *Auckland Star*, 30 August 1982; cf. letter, dated 16
    August 1980, from Captain Walther von Zatorski, Osterholz-Scharzbeck, Germany, to Mr M.K.
    Fitzgerald, Curator of Colonial History, National Museum of New Zealand, Wellington, in
    Auckland Institute and Museum, Reference File no. 849.
77 Von Luckner [note 4], pp. 255f and 296.
78 Rühen [note 9], p. 23.
79 Rühen [note 9], p. 45.
80 In this connection it is interesting to note the comments of the New Zealand Deputy Chief
    Postal Censor, W.A. Tanner, in a letter of 28 November 1919 to Brigadier-General George
    Richardson of Defence Headquarters, accompanying a picture purporting to show von Luckner
    as a Maori chief: 'This picture and the accompanying description is typical of the character of
    our former Prisoner of War, who might well be called "Baron Munchausen [*sic*] the Second".
    His self-esteem, as has been noted in the past from his letters, is very considerably above the nor-
    mal and his sense of truth, primitive' (National Archives of New Zealand, Wellington, ref. AAAB
    482 70 L).
81 Henry Newbolt [note 20], pp. 195 and 197.
82 Shirley Maddock, *Islands of the Gulf* (Auckland, 1983, rev. edn), pp. 57f.
83 *New Zealand Herald*, 4 May 1938.

5

Major Geoffrey Bedding

GRAEME HORNE

After staunchly resisting the onslaught of German paratroopers on the island of Crete one day in May 1941, Major Thomas Geoffrey Bedding had found himself and his troops completely isolated from other Allied forces by terrain and severed communication links. It was shortly after making efforts in a local post office to try to establish contact with other Allied units that Bedding's adventures as a POW (prisoner of war) were to begin. The post office was bombed by what he believes to have been a Junkers dive bomber, and, after being dug out of the rubble by his troops, he re-entered the battle, confused, his head spinning, and with a ruptured right ear drum. Austrian Alpine troops had now arrived on the scene to reinforce the struggling German units. Major Bedding became, in his words, 'engaged in a pretty grim sort of a scrum',[1] which ended with him being taken prisoner. His experiences towards the closing stages of the war, however, would take quite a different direction, and one that could be said to foreshadow the good relations that New Zealand and Germany have enjoyed in the post-war era.

Bitterly disappointed at being captured, Major Bedding was held as a POW on the island of Crete until late 1941. During his captivity there his early feelings of bitterness towards the Germans grew as he witnessed such horrific events as Cretans being marched off, led by ropes tied around their necks, into the sandhills where 'they obviously dug graves, and then you heard a couple of bursts of Tommy-gun fire and that was that'. The conduct of some German soldiers also left a lot to be desired. Such actions as the plundering of Cretan villages for booty to send back to Germany were a common occurrence. However, once Major Bedding found himself among different Germans, where that sort of thing was not happening, his feelings towards them began to change.

After being transported from Crete to Germany, Major Bedding spent time in several locations as a POW, and his impressions of his captors were mixed. During his time at a camp in Lamsdorf, for instance, he encountered a number of German troops who had been invalided from the Russian front. Some of them were rough types, obviously soured by their experiences in Russia, 'and a lot of that rubbed off on us'. But with more than a metre of snow on the ground and nowhere to go, escape was almost impossible.

Major Bedding's time at Spangenberg contributed to his changed attitude towards the Germans. Bedding recalls standing in the camp exercise ground, where townsfolk who were passing by would sometimes pause to watch the prisoners' activities. What Bedding saw in their eyes was a genuine curiosity, and certainly not the malice one might have expected.

In early 1944 Major Bedding's story took a significantly new turn. A notice was published in the camp where he was held calling for volunteers with any teaching experience to assist in a camp with a large number of evacuated Channel Island children. Having previously worked as a physical education instructor in New Zealand, Major Bedding decided to volunteer. However, when he reached his destination, Bad Soden, he found that he had not been sent to a children's evacuation camp but rather to an Allied POW eye hospital and Braille school. The eye hospital was run by a British doctor, Major David Charters, and included a French-run dental unit. Major Bedding was to stay in Bad Soden for the remainder of the war and look after administration and discipline. In addition, he was also responsible for organising the prisoners' recreation.

The prisoners gathered news about what was happening in the war from a number of sources, including a wireless, French forced labourers who came into the camp for treatment, discussions with each new prisoner who entered the camp, and German-speaking POWs who would keep up with the often inaccurate German newspaper reports and maps, thus gauging reality by reading between the lines. By mixing the news from all these sources, a reasonably accurate idea of the war's progress was ascertained: all was not going well for Nazi Germany. Indeed, Germany's poor situation in the final days of the war would, on one extraordinary evening, see Major Bedding meet a few local Germans and thus become involved in a series of events that ultimately led to him embarking on a mission to save two German towns from destruction.

One evening in March 1945, the Mother Superior of the nursing sisters who worked in the camp approached Majors Bedding and Charters, and asked them to come to the cellar of the hospital at once. To their surprise, the officers found a small delegation of three townsfolk, led by Herr Körling, the local mayor, waiting for them.[2] The purpose of their visit was their wish to surrender Bad Soden to the two majors as they did not want to see their old town, which had a long history, destroyed by the advancing Americans. They also promised to deal with whatever Nazis there were in the town, and added that there were very few soldiers in the area and that these would put up little resistance anyway.

At first sceptical, Bedding said that he, as a prisoner, could not accept the surrender. However, he acknowledged that the Americans were closing in and agreed to write a letter expressing the wishes of the delegation and to make three copies of it.[3] Each of the three Germans took a copy with him and set off to meet the advancing Americans as far from the town as possible, in the hope that at least one of the three might get through with the message. The letter was delivered successfully, and the Americans advanced cautiously—no shots were fired.

When asked why he agreed to help the enemy in the closing stages of the war, after having been imprisoned by Nazi Germany from mid 1941, Major Bedding replied that it was done as much for the good of his own men as

The bearer of this note represents the CIVIL POPULATION
of the two villages of Bad Soden and Salmunster. The
Population is Roman Catholic and anti-Nazi with the exception of about one dozen individuals.

It is the wish of the people that the villages be
surrendered without fighting especially as they contain
both German and Prisoner of War Hospitals.

We guarantee the personal integrity of the bearer
and we hope that you will be able to occupy the villages
without action .

We are informed that there are about 60 German
Soldiers in the villages at present, that they will offer no
resistance and that the Civilian Authorities will take every
possible step to prevent any activity on the part of the few
remaining Nazis.

(G. Bedding) Major. N. Z. E. F.
Senior British Officer.

Prisoner of War Hospital.
Bad Soden. SALMUNSTER.

2130 hours.
30th. March. 1945.

(D. L. Charters) Major. R. A. M. C.
Senior British Medical Officer.

A copy of the note that accompanied the three men from Bad Soden entrusted with meeting the advancing American troops. (Dokumentation zur 50. Wiederkehr der Rettung des Dorfes Ahl vor der Zerstörung, *Bad Soden-Salmünster, [1996]*)

for the locals. He explained that had the hospital, with more than a hundred Allied patients in it, taken just one shell, the result would have been chaos. Many wounded would have had to be moved by only a handful of able-bodied men. Even if they managed to evacuate everyone, he questioned where they would have gone. The position was, he deemed, untenable. It was as much for the benefit of themselves as for the locals of Bad Soden that there should be no fighting. In saying that, however, Major Bedding also stated that some locals came into the camp on a fairly regular basis and chatted with the prisoners and were generally fairly friendly. 'We formed the impression they'd had a gutsful of the war': they wanted it finished and asked for help, 'and naturally you say "Yes, of course we'll help you"'.

Indeed, Major Bedding recalled that the French dental hospital, which lay below theirs, bore the brunt of the Germans' attention. The guards were either too old for front-line service or were injured in some way so as to make them unfit for that kind of fighting. Some of them even became friends. 'Two of them were POWs in Scotland in World War I, and never could forget being given porridge and bacon and eggs for breakfast.' There was one guard, however, whom Bedding and his companions treated with caution—'Bomb Happy Fred', who, Bedding believes, had lost his mother, father, grandfather, grandmother, brothers, and sisters all in one air raid. 'Bomb Happy Fred', said Bedding, 'had a chip on his shoulder, and no one could blame him.'

Major Bedding acknowledged that he was treated well in Bad Soden. One thing he could never understand, however, was why so many local citizens were allowed into the camp almost at will. The only explanation seemed to be the fact that there was a chapel in the camp grounds. Mainly the elderly came along to the services, and it was these people who helped to change Major Bedding's feelings towards his captors. While the guards were looking the other way, the visitors would often talk to the prisoners. Major Bedding was never sure why, whether it was for reasons of religion or because most of them had seen one world war and were frightened, now that the end was again not too far away.

Twelve hours later, after being released by the Americans in Bad Soden, Major Bedding learned that they were seeking revenge for the killing by the SS of an American scouting party, which had been on a mission in the nearby village of Ahl. The Americans were going to flatten the township in response.

Once again, Major Bedding was approached by a small group of Germans in need of help. They had heard how he had helped to save Bad Soden and wanted him to do the same for Ahl.[4] Not approving of the Americans' thirst for revenge, he agreed to do what he could to help, but it proved difficult. Major Bedding was unable to dissuade the local American commander, a colonel, who remained intent on levelling the village, but was sent nevertheless to meet the American regional commander. The latter, a general, was also unmoved by Bedding's pleas and backed the position of his local commander. However, the general called in his second-in-charge, a Major Kalkstein, with whom Bedding continued to put his argument. Eventually Bedding managed to persuade him that to flatten the town of Ahl 'was plain bloody stupidity'.

Major Bedding recalls that his final argument with Major Kalkstein was that if it were happening to him in his country, he would be doing just as much to save the village. Major Kalkstein took the argument to the general, who finally countermanded the order. The offensive against Ahl was cancelled. Major Bedding recalled that 'when you see buildings like that, and when you consider our history is not even a fifth of that age—you get a hell of a big respect for that'. Indeed, Bedding saw the history that surrounded him as something quite profound.

In the days that followed, Bedding was made part of AMGOT (Allied Military Government of Allied Territories). His tasks included the calling in of all radio sets, binoculars, telescopes, swords, daggers, bayonets, and firearms. His responsibilities also included the inspection of water and power supplies. In this period a gesture was made by the local head forester that Bedding has not forgotten: the forester thanked him and handed him his dress dagger, insisting that he did not want the Americans to get hold of it.[5] Bedding also received a letter of thanks from Dr Heinz Adam, a member of the initial delegation from Bad Soden.[6]

After he was settled again in New Zealand, Major Bedding maintained correspondence with some of the people he had met during his time at Bad Soden and Ahl. He visited the area again for the first time after the war in 1970, and a couple of receptions were held for him by the local community, whose members regarded him as the saviour of the towns. In 1995, on the fiftieth anniversary of the ending of World War II, Bedding returned to the area again at the invitation of the local communities, who had combined

Geoffrey and Mary
Bedding, 1996.
(Graeme Horne)

to assist with his travel expenses to Germany. He was officially honoured for having saved Bad Soden and Ahl, and was the guest at numerous functions held in his honour, one of which included the unveiling of a fountain dedicated to him.[7] He was also made the first honorary citizen of Bad Soden-Salmünster.[8] Although seen as a hero by the people of Bad Soden and Ahl, Bedding is reluctant to see himself in this light.[9]

Today Major Bedding bears no grudge against the Germans. Indeed, he has a great deal of respect for Germany and the Germans, and is greatly impressed by their progress since the end of World War II. Instead, he puts the war down to an unfortunate turn in history. Germany, he said, was left in a poor state after World War I. The Germans, he feels, were ready to accept anyone who offered any hope for a better existence. There was the additional factor of what he calls the psychological 'hype'—in other words, the brainwashing—of the country's youth, which, he believes, converted many to the theory of the 'master race'.

Certificate of honorary
citizenship conferred on
Major Bedding, Bad
Soden-Salmünster, 1995,
in recognition of his role
in the bloodless surrender
of Bad Soden and the
saving of Ahl from
destruction, Easter 1945.
(G. Bedding)

Urkunde

über die Verleihung der Ehrenbezeichnung Ehrenbürger

Aufgrund des Beschlusses der Stadtverordnetenversammlung der Kurstadt Bad Soden-Salmünster
vom 19. Dezember 1994 wird

Herr Major a. D.
Thomas Geoffrey Bedding

geboren am 18. November 1909

zum

Ehrenbürger

ernannt.

Die Ehrung erfolgt in Würdigung seiner besonderen
Verdienste um die gewaltlose Übergabe
der Stadt Bad Soden und die Bewahrung der
Gemeinde Ahl vor der totalen Zerstörung
an Ostern im Jahre 1945.

Bad Soden-Salmünster, 1. April 1995

Für die
Stadtverordnetenversammlung:

(Ewald Wolf)
Stadtverordnetenvorsteher

Für den Magistrat:

(Döring)
Bürgermeister

A fitting conclusion to the war for Major Bedding was perhaps a letter dated 7 April 1945 from the mayor of Bad Soden, which honoured Major Bedding by having the street where he spent his time in Bad Soden as a POW, and which forms a link between Bad Soden and Ahl, named after him.[10] The words of the mayor expressed, along with the dedication of the street, his hopes that the major would depart a friend of the town of Bad Soden and that the people of Bad Soden had in the wider sense contributed to the reconciliation of nations.

1 This chapter is based on an interview with Major Bedding that took place in Masterton on 22 February 1996. Unless indicated otherwise, all quotations in this chapter are taken from this interview.

2 Dr Heinz Adam and forester Anton Kramer were the other two members of the delegation. See *Gelnhäuser Neue Zeitung*, 1 April 1995 ('Major Bedding besuchte Vinzenzheim. Sein größter Wunsch: den Keller sehen'. This particular article, along with other documents relating to the saving of Bad Soden and Ahl by Major Bedding, can be found in the 'Dokumentation zur 50. Wiederkehr der Rettung des Dorfes Ahl vor der Zerstörung 1945–1995', edited by Marianne Sperzel and Ewald Wolf, Bad Soden-Salmünster [1996]).

3 The letter, signed by Majors Bedding and Charters, was written at the Prisoner of War Hospital, Bad Soden-Salmünster, at 2130 hours on 30 March 1945, and reads as follows:

> The bearer of this note represents the CIVIL POPULATION of the two villages of Bad Soden and Salmünster. The Population is Roman Catholic and anti-Nazi with the exception of about one dozen individuals.
>
> It is the wish of the people that the villages be surrendered without fighting especially as they contain both German and Prisoner of War Hospitals.
>
> We guarantee the personal integrity of the bearer and we hope that you will be able to occupy the villages without action.
>
> We are informed that there are about 60 German Soldiers in the villages at present, that they will offer no resistance and that the Civilian Authorities will take every possible step to prevent any activity on the part of the few remaining Nazis. (Dokumentation [note 2])

4 See *Gelnhäuser Neue Zeitung*, 4 April 1995 ('Ahl wäre Erdboden gleichgemacht worden—wäre da nicht Major Bedding gewesen: Zeitzeugen erzählten, wie Bürger mit Sack und Pack aus Ahl flüchteten: Ehrenbürger überreichte einen Bildband über seine neuseeländische Heimat'). See also *Kinzigtal-Nachrichten*, 4 April 1995 ('Herzlicher Empfang für Bedding und seine Familie' in Dokumentation [note 2]).

5 *Gelnhäuser Neue Zeitung*, 29 March 1995 ('Major Bedding und die sagenhafte Geschichte vom Dolch des Försters', in Dokumentation [note 2]).

6 Dr Heinz Adam's letter, dated 7 April 1945, with original capitalisation retained, reads as follows:

> Dear Sir, Dear Major Bedding,
>
> On the occasion of Your friendly help to surrender the village of Bad-Soden without action, I personally desire to thank You once more and to give You a little present for remembrance this day.
>
> If it is possible, I shall come to You now, and wait for Your information, conveyed by the bearer of this letter.
>
> With respectful greetings
> Your
> [Dr Heinz Adam]. (Dokumentation [note 2])

7 Interview with Major Bedding, broadcast on Television New Zealand, '60 Minutes', 23 April 1995. See also *Kinzigtal-Nachrichten*, 3 April 1995 ('Feierlichkeiten aus Anlaß des "Verlobten Tages"/Bedding-Brunnen eingeweiht: Zeichen der Dankbarkeit').

8 See *Kinzigtal-Nachrichten*, 31 March 1995 ('Major Bedding wird Ehrenbürger: Verdienste um die Gewaltlosigkeit'); *Kinzigtal-Nachrichten*, 3 April 1995 ('Besondere Ehrung: Bedding

Ehrenbürger'); *Gelnhäuser Neue Zeitung*, 3 April 1995 ('Bedding ist Ehrenbürger'); *Kinzigtal-Nachrichten*, 5 April 1995 ('Major a. D. Bedding trug sich ins Goldene Buch der Stadt ein: Namenszug und Foto'). The official certificate declaring Major Bedding an honorary citizen of Bad Soden-Salmünster, dated 1 April 1995, is reproduced in the Dokumentation [note 2].

9 Television New Zealand interview [note 7].

10 The letter is reproduced in full in the Dokumentation [note 2]. The renaming of the street as 'Major Bedding-Straße' was cancelled by the Americans who occupied the zone; however, the Germans reinstated the new name once the Americans left (Television New Zealand interview, [note 7]).

Major Geoffrey Bedding died on 2 June 1998. This chapter is dedicated to his memory.

Part 2

The German connection in the arts

Introduction

JAMES N. BADE

The German connection with New Zealand has traditionally been strong in the arts, particularly in the visual arts, music, and literature.

Leonard Bell's chapter on the impact of German-speaking immigrants on art, photography, and the crafts in New Zealand might surprise those who were not aware of the range and diversity of the German contribution to an area that has hitherto been all too often regarded as monocultural 'Pakeha' art. Separate chapters are devoted to Margot Philips and Friedensreich Hundertwasser. As Margaret Sutherland writes, without Margot Philips the history of art in the Waikato would look quite different, and one should add that Margot Philips' contribution to New Zealand art generally should clearly not be underestimated. Friedensreich Hundertwasser is well known as the eccentric Viennese artist and architect who sometimes likes to spend part of the year on his environmentally friendly farm in the Kaurinui Valley. Most New Zealanders would agree with Hansgerd Delbrück and Leonard Bell that Hundertwasser's koru design for an alternative New Zealand ensign is one of his best works.

Lauren Jackson's chapter on twenty years of contact between the New Zealand and German film industries highlights the German interest in New Zealand film-making over recent years, which started with the screening of New Zealand films at German film festivals and on television, and culminated in German–New Zealand collaboration in a number of films.

James Braund concentrates on two forms of literary contact between New Zealand and German-speaking Europe: New Zealand authors who have an interest in Germany or German literature, and German writers who have featured New Zealand in their works. An example of the latter is the celebrated German poet Karl Wolfskehl, who spent the last ten years of his life in Auckland. Karl Wolfskehl is often overlooked in New Zealand literary surveys, and Friedrich Voit's chapter puts Wolfskehl in his proper perspective as a major literary contact between New Zealand and German literature.

John Mansfield Thomson examines the impact of post-war German composers on New Zealand musicians and composers, and touches on the role of visiting German musicians in enriching New Zealand musical life. As Thomson mentions, refugees from Nazi Germany contributed significantly to the musical life in this country. (See also the chapters on Denis Adam and

Arthur and Lisl Hilton in part 4.) One of the most notable refugee musicians was the cellist Marie Vandewart Blaschke, who is discussed in a
chapter by Maja Beutler and Kathryn Smits. Like Maria Dronke, Marie
Vandewart Blaschke had already established a reputation in Berlin in her
chosen *métier* before she was forced to leave Germany because of her Jewish
heritage. Peter Vere-Jones' comment in his chapter on Maria Dronke, for so
many years a leading light in voice production, speech, and drama, holds true
for many of the refugees from Nazi Germany who settled in this country,
but particularly those involved in the arts: Germany's loss was New Zealand's
immeasurable gain.

6

Art, photography, the crafts, and German-speaking immigrants

LEONARD BELL

Cultural histories have not adequately recognised the cumulative impact on, and seminal and continuing importance for, developments in New Zealand visual arts—especially since the 1940s—of German-speaking immigrants in the twentieth century. Indeed, the very numbers and diversity of such people might surprise some readers, in particular those who have been inclined to view Pakeha culture and society as homogeneous and unified in ethnic origins and language. This chapter aims to enlarge the picture. It is not a comprehensive survey or listing of all the German-speaking artists, photographers, craftspeople, and art collectors who have been active in New Zealand since 1900.[1] Rather it sketches in, of necessity in a summary manner, those areas of activity and interaction in the arts in which German-speaking immigrants either were or are major and influential participants, or produced work that can be seen to articulate prime concerns of New Zealanders generally—notably the dynamics and complexities of displacement and indigenity, of being 'new' to a country and attempting to make a home for oneself there.

The use of the term *German-speaking* does not entail or imply any necessary uniformity or homogeneity among the people so characterised. Quite the contrary, they comprise a varied and heterogeneous grouping in several fundamental respects: ethnically and culturally, in the kinds and styles of visual art in which they are engaged, and in their reasons for coming to New Zealand. Changes in immigration policies have played a major role. Since it was almost impossible for people from German-speaking countries to emigrate to New Zealand between World War I and the early 1930s, German-speaking artists were, not surprisingly, a rarity in New Zealand in that period. The admittance of Central European refugees from Nazism in the 1930s and 1940s—most but not all of whom were Jewish—radically altered this state of affairs. And the substantial increase in the numbers of German-speaking artists, photographers, and craftspeople residing in New Zealand since the mid 1980s correlates with the major increase in the number of German-speaking immigrants generally in that period.

Many Central European people in the nineteenth and twentieth centuries could speak two or more languages as a matter of course—a consequence of the complexities of ethnic, social, and political interactions and the frequent shifts in national boundaries in Central Europe during that time. In particular, while Czech Jews were primarily German-speaking until the end of World War I, those born or educated after that war were Czech as well as German speakers. Hence my references to people of Czech–Jewish origin—people whose lives and use of languages testify to the permeability of boundaries of various kinds and to the energies and creativity that can be generated by linguistic and cultural mixing. One Czech- and German-speaking refugee to New Zealand, Fred Turnovsky, described such people as 'hybrids', that 'yeast that makes a society interesting'.[2] I would characterise that 'yeast' as an invaluable catalyst for the cultural and social diversification and enrichment of a society. That has been demonstrably the case in this country, as what most of the people described in this chapter brought to New Zealand was an invigorating difference from prevailing norms, an openness, even if of necessity, to what was new and different to them and an adeptness, sometimes painfully acquired, in adapting, productively and imaginatively, to life and work in a variety of sociocultural and linguistic environments.

Not that Dr Max Herz's comments on colonial arts, written in New Zealand, in his *Das heutige Neuseeland: Land und Leute* (1908; English edition: *New Zealand: The Country and the People*, 1912), fit that profile. Herz, an advocate of 'the new spirit of art, which strives to express our modern sentiments in modern forms, strong and simple', wrote derisively about European art, architecture, and design in New Zealand—of art galleries 'where soiled canvas hangs like washing on a clothes-line; of "his" [the colonist's] architecture and … furniture [which] carry the stamp of deadly monotony in design'.[3] In contrast, however, Herz wrote enthusiastically and positively about Maori art. He was the first writer to attempt an analysis of the formal properties and symbology of kowhaiwhai (rafter painting) and carving from an informed modernist primitivist perspective. For instance, of that characteristic element in much Maori art, the spiralling koru motif, Herz wrote: 'The coil … the favourite means of ornament … found in the art of all prehistoric people … Is this a recollection of the childhood days of the world?'[4]

This interpretation of Maori art links Herz to the only known German professional artist active in New Zealand in the early twentieth century, Wilhelm Dittmer (1868–1909). Dittmer, resident here from 1898 to 1905 and best known now for his illustrated book, *Te Tohunga: The Ancient Legends and Traditions of the Maori* (1907), featured in *The German Connection: New Zealand and German-speaking Europe in the Nineteenth Century*,[5] and thus will only be dealt with briefly here. Dittmer did not share Herz's dyspeptic view of colonial culture. On the contrary, he was a well-known and important participant in the art and museum worlds, both as a painter and illustrator, for his Maori subject pictures and for his portraits of both Maori and Europeans.[6] Travelling to Europe in 1905 to seek a publisher for his *Te Tohunga* text and drawings, and to exhibit his New Zealand work in Germany, Dittmer had planned to return and make his home in New Zealand. In relation to this, his *Te Tohunga* illustrations, in which he 'married' elements from Maori art and European Art Nouveau and Symbolist forms and motifs, could be regarded as the first and pioneering attempt by a professional artist in New Zealand both to indigenise the modern and to modernise the indigenous.

Dittmer was a lone figure in New Zealand art in this period in this respect, although several New Zealand-born artists either of German parentage, like Armin Schmidt,[7] or with German family connections, like Mina Arndt, trained in Germany before World War I and would have had ample opportunities to familiarise themselves with Herz's 'new … modern … spirit of art'. Arndt (1885–1926) is now recognised as an important figure in developments in New Zealand art in this respect. For instance, she was invited by the renowned German–Jewish printmaker, Hermann Struck, to study etching in his Berlin studio in 1906; between 1911 and 1914 she had a studio in Berlin and took further classes with Lovis Corinth, one of the key figures in the 'modern movement' in Germany.[8] Although she returned to New Zealand after the outbreak of war, her New Zealand art, which was not exhibited publicly in any quantity until the early 1960s, manifests the imprint of these experiences.

Wilhelm Dittmer: *Knighthood of Dr Logan Campbell, Auckland's Leading Citizen*. Drawing in the *New Zealand Graphic*, 14 June 1902.

Another German-speaking immigrant or temporary resident, Julius Geissler, about whom little is known, produced a number of pen and ink drawings representing aspects of immigrant and pioneering life in New Zealand. While probably an amateur rather than a professional artist, Geissler's four-part *Making a New Zealand Home* (1919) succinctly narrates a progression from *Primaeval Bush* through the clearing of that bush, leaving the *Charred Remains of the Forest* to a culmination in *The Settler's Homestead*.[9] This series exemplifies a stock theme commonly found in settler–colonial societies' depictions of themselves. A more personalised representation of home-making in the 'new' country is Geissler's *View of C. and M. Geissler's Farm, Warkworth* (1918). This features a homestead surrounded by ordered and fenced pastures, orchards, and gardens, all framed by the foreground kauri trees (actually two separate views of the same tree). The giant trunk on the right has the title and inscription in English and German, while at the foot a small figure—the artist himself?—is shown completing that inscription, *Dreissig Fuss Umfang* ('thirty feet in circumference'); in tagging this uniquely New Zealand feature, he is thus marking his presence in the land and making it, or attempting to make it, his own.

Julius Geissler, *View of C. and M. Geissler's Farm, Warkworth, 1918*. Pen and ink, 30.4 x 44.6 cm. *(Auckland Art Gallery)*

To the best of my knowledge, no professional German-speaking painters or sculptors settled in New Zealand in the interwar period. Several immigrants of the 1930s took art classes and became artists here, however. Frank Gross (1908–63) was born in Vienna, studied fashion design there and in Paris and London, and worked in the fur trade. In New Zealand from 1934, he studied at the Elam (Auckland) and Dunedin Schools of Art, and exhibited his work regularly in Dunedin from the mid 1940s to 1953 and from 1954 until his death in Christchurch. From 1960 he was an art tutor for Adult Education at Canterbury University.[10] In what was generally a conservative cultural climate, in which very few painters could be full-time professionals, Gross was a well-known member of a number of artists' associations considered to be 'modern' and committed to the 'new'—the Independent Group in Dunedin and the Group in Christchurch. His work was praised and regularly reproduced in art periodicals in the 1940s and 1950s, and included in an exhibition of New Zealand art that toured the USSR in 1959. However, Gross, undeservedly, has not been included in the general histories of New Zealand art published from the 1960s. His painting and drawing, informed by a knowledge of Cubism and Expressionism, were characterised by strong, sometimes broadly sweeping lines and by what one reviewer saw as 'vigorous brushwork' and an 'almost aggressive use of colour'.[11] Gross's choice of subject and motif was varied—rural, suburban, urban, and industrial environments—and could be strikingly unconventional: images of hydroelectric power stations, service stations, or picture theatres at night, and paintings inspired by Maori rock art.

Frank Gross, *Chained River*, 1957. Chalk and wash, 44.7 x 57.3 cm. *(Dunedin Public Art Gallery)*

Margot Philips (1902–88), a refugee from Germany who arrived in New Zealand in 1938, came later to painting as a student at summer schools at the Auckland Art Gallery during the 1950s. However, stimulated there by the tuition of Colin McCahon, probably New Zealand's most esteemed painter, Philips produced an impressive body of work, exhibited widely in the 1960s and 1970s, and was celebrated in major art museum retrospectives in 1983 and 1987.[12] Even if technically and formally less accomplished than Gross, her paintings can have an expressive idiosyncrasy and quiet intensity that is memorable. While their profusions of often rich greens and rhythms of the landforms generally bring to mind New Zealand landscapes, Philips's paintings were not in fact depictions of specific, identifiable locations. Rather, worked from memory, they were imaginative and composite constructions, which depicted the 'inner' as much as the 'outer'. Her painted 'places' were almost invariably viewed from above and shaped as sweeps over land, empty of people, towards distant hills in a manner that is both decorative and suggestive of latent agitation. In contrast to Geissler's images, in Philips's paintings, even if they include the occasional small building and indications of agricultural activity, it would seem that humans have an uncertain hold. That quality links her work to German Romantic landscape imagery of the mid-nineteenth century, and is also metaphorically suggestive of Philips's own situation as a refugee—'alien', unsure of her place. Her practice of painting, however, perhaps became a way of mediating her dilemma—a means by which she asserted her difference as well as acclimatising herself to New Zealand.

A refugee Czech architect and writer, Frederick Ost (1905–85), who arrived in New Zealand via England in 1940, had also trained as a painter and graphic artist in Ostrava. Two books reproducing his drawings were published here: *My Little Book of Swallows with Verse and Pictures* (1941) and *Tikis: Impressions in Black and White* (1946). His illustrations were included too in books of his and of other poets in the same period. However, his most substantial book of drawings, *Die Aotearoa Tiki Botschaften*, with sixty-one images, was published in Austria in 1984. Ost's art and writing is, undeservedly, hardly known or remembered in New Zealand now. Yet he was ahead of his time in a number of respects. One of his favoured motifs or starting points in his image-making were Maori tiki, which he reshaped in terms of Central European Cubism and Expressionism—a syncretic method or approach new to New Zealand art and graphics in the mid 1940s. His *Tiki in Mirror* (1946), retitled as *Metamorphose des Tiki I* in the 1984 book, is a sophisticated composition in which the doubling and separation of forms are intriguingly suggestive, socially and psychologically.[13] The other books Ost had published in New Zealand provide further evidence of his energies and versatility in a sometimes unreceptive environment: his *One Amongst Us: A Ballad* (1944) and *Three Essays on Czech Poets* (1944), as well as the books he edited, *Poems from Allied Nations* (with Noel Hoggard, 1944) and *The Vltava Still Sings: Modern Czech Verse* (with Ronald Meek, 1945).

One leading German professional painter of the early 1930s did, unwittingly and indirectly, play a key role in emerging New Zealand modernist art of the 1930s and 1940s without ever setting foot in the country. Hans

Frederick Ost, *Tiki in Mirror* in *Tikis: Impressions in Black and White*, Wellington, 1946.

Hofmann (1880–1966), who had run a prestigious art school in Munich, shifted to the USA in 1932. A New Zealand-born pupil at that school, Flora Scales, transmitted his ideas and methods to a young aspiring artist in Nelson, Toss Woollaston, a pioneer of the 'modern' in New Zealand. Woollaston regards the Hofmann 'factor' as the crucial determinant in the direction of his painting,[14] an attribution that might very well have perplexed Hofmann himself.

Another Hofmann, however, who came to New Zealand as a refugee from Czechoslovakia in 1940, helped to introduce modernist approaches here in a more straightforward manner in the practice of photography. Frank Hofmann (1916–89), born in Prague and a member of the Prague Photographic Society, quickly found employment as a commercial photographer in New Zealand, initially as a freelance photojournalist, then in studios in Christchurch, Napier and, from 1941, Auckland, where he worked first for the important photographer Clifton Firth before establishing his own firm, Christopher Bede, in the early 1950s. The firm became nationally well known for its portrait work. Hofmann had wide-ranging artistic, literary, and musical interests and involvements: he helped to found (and played in) the Auckland String Players, which later evolved into the professional Auckland Philharmonia orchestra; he also helped to found the politically radical periodical *Here and Now* (1949–57); he participated in the 'new' and abstract Contemporary Artists shows at the Auckland City Art Gallery in 1950 and 1951; and he also worked with 'progressive' and innovative architects such as Vernon Brown and the Group, producing photographs of their buildings for periodicals like *The Arts Yearbook* and *Home and Building* in the 1940s, 1950s, and 1960s. His first solo exhibition was mounted by the Photographic Society of New Zealand in 1959, although his second in 1963 and third in 1987 were held in leading commercial galleries, John Leech and Aberhart North respectively. Full recognition of the high quality, historical importance, and artistry of his photography came with a retrospective exhibition of four decades of his work shown at New Zealand's major public art galleries in 1989–90.[15]

Hofmann's photographic output was wide and varied in terms of subject. Besides images in such standard genres as portraiture, architecture, landscape, and travel abroad, some of his most striking photographs focus on a single motif—flowers, shells, a lamp, a clothesline, a toy car, for instance—with an acuity of vision and attention to shape, pattern, texture, detail, and lighting that can take on an almost abstract quality. This points to his close familiarity with the 'New' photography of pre-war Europe—the work of Kertész, Moholy-Nagy, and Rodchenko, for example—and to his general adherence to Modernist principles. His photographs were invariably carefully calculated and composed constructions, made rather than taken, in which a concern with formal and symbolic values was paramount. His best photographs can feature unusual angles and viewpoints and a 'musical' sense of interval and rhythm, by which the ordinary and ever-present is made, and seen, anew and afresh.

Another highly skilled photographer whose work, unlike Hofmann's, is little known in 'fine art' milieux in New Zealand was Richard Sharell

Photograph by Frank Hofmann: *Helen Shaw,* 1950. *(Peter Ireland)*

(1893–1986), who came here in 1940 after several months' incarceration in Dachau following the Nazi invasion of Austria in 1938. Born in Graz, Austria, Sharell had teaching qualifications in natural history, art, and handicrafts and had been a leading figure in educational reform in Austria—for instance, as director for eleven years at the Evening Schools (People's University) in Graz. In Wellington he worked for the Correspondence Schools from 1943 to 1955,[16] in particular in the field of natural history, a discipline in which he put his photographic talents to outstanding use. For instance, in 1957 he was the first person to photograph hatching eggs of that prehistoric reptile unique to New Zealand, the tuatara. His pioneering book, *Tuataras, Lizards and Frogs of New Zealand,* illustrated with about sixty of his photographs, was published in 1966, and was followed by his *New Zealand Insects and Their Story* in 1971 (with a revised edition in 1982), also replete with his photographs. Both books were praised for their exemplary texts, both scientifically rigorous and accessible to lay people, and for their photographs.

Photograph by Richard Sharell: *Tui,* 1945. *(Eva Sharell)*

The photographic image was fundamental to Sharell's quest to make his subjects known and visible, and these photographs are characterised by their attention to form, pattern, colour, texture, and detail—that is, by a self-conscious aesthetic dimension, which Sharell believed was inseparable from his scientific work.[17] He belonged to a long line of German-speaking naturalists going back to Alexander von Humboldt, for whom art and science had a necessary complementary relationship. Sharell's photographs indicate too his familiarity with the 'New' photography of interwar Central Europe—particularly Albert Renger-Patzsch's *Die Welt ist schön* (1928),[18] in which unusual camera angles, oblique lighting, and carefully calculated compositions were geared to the revelation of the wondrous in the ordinary and the natural.

Sharell's photography was not restricted to natural history. Both in Austria and in New Zealand, he made photographs of people, landscapes, and atmospheric phenomena. He had exhibited at the Third International *Fotoaustellung* (Photographic Exhibition) in Vienna in 1934, and from 1940 compiled a private portfolio titled *With Eyes and Heart*. A selection of these works, as well as other Austrian-made images, was shown posthumously at the Exposures Gallery, Wellington, in 1989—his only exhibition in an 'art' institution in New Zealand.

Several other German-speaking emigrés worked as commercial photographers in New Zealand. For instance, a husband and wife partnership, the Müllers, believed to have been left-wing anti-Nazi activists, had a studio in central Auckland in the late 1930s. Franz Barta (1908–85), a refugee from Austria, was a well-known and highly regarded photographer in Dunedin from 1944 to 1976. A well-known photographic studio in Auckland from about 1940 to the mid 1960s, Bettina, was run by Inge Bytinner, a refugee from Germany or Austria.[19] And Gregory Riethmaier (b. 1913), who came to New Zealand with von Luckner in 1938 and stayed, worked after the war as a portrait photographer, including a period with Hofmann's Christopher Bede, before becoming a photographer with the government National Publicity Studios, based in Auckland, from 1959 until his retirement. His work was diverse in subject, with his photographs used, for instance, by the National Airways Corporation and the National Travel Association and by

Photograph by Gregory Riethmaier: Gerald Lee (president of the Grand Opera Society), Kiri te Kanawa, and accompanist, before a performance at the Royal Commonwealth Society, Auckland, 1965.
(G. Riethmaier Collection)

periodicals such as the *New Zealand Journal of Agriculture*, the *Listener*, and *Te Ao Hou: The New World* for the Maori Affairs Department. While he was primarily a photojournalist, a selection of his work was included in a major international exhibition, 'The Best Pictures of the World', in the Hague in 1964. Four books of his photographs published between 1964 and 1973.[20]

The eminent architect Ernst Plischke dedicated his book *On the Human Aspect in Modern Architecture* (1969) to his wife Anna: 'All my buildings and also this book were only made possible by [her] untiring cooperation.'[21] It is little known now that the Vienna-born Anna Plischke (formerly Lang-Schwizer) (1896–1983) was a highly regarded practitioner of landscape or garden design, although professional opportunities were limited in New Zealand in the 1940s and 1950s. She planned gardens for houses designed by Ernst Plischke. One of her works, however, was widely known: the design for her own garden in Brooklyn, Wellington, the layout for and seven photographs of which accompanied her detailed essay, 'A garden for pleasure', in the *New Zealand Design Review* in 1951. Her approach to garden design emphasised the need to attend to the individual peculiarities of the site and the 'preferences of the owner': 'With every plant I ... try to find the place where it looks best ... Tidiness should not be overdone ... I prefer a much wilder effect'[22]—probably not a conventional orientation in New Zealand suburbia of the 1950s.

Anna Plischke, layout of garden in 'A garden for pleasure', *New Zealand Design Review*, 3(6) May–June 1951, p. 140.

Odo Strewe (1910–86), another refugee from Germany in 1938, made a reputation in the 1950s and 1960s as a landscape and suburban garden designer in Auckland and for his children's adventure playgrounds. His were self-consciously modern gardens, with a primary architectonic and sculptural dimension in his use of walls, pergolas, pavilions, and patios, and with the selection and placement of plants such as taro, the rubber plant, and the fruit salad plant to highlight qualities of shape, form, texture, and surface.[23] Strewe was also well known in the 1960s as an unorthodox left-wing protester and provocateur. These activities extended to anti-war poetry and play-writing: his *Six Political Poems* (Auckland, c. 1969), which included caricatures and photomontages by two younger New Zealand-born artists of German descent, Chris Grosz and Chris Strewe, and his *Anzac* and *Excreta*, 'experimental' plays produced by the Auckland Living Theatre Troupe in 1973.[24]

A very different contribution to the arts, which is still not as widely known as it merits, was made by Dr Walter Auburn (1906–79). Born in Cologne, he and his wife Lore, who was also a doctor, left Germany after Jewish doctors were dismissed from their hospital positions in 1933. In 1948 they emigrated from Britain to New Zealand, where Dr Auburn had a long medical career, first in private practice and later as director of the Student Health Services at the University of Auckland and the North Shore Teachers' Training College. From 1956 he began collecting 'old master' prints, woodcuts, engravings, and etchings, eventually building up a superb collection, the largest and most comprehensive of its kind in Australasia. His focus was mainly, although not exclusively, on works from the late sixteenth to the eighteenth centuries. Its prime strengths lay in its holdings of Stefano della Bella, Wenceslaus Hollar, Giovanni Piranesi, and Jacques Callot.[25] From the outset Dr Auburn had a close association with the Auckland Art Gallery. In 1960 he was appointed honorary consultant to the Prints and Drawings Department. He played an active role in several exhibitions that toured nationally and drew extensively on works from his collection, as well as presenting lectures. While he had loaned and given prints as gifts to the gallery from the late 1950s, towards the end of his life he made a bequest of 1,143 works (now in the gallery's care) to be held in trust for the people of Auckland, the place 'where he had had such a full life'.[26] The gallery later bought a further 200 works from his estate and dedicated a gallery in his name in recognition of these invaluable resources and Dr Auburn's long-standing promotion of art history and the visual arts (he had also helped found the New Zealand Print Council in 1967).

Another person who left Germany before World War II but only came to New Zealand after the war, and who played a seminal and pioneering role in the arts here, is the fabric artist and designer Ilse von Randow. Born in Giessen in 1901, von Randow, a fine arts graduate, went to China with her then husband, a German diplomat, in 1930. Initially a painter, she became a professional designer and weaver in Shanghai in the 1940s, producing a wide range of products.[27] She brought a loom with her to New Zealand and, despite being told it would be impossible to make a living as a weaver, she quickly established herself as a notable figure in the contemporary art world. While exhibited at the Auckland Society of Arts, her work attracted the attention of Eric Westbrook, director of the Auckland City Art Gallery, where she was to have a studio, do work for the gallery (in particular, weaving large woollen curtains), and to exhibit further and give weaving demonstrations, for instance, a joint show with the potter Len Castle in 1955[28] and in the 1959 Exhibition of New Zealand Crafts. She was one of the founders of the Handweavers and Spinners Guild in 1953 and was perhaps the key figure in the professionalisation, teaching, and promotion of the fabric arts in the 1950s and 1960s. Her own work—for instance, tablecloths, mats, bedspreads, wall hangings, and pictorial pieces, such as the batik, *The Coming of the Maori*—was wide-ranging and at times experimental and innovative in style and use of materials.

While she has been credited with bringing 'modern ideas to [the] emerging craft',[29] in fact her work was characterised by an openness to, indeed an 'interweave' of, elements from various cultural traditions, such as Central European, Chinese, Maori—an instance of the invigorating hybridisations that can result when different cultures intersect. After she left New Zealand for Britain in 1967, her work dropped out of sight until its re-emergence and recognition for its qualities in a major exhibition, 'The 1950s Show', at the Auckland City Art Gallery in 1992, shortly after von Randow's own return here in 1991.[30]

The next generation, those who were born or grew up after the war, have been as diverse as their predecessors in personality and background and in the kinds and styles of art they have engaged in. And there have been a lot of them, of whom only a selection of the more prominent can be profiled in this chapter. Another German weaver, Anna Correa-Hunt (d. 1990), who settled with her family in New Zealand in 1965, made a significant contribution to the development of the craft here. Born in Hamburg, trained in Bremen, and once employed in a therapeutic workshop for handicapped children in Austria, she introduced weaving courses at Nelson Polytechnic in 1974. These courses have evolved into a two-year diploma course for aspiring teachers and professionals.[31]

Heribert (Harry) Sangl (b. 1928) came from an ethnic German family that shifted from Czechoslovakia to Germany after the war. He studied at the Munich Academy of the Arts and became a professional portrait painter. In 1964 he married a New Zealander. On a visit to New Zealand in 1969, noting that there were no professional portraitists, he saw an opportunity to ply his trade and emigrated the following year. Since then his output has been prolific—reportedly 800 paintings completed between 1970 and 1980.[32] He has painted numerous portraits of dignitaries and powerful people, both local (e.g. the long-time mayor of Auckland, Sir Dove Myer Robinson) and foreign (e.g. Walter Scheel, President of the Federal Republic of Germany), but he came to wider public prominence with portraits of elderly Maori with moko, inspired by the paintings of C.F. Goldie (1870–1947). These were initially known and seen through colour reproduction in his book, *The Blue Privilege: The Last Tattooed Maori Women: Te Kuia Moko* (1980). While some critics have contested the artistic quality of these works,[33] they also have their admirers, including some Maori and museum professionals. Thirty-four of Sangl's Maori portraits were exhibited at the Museum of New Zealand in 1995, while their original purchasers, Brierley Investments Ltd, set up a trust to administer the collection—a facet, it would seem, of Brierley's partnership with Maori iwi in the fisheries business.[34]

Harry Sangl, *Makareta Hose*, plate 18, *The Blue Privilege: The Last Tattooed Maori Women: Te Kuia Moko*, Auckland, 1980.

The internationally well-known artist Friedensreich Hundertwasser has indeed lived and worked in New Zealand since his highly popular 1973 travelling show. However, his subsequent art and design, with the exception of his alternative New Zealand flag piece, have made little impact in fine art and design milieux here. His flag is one of his best works. It has a clarity, succinctness, and elegance usually lacking in his more typically brightly, even luridly, coloured pictorial profusions of predominantly spiralling forms. Hundertwasser's devotion to spirals, which embody for him 'all of nature, all of creation',[35] links his art, rather like Wilhelm Dittmer's, to turn-of-the-century Austrian Art Nouveau or Jugendstil and to traditional Maori art. Hundertwasser's subscription to a kind of pre-modern and primitivising idealism, combined with an apparent view of rural New Zealand as a latter-day South Seas Paradise, leaves him an idiosyncratic figure somewhat out of touch with the contemporary New Zealand he has made his part-time home—the perhaps more hard-headed New Zealand in which his 'soft' romanticism can echo colonial exoticism.

In contrast, younger German-speaking immigrant artists like Siegfried Köglmeier and Peter Schoenauer are more attuned to the contemporary, modern, and post-modern in both art and culture generally in New Zealand. Köglmeier (b. 1953) lived for eight years in a displaced persons' camp in Bavaria after his family fled East Berlin in 1961. After studying graphic design in Munich, he worked variously as an interior designer, sign-writer, draughtsman in an archaeological museum, and artist. In 1983 his travels brought him to New Zealand, where he stayed, based in Dunedin.[36] He has become a very productive and respected artist, exhibiting frequently throughout the country.

Köglmeier's work has been diverse in genre and use of materials, extending to painting, sculpture (both site-specific and for galleries), installations, and performance pieces. His *Travel Work*, executed shortly after his arrival, involved a non-stop walk from Wellington to Picton (on the ferry—not the water) and its documentation. The 1989 *Floor Piece* featured an intricate arrangement of about 3,000 sticks, his *Shattered Dreams* (1991)—'we learn to live in flux'[37]—a multi-unit orchestration of pottery fragments, while his *Cloudscape* (1994) comprised numerous tiny silver-grey 'clouds' equidistant from each other on a gallery wall—'You can't shape a cloud. It is moving and changing all the time'.[38] Cement tiles and stone have also played roles in his invariably beautifully crafted and emotionally and intellectually suggestive works. Fundamental to them is a sophisticated 'play' at the interface of the natural and artificial, the random and ordered, wholeness and rupture, the occupation of a space and displacement. These characterising tensions and interactions, a concern with shifting states, might originate in his own experiences, but Köglmeier's work is shaped not in a self-centred and expressionistic manner but in terms of people's experiences and perceptions of environments and landscapes, inner and outer, generally. It is at once both poetic and detached.

The 'lyric abstract'[39] paintings of Peter Schoenauer (b. 1947), who exhibited frequently in Germany before taking up New Zealand residence in 1981, are more expressively and seemingly intuitively worked. Typically multilayered, with materials such as shell, cloth, gold powder, and brass admixed with the paint in the interests of resplendence of colouristic and textural effects, Schoenauer's works have found niches in a variety of venues

Siegfried Köglmeier, *Shattered Dreams*, 1991. Appr. 2000 mm. Plaster, acrylic paint, graphite, ink. *(S. Köglmeier)*

from fine art galleries to popular art markets and restaurants. He, too, has not remained within conventional boundaries.

Another well-known figure in the world of painting and the arts generally in New Zealand, although not a painter himself, is Swiss-born Kobi Bosshard (b. 1939). Immigrating in 1961, he married a New Zealand woman, with whom he opened a commercial gallery in Dunedin, which for many years was a leading showcase for contemporary arts. Bosshard himself, a graduate of the School of Applied Arts in Zürich, who had worked with the important Swiss jewellery designer Burch-Korrodi,[40] has long been a highly regarded jewellery maker. The impact of his work has been fundamental to the development of quality jewellery arts in New Zealand.

Boundaries between 'fine arts' and 'crafts' have been questioned and unstable at least since the mid nineteenth century. A category, 'art furniture' for instance, was designated then, of which a talented German-speaking practitioner was Anton Seuffert (1825–87), who had an acclaimed career in New Zealand.[41] Another recent German immigrant (in 1986), Detlef Klein, is a master craftsman and conservator now working at the Science Centre and Manawatu Museum. As his first job in New Zealand, Klein restored a cabinet (now in the Museum of New Zealand) by Seuffert, about whom Klein had been ignorant before immigrating. Several other recent German immigrants have specialised in the production of high-quality furniture in both traditional and post-modern styles, for example, Uwe Steidinger, who makes stunning reproduction Biedermeier pieces, and Jürgen Thiele, whose display cabinet *Homage to New Zealand* (c. 1988) is wittily made from such iconic New Zealand construction materials as corrugated iron and wooden '4 x 2s'. The door handles, however, are German-made golf balls. An intriguing 'reversal' and another testimony to the fruitful consequences of cultural mixings has been the work of non-German New Zealander, Paul Downie. He makes internationally renowned eighteenth-century German-style harpsichords, which are exported to Germany and elsewhere in Europe. Downie needed to become fluent in German in order to read original plans.[42]

The processes by which 'foreigners' find or seek to find a place in a country, or by which people regarded as 'outsiders' relate to the mainstream cultures of a society, are explored in the works and epitomised by the careers of two professional photographers who settled in New Zealand in the late 1980s. Arno Gasteiger, born in Innsbruck, Austria, in 1962, came here in 1988. Now photographic editor for the *New Zealand Geographic*, his work has been widely published and exhibited internationally. His series on the Maori Black Power group depicts its members—men, women, and children—'at home' as orderly social beings in contrast to their popular stereotyping as dangerous and asocial. This photo essay was one of six in *New Zealand—By the Way: Immigrant Photographers & Photographs of Immigrants* (1996), a project initiated and edited by Jenner Zimmermann, born in 1950 in Munich and resident in New Zealand since 1989.[43] For Zimmermann, whose photographs have been extensively published and exhibited internationally, and who was hitherto best known for his books on the people of India, *New Zealand—By the Way* constituted an attempt to address the nature

Jürgen Thiele, display cabinet, *Homage to New Zealand*, 1988. Corrugated iron, New Zealand pine, and glass. *(Auckland Library)*

Photograph by Jenner
Zimmermann: *Jetty,
Herne Bay, Auckland,
1991. (J. Zimmermann)*

and problematics of social and cultural identity. His own photographs, of both the urban and the rural, function as encounters with peoples and places, as if he were seeking to isolate a distinctive 'feel' for, or sense of, being here that was different from elsewhere.

In his introduction, Zimmermann noted experiences common to many immigrants to New Zealand in the twentieth century: an initial suspicion of, or resistance to, their difference, an unwillingness among the New Zealand-born to recognise what immigrants or 'foreigners' have contributed and that for a long time New Zealand has in fact been socially and culturally diverse. Yet, his project completed, Zimmermann can observe: 'As an emigrant from Germany, a society of at times immovable self-satisfied certainty, I am excited to be in a land [New Zealand] where change and question is possible.'[44] That assessment contrasts markedly with Max Herz's 1908 view of European society in New Zealand, at least in cultural matters, as being hidebound, rigidly resistant to the new. If these contrasting opinions do indicate radical shifts of consciousness and behaviour in New Zealand society over the twentieth century, a greater openness now to the value of cultural and social differences, and less pressure to conform to homogeneous norms, then major stimuli for these shifts have been the lives and works of diverse German-speaking immigrants here and their impact on other New Zealanders.[45]

1 Space constraints disallow the inclusion of architects and town-planners, who warrant a chapter of their own. In particular, notable German-speaking architects who came to New Zealand as refugees from Nazism include, besides Ernst Plischke, Henry Kulka, Helmut Einhorn, Frederick Newman, Ernst Gerson, Fritz Farrar, Imre Porsolt, Max Rosenfeld, and Gerhard Rosenberg. Kulka, Porsolt, and Rosenfeld were Czech nationals.

2 Fred Turnovsky, *Turnovsky: Fifty Years in New Zealand* (Wellington, 1990), p. 25.

3 Dr Max Herz, *New Zealand: The Country and the People* (London, 1912), pp. 189 & 350. Herz lived and worked as a doctor in Auckland from 1907 to 1911.

4 Herz [note 3], p. 49. The New Zealand periodical, the *Triad* (1 February 1907), pp. 5–7, included extracts on Maori art from Herz's 'book on New Zealand soon to be published in Germany'.

5 Leonard Bell, 'German-speaking artists in New Zealand', in James N. Bade (ed.), *The German Connection: New Zealand and German-speaking Europe in the Nineteenth Century* (Auckland, 1993), pp. 107–9.

6 For a fuller account of Dittmer's New Zealand work and career see Leonard Bell, *Colonial Constructs: European Images of Maori 1840–1914* (Auckland, 1992), pp. 222–55.

7 For Armin Schmidt (1866–1957), see *Early Identities: An Exhibition of Portraits held at the Auckland City Art Gallery*, 1955, pp. 57–8.

8 See Anne Kirker, *New Zealand Women Artists: A Survey of 150 Years* (Sydney, 1993), pp. 55–8.

9 Included in the exhibition '200 Years of New Zealand Landscape Art' (Auckland City Art Gallery, 1990). See also the Auckland City Art Gallery file on Geissler.

10 For Gross's biographical details, see H.V. Miller, 'Frank Gross', *Arts in New Zealand*, vol. 17, no. 5 (September–October, 1945), pp. 40–1; and Gordon Brown, *New Zealand Painting 1940–1960: Conformity and Dissension* (exhibition catalogue, Wellington, 1981), p. 102, and the Hocken Library file on Gross.

11 H.V. Miller [note 10], p. 40. Thanks to Jean Gross and Madeleine McFadden, his daughter, for discussion of Frank Gross's work and career.

12 *The Paintings of Margot Philips: A Waikato Art Museum Exhibition* (Hamilton, 1983; catalogue essay by Janet Paul); and *Margot Philips—Her Own World* (Hamilton, 1987; includes Tim Walker and Margot Philips, 'The painter's life'). See too, Janet Paul, 'Margot Philips', *Art New Zealand*, 46 (Autumn, 1988), pp. 84–7.

13 See Leonard Bell, 'A series of displacements: An introduction to the art of Frederick Ost (1905–85)', *Art New Zealand*, 85 (1997), pp. 64–8; and Leonard Bell, '"A stranger arrives": The art and writing of Frederick Ost in New Zealand' (paper delivered at the symposium 'Exul Poeta: Karl Wolfskehl Leben und Werk im Exil 1933–48', University of Auckland, 31 August–3 September 1998).

14 See, for example, Gordon Brown and Hamish Keith, *New Zealand Painting: An Introduction* (Auckland, 1969), pp. 152f.

15 *Object and Style: Photographs from Four Decades: 1930s–1960s* by Frank Hofmann (exhibition curator, Peter Ireland), Wellington, 1989. See too, Reimke Ensing, 'The photographs of Frank Hofmann', *Art New Zealand*, 46 (Autumn, 1988), pp. 94–7, and 'Frank Hofmann (1916–1989)', *Art New Zealand*, 52 (Spring, 1989), p. 51, and Hamish MacDonald, 'Frank Hofmann, photographer', unpublished research essay, Fine Arts Library, University of Auckland, HOPINZ [19] 88–19. Thanks to Stephen Hofmann for discussion of his father's work.

16 For biographical details, see 'A gift from Hitler', *New Zealand Listener*, 17 August 1945, and Richard Sharell, *New Zealand Insects and Their Story* (Auckland, rev. edn 1982), (frontispiece). Thanks to Eva Sharell for discussion of her father's work.

17 Sharell [note 16], p. 251.

18 See William Main, *Richard Sharell 1893–1986: Catalogue of Original Prints 1929–40* (Exposures Gallery, Wellington, 1989).

19 Thanks to Tom Hutchins for information on the Müllers and Inge Bytinner, and to Gregory Riethmaier for advice on Inge Bytinner. Otherwise at the time of writing little biographical information had been located.

20 Thanks to James Bade and Gregory Riethmaier for advice. His books are a photo essay, *Rebecca and the Maoris* (Wellington, 1964); *Auckland: Gateway to New Zealand* (Auckland, 1968; text by R.L. Bacon); *Auckland Town and Around: North Cape to National Park* (Auckland, 1973; text by R.L. Bacon); and *Samoa ma le fa'a Samoa* (Auckland, 1973; text by Richard A. Goodman).

21 E.A. Plischke, *On the Human Aspect in Modern Architecture* (Vienna, 1969), p. 7.

22 Anna Plischke, 'A garden for pleasure', *New Zealand Design Review*, vol. 3, no. 6 (May–June, 1951), pp. 139–43. For photographs and the layout of another garden designed by Anna Plischke, see E.A. and Anna Plischke, 'Sunroom and a garden', *New Zealand Design Review*, vol. 4, no. 4 (August–September 1952), pp. 82–5. For advice on Anna Plischke, thanks to Henry Lang (her son), Janet Paul, and Roger Parsons.

23 For biographical details, see Odo Strewe's obituary, *New Zealand Herald*, 29 July 1986; and Sally Griffin, 'The fifties show', *Republican*, no. 79 (March 1993), pp. 16–17. For Odo Strewe's garden designs and his writings about modern garden design, see Douglas Lloyd Jenkins, 'Odo Strewe:

Modern homes: modern gardens', in Matthew Bradbury (ed.), *A History of the Garden in New Zealand* (Auckland, 1995), pp. 162–71.

24 An article on these plays appeared in the *New Zealand Herald* of 21 April 1973.

25 See Andrew Bogle, 'Walter Auburn: The man and his collection' (typescript), Auckland Art Gallery Research Library file. This file includes Dr Auburn's 'Personal memoir' (typescript) and Lore Auburn's additional biographical details.

26 Lore Auburn [note 25].

27 For biographical details see Ross Fraser, 'Keeping up with the arts: Weaver Ilse von Randow plies ancient handcraft', *Home and Building*, 1 May 1954, pp. 49–53; Kathryn Webster, 'Still weaving magic at 90', *Bays and Remuera Times*, 21 October 1992, p. 16; and Douglas Lloyd Jenkins, 'Ilse von Randow and mid-century weaving in New Zealand (1950–67)', MA thesis, University of Auckland (forthcoming). Another person who came to New Zealand from China after the war, in 1949, was Grete Graetzer (1901–68), who had emigrated to China with her doctor husband after the Nazis occupied Austria. Trained at the School for Applied Arts in Vienna, she became a well-known painter in Dunedin, and bequeathed many of her works to the Dunedin Public Art Gallery and the Hocken Library.

28 For a review of this exhibition see Charles Bond-Smith, 'A joint exhibition of weaving and pottery by Ilse Von Randow and Leonard Castle', *Home and Building*, 1 November 1955, pp. 70–3. Thanks to Alexa Johnston for the *Home and Building* references.

29 Anne Field, 'History of New Zealand weaving' in Jean Abbott and Shirley Bourke (ed.), *Spin a Yarn Weave a Dream: A History of the New Zealand Spinning, Weaving and Woolcraft Society Inc. 1969–94* (Auckland, 1994), p. 16.

30 See *Home and Building*, souvenir edition, 'The 1950s Show' (Auckland City Art Gallery, 1992).

31 Abbott and Bourke [note 29], pp. 55 & 57.

32 For biographical details, see the article by Reg Chapman in the *New Zealand Herald*, 19 July 1980.

33 For example, Jane Sayle in a review of the exhibition in *Art New Zealand*, 76 (Spring 1995), p. 40.

34 See 'Historic Moko exhibition opens', *Museum of New Zealand News*, June 1995. *The Blue Privilege* included essays by Merimeri Penfold and David Simmons.

35 Harry Rand, *Hundertwasser* (Cologne, 1991), p. 54.

36 Köglmeier's work has been widely and invariably positively reviewed in newspapers, art columns, and art periodicals. See, in particular, David Eggleton, 'Polar opposites: German sculptor: Siegfried Köglmeier', *Art New Zealand*, 62 (Autumn, 1992), pp. 42–5; and Louise Wilton, 'Dunedin', *Art New Zealand*, 61 (Summer, 1991–92), p. 30.

37 Köglmeier in Wilton [note 36], p. 31.

38 Köglmeier in 'Visions of tiki and clouds', *Dominion*, 5 March 1994.

39 Schoenauer in 'Peter Schoenauer exhibition: Chez Daniel restaurant', *Art News Auckland*, vol. 13, no. 2 (Winter 1993), p. 31.

40 Doreen Blumhardt, *Craft New Zealand, and the Art of the Craftsman* (Wellington, 1981), p. 280. See, too, Peter Cape, *Artists and Craftsmen in New Zealand* (Auckland, 1969), pp. 135 & 138. Other German-speaking craftspeople included in Blumhardt's book were the fabric artist Pitt Henrich and the goldsmith Guenther Taemmler.

41 See Bell [note 5], pp. 115–16 for biographical references.

42 Thanks to Detlef Klein for advice on these and other German-speaking furniture makers who live in New Zealand, such as Roland Seibertz and Martin Wenzel. See Peter Shaw, 'Art affairs', *Pacific Way* (February 1989), p. 18, on Thiele and Wenzel's training and work in Germany and New Zealand otherwise. Thanks to Dorothée Justi for advice on Jürgen Thiele.

43 For Gasteiger and Zimmermann's biographical details see Jenner Zimmermann (publishing coordinator), *New Zealand—By the Way: Immigrant Photographers and Photographs of Immigrants* (Auckland, 1996), p. 127. Note too Gasteiger's *Rotorua: Palette of the Gods: Photographs* (Auckland, 1997).

44 Zimmermann [note 43], p. 6.

45 Thanks to Gregory Riethmaier, Harry Sangl, Siegfried Köglmeier, Jürgen Thiele, and Jenner Zimmermann for permission to reproduce their works.

7

Literary points of contact

JAMES BRAUND

Students of New Zealand literature, particularly those whose academic upbringing has emphasised the debt of New Zealand writers to the literatures of English-speaking countries, might be somewhat surprised to learn of the influence of Germany and German literature on many twentieth-century New Zealand authors; indeed, it would not be unreasonable to say that New Zealand and Germany are bound by more literary ties than one might expect from two countries situated on opposite sides of the globe that do not share a common language and have found themselves at war with one another twice in the twentieth century.

The literary points of contact between Germany and New Zealand in fact take a number of forms, not all of which, unfortunately, can be discussed here for reasons of space. The following overview will therefore consider what might be fairly described as the two most obvious forms of literary contact: the various New Zealand authors, usually (but not always) former visitors to Germany, whose literary efforts have from time to time reflected an interest in some aspect of German literature, culture, or society; and a small group of German writers who, through their works or their presence in New Zealand, could perhaps be said to have secured a modest place for New Zealand and its literature in the broader German consciousness.

New Zealand writers, Germany, and German literature

The list of New Zealand writers who have spent extended or repeated periods of time in Germany is a long one, and includes such names as novelist William Satchell (1861–1942); short story writer Katherine Mansfield (1888–1923); poet, editor, and critic Charles Brasch (1909–73); critic James Bertram (1910–93); poet Hone Tuwhare (1922–); novelist and journalist James McNeish (1931–); and poet Cilla McQueen (1949–). Most of these writers have, at one time or another, written about their experience of Germany and its people, with their individual impressions finding expression in a variety of literary forms. Mansfield's recollections of life in a Bavarian resort town, for instance, come through in her first published collection of short stories, *In a German Pension* (1911); Tuwhare has published several poems, occasionally incorporating German words and phrases, that recall time he spent in Germany;[1] Brasch and Bertram have both written of their experiences in Germany in their respective autobiographies;[2] McNeish's essay 'The man from nowhere', a summary, in diary form, of his research on the athlete Jack Lovelock conducted in Berlin in late 1983, could be described as an example of literary travel writing;[3] and McQueen recalls her stay in the same city in the summer of 1988 in her extended prose poem, *Berlin Diary* (1990).[4]

Of all the writers referred to above, however, three in particular— Satchell, Mansfield, and Brasch—and at least one other prominent New Zealand author—Janet Frame (1924–)—have produced works that reflect more than just a passing interest in some aspect of German literature or culture.

The first of these, the British-born Satchell, had been a student at the University of Heidelberg in the late 1870s, where he seems to have become acquainted with German literature and philosophy, but in particular with German Romanticism, the mannerisms of which would remain noticeable throughout his *oeuvre*.[5] In his collection *Will O' the Wisp* (1883), for instance, an early anthology of ballads and prose tales that might well contain material dating back to his Heidelberg period, Satchell is clearly under the sway of the Romantic movement; indeed, Satchell's biographer Phillip Wilson goes so far as to describe perhaps the best tale in the collection, a morbid, super-natural romance entitled *The Black Mirror*, as being 'almost worthy of the great E.T.A. Hoffmann himself'.[6] Elements of German Romanticism are also apparent in Satchell's last and best-known novel, *The Greenstone Door* (1914),[7] and here, as in a number of his works, Satchell's concept of human-ity remains a mixture of his youthful reading of German poets and philoso-phers with his actual observations of men and women living in the frontier settlements of the New Zealand bush.[8] Indeed, *The Greenstone Door* must be the only novel set against the backdrop of the New Zealand Land Wars in which secret messages are written in German, two of the central characters discuss Schiller's famous poem 'The Song of the Bell' (1799), and the same ballad (in the original German, no less) is cited as a kind of epitaph to the book!

The various literary, cultural, and personal ties of Katherine Mansfield to Germany, particularly during the earlier part of her literary career, are prob-ably more numerous than those of any other New Zealand writer to date, yet with the notable exception of her early short story collection, *In a German Pension*, almost of all of her German connections remain relatively unknown. For instance, an elder cousin of Mansfield, Mary Annette Beau-champ, had married a German count, Henning von Arnim, in 1887 and settled with him in Pomerania, where, writing under the pseudonym of 'Elizabeth', she had achieved enormous international success around the turn of the century with a series of light-hearted semi-autobiographical novels, some of which were set in Germany.[9] Indeed, it is possible that the success of Mansfield's elder cousin might well have inspired her to become a writer in the first place,[10] and it has even been suggested that some of 'Elizabeth's' German novels might have had a direct influence on some of Mansfield's own early literary efforts.[11]

As a pupil at London's Queen's College (1903–06), Mansfield had been an avid student of German and, both during this time and immediately after, seems to have associated Germany primarily with things Romantic.[12] This would appear to be reflected not only in an abiding taste for the music of Wagner that she begins to display around this time—allusions to his operas appear in both the *Juliet* fragment[13] (1907) and the so-called Urewera Notebook[14] (also 1907)—but also in the German poets she read during this period, in particular Heine,[15] Mörike,[16] and Dehmel.[17]

Katherine Mansfield, 1911. *(Alexander Turnbull Library, Ref. no. F-2590-1/2)*

The German whom Mansfield appears to have admired more than any other, however, especially in the early part of her literary career, was Nietzsche.[18] Allusions to the philosopher and his works can be found in Mansfield's stories and letters,[19] while some of her early characters have a decidedly Nietzschean aspect to them.[20] There is even something almost Nietzschean about certain phases of Mansfield's own life, first as the young and 'ardent disciple of the doctrine of living dangerously',[21] and later as the ailing writer who, following Nietzsche, comes to acknowledge the link between illness and creativity.[22] Mansfield's acquaintance with Nietzsche, which can be traced at least as far back as 1907,[23] would almost certainly have deepened around 1910–11, the period in which her association with the London magazine, the *New Age*, was at its height. The weekly had, after all, been one of the first magazines of its day to proclaim the importance of Nietzsche,[24] especially in the period 1907–13.[25] Furthermore, its editor from 1907 onwards, A.R. Orage, whom Mansfield would later credit with teaching her how to write and think,[26] was one of the period's leading English propagandists for Nietzsche.[27]

Mansfield's close association with the Nietzscheans who worked in the offices of the *New Age* was in many respects just one instance of how, throughout a large part of her adult life, she would find herself in the company of acquaintances and colleagues in a better-than-average position to appreciate German literature and thought. Perhaps the most conspicuous example of such a person was none other than D.H. Lawrence. Given the task of reviewing German books for the *Blue Review*, the short-lived literary magazine that Mansfield edited with John Middleton Murry, he penned the earliest known English-language review of Thomas Mann's classic novella, *Death in Venice* (1912).[28]

Charles Brasch is perhaps best known in New Zealand literary circles as a poet and as founder and editor for twenty years of the literary quarterly, *Landfall*. What is not widely known about him, however, is that he seems to have kept an interested eye on contemporary developments in German literature,[29] and throughout his adult life read and admired—and was evidently influenced by—a number of well-known German poets.[30] The most important names among them are Goethe,[31] Hölderlin,[32] Günter Eich,[33] Johannes Bobrowski (whom Brasch enthusiastically recommended to friends of his who could read German),[34] and Peter Huchel (whom Brasch met personally at the 1972 Poetry International in Rotterdam).[35] The German poet whom Brasch admired above all, however, was Rilke. Brasch had been introduced to his poetry by a relative in 1928, and quickly set about acquiring various works by the poet: a collection of selected poems (in an Insel Verlag pocket edition), the *Letters to a Young Poet* (1929), the *Duino Elegies* (1923), the *Notebooks of Malte Laurids Brigge* (1910), and the *Sonnets to Orpheus* (1923).[36] Of Rilke's poetry in particular, Brasch writes:

Charles Brasch. *(Hocken Library)*

I read him fairly steadily and was preoccupied with him throughout the thirties and indeed longer. I was captivated first by the exquisite rhythms and verbal music of his earlier work. And by his attitudes, which rhythm and language expressed so well, deeply poetical, touchingly, romantically melancholy … In those years, Rilke spoke for me intimately … I must have written many poems which in a blurred watery way closely reflected his …[37]

James Bertram, Brasch's friend and biographer, sees the latter's Rilke phase as reaching its culmination in the sequence 'The Estate', published in 1957, but composed over a long period beforehand.[38]

The debt of Janet Frame to German literature is in some respects perhaps just as significant—and just as extensive—as that of Charles Brasch. Frame's earliest contact with German literature, indeed, her first real contact with literature as such, was her childhood discovery of a copy of Grimms' fairytales. This discovery is recalled on more than one occasion in her autobiographical writings[39] and further attested to by the various allusions to Grimms' tales throughout her fiction, especially in her first novel, *Owls Do Cry* (1957), where we find numerous references to such well-known tales of the Grimms as *Rapunzel*, *Tom Thumb*, *Cinderella*, and *Rumpelstiltskin*.[40]

Probably an even greater German literary influence on Frame's writing, however, has been the poetry of Rilke,[41] her interest in which can be traced back to the very beginnings of her literary career.[42] A number of obvious clues in Frame's novels, particularly the earlier ones, bear testimony to her reading of the poet, among which are some direct quotations (the *Sonnets to Orpheus* are cited in *Faces in the Water* and in *The Edge of the Alphabet*, first published in 1961 and 1962 respectively), as well as some of the names she gives her characters. Daphne, the narrator in *Owls Do Cry*, for instance, appears to take her name from the mythological figure referred to the *Sonnets to Orpheus*, while her brother Toby, who appears both in the same novel and in *The Edge of the Alphabet*, might well be named after Tobias, who is mentioned in the second of the *Duino Elegies*.[43] More importantly, however, one recognises in Frame's works a number of recurring themes that can also be seen in Rilke. The belief in the need to accept death as a 'complementary pole' to life is but one concern she shares with the poet;[44] and a further point in common is the penetrating insight of both authors into the mind of the twentieth century—an age characterised by war, organised death, and creeping industrialisation.[45]

German writers, New Zealand, and New Zealand literature

The presence of New Zealand or New Zealand subjects in creative works by German-speaking authors, that is, in prose fiction and poetry, is a comparatively recent phenomenon. Until the mid twentieth century, New Zealand's presence in writing by Germans was restricted almost exclusively to works of a documentary nature, such as scientific literature and travelogues. Probably the most important contributions to this area of activity were Georg Forster's *A Voyage Round the World* (1777; German version: *Reise um die Welt*, 1778–80), which includes an account of his three visits to New Zealand in 1773 and 1774 as part of Cook's second voyage; Ernst

Dieffenbach's two-volume *Travels in New Zealand* (1843), which summarises his findings between 1839 and 1841 as a naturalist for the New Zealand Company; and Ferdinand von Hochstetter's monumental *Neu-Seeland* (1863; English version: *New Zealand*, 1867), which was based largely on observations made during of his excursions through parts of New Zealand between December 1858 and October 1859, and which is perhaps the most thorough nineteenth-century monograph to deal exclusively with this country.[46] There was, of course, an occasional exception to this impressive tradition of scientific and descriptive works about New Zealand, a notable example being Gottfried August Bürger's poem 'Neuseeländisches Schlachtlied' (1782).[47] However, it was not until the arrival of the German–Jewish poet Karl Wolfskehl in Auckland in July 1938 that the general depiction of New Zealand by German writers began to move from purely descriptive or documentary works towards works of a more imaginative nature.

Wolfskehl, who arrived in New Zealand as a Jewish refugee from Fascist Europe and who spent the final ten years of his life in this country, the last two of those as a naturalised citizen, is a man of many paradoxes.[48] On a purely personal level, for instance, he had been a wealthy and popular figure in Munich literary circles at the turn of the century, yet died lonely and impoverished in virtual obscurity in an English-speaking land on the opposite side of the world. It was in precisely these depressing circumstances, however, that he not only wrote what he considered his best poetry (a large portion of which would only appear posthumously)[49] but also engaged in a moving and extensive correspondence with old friends around the world. Indeed this correspondence, when first published in the late 1950s, seemed likely to upstage his efforts in his chosen literary *métier* of poetry.[50] Wolfskehl is now regarded as one of the most important figures in twentieth-century German literature, yet in the land that welcomed him as a refugee and in which he now lies buried, his literary and intellectual talents remain, as they did in the late 1930s and most of the 1940s, virtually unknown except to a small circle of friends and initiates. Several factors might well explain this situation. The fact that Wolfskehl, although proficient in a number of languages, both ancient and modern, continued to write poetry in his native German while residing in a predominantly English-speaking environment—and a very monocultural, monolingual, and provincial one at that—doubtless played a major part in his relative obscurity in New Zealand.[51] But even if Wolfskehl had tried to write extensively in English, it is doubtful whether the subject matter of his poetry would have appealed to a wide New Zealand audience, as most of the verse he produced in the course of his ten-year sojourn actually contains very little direct reference to New Zealand, which is alluded to rather than mentioned directly.[52] Indeed, the theme that preoccupied Wolfskehl first and foremost throughout this period (and quite understandably, given his personal situation) was the anguished lot of the exile—something that would naturally explain his continued identification with the biblical figure of Job, the archetype of the sufferer in Western literature.[53]

A further factor that might well have worked against Wolfskehl finding a wider reception in New Zealand was the very cultural and intellectual tradition that he personally embodied: as someone who described himself as 'jüdisch, römisch, deutsch zugleich' ('Jewish, Roman, German at the same time'),[54] and who prided himself, justifiably, on being well acquainted with the respective cultures suggested by each of these three labels, Wolfskehl had the misfortune to arrive in New Zealand at a time when its leading literary figures were seeking to establish a uniquely indigenous literary identity. (Indeed, if he were to arrive in New Zealand today, his intellectual and cultural outlook would be probably be criticised as being 'Eurocentric'.)

The sad irony underlying this unashamedly pro-European intellectual focus was that it was precisely Wolfskehl's encyclopedic knowledge of European cultures, literatures, and languages that played such a crucial part in stimulating the interest and friendship of the leading New Zealand writers of the day. Wolfskehl was befriended and admired by such local literary figures as A.R.D. Fairburn (1904–57), Allen Curnow (1911–), Denis Glover (1912–80), and in particular Frank Sargeson (1903–82) and R.A.K. Mason (1905–71).[55] He was clearly impressed by the various talents of these writers, and repeatedly sought to recommend them to his friends and literary colleagues overseas.[56] But however much these younger writers valued and respected Wolfskehl as both an authority on and the embodiment of the best of European culture, his relationship with them was destined to remain more one of an erudite conversation partner among curious fellow intellectuals than of a teacher among pupils.[57] This, together with the obvious language barrier, might well explain why Wolfskehl has left no appreciable mark on either the above or indeed any subsequent New Zealand writers.

The circumstances of Wolfskehl's arrival and subsequent stay in New Zealand—a refugee from Fascist Europe whose further movements were effectively curtailed by the events of World War II—and the length of his stay in this country—almost ten years—make him very much an exceptional figure among subsequent German-speaking literary visitors to these shores, all of whom would visit for a relatively short period and few of whom could hope to rival his stature within German literature. Arranged visits by German-speaking writers to New Zealand—whether under the auspices of cultural organisations such as the Goethe Institut or in order to attend events such as arts festivals or writers' conferences—did not really commence as such until the 1960s, more than a decade after Wolfskehl's death. By the late 1980s and early 1990s, however, visits by German-speaking authors had become so frequent that one could almost say they were occurring on a regular basis. These literary visitors have included such well-known authors as Siegfried Lenz, who visited New Zealand in 1968; Adolf Muschg (1980); Gerhard Köpf (1988, 1989, and 1990); Jurek Becker (1990); Günter Kunert (1992); and Hans Magnus Enzensberger (1996).[58] Lenz, Köpf, and Enzensberger have the additional distinction of having had some of their works published (in translation) in *Landfall* in the year (or years) of their visits.[59]

Of these recent literary visitors, Gerhard Köpf deserves special mention, inasmuch as he is the only one of the above-mentioned writers who has shown an abiding interest in New Zealand literature. In fact he is probably the only German writer who can claim to have produced not one but three major works of his own that could be said to be indebted to New Zealand literature. Köpf, an admirer of novelist Maurice Shadbolt (1932–) for many years and a personal friend of his since the late 1980s, makes no secret of his deep respect for the Auckland writer's works,[60] above all for the latter's novel *Among the Cinders* (1965; revised edition 1984), which he counts among his favourite books.[61] Indeed, this particular work, and Köpf's discussions with Shadbolt about it, inspired Köpf's short novel *Bluff, oder das Kreuz des Südens* (1991).[62] Readers acquainted with Shadbolt's book will recognise a number of familiar features in Köpf's *Bluff*, not least of which is the same basic story-line.

Gerhard Köpf. *(Anita Schiffer-Fuchs)*

As is the case with *Among the Cinders*, *Bluff* is a first-person narrative related from the point of view of an adolescent narrator, who, while seeking to come to terms with the death of a friend, is taken off one summer on a journey of self-discovery by an irascible, headstrong grandfather. Köpf's translation of the basic plot of Shadbolt's novel of initiation to a German setting contains a number of interesting features (e.g. Nick Flinders' Maori friend in *Among the Cinders* becomes a post-unification 'Ossi' in *Bluff*),[63] but, compared with the original work, his novel suffers somewhat in its inability to recreate convincingly many of the distinctly New Zealand elements present in the original novel. Probably the most obvious example in this regard is the relative absence in *Bluff* of the picaresque character that comes across so strongly in Shadbolt's novel. For obvious reasons, it is much harder for two characters in a German setting to 'go bush', as it were, than it is for characters in a New Zealand one, although Köpf does compensate well by giving the idea of an escape into the wilderness, which plays such a central part in *Among the Cinders*, a rather more allegorical treatment in *Bluff*. This, of course, is suggested in the very title of the book: the 'Southern Cross'(referring to the constellation and to a signpost located at the town of Bluff in the far south of New Zealand) not only represents, in a purely geographical sense, the furthest possible point from the drudgery of the narrator's home town of Thulsern, it also symbolises, inasmuch as he constantly aspires to see it, his urge to escape from his stifling home surroundings.

Front cover of Gerhard Köpf's novel, *Bluff oder das Kreuz des Südens* (1991).

Köpf returns to the basic plot 'formula' of Shadbolt's novel in his most recent novel *Nurmi, oder die Reise zu den Forellen* (published in 1996, but begun in 1993). As is the case with *Bluff* and *Among the Cinders*, *Nurmi*, too, is essentially a story about initiation into adulthood, as told (again in the first person) by an adolescent male, who, as he tries to get over a personal loss, is taken by an older male relative on an adventure into the wilderness one summer. However, the loss alluded to is the narrator's loss of his first real love to a school friend, the elder male relative is an uncle (not a grandfather), and the great adventure into the wilderness is not into the New Zealand bush or south towards the Southern Cross, but north into the wilds of Finland.

Perhaps Köpf's most ambitious experiment with New Zealand literature, however, can be found in his novel, *Der Weg nach Eden* (1994). The narrative involves a man reminiscing on his travels around the world, in the course of which he has visited a number of exotic places that his deceased grandmother always wanted to see while she was still alive but never managed to do so. Two of the stations in the narrator's travels had been in New Zealand: one of these was Takapuna, the other Opononi. In the episode 'Takapuna', the narrator remembers how a good New Zealand friend of his, known only as Kevin (but who bears a certain resemblance to Auckland poet Kevin Ireland), once took him along to 14 Esmonde Road, Takapuna, to visit an elderly Frank Sargeson. The encounter is obviously fictional, of course, but it provides Köpf with the opportunity to give his German readers a brief but remarkably accurate biographical sketch of the famous New Zealand writer and to quote from what is clearly the German version of two of the real Frank Sargeson's stories.[64] We see something equally fantastic in the episode 'Opononi', where Köpf once again blends reality, make-believe, and someone else's fiction. Here the narrator recalls meeting his good friend Maurice Shadbolt and how the latter took him on a day trip to Opononi; as the narrator reflects on his and Shadbolt's exploration of this special place in New Zealand folklore, Köpf again takes the opportunity to draw heavily on the German version of another work of New Zealand fiction—in this case Shadbolt's novel, *This Summer's Dolphin* (1969).[65]

Audacious though this large-scale quotation from the works of another author might seem to some readers, Maurice Shadbolt and Frank Sargeson are by no means the only New Zealand writers whose works have been adapted in this fashion by German-speaking authors, nor is Gerhard Köpf the only practitioner, in the larger context of New Zealand–German literary relations, of this type of adaptation. In the mid 1980s alone, no fewer than three German-language novels were published that made extensive use of both the works and the life of perhaps New Zealand's most famous writer, Katherine Mansfield. They were: *Kopfschmuck für Mansfield* (1985), by the Austrian writer Erwin Einzinger; *Die Kränkung* (1987), by Evelyn Schlag, another Austrian;[66] and *Aus tausend grünen Spiegeln* (1988), by the former East German writer Christa Moog.[67]

Common to all three of these novels, apart from their unconcealed fascination with Mansfield and her works, is the fact that in each of them the narrator (or the protagonist) identifies strongly in some deep way with the famous New Zealand writer. In Einzinger's novel, for instance (certainly the most technically ambitious of the three), the protagonist/narrator Sandbach tries to gain some sense of direction in his life through the act of writing, and the writer by whom he seeks to orientate himself is Mansfield. Much as Mansfield did in real life, Sandbach also experiments with different identities both in his writing and in his life as a means of acquiring a better knowledge of himself.

Evelyn Schlag's novel is rather more imaginative in its approach. As is the case in *Kopfschmuck für Mansfield, Die Kränkung* is again about a process of self-discovery—in this case, the self-discovery of a young female writer who seeks to come to terms with illness and a failing relationship. Throughout these crises, the narrator is attended by the figure of Katherine Mansfield, who maintains a constant presence as a kind of ghostly alter-ego (we are reminded more than once that 'Kathleen', as Mansfield is referred to throughout the novel, has in fact been dead for more than sixty years). The narrator shares not only her occupation as a writer with her famous literary counterpart but also illness (she too falls ill with tuberculosis, although not fatally, as Mansfield did) and alienation from her husband 'Jack'. Her increasing estrangement from Jack can be interpreted as reflecting the emotional gulf that started to open up between Mansfield and John Middleton Murry.

Christa Moog's novel is probably the most interesting—and certainly the most readable—of the three. Clearly very autobiographical in nature, *Aus tausend grünen Spiegeln* is a kind of travelogue and literary investigation combined, consisting entirely of diary entries and letters written by an otherwise anonymous narrator, a former resident of the GDR, to a friend still living in that country, as the narrator visits a number of places lived in and visited by Katherine Mansfield in her search for health, happiness, and ideal conditions for writing—countries such as France, England, Germany, Switzerland, and above all New Zealand, where about a third of the book is set. As the narrator retraces Mansfield's wanderings, she also engages in much personal research into (and speculation on) the life and writings of the New Zealand writer and, in the course of her investigation, gets to read not only much of Mansfield's fiction and more personal writings but also some of the standard secondary literature on her as well. Indeed, the narrator of Moog's novel even manages to have discussions with such well-known Mansfield scholars and biographers as Ian Gordon, Margaret Scott, Antony Alpers, and Claire Tomalin!

As the novel progresses, we begin to sense the reason for Moog's extensive reference to and quotation from the creative and autobiographical works of Katherine Mansfield. Underlying her narrator's attempts to retrace Mansfield's footsteps and to learn more about the latter's life and works (and how the works arose) there is a secret identification with the writer, born of the fact that the narrator, a recent arrival from the former East Germany, now finds herself as a kind of exile from the country of her birth, as indeed the young Katherine Mansfield found herself after her departure from New Zealand to Europe in 1908.[68] Like the real Katherine Mansfield, Moog's narrator (and, we presume, Moog herself) is a woman trying to come to terms with a bewildering range of experiences suddenly at her disposal now that she has 'escaped' from the restrictions of her former homeland—and with the equally bewildering range of emotions that accompany this great personal break, among them the perhaps paradoxical but obviously heart-felt longing for friends and familiar places left behind.[69] What this all implies, of course, is that in trying to learn more about the life and works of the real Katherine Mansfield, Moog's narrator has not only acquired a greater measure of self-knowledge; she has, in the process, also found a kind of literary *Vorbild* with which she can identify and, so we presume, orientate her life in later years.[70]

Conclusion

New Zealand–German literary ties have reached a point few commentators could have foreseen at the end of the nineteenth century—a time when

William Satchell, probably the only New Zealand writer of that era who could claim any real German connection, was still to produce his most 'German' work, *The Greenstone Door*, and the arrival of Karl Wolfskehl, the first modern German-speaking author to create anything remotely resembling a niche for New Zealand in the broader German literary consciousness, still lay four decades in the future. Indeed, it was as recently as the mid 1950s that a young Auckland academic by the name of John Asher, later to become the first Professor of German at the University of Auckland, wrote almost despairingly of the likelihood of a New Zealand subject ever being the theme of a major literary work in the German language.[71]

Despite these relatively inauspicious beginnings, however, New Zealand literature has, in the course of the twentieth century, amassed a substantial body of works that have been inspired by Germany and its literature, and, similarly, the literatures of German-speaking Europe have also acquired a small selection of literary works that are concerned with New Zealand and New Zealand themes. Given these developments, and given also the continuing interest in both New Zealand and Germany in the literature of the other country, one could conclude that the future of literary ties between these two opposite parts of the globe has never seemed brighter.

1 See, for instance, 'Monika' and 'Tour bus minutiae, and commentary: West Berlin, 1985', both in *Tiwhare, Short Back and Sideways* (Auckland, 1992), pp. 20f & 28f.

2 See Brasch, *Indirections: A Memoir 1909–1947* (Wellington, 1980), pp. 167, 168, & 171; and Bertram, *Capes of China Slide Away: A Memoir of Peace and War 1910–1980* (Auckland, 1993), pp. 77–80. Bertram, although perhaps best known as one of New Zealand's leading literary critics, was also an occasional poet in his own right and published translations of such German poets as Goethe, Mörike, and above all Rilke; see for instance his translations in *Rostrum* 7 (1946), pp. 8–10, and *Landfall* 3 (1949), pp. 109–11, but in particular his collection *Occasional Verses* (Wellington, 1971), pp. 35–9.

3 See McNeish, *The Man from Nowhere and Other Prose* (Auckland, 1991), pp. 1–66.

4 The continuing fascination of certain New Zealand writers with Berlin is attested to by the use of the city as the setting for *Wormwood*, the first novel of poet, playwright, and artist (and former resident of Berlin) Bill Direen (1957–), which has appeared in *Sport* 18 (Autumn 1997), pp. 53–119.

5 See Phillip Wilson, *William Satchell* (New York, 1968), pp. 7, 20, 24, & 54.

6 Wilson [note 5], pp. 22 & 53f.

7 Wilson [note 5], p. 132.

8 Wilson [note 5], p. 137.

9 See Antony Alpers, *The Life of Katherine Mansfield* (London, 1980), pp. 6 & 16, but in particular Karen Usborne, *'Elizabeth': The Author of Elizabeth and Her German Garden* (London, 1986). 'Elizabeth's' first novel, *Elizabeth and Her German Garden*, was first published in September 1898 and, by May 1899, was about to appear in its twenty-second edition.

10 Alpers [note 9], pp. 16 & 32f; cf. Charanne Carroll Kurylo, 'Chekhov and Katherine Mansfield: A study in literary influence' (PhD dissertation, University of North Carolina, Chapel Hill, 1974), p. 56.

11 Mansfield's story 'Die Einsame' ('The Lonely One'), for instance, which appeared in the *Queen's College Magazine* in March 1904, seems to have taken its title from Elizabeth's *The Adventures of Elizabeth in Rügen*, published a month before (Alpers [note 9], p. 33), while some of the stories in *In a German Pension* would appear to have parallels with both this novel and *Elizabeth and Her German Garden*; on this matter, see Kurylo [note 10], p. 86.

12 Ruth Elvish Mantz and John Middleton Murry, *The Life of Katherine Mansfield* (London, 1933), p. 208; see also Mansfield's letter to Sylvia Payne of 24 January 1904, in Vincent O'Sullivan and

Margaret Scott (ed.), *The Collected Letters of Katherine Mansfield*, vol. 1, 1903–17 (Oxford, 1984), p. 10.

13 The opera referred to is *Tannhäuser*; see 'The unpublished manuscripts of Katherine Mansfield. 1. Juliet', edited by Margaret Scott, *Turnbull Library Record* 3 (1970), pp. 20f.

14 References are made in passing to *Tannhäuser* and the *Ring*: see Ian A. Gordon (ed.), *Katherine Mansfield: The Urewera Notebook* (Wellington/Oxford, 1978), pp. 20, 74, & 80.

15 See Sir Harold Beauchamp (with a chapter on Katherine Mansfield contributed by G.H. Scholefield), *Reminiscences and Recollections* (New Plymouth, NZ, 1937), p. 194.

16 See for instance Mansfield's letter to S.S. Koteliansky of 17 May 1915, in O'Sullivan & Scott [note 12], pp. 191f.

17 Mantz & Murry [note 12], p. 207f.

18 See e.g. Sydney Janet Kaplan, *Katherine Mansfield and the Origins of Modernist Fiction* (Ithaca, NY, 1991), p. 132. As an entry in Mansfield's *Journal* from 1915 would appear to indicate, Mansfield seems to have lost her early enthusiasm for Nietzsche in later years, although it is significant nevertheless that just a few months before her death she can still recall precisely when Nietzsche's birthday falls. See the entries for 1 February 1915 and 15 October 1922, in John Middleton Murry (ed.), *The Journal of Katherine Mansfield. Definitive Edition* (Auckland, 1984), pp. 73 & 335.

19 Nietzsche's name is mentioned in passing in the early story 'In a Café' (1907), while his tract, *The Birth of Tragedy* (1872), might well be alluded to in the story 'Violet' (1913). On the latter, see Alpers [note 9], p. 119. Mansfield also alludes to *Human, All-Too-Human* (1878) in her letter to Lady Ottoline Morrell of about 8 March 1919; see Vincent O'Sullivan and Margaret Scott (ed.), *The Collected Letters of Katherine Mansfield*, vol. 2, 1918–19 (Oxford, 1987), p. 307.

20 The eponymous heroine of the *Maata* fragment (1913), for instance, has been described as 'a Nietzschean figure who makes her own fate, without regard for morality or kindness' (Claire Tomalin, *Katherine Mansfield: A Secret Life* (London, 1987), p. 120), while the Advanced Lady in Mansfield's story of the same name (1911) utters 'a thinly-veiled Nietzschean definition of feminists'; see Sophie Tomlinson, 'Mans-Field In Bookform', *Landfall* 39 (1985), p. 483.

21 This description of Mansfield comes from Murry [note 18], p. ix; cf. Nietzsche's *The Gay Science* (1887), Bk. 4, § 283.

22 Clare Hanson and Andrew Gurr, *Katherine Mansfield* (London, 1981), pp. 57f; cf. the Epilogue of Nietzsche's *Nietzsche contra Wagner* (1895).

23 See Beauchamp/Scholefield [note 15], p. 194.

24 David S. Thatcher, *Nietzsche in England 1890–1914: The Growth of a Reputation* (Toronto, 1970), p. 262.

25 Thatcher ([note 24], p. 235) notes that during this particular period, the *New Age* carried some eighty items relating to Nietzsche, ranging in importance from extensive articles and book reviews to readers' comments in the correspondence pages.

26 See Mansfield's letter to A.R. Orage of 9 February 1921, in Vincent O'Sullivan and Margaret Scott (ed.), *The Collected Letters of Katherine Mansfield*, vol. 4, 1920–21 (Oxford, 1996), p. 177.

27 Thatcher [note 24], p. 262. Orage was also the author of two small but widely read books on Nietzsche: *Friedrich Nietzsche: The Dionysian Spirit of the Age* (1906), and *Nietzsche in Outline and Aphorism* (1907).

28 Alpers [note 9], p. 157; and Tomalin [note 20], p. 117.

29 See for instance Brasch's essay 'Poetry and politics' in J.L. Watson (ed.), *The Universal Dance: A Selection from the Critical Prose Writings of Charles Brasch* (Dunedin, 1981), pp. 195f. One of the magazines Brasch had considered as a possible model for *Landfall* was S. Fischer's *Neue Rundschau*; see Brasch [note 2], p. 390.

30 See in particular James Bertram, 'Joining in the universal dance of art: Charles Brasch and German lyric', in Hansgerd Delbrück (ed.), *Sinnlichkeit in Bild und Klang: Festschrift für Paul Hoffmann zum 70. Geburtstag* (Stuttgart, 1987), pp. 17–23.

31 Ian Milner, 'Conversation with Charles Brasch', *Landfall* 25 (1971), p. 371; cf. Bertram [note 30], pp. 19–21.

32 Milner [note 31], p. 369.

33 Cf. Brasch [note 29], pp. 195f.

34 James Bertram, *Charles Brasch* (Wellington, 1976), p. 42.

35 Brasch's impression of Huchel is recorded in his letter to Ruth Dallas of 28 June 1972, quoted in Dallas, *Curved Horizon: An Autobiography* (Dunedin, 1991), p. 160. Brasch also translated some of Huchel's poems; they were published in *Islands* 2 (1973), pp. 31–5.

36 See Brasch [note 2], pp. 174f & 191. Translations by Brasch of extracts from *Letters to a Young Poet* appeared in the second number of the celebrated Auckland University student publication, the *Phoenix*, and might well be one of the earliest English versions ever made of this influential work; see Brasch, 'Letters to a young poet', *Phoenix*, vol. 1, no. 2 (1932), pp. 18–21, and Bertram [note 34], p. 8.

37 Brasch [note 2], p. 191. Bertram ([note 30], p. 18) provides a list of some of the poems by Brasch that he believes have been influenced by Rilke.

38 See Brasch's *The Estate and Other Poems* (Christchurch, 1957), pp. 36–59; cf. Bertram [note 30], p. 19.

39 See 'Janet Frame on *Tales from Grimm*', *Education* vol. 24, no. 9 (1975), p. 27; but in particular Frame's *To the Is-Land: An Autobiography* (London/Auckland, 1984), pp. 78–80; cf. also Martin Sutton, 'Märchen der Brüder Grimm in Neuseeland und Polynesien: Ein erster Bericht', *Brüder Grimm Gedenken* 8 (1988), pp. 352f.

40 Judith Dell Panny also sees echoes from Grimms' tales in *The Adaptable Man* (1965) and *Intensive Care* (1970); see Panny, *I have What I Gave: The Fiction of Janet Frame* (Wellington, 1992), pp. 73 & 119.

41 See Jeanne Delbaere-Garant, 'Daphne's metamorphoses in Janet Frame's early novels', *Ariel* 6 (1975), pp. 23–37; and Patrick Evans, *Janet Frame* (Boston, 1977), pp. 33–9.

42 Indeed, an English version of the *Sonnets to Orpheus* was one of Frame's constant companions throughout the eight years she spent in a mental hospital in the late 1940s and early 1950s. See Frame, 'Memory and a pocketful of words', *Times Literary Supplement*, 4 June 1964, p. 487.

43 Delbaere-Garant [note 41], pp. 34f; cf. Evans [note 41], pp. 37f.

44 Evans [note 41], p. 38.

45 Evans [note 41], pp. 36, 39.

46 For a fuller discussion of these three naturalists, see respectively: John A. Asher, 'Georg Forster', Gerda Bell, 'Ernst Dieffenbach', and Les Kermode, 'Ferdinand von Hochstetter', in James N. Bade (ed.), *The German Connection: New Zealand and German-speaking Europe in the Nineteenth Century* (Auckland, 1993), pp. 126–33, 134–44, & 152–61.

47 See Hans-Werner Nieschmidt, 'Bürgers "Neuseeländisches Schlachtlied": Zur Aufnahme Neuseelands in die deutsche Dichtung', *Zeitschrift für deutsche Philologie* 90 (1971), pp. 186–91.

48 Wolfskehl is discussed at greater length in chapter 10. See also Paul Hoffmann, 'A German poet in New Zealand', *Landfall* 23 (1969), pp. 381–91.

49 Wolfskehl felt that his last poems were among his best; see his letter to Emil Preetorius of 23 January 1948, in Karl Wolfskehl, *Briefe aus Neuseeland*, ed. Cornelia Blasberg, with an introduction by Paul Hoffmann (Darmstadt, 1988), vol. 2, p. 958. For an early assessment of Wolfskehl's poetry, see e.g. John Asher, 'Wolfskehl in exile', *AUMLA* 9 (1958), pp. 65–70.

50 Wolfskehl's correspondence from New Zealand has appeared in two editions: *Zehn Jahre Exil. Briefe aus Neuseeland*, ed. Margot Ruben (Heidelberg/Darmstadt, 1959—the edition referred to here), and the larger, more recent two-volume edition *Briefe aus Neuseeland* (see note 49). The first edition of 1959 was widely discussed and quickly sold out. Some commentators even hailed it as being, along with Thomas Mann's novel *Doktor Faustus* (1947), the most important literary testimony to German *Exilliteratur*. See Margot Ruben, 'Karl Wolfskehl. Exul Immeritus. Erinnerungen an Neuseeland', in Paul Gerhard Klussmann (ed.), *Karl Wolfskehl Kolloquium. Vorträge—Berichte—Dokumente* (Amsterdam, 1983), p. 57.

51 Wolfskehl's few attempts to write verse in English—a language of which he had an excellent command—were not successful, as were his attempts to translate some of his own poems into English. See John Asher, 'Das "letzte Inselriff" in der deutschen Dichtung', in Institut für Auslandsbeziehungen, *Mitteilungen* 6 (Jan.–Feb. 1956), p. 47.

52 One notable exception, of course, is his poem 'Glocke vom Strand' (1941), which relates the poet's discovery of a small metal bell on Auckland's St Heliers Beach. See Wolfskehl, *Sang aus dem Exil* (Zürich, 1950), p. lxxvii.

53 See e.g. Wolfskehl's letter to Kurt Frener of 13 September 1946, in Wolfskehl [note 49], vol. 2, p. 909.

54 The description occurs in the cycle *Mittelmeer, oder die fünf Fenster;* see Wolfskehl [note 52], p. xliv.

55 On Wolfskehl's friendship with these New Zealand writers, see e.g. Asher [note 51], p. 47; Hoffmann [note 48], pp. 384f; and Ruben [note 50], p. 52f. Sargeson's friendship and sudden break with Wolfskehl has been discussed both by Sargeson himself and by such commentators as Margot Ruben, Nelson Wattie, and Michael King. See, respectively: Frank Sargeson, *More Than Enough: A Memoir* (Wellington, 1975), pp. 102–14; Ruben [note 50], pp. 57f; Nelson Wattie, 'Frank Sargeson's encounter with Karl Wolfskehl', in Nelson Wattie, *Two Essays* (Stout Centre Occasional Papers), no. 1 (November 1991), pp. 35–48; and Michael King, *Frank Sargeson: A Life* (Auckland, 1995), pp. 222–8.

56 See e.g. his letters to Helmut von den Steinen of 18 April 1944, Kurt Heinrich Wolff of 14 September 1943, and Ottilie Binswanger of 2 March 1943 in, respectively, Wolfskehl [note 49], vol. 1, pp. 228, 474, & 524.

57 If anything, Fairburn and, in particular, Sargeson seem to have done more to enlighten Wolfskehl about the latest developments in contemporary English, American, and New Zealand literature than he managed to instil in his New Zealand literary friends a wider knowledge of European literature. See e.g. Hoffmann [note 48], pp. 384f.

58 Information kindly supplied by Mrs Janet Kelsey (University of Auckland).

59 See Lenz, 'The sixth birthday', *Landfall* 22 (1968), pp. 157–64; Köpf, 'Borges does not exist', *Landfall* 42 (1988), pp. 139–48, and his two stories 'Prison Mail' and 'A Sad Story Without Solace', *Landfall* 44 (1990), pp. 210–13 and 213–18; and see also Enzensberger, 'Carry on, Gutenberg!' and 'Three poems', *Landfall* n. s. 4 (1996), pp. 75–85 and 85–7.

60 See Köpf, 'Bricks and mortar: Über Maurice Shadbolt', in *Aotearoa Neuseeland (Chelsea Hotel: A Magazine for the Arts*, Eggingen, Germany), vol 3, no. 5, 1994, pp. 114–17, but in particular pp. 114f.

61 Köpf [note 60], p. 115.

62 See the interview with Köpf in Franz Loquai (ed.), *Gerhard Köpf* (Eggingen, 1993), pp. 130f. Köpf's dedication in *Bluff*, incidentally, reads as follows: 'With Gratitude/To my Friend Maurice Shadbolt/From an opposite Country/Where Water spirals and the Moon waxes otherwise/And all the wild Way Among the Cinders' (Gerhard Köpf, *Bluff oder das Kreuz des Südens,* Weinheim/Basel, 1991, p. 2).

63 This particular change appears to have been suggested by Shadbolt in a private conversation with Köpf. See Loquai [note 62], p. 130f.

64 The two stories in question are the German versions of 'A Piece of Yellow Soap' and 'Cats by the Tail', both of which were first published in 1935. These appeared in Sargeson's collection *That Summer and Other Stories* (London, 1946), the German version of which (*Damals im Sommer. Gesammelte Erzählungen,* Munich, 1968) is one of the works that Köpf lists among the many 'sources' of his novel. See Köpf, *Der Weg nach Eden* (Munich/Zürich, 1984), p. 300.

65 *Der Sommer des Delphins* (Hamburg, 1973) is another of the various works by other authors listed by Köpf among the 'sources' of *Der Weg nach Eden;* moreover, Maurice Shadbolt is one of the select handful of people whom Köpf specifically thanks for ideas and encouragement offered in the writing of the novel. See Köpf [note 64], p. 301.

66 See Willy Riemer, 'Evelyn Schlag's *Die Kränkung*: Resurrecting Katherine Mansfield', *Modern Austrian Literature* 26 (1993), pp. 107–25.

67 See Alison Lewis, '"Foiling the censor": Reading and transference as feminist strategies in the works of Christa Wolf, Irmtraud Morgner, and Christa Moog', *German Quarterly* 66 (1993), pp. 381–3.

68 Lewis [note 67], pp. 381f.

69 Lewis [note 67], ibid.

70 Lewis [note 67], p. 382.

71 Asher [note 51], p. 43.

8

German influences on
New Zealand music

JOHN MANSFIELD THOMSON

It is difficult to isolate the essentially German strands of a musical tradition that has close links with Austria and forms part of the overall culture of Central Europe.

> Geographical concepts are flexible [writes the German critic Hans-Heinz Stucken-schmidt]. Lines of demarcation shift with the course of history, peoples and civilisations migrate, merge and go their separate ways again, forming new national sentiments and borders ... Even when an obvious rapport exists as between the musicians of Austria and Germany, there are always elements of diversity, as there has been between these two countries since Wagner.[1]

He comments on the technical and stylistic affinities that composers Richard Strauss and Max Reger share with Gustav Mahler, 'though each of them speaks in his own unmistakable musical idiom'.[2] Until the innovations of post-World War II composers such as Boulez and Stockhausen, German influence on New Zealand composers and audiences in the twentieth century proved minimal, being overshadowed by the British tradition of Elgar, Vaughan Williams, Holst, and Britten. Hindemith's rejection of romanticism and adoption of the philosophy of *Gebrauchsmusik* ('music for use') had its followers, particularly on account of his pedagogical works. Similarly Carl Orff's *Das Schulwerk* (1930–33) attracted educationists. Boris Blacher, Karl Amadeus Hartmann, Werner Egk, Wolfgang Fortner, Giselher Klebe, and Hans Werner Henze, for instance, entered the repertoire, but they were not generally well-known names.

The dominant position of German music in the nineteenth century had already made its mark in New Zealand through its composers and great conservatoriums, including those of Dresden and Leipzig. In this tradition the Nelson School of Music, founded in 1894 by Michael Balling (1866–1925), the notable German conductor, viola player, and editor of Wagner, has miraculously survived and has developed innovatory functions and occasions, such as its composer workshops and summer festivals.[3] The lyrical Leipzig-influenced, conservative late nineteenth-century musical style of the pioneer New Zealand–Australian composer Alfred Hill (1870–1960) reaches audiences today through CD recordings. On occasion, an early work such as his cantata *Hinemoa* (1896) is revived as part of our historical heritage.[4] His programmes for the Christchurch International Exhibition Orchestra of 1906–07, which he conducted, show their affinity with those he had heard as a student in Leipzig when playing in the string section of the celebrated Gewandhaus Orchestra.

In the twentieth century it is the post-war German composers who have had the greatest impact on their New Zealand contemporaries. The summer schools at Darmstadt, which began in 1946, and the annual festival at Donaueschingen, revived in 1950, became symbols of the new movement and attracted musicians from all over the world, including New Zealand. Professor Frederick Page (1905–83), a born member of the avant-garde in literature and art as much as music, led the way. Having established Victoria University's Music Department in 1946, he turned it into the country's leading composition school, with Douglas Lilburn and other composers on the staff. In 1958 Richard Hoffmann, a member of a German immigrant refugee family in New Zealand, who had been Schoenberg's amanuensis, persuaded Page to visit Darmstadt and Donaueschingen. In his autobiography *A Musician's Journal* (1986), Page describes what happened:

Caricature of Frederick Page by Juliet Peter. *(J.M. Thomson Collection)*

It was a vintage year with Nono, Stockhausen, Pousseur, Maderna, Cage, lecturing, demonstrating, talking about music. As New Zealand President of the ISCM (International Society for Contemporary Music) I was made welcome: all doors were opened, a New Zealand flag was run up, and when it became known that I had played the Berg Sonata in remote New Zealand as early as 1942, I was pointed out as a matter of wonder. … It was the conviction of the players, the enthusiasm of the students that was so exciting with their certainty that a new land had been reached … Darmstadt gave my ears a good shake-up and I've had no cause to backtrack on my sentiments. [5]

In New Zealand, Frederick Page wrote a series of articles on the new music for *Landfall* and broadcast the works of Boulez, Stockhausen, Feldman, Cage, Maderna, and many others. By now, several of these composers had become personal friends whom he visited on his quite frequent European tours. He had a profound influence on the young generation in his classes, urging his students to listen with an open mind. The composer Jenny McLeod (b. 1941) and musicologist/composer Robin Maconie (b. 1942) are outstanding exemplars of this approach.

Frederick Page and Gillian Weir, 1983. *(John Casey. J.M. Thomson Collection)*

Although Jenny McLeod's principal European teacher was Olivier Messiaen at the Paris Conservatoire, she followed her studies with him by spending time with Boulez in Basel and with Stockhausen in Cologne in order to come to terms with the European avant-garde. Her work for small ensemble *For Seven* (1966) was much praised when performed in Europe. She herself described it as 'an avant-garde European piece in the approved manner'.[6] On her return to New Zealand and her appointment as Lecturer in Music at Victoria University of Wellington, she brought back the ideas of Messiaen, Boulez, and Stockhausen. At Frederick Page's request, she rewrote the entire Victoria University music curriculum and degree regulations, placing a strong emphasis on musical analysis and the study of twentieth-century music. Much of this was already in place by the time she was appointed professor in 1971 and had attracted senior students from other parts of the country, such as Gordon Burt and Denis Smalley from Canterbury. Although she is especially interested today in Maori and Pacific music and in the Dutch composer Peter Schat's 'Tone Clock' theory, the impetus for her deep involvement in experimental techniques derived initially from Frederick Page and his enthusiasm for the music he had heard in Darmstadt and Donaueschingen.

Following studies with Messiaen in Paris, Jenny McLeod's contemporary, Robin Maconie, joined Stockhausen's classes in Cologne in 1964–65, and those of Zimmermann and Pousseur. A decade or so later, he wrote a definitive book, *The Works of Karlheinz Stockhausen*.[7] He found himself in the classic situation described by Schoenberg: 'Somebody had to do the job and no-one else would, so it fell to me.'[8] Maconie was determined to show that even the most difficult new music could be defended as rational and coherent:

Despite the range and strength of loyalty his music inspires, it is still true, I fear, that the impact of Stockhausen's music is something difficult for most listeners, including composers, to comprehend. In part this is a problem created by a consumer culture. People are disturbed by the music and they want to know why they can be profoundly touched by a musical experience that is not entertaining in any conventional way.[9]

Left: Jenny McLeod. *(Neville Glasgow Collection)*

Right: Robin Maconie and Karlheinz Stockhausen at the composer's house, Kürten, Germany, December 1991. *(J.M. Thomson Collection)*

Maconie followed this by compiling a series of lectures and interviews entitled *Stockhausen on Music* (1989), based on those the composer gave during his first visit to Britain in 1971, amplified by a number of questions and answers (recorded in 1981) in which Maconie sought to draw him on a range of practical and slightly more technical issues.[10] As Stuckenschmidt wrote in 1970: 'Radical, volatile and provocative, Stockhausen has aroused the approval of a rebellious rising generation in many parts of the world. Where it will all lead to is anybody's guess.'[11] The question remains open to this day.

Another contemporary, Annea Lockwood (b. 1939), completed her training in the somewhat staid academic background of the University of Canterbury, which nevertheless gave her warm support. In London on an Arts Council bursary, her composition teacher, Peter Racine Fricker, pointed her in the direction of Darmstadt in 1962, and in 1963–64 she took classes in instrumental composition with Gottfried Michael Koenig (b. 1926) in Cologne, where she heard 'a magnificent series of new music concerts by the Westdeutscher Rundfunk'.[12] Koenig's 'very precise organisational mind provided fine teaching of structural aspects, and working in the CEM studios [in Bilthoven, Holland] opened up all those alternative fields of sound sources'.[13] It proved the most productive year of her musical education, which led to her becoming internationally known for her experimental mixed-media works.

Among the German-born artists who visited New Zealand this century, the pianist Wilhelm Backhaus (1884–1969), a giant of his time, stands out. In 1926, he arrived with his own piano and his famous piano stool, which was fitted with a spirit level to make it adjustable to any stage. Described by Frank Dawes in the *New Grove* as 'the last exponent of the great Leipzig tradition of pianism',[14] Backhaus won fresh renown in the latter part of his life as a Beethoven specialist.

Although individual German musicians came here infrequently, the Music Federation (now Chamber Music New Zealand) brought out a number of ensembles ranging from the Koeckert Quartet (1955) and the Berlin Chamber Orchestra (1961) to the Melos Quartet (1978). The Stuttgart Youth Chamber Orchestra (1975) raised the money for its rewarding tour by its members' own efforts. The German Touring Opera Company of Berlin (1971) with Carl Orff's own arrangement of his *Die Kluge* won a warm response.

Very few German soloists have appeared with the New Zealand Symphony Orchestra; however, in 1966 Franz-Paul Decker became its principal guest conductor. In his history of the Sydney Symphony Orchestra, *Play On!*, Phillip Sametz describes him as 'one of the great eccentrics of the conducting firmament, a fiery Wagnerian with a tremendous sense of architecture in big works'.[15] He has given memorable interpretations of Mahler and Bruckner with the New Zealand Symphony Orchestra, and in 1997 conducted a concert performance of Wagner's *Rheingold*.

The Goethe Institut, based in Wellington, which began its cultural work in 1980, has presented a number of outstanding musicians in a variety of fields. The twentieth-century music specialist, the pianist Herbert Henck, who toured in 1983, included Stockhausen's last *Klavierstücke* in his programmes—an interpretation of electrifying intensity. He also played works by Wolfgang Rihm and Walter Zimmermann. In 1984 the Reger Trio toured, and in 1988 the Pocket Opera Company of Nuremberg took part in the biennial Wellington International Festival of the Arts. Today's focus is on contemporary music and jazz.

Refugee musicians from Nazi Germany in the late 1930s and early 1940s have contributed significantly to New Zealand's own burgeoning musical culture. They have included the violinist Erika Schorss, who played in the New Zealand Symphony Orchestra, and the cellist Marie Vandewart Blaschke, who had studied at the Berlin Hochschule für Musik under Hindemith and became a central figure in the concerts given by the newly formed Wellington Chamber Music Society.

As the dominant influences of Darmstadt and Donaueschingen have been absorbed and reflected in countless ways throughout the world, one speculates on what fresh manifestations of the Germanic tradition will emerge. Although other schools have sprung up, such as that of the American West Coast minimalists, it is impossible to believe that the culture that produced Bach, Beethoven, Wagner, Strauss, Hindemith, Kurt Weill, and Stockhausen will not bring forth such powerful figures in the future as it has done in the past.

1 H.-H. Stuckenschmidt, *Twentieth Century Composers*, vol. 2, *Germany and Central Europe* (London, 1970), p. 11.

2 Ibid.

3 See John Mansfield Thomson, 'The era of Michael Balling: 1893–96' in Shirley Tunnicliff (ed.), *Response to a Vision: The First Hundred Years of the Nelson School of Music* (Nelson, 1994), pp. 37–53; John Mansfield Thomson, 'Michael Balling' in James N. Bade (ed.), *The German Connection: New Zealand and German-speaking Europe in the Nineteenth Century* (Auckland, 1993), pp. 119–25; and John Mansfield Thomson, 'From Bayreuth to the Ureweras: Michael Balling and the revival of the viola alta', *Turnbull Library Record*, vol. 23, no. 2 (1990), pp. 157–68.

4 See John Mansfield Thomson, *A Distant Music: The Life and Times of Alfred Hill 1870–1960* (Auckland, 1980). *Hinemoa* was performed in Wellington as part of the 1990 sesquicentenary celebrations.

5 Frederick Page, *A Musician's Journal: 1905–1983*, edited and arranged by J.M. Thomson and Janet Paul (Dunedin, 1986), pp. 106f.

6 John Mansfield Thomson, *Biographical Dictionary of New Zealand Composers* (Wellington, 1990), p. 98.

7 Robin Maconie, *The Works of Karlheinz Stockhausen* (Oxford 1976; rev. edn Oxford 1990).

8 See Thomson [note 6], p. 102.

9 Maconie [note 7], 1990 edn, p. vii.

10 Karlheinz Stockhausen, *Stockhausen on Music: Lectures and Interviews compiled by Robin Maconie* (London & New York, 1989).

11 Stuckenschmidt [note 1], p. 212.

12 Thomson [note 6], p. 91.

13 Ibid.

14 *The New Grove Dictionary of Music and Musicians*, ed. Stanley Sadie (London, 1980), vol. 2, p. 3.

15 Phillip Sametz, *Play On!* (Sydney, 1992), p. 306.

9

The film connection

LAUREN JACKSON

Since the late 1970s, when New Zealand's small feature film industry entered a growth phase, German film distributors, producers, directors, festival organisers, and audiences have demonstrated a remarkable interest in our films. New Zealand films have been invited to German film festivals, where some have won prizes. Individual titles have been bought for cinematic release and/or television broadcast in Germany. A complete 'season of New Zealand films' has been presented on German television and in movie theatres. Members of the German film industry have visited New Zealand to compare our nation with our cinematic representation of it. Some German directors have stayed to work here. Finally, German funding bodies and producers have invested in the New Zealand film industry in the form of German–New Zealand co-productions.

It was not so much through effective marketing but by good fortune that New Zealand's films came to Germany's attention in the late 1970s. David Blythe's first feature *Angel Mine* (1978) was invited to screen at the 28th Mannheim Film Festival in late 1979 as a result of a screening in New Zealand for visiting Polish director Krzysztov Zanussi, who was impressed by the film and recommended it to the Mannheim organisers.[1] New Zealand producers were very active as individuals in the marketing of films. Bruce Morrison returned from an 'overseas selling trip'[2] at the end of 1979, having sold his documentary film *Red Deer* (1979) to NDR (Norddeutscher Rundfunk), among other foreign stations, for television broadcast. A few weeks later, in early 1980, a documentary directed by John O'Shea for his company, Pacific Films, won second prize at a Berlin film festival run in conjunction with Berlin's 'Green Week'. The film, *Cows, Computers and Customers* (1979), had been made for the New Zealand Dairy Board.[3] In time O'Shea would become one of the main links between the New Zealand and German film industries.

Half way through 1981 a jubilant headline on the front page of the New Zealand Film Commission's publication, *New Zealand Film*, trumpeted: 'BREAK-THROUGH YEAR FOR NEW ZEALAND FEATURES IN INTERNATIONAL MARKETS.'[4] This was the second year New Zealand features had been taken to the international film market at Cannes. Among the many overseas sales the article reported were 'Six New Zealand features sold for TV transmission in Germany'.[5] Out of the UK, the USA, Germany, the Soviet Union, Spain, Sweden, and India, Germany was the biggest buyer of New Zealand films.[6] Bought for television transmission were: *Beyond*

Reasonable Doubt[7] (West and East Germany), *Pictures*,[8] *Sleeping Dogs*[9] (West and East Germany), *Smash Palace*,[10] *Skin Deep*,[11] and *Sons for the Return Home*.[12] *Skin Deep* also gained a cinema release in Germany, and similar negotiations were proceeding for *Smash Palace*.[13] The same year, director Sam Pillsbury's film *The Scarecrow* (1982) was bought by Janus Film of Frankfurt for theatrical and television release in Germany.[14] Germany thus became one of the first countries to be exposed to a broad range of films from New Zealand's 'new wave'.

Also in 1981 it was announced that *Pictures*, produced by John O'Shea, had been chosen for screening at the 1982 Berlin Film Festival.[15] That year, the festival director, Moritz De Hadeln, had visited New Zealand and spent two days with the Film Commission. At the time, he told the Wellington *Evening Post*: 'New Zealand is very innovative in its film-making. … You have your own sort of humour, your own history and traditions, all of them unknown to us.'[16] *Pictures* was perhaps less innovative for its style than for its subject matter—the interaction between Maori and Pakeha in nineteenth-century New Zealand, explored through the story of two brothers, pioneer photographers who disagreed about how to photograph Maori subjects. This was the first New Zealand feature film to be screened at the festival, and, according to reports, it attracted considerable interest. *New Zealand Film* reported: '*PICTURES* was shown in the information section at Berlin, in a print especially subtitled in German. After each screening Film Commission Marketing Director Lindsay Shelton … answered many questions about the film, its story and its backgrounds, which were seen as particularly exotic by the German audiences.'[17]

This festival marks the beginning of a tradition: the German perception of New Zealand films as providing images from an exotic, culturally distant

Still from *Pictures* (1981, dir. Michael Black). *(NZ Film Commission)*

land. The fascination of this 'otherness' seems to have shielded German audiences from the harsh critique levelled at European colonisers throughout the film. Whereas films with this kind of political message have sometimes aggravated Pakeha New Zealand viewers, the same films have often been received in Germany with interest and admiration. Merata Mita's films, for example, have attracted much controversy in her own country. *Patu!* (1983), her documentary on the Springbok Tour, was considered by television executives to be so inflammatory that it was not broadcast in New Zealand for a decade. Yet in 1983 her twenty-seven-minute documentary about the police arresting Maori land rights demonstrators, *Bastion Point— Day 507* (1980, co-directed by Leon Narbey and Gerd Pohlmann)[18] won first prize in the international jury section of the Oberhausen Film Festival in West Germany.[19]

By this stage, interest in New Zealand film-making had grown strong enough to warrant a New Zealand season of feature films screening on ZDF (Zweites Deutsches Fernsehen) in September and October of 1982. The films screened were *Skin Deep, Goodbye Pork Pie,*[20] *Sleeping Dogs, Smash Palace, Pictures,* and *Beyond Reasonable Doubt.* The fact that each film attracted about five million viewers must have seemed phenomenal considering that New Zealand's population at the time was only three million. An introductory documentary on New Zealand and its film industry had already been shot here in April 1982 by a German film crew.[21] The ZDF season elicited a strong response from the German media, with a number of feature articles appearing in publications such as *Die Welt, Die Zeit, Frankfurter Allgemeine,* and *Stuttgarter Zeitung.* Hans Blumenburg, writing for *Die Zeit,* commented: 'In the culture pages of European newspapers, there has been no place for New Zealand till now.'[22] The New Zealand film industry's eagerness to hear Germany's feedback is demonstrated by *New Zealand Film*'s lengthy translations of critics' responses in two consecutive issues.[23] In general, the critics responded to three elements of the films: their 'authenticity',[24] comparing their style to English realism of the 1950s;[25] the dichotomy between the paradisal setting and the tone of social disillusionment;[26] and the frequent appearance of an anarchistic protagonist who suffers from 'island madness and paranoia'.[27] They also praised the 'soothing human touch'[28] of the films and the directors' mastery of film conventions.[29]

As a consequence of this media attention, German directors and producers began to regard New Zealand as a potential co-production partner. In fact, by the end of 1982 a co-produced six-part television series entitled *Jack Holborn* had already been completed. It was produced by Aucklander Jack George in association with TV60 of Munich and screened by ZDF.[30] The director was German—Sigi Rothmund—and the cast included a number of New Zealanders. It was filmed at Northern Television's Auckland studios with location shooting in Rarotonga and Yugoslavia. Germany's growing awareness of New Zealand as a film-making nation had been welcome news to George, who had been trying to get co-production deals with German companies off the ground since 1980.[31]

Another producer who had been working on co-production deals during this time was John O'Shea. In early 1979 *New Zealand Film* reported:

'John O'Shea of Pacific Films is making a rapid visit to Britain, West Germany and the United States to discuss various film projects.'[32] At the beginning of 1980, Maurice Shadbolt 'announced that his novel *Among the Cinders* had been bought by a German film company'.[33] Shadbolt's novel, originally published in 1965, had been translated into German and published in 1971 as *Und er nahm mich bei der Hand*. It had enjoyed great success in Germany and was one of *Der Spiegel*'s bestsellers for months,[34] thus proving to be 'rather spectacularly more successful than the original English language editions had been'.[35] The German translation of *Among the Cinders*, however, was in fact based on a somewhat revised version of the English original—Shadbolt had made some changes to it for his German translator[36]—and the story itself was to undergo a few more changes when John O'Shea's Pacific Pictures, together with NDR of Hamburg, produced *Among the Cinders* as a film in 1983 (released 1984).

The film's director was German film-maker Rolf Haedrich, who told the *Evening Post* that when he read the translation of Shadbolt's novel 'he found it moving, and it made him identify with the central character like a father with a son'.[37] John O'Shea reassured the paper that '*AMONG THE CINDERS* will be a New Zealand film, with a wholly New Zealand cast and almost wholly New Zealand crew. "The Germans are pleased to be associated with the New Zealand film industry," he said. "The success of New Zealand films overseas has brought about this feeling." '[38]

O'Shea and Haedrich collaborated on the screenplay, with Haedrich flying to New Zealand for talks in April of 1982 and O'Shea flying later to Hamburg to complete the script. In 1980 the German critic Hans Blumenburg had advised the New Zealand Film Commission not to give money 'to international co-productions, which can get money elsewhere'.[39] Accordingly the commission had adopted the policy of supporting a production 'only when it is "satisfied that the film has or is to have a significant New Zealand content" in terms of subject-matter, locations and the nationality of crew and backers'.[40] *Among the Cinders* did receive funding from the commission because, as Nicholas Reid suggests, it was 'adapted from an important New Zealand novel reeking of Kiwi concerns'.[41]

Still from *Among the Cinders* (1983, dir. Rolf Haedrich). *(NZ Film Commission)*

Indeed, both the book and the film explore some typical 'New Zealand' issues. An adolescent boy, Nick Flinders, struggles to come to terms with the death of his best friend, Sam Waikai. He spends his summer holidays with his grandfather physically recuperating from the accident that hospitalised him and killed his friend. Issues of New Zealand race relations arise, as Sam is Maori while Nick is Pakeha. Nick feels the need to escape his tiny rural town of Te Ika, perhaps suffering from 'island madness', to use a Blumenburg term. Nick is a teenage version of a 'Man Alone' character (from the famous New Zealand novel of that name by John Mulgan) while his grandfather is a much older version.

Yet German elements not present in the book have been slipped into the film, presumably to please German investors and audiences. Nick's mother becomes German in the film. As in the novel, Grandfather Flinders upsets her when he insists on coming to visit Nick. In the book she protests: 'I can't stand it ... Him and his foul mouth'[42] whereas in the film she proclaims, 'Mein Gott ... I did not come to New Zealand to be abused by this monster.' In the novel, a minister who comes to visit Nick in hospital tries to persuade him that God loves humans: 'He sent His only son to die for us.'[43] Yet Nick has little faith in either God or humans, and replies: 'I don't see what's so great about that either. A lot of people have sent their sons off to die, some way or other.'[44] On screen, Nick's expression of disillusionment is more impassioned. He explains his horror at the human race and his lack of religious belief by describing what he knows about the Holocaust.

There is no indication that *Among the Cinders* ever had a theatrical release in Germany, although it was invited to special screenings at the Berlin festival in 1984. While the film does not appear to have enjoyed much box-office or critical success (Reid describes it as a 'lacklustre version of a good novel'),[45] it has significance as the first New Zealand–German feature co-production, and paved the way for O'Shea's later co-productions.

The film that put New Zealand on the film-making map once and for all as far as Germany was concerned was Vincent Ward's *Vigil* (1984)—New Zealand's first film in competition at Cannes. In early 1985 Futura Films released it in Germany, intending it to be screened in 'more than 50 German

Still from *Among the Cinders* (1983, dir. Rolf Haedrich.) *(NZ Film Commission)*

Still from *Vigil* (1984, dir. Vincent Ward.) *(NZ Film Commission)*

cities over the first six months of its theatrical release'.[46] Ward, an art school graduate, represented a new breed of New Zealand film-maker. In contrast to the so-called 'Cowboys of Culture' (a term employed to describe directors such as Geoff Murphy and Roger Donaldson), the younger directors of the 1980s were strongly interested in European films and art movements. Elements of the German traditions of Expressionism and 'Innerlichkeit' found their way into *Vigil*, to the delight of German critics and audiences. 'Vincent Ward's film lives from its stupendous nature shots,' noted *Die Welt*. 'Obviously German directors of the 1920s and 1930s stood as godfather.'[47] Nearly every German critic marvelled at 'the tremendous strength and power' of Ward's imagery,[48] which was both 'menacing' and 'mythical'.[49] As usual, 'exotic'[50] was a word that sprang to the reviewers' minds as they searched for a way to describe the film and its 'wild, overpowering'[51] landscape: 'New Zealand is an unusual piece of earth, which in the film gives an impression of a mixture of Scotland's highlands and the green of Ireland.'[52] One can imagine that New Zealand's rural landscape must have seemed just as foreign to Vincent Ward's mother when she arrived here as a German–Jewish refugee and became the wife of a farmer.

Yvonne Mackay's feature film *The Silent One* (1984) also drew praise from German newspapers in 1985 when it won first prize at the Frankfurt Festival of Films for Children and Young People. Eva Maria Lenz enjoyed the 'Exotic scenes and equally exotic insights … offered in *THE SILENT ONE*, an orgy of sea and sky'.[53] Aside from the usual drawcard of exoticism, the film pleased its young German viewers because it could 'take them outside Germany without ending up in some fairytale forest'.[54] Meanwhile, to the general New Zealand public of 1985, local films were not 'exotic' because they could not transport New Zealanders out of their country. Indeed, the public was so afflicted by 'cultural cringe' that producers John Maynard and Bridget Ikin would not release a film like *Vigil* until it had received critical acclaim in Europe. Only then were local audiences confident of its worth as a film. Most pages of *New Zealand Film* consisted of reports of overseas enthusiasm for our films, which functioned as both encouragement and vindication of New Zealand as a film-making nation. (This is still the case today.) Therefore the following 1985 report must have greatly heartened the film-making community:

A New Zealand Film Week was presented in Berlin in April. Thirteen films were shown, at a total of 21 screenings at the cinema Filmbuhne amm [*sic*] Steinplatz. Capacity audiences were attracted for *VIGIL, CONSTANCE, GOODBYE PORK PIE,* and *OFF THE EDGE.* … During the film week, a photographic display about New Zealand was exhibited in the cinema foyer, and an information stand about New Zealand was set up.[55]

New Zealand was beginning to realise the effectiveness of films in encouraging tourism. The film industry made frequent use of this argument in attempts to gain increased funding from the government.

The following year, New Zealand film societies demonstrated a reciprocal interest in German film when they brought Eva Orbanz, curator, Stiftung Deutsche Kinemathek, and member of the FIAF[56] executive, to New Zealand to spend time at the National Film Archive during the 1986 FIAF Congress. Orbanz selected and introduced 'Origins of the German cinema 1895–1927', programmes screened by the Film Archive in Wellington and Auckland. The Goethe Institut co-sponsored this event with the Film Societies and Film Archive.

John O'Shea was again busy in 1987, producing Maori film-maker Barry Barclay's first feature, *Ngati* (1987). Of the experience he said: 'Having worked in recent years on New Zealand stories with German and French film makers, it has been an occasion for rejoicing to be able to return to a more obviously indigenous subject.'[57] Yet it would not be long before O'Shea's Pacific Films would work on a joint New Zealand–German production, again directed by Barclay. In the meantime, the continued appreciation of New Zealand films in Germany meant that it was no longer headline news when German companies purchased the German rights to them. At the Hof Film Festival in 1989, Vincent Ward's second feature, *The Navigator* (1989), was hailed as a 'cinematic tour de force'.[58] A season of twenty New Zealand feature films, entitled 'Filme vom anderen Ende der Welt', toured West Germany in November 1989, organised by the Hamburg Film Institute in association with the New Zealand Film Commission and the New Zealand Film Archive. By the start of August 1991, close to 100,000 viewers had seen one of the sixteen prints of Jane Campion's *An Angel at My Table* (1990) circulating in Germany.[59]

While it is true that *New Zealand Film* concentrates on the most positive reviews, the impression the reader gleans of strong German interest in New Zealand films is not incorrect. Proof came in the form of an invitation to Te Manu Aute (a group of Maori film-makers and artists) from the West Berlin state film fund. If the group could 'come up with a story which somehow married Berlin and the Maori world, they would consider investing in it'.[60] Thus *Te Rua* came to be made in 1990 with backing from the New Zealand Film Commission and the Berlin Senate and Film Commission. O'Shea was deeply impressed by the German support and hoped that this project would avoid the usual co-production problems of cultural compromise: 'There was simply no other city in the world where we could have made it … The Berliners backed us knowing the film was opening up a major issue about indigenous rights to cultural materials.'[61]

Indeed, had *Te Rua* been produced and shot solely in New Zealand, it would have been a very different film. The story follows the journey of a

Still from *Te Rua* (1990,
dir. Barry Barclay.) *(NZ
Film Commission)*

group of Maori to Berlin, where they try to reclaim three of their ancestral
carvings. The carvings had been stolen from the (fictional) Uritoto marae
150 years earlier by two men—one Maori and one German—and are now
stored in the basement of a Berlin museum. The Maori activists seize three
busts from a park, to draw a parallel between the cultural significance of these
sculptures for Germans and the spiritual value of the Maori carvings for the
Uritoto marae. The same effect could not have been achieved had the action
taken place in Auckland, where European art is not generally valued in the
same way. The Berlin shoot took place in the midst of the reunification of
East and West Berlin, and many of the German extras cast for the scenes of
conflict were activists who had been involved in the protests that preceded
the fall of the Berlin Wall.[62] Thus the Berlin scenes were charged with a
revolutionary energy that would have been difficult to evoke in Auckland.

The film employs a reflexive narrative technique that could be called
Brechtian. The camera is visible in the opening shots of the film, and Matiu
Mareikura appears as the storyteller to ask: 'Are you rolling?' A group of
Maori then perform a haka to camera. On another occasion, Vanessa Rare's
character speaks directly to the viewer about the cultural exploitation of
Maori. These episodes momentarily create a 'Verfremdungseffekt' (alienation
effect). However, Barclay has his own motivation (rooted in Maori culture)
for using this style, in aiming to construct the narrative around the community rather than individual protagonists. He is also emulating the Maori style
of oral storytelling.[63] The Berlin sequences follow a more traditional narrative style, yet one is again reminded of Brecht when Rewi (played by Wi
Kuki Kaa) climbs a stepladder and demands that the director of the Berlin
museum does the same[64] so they can be 'on the same level' to negotiate the
exchange of the busts for the carvings. This is didactic street theatre in the
spirit of Brecht, set in his own city—East Berlin.

Barclay told the *Christchurch Press*: 'I have enormous respect for our Berlin
collaborators for taking on the film, because we couldn't do it in London,
Washington, Paris or Wellington because it's threatening … If you challenge
the right of an entire culture to have guardianship or ownership over part of
a culture, then a multi-million dollar industry falls down.'[65]

Yet the German response to the film was not entirely supportive. The
German museum curator is seen as a man void of his own culture, who leads
a vampire-like existence, sapping spiritual strength from the artefacts of
indigenous peoples that he keeps stored in the basement. Eventually, however, he agrees to return the Maori carvings. Although approval to film at
West Berlin's Ethnographic Museum had been given, the museum director
suddenly withdrew permission. Fortunately, production manager Katrin
Schlosser was able to obtain permission to film in an East Berlin museum.[66]
There were other negative responses to *Te Rua*, which Barry summed up as
follows: 'Your film implies that we have no spirituality. But we have deep
feelings about our art works too. That should have been in the film, otherwise we don't feel part of it.'[67] Here was a New Zealand film that had
moved out of the realm of the 'exotic' and hit close to home. *Te Rua* has
not been released in Germany.[68] When screened in New Zealand, it produced an equally uneasy response.

Still from *Flight of the Albatross* (1996, dir. Werner Meyer.) *(NZ Film Commission)*

Since 1991, another four feature films have been made in New Zealand with financial backing from German companies. The popularity in Germany of Jane Campion's *The Piano* (1994), Peter Jackson's *Bad Taste* (1988) and *Braindead* (1993), Peter Wells' and Stewart Main's *Desperate Remedies* (1993), and Lee Tamahori's *Once Were Warriors* (1993) has encouraged German investment in New Zealand films. Hanno Huth of Senator Films helped fund Peter Jackson's *Heavenly Creatures* (1994), Grant La Hood's *Chicken* (1996), and Tony Hiles' *Jack Brown, Genius* (1995), although none of the three films has any German content. Neither *Chicken* nor *Jack Brown, Genius* has done well at the box office, and it remains to be seen whether Senator Films will continue to invest in New Zealand films. *Flight of the Albatross* (1996), directed by Werner Meyer (a German) and funded by the New Zealand Film Commission, Avalon Studios, ZDF, and the Berlin Film Commission, also did disappointing box-office business. The story revolves around the relationship between a Maori boy (Taungaroa Emile of *Once Were Warriors*) and a German girl (Julia Brendler), and is set on Great Barrier Island. The screenplay was adapted by Riwia Brown (the screenwriter of *Once Were Warriors*) from Deborah Savage's novel, which already had the German elements that must have attracted the German investors.

Clearly, international co-productions do not always 'gel'. Lately, the most successful contacts have been through screenings of New Zealand short films. In June 1996, the Hamburg Short Film Festival featured three general programmes of New Zealand shorts, with a few entered in competition. Kurzfilme has also released a compilation of New Zealand shorts.[69]

There can be no doubt that since New Zealand took its first tentative steps towards establishing its own film industry in the late 1970s, the German industry has observed our progress keenly. Germany has been attracted to our films because it considers the indigenous people and landscapes of New Zealand 'exotic', yet there is at the same time an element of familiarity in the European characters and their society. New Zealand stories have the passion and the angst of a nation still struggling to develop its identity. Bringing the two countries together in co-productions has been a very interesting but complex process of cultural negotiation.

Whether or not we agree with Germany's perception of our films, one thing is clear: Germany has aided our film industry in numerous ways. It has contributed financially, creatively, and by encouraging us to believe in our own product. Every time a German company snaps up the German rights to a film, every time New Zealand work is shown at festivals and on German television, and every time one of our films wins a German award, we are reminded that someone out there is interested and watching.[70]

1 *New Zealand Film*, no. 3 (June/July, 1979), p. 3.
2 *New Zealand Film*, no. 6 (November/December, 1979), p. 7.
3 *New Zealand Film*, no. 7 (January/February, 1980), p. 4.
4 *New Zealand Film*, no. 13 (April/May/June/July, 1981), p.1.
5 Ibid.
6 Publications before the reunification do not always differentiate between East and West Germany. Where possible, I will indicate which German state is being referred to.
7 Dir.: John Laing, 1980.
8 Dir.: Michael Black, 1981.
9 Dir.: Roger Donaldson, 1977.
10 Dir.: Roger Donaldson, 1982.
11 Dir.: Geoff Steven, 1979.
12 Dir.: Paul Maunder, 1979.
13 *New Zealand Film*, no. 13 (April/May/June/July, 1981), p. 2.
14 *New Zealand Film*, no. 15 (November/December, 1981), p. 3.
15 Ibid, p. 4.
16 Quoted in *New Zealand Film*, no. 15 (November/December, 1981), p. 8.
17 *New Zealand Film*, no. 16 (March/April, 1982), p. 6.
18 Gerd Pohlmann was born in West Germany and is a graduate of the Berlin Film School. He has lived and worked in New Zealand as a film-maker since the late 1970s, and has been influential in the making of political documentaries.
19 *New Zealand Film*, no. 20 (May/June/July/August, 1983), p. 14.
20 Dir.: Geoff Murphy, 1981.
21 *New Zealand Film*, no. 17 (May/June/July/August, 1982), p. 6.
22 Undated review in *Die Zeit*, translated and quoted in *New Zealand Film*, no. 18 (September/October/November/December, 1982), p. 8. Blumenburg had in fact visited New Zealand in November 1980 when he saw and was impressed by *Goodbye Pork Pie*. He also noted: 'There are several gifted film-makers who need Government funding' (*New Zealand Film*, no. 11 (November/December, 1980), p. 10).
23 See *New Zealand Film*, no. 18 (September/October/November/December, 1982), p. 8, and no. 19 (January/February/March/April, 1983), p. 11.
24 See the undated review by Margarete Schwarzkopf in *Die Welt*, translated and quoted in *New Zealand Film*, no. 18 (September/October/November/December, 1982), p. 8.
25 Undated review in the *Frankfurter Allgemeine Zeitung*, translated and quoted in *New Zealand Film*, no. 19 (January/February/March/April, 1983), p. 11.
26 Undated review by Hans Blumenburg in *Die Zeit*, translated and quoted in *New Zealand Film*, no. 18 (September/October/November/December, 1982), p. 8.
27 Ibid.
28 Schwarzkopf [note 24], p 8.
29 Undated review in the *Frankfurter Allgemeine Zeitung*, translated and quoted in *New Zealand Film*, no. 19 (January/February/March/April, 1983), p. 11.
30 *New Zealand Film*, no. 18 (September/October/November/December, 1982), p. 15.
31 See *New Zealand Film*, no. 11 (November/December, 1980), p. 5.
32 *New Zealand Film*, no. 2 (April/May, 1979), p. 5.
33 *New Zealand Film*, no. 10 (August/September/October, 1980), p. 6.
34 *New Zealand Film*, no. 19 (January/February/March/April, 1983), p. 9.

35 Maurice Shadbolt, *Among the Cinders* (Auckland, rev. edn, 1984), p. 6 (author's note).

36 Ibid. According to Shadbolt, the second (revised) edition of *Among the Cinders*, as published in 1984, 'substantially follows the changes made for my German translator'.

37 Quoted in *New Zealand Film*, no. 19 (January/February/March/April, 1983), p. 9.

38 Ibid.

39 Undated item in the *Dominion*, quoted in *New Zealand Film*, no. 11 (November/December, 1980), p. 10.

40 Nicholas Reid, *A Decade of New Zealand Film: Sleeping Dogs to Came a Hot Friday* (Dunedin, 1986), p. 16.

41 Ibid.

42 Shadbolt [note 35], p. 69.

43 Shadbolt [note 35], p. 45.

44 Ibid.

45 Reid [note 40], p. 142.

46 *New Zealand Film*, no. 25 (April, 1985), p. 11.

47 Undated review in *Die Welt*, translated and quoted in *New Zealand Film*, no. 26 (September, 1985), p. 8.

48 Undated review in the *Düsseldorfer Nachrichten*, translated and quoted in *New Zealand Film*, no. 26 (September, 1985), p. 8.

49 Undated review in the *Berliner Morgenpost*, translated and quoted in *New Zealand Film*, no. 26 (September, 1985), p. 8.

50 Ibid.

51 Undated review in *Der Tagesspiegel* (Berlin), translated and quoted in *New Zealand Film*, no. 26 (September, 1985), p. 8.

52 Undated review in the *Ruhr-Nachrichten* (Dortmund), translated and quoted in *New Zealand Film*, no. 26 (September, 1985), p. 8.

53 Undated review in the *Frankfurter Allgemeine Zeitung*, translated and quoted in *New Zealand Film*, no. 25 (April, 1985), p. 14.

54 Undated review by Oliver Tolmen in the *Frankfurter Rundschau*, translated and quoted in *New Zealand Film*, no. 25 (April, 1985), p. 14.

55 *New Zealand Film*, no. 26 (September, 1985), p. 13.

56 International Federation of Film Archives (translated from the French).

57 *New Zealand Film*, no. 28 (April, 1986), p. 12.

58 Christian Winterfeldt, reviewer for the *Kölner Stadt-Anzeiger*, as reported in *New Zealand Film*, no. 36 (March, 1989), p. 2.

59 *New Zealand Film*, no. 44 (September, 1991), p. 9.

60 Barry Barclay, 'Amongst landscapes', in Jonathon Dennis and Jan Bieringa (ed.), *Film in Aotearoa New Zealand* (Wellington, 1992), p. 127.

61 *New Zealand Film*, no. 43 (May, 1991), p. 3.

62 *New Zealand Film*, no. 41 (October, 1990), p. 11.

63 Undated review by Costa Botes in the *Dominion*, quoted in *New Zealand Film*, no. 44 (September, 1991), p. 6.

64 Ibid.

65 Quoted in *New Zealand Film*, no. 44 (September, 1991), p. 6.

66 *New Zealand Film*, no. 41 (October, 1990), p. 10.

67   Barclay [note 60], p. 128.

68 *New Zealand Film*, no. 43 (May, 1991), p. 3.

69 *Onfilm*, April 1996, p. 5.

70 I would like to thank Associate Professor Roger Horrocks (University of Auckland) for his editorial advice and assistance.

10

Karl Wolfskehl

FRIEDRICH VOIT

I am coming to a new country, an entire new world, a new mentality and outlook, and I am enormously interested at the prospect.

This optimistic and positive statement by Karl Wolfskehl appeared in the *New Zealand Herald* on Monday, 4 July 1938, the day after his arrival in New Zealand. More than six feet tall, with a lively temper, and radiating a powerful personality despite suffering from almost complete blindness, Wolfskehl looked even at the age of 69 very much like a poet, with his striking appearance and long hair. While his arrival did not go completely unnoticed, hardly anyone in New Zealand knew of Karl Wolfskehl—a popular figure at the centre of the literary circles of Munich, a close friend of Stefan George, and well known to Hugo von Hofmannsthal, Rainer Maria Rilke, and Thomas Mann—nor did anyone know anything of Wolfskehl the eminent scholar and famous book collector. His poetry was even less well known.[1] For New Zealanders, Karl Wolfskehl was merely an obscure European poet, fleeing from the Nazi regime because of his Jewish origins.

Born in Darmstadt in 1869, Wolfskehl was brought up in a wealthy upper-class family. After his study of German literature in Berlin, Leipzig, and Giessen, where he submitted his doctoral thesis on an aspect of Germanic mythology, he did not need to pursue a regular career, for he had the means to devote his time to his poetic and private scholarly interests. His meeting in 1893 with Stefan George—Germany's most enigmatic poet— was an experience that would have a profound effect on his later life. In George he recognised the beginning of a new epoch in German poetry and of 'a national revival through an élite and the power of the mind'.[2] Wolfskehl upheld this conservative utopian vision throughout his life.

In 1898 he married Hanna de Haan and settled in Munich, where his house soon became a focal point in the cultural scene of the city, and remained so for many years. Much of Wolfskehl's wealth was lost in the inflation after World War I, and he was forced to earn a living. While his wife and their two daughters moved into a small baroque villa in the village of Kiechlinsbergen (Baden), he spent several years in Italy teaching as a private tutor before returning to Munich in 1925, where he established himself as an essayist writing for newspapers and periodicals.

Very early on, Wolfskehl sensed the menace implied in the rise of Fascism in Germany, not only as a threat to his own life but also as a movement that spelled disaster for the spiritual and cultural values of European humanism, which formed the foundation of his intellect. When, in the 1930s, he felt Europe was about to be drowned in a turmoil of Fascist brutality and another world war, Wolfskehl decided to leave Europe. He explained this, years later, in a letter to a friend:

I actually had emigrated [from Germany] as early as October 1931, had moved to Italy … I have always felt at home in Italy. But then, when Fascism became more and more pronounced and more threatening, competing with its terrible northern twin even in the most inhumane aspects, when it began to assume characteristics similar to Nazism, I decided to leave Europe completely, and I chose this island-country of which I only knew at the time[3] that it was a country of strange birds, of the kiwi and the kea, and that it was the home of an indigenous population with a cultural past full of the most strange but unique kind of beauty, with lovely bays, evergreen forests and a pleasantly temperate climate. More than all that, what attracted me was that New Zealand is further away from Europe than any other inhabitable place on the globe, thus epitomising distance to me.[4]

On arrival Wolfskehl and Margot Ruben, who had been living with him since 1934 and who was to share with him the ten years in exile in New Zealand, had only a tourist visa. At that stage, they had envisaged staying in the Antipodes for some period and then travelling on or, if the political situation should permit it, returning to Europe. Initially, he did not see himself as a refugee in exile. In his poetic imagination, New Zealand had become a symbolic counterpart to Thule, the legendary northern-most land of ancient belief. New Zealand, the 'Anti-Thule', as he called it, seemed to him a promised land, blessed by nature and with a favourable climate, and, even more significantly, a land free of the evil and all-pervasive atmosphere of Fascism, which threatened to suffocate his creativity.

On his way to New Zealand, Wolfskehl had to stop off in Sydney for a week to wait for the *Awatea*, the ship that brought him to Auckland. The days in Sydney proved to be an extremely pleasant and stimulating experience.[5] The lively cultural life of the city impressed him, and he also, quite unexpectedly, made the acquaintance of people whose intellectual interests were similar to his own. He had intended to return to Sydney after his stay in New Zealand, for he soon felt that Auckland did not offer a particularly welcoming or inspiring environment. But political developments overtook him and his companion: in autumn 1938, Italy expelled all Jews, and Australia refused him a residence permit. Suddenly Wolfskehl and Ruben found themselves as refugees in need of a host country. It was only through the recommendations of friends abroad (among them Thomas Mann) and the support of some helpful New Zealanders who offered to act as their guarantors (the surgeon, Dr Douglas Robb, and the professor of English literature, Arthur Sewell) that, in January 1939, they finally obtained residence permits from the New Zealand Government.

They spent their first weeks in Auckland in a small boarding house, the Hotel Stonehurst in Symonds Street, before they sought more permanent accommodation. Soon it became obvious that the small annuity Wolfskehl was counting on from the sale of his valuable book collection would only allow a very modest standard of living.[6] But they managed to find a comfortable little flat in Mount Eden, where they lived from September 1938 to October 1941. The house had a small garden, which the poet cherished because of a fig tree in it. He addressed this fig tree as a fellow exile from the Mediterranean in a poem he wrote a few weeks after they had moved in. The poem reflects how he felt and started to see himself; the following are the last two stanzas:

> Bist in der Fremde, Freund, Meerinselkinder,
> Die dich verpflanzten, hassen dein Gezack.
> Gestutztem Rasenplan fügst du dich minder,
> Und Feigen sind doch wohl nicht ihr Geschmack.
>
> Darbst nicht allein, wir beide sind gestrandet.
> Leben, gedeihn wir? Gelt, wir spürens kaum.
> Wer in der Heimat kargstem Karst versandet
> Zog bessres Los. Ists nicht so, Feigenbaum?
>
> You are a stranger, friend! These islands' children,
> Transplanting you, dislike your crooked lines.
> You care not to conform to shaven lawns,
> Figs cannot be—how could they—to their taste!
>
> You suffer not alone. We both are stranded.
> Say: do we flourish? Do we live? Who knows!
> To wither in the scantiest sand of homeland
> What kinder lot! Is it not so, my tree?[7]

   Wolfskehl and Margot Ruben made a number of acquaintances, but there were few among them with whom they could share their intellectual interests in a deeper way. In this respect, he soon felt isolated, deprived of congenial stimuli, and thus was thrown back entirely on his own rich inner resources. He was compensated only by his enjoyment of the natural environment, the lush vegetation, the clear air, and the often brilliant quality of

Karl Wolfskehl under the fig-tree, Esplanade Road, Mount Eden. *(Maja Blumenfeld. Blumenfeld Family Collection)*

the natural light, and it filled him with satisfaction to see that his creative powers were by no means diminishing. The initial lack of inspiring contacts is scarcely surprising, considering that for the average New Zealander at the time, he must have been a rather curious, indeed, slightly suspicious, character: he had no occupation in the normal sense of the word, nor did he run a business of any sort; instead, he devoted all his time to so-called intellectual interests.

This situation remained much the same for the couple's first few years in New Zealand. In time, however, Wolfskehl found friends among fellow exiles and among New Zealanders, in particular younger writers. His small circle of friends became wider when he undertook his first and only extended journey within New Zealand in February and March 1941. Friends—Caesar and Hanna Steinhof,[8] who had moved from Auckland to Dunedin the previous year, and Otti and Paul Binswanger,[9] two German refugees who lived in Christchurch—had invited him to stay with them during the summer months. Wolfskehl's trip to the South Island was to be one of the happiest periods of his time in New Zealand, due mainly to the many new connections and friendships that this trip brought him.

Although his thinking and his poetry were deeply rooted in the traditions of European culture and literature, Wolfskehl was nevertheless eager to learn about the literature of his host country. He showed a keen and lively interest in the work of poets and writers in New Zealand, and got to know a number of them personally in the early 1940s. The Binswangers introduced him to a group of writers around the Caxton Press—the publisher and poet Denis Glover, the graphic artist Leo Bensemann, and the then little-known poet Allen Curnow—but for some reason he did not meet the philosopher Karl Popper, who was then teaching at Canterbury University College. Around the same time, Wolfskehl made the acquaintance of the poet A.R.D. Fairburn in Auckland, and an even closer friendship developed some months later between him and the poet R.A.K. Mason and the writer Frank Sargeson. Within a short period, Wolfskehl had established lively contacts with key figures of the New Zealand literary avant-garde.

As this interest and his friendships with New Zealand writers indicate, Wolfskehl by no means withdrew into himself, nor were his energies absorbed by memories of Europe alone. Wolfskehl, as a poet, scholar, and an important representative of European culture, became for the young writers and intellectuals an intermediary between the old and the new world. For those who got to know him, Wolfskehl was an engaging conversationalist, an inexhaustible first-hand source of knowledge on European literature. Conversely, in his letters to friends overseas, he repeatedly called attention to New Zealand writers whom he regarded as important. The writer whose works Wolfskehl valued most highly was, according to Margot Ruben, R.A.K. Mason, but paradoxically Wolfskehl never mentioned him in his letters.[10] It was characteristic of Wolfskehl not to talk openly about what moved him most.

Wolfskehl's relationship with New Zealand writers was one of mutual attraction and appreciation. He shared with them his experience and knowledge, and in return he was introduced to literary fields virtually unknown to him. Fairburn dedicated his *Poems 1929–1941* (1943) to Wolfskehl, but the literary figure who grew closest to him in the period 1942–44 was Frank Sargeson.[11] Although one cannot say that he exercised any direct influence on the works of the New Zealand writers and poets he met, Wolfskehl was, nevertheless, a most distinctive personal experience for every one of them.

Over the years that followed, life in New Zealand became more and more difficult for Wolfskehl. Apart from the recurring lament in his letters at being separated from his European friends, complaints about his worsening blindness and health escalated in the course of his wartime correspondence. His blindness forced him to rely on others for reading and dictation. Until the autumn of 1943, he and Margot Ruben lived together, with only a short interruption: Margot took care of household affairs and acted as his secretary and assistant. This changed, however, when—for personal and financial reasons—she increased her private teaching of languages and later took on a job as a teacher at the University Coaching College. She continued to visit Wolfskehl almost daily for dictation or to read aloud to him, but from September 1943 onwards Wolfskehl lived as a private boarder—a situation he could never really get used to. Usually restricted to a single room in a boarding house, he awaited eagerly the visits of his regular callers. Among them were Paul Hoffmann, frequently referred to in Wolfskehl's letters as a young German scholar from Vienna,[12] and Pia Richards, who had come to New Zealand from England.[13]

Wolfskehl never withdrew completely from his immediate contacts—his various landlords, or the families in the different places where he lived. But in surroundings such as these it became all too clear just how much of a stranger—indeed, how much of an incomprehensible figure—he remained for 'normal' New Zealanders. He was virtually an enigma to most. Wolfskehl himself, at least according to his letters, seems to have accepted this state of affairs quite calmly. He gives detailed, amusing, and ironic descriptions of two households in particular, one of which he christened the 'House of Saint Noisius' because of his lively and chaotic fellow residents, and another—characterising his somewhat pretentious middle-class landlady—the 'House of the indignant bum'.

Although Wolfskehl got on quite well with people on an everyday basis, he was able to share his real self with only a few. These he found mainly among other German–Jewish refugees, such as the Blumenfeld family, with whom he often celebrated Jewish festivals (like the Seder), or Alice and Wolf Strauss,[14] who had originally come from Czechoslovakia and who became valued friends.

Considering these circumstances, it is surprising that Wolfskehl was able to achieve such a substantial poetic *oeuvre* during the ten years of his exile. He composed and completed three major cycles of poems (*Mittelmeer oder Die fünf Fenster* ['The Mediterranean or The Five Windows'], *INRI oder Die vier Tafeln* ['INRI or The Four Tablets'] and *Hiob oder Die vier Spiegel* ['Job or The Four Mirrors']); he revised the long poem 'An die Deutschen' ('To the Germans'); and he also wrote a considerable number of individual poems.

The end of the war meant an improvement in Wolfskehl's personal situation. He was again able to exchange letters with his family, his wife, and

Karl Wolfskehl with Alice Strauss (left) and Margot Ruben in Queen Street, Auckland. *(W. Strauss Collection)*

their two daughters—they had all survived the war. But news also reached him that confirmed some of his worst fears and thus increased his emotional distance from Germany. He learned that his home town, Darmstadt, had been almost completely destroyed and that his parents' house and the home of his youth had been razed to the ground. Worse was to come: he learned that his brother had not died a natural death, as he had believed until then, but that he had been killed in a concentration camp. Most painful of all was the news of the death of his wife in 1946, before he was able to see her again. In 1946, Wolfskehl applied for naturalisation, and in July of that year he became a New Zealand citizen. He accepted citizenship with a deep sense of gratitude towards this country: '[T]his country, whose hospitality I am now enjoying for the ninth year, and which has allowed me to spend my days unhampered …, even in the tensest moments, deserves the gratitude which I freely render.'[15]

After becoming a naturalised New Zealander, Wolfskehl hoped he might one day be able to visit Europe once more—even if only temporarily—in order to see at least a few of his friends in Switzerland and Germany again, although he was probably aware that his age, health, and finances would no longer permit such a journey. In the early post-war years, this hope diminished even further as his health continued to deteriorate. At the beginning of 1947, Wolfskehl broke his foot but managed to recover quickly. More serious than this broken limb, however, was his worsening heart condition.

In the final months of his life, Wolfskehl, together with Margot Ruben, prepared and planned the content of a future definitive edition of his *oeuvre*. But he was not able to complete this task. He had, however, the satisfaction of seeing interest in his work reawaken in Europe. He had already put together the first manuscript for an edition of his poems written in New Zealand; it was eventually published in 1950 under the title *Sang aus dem Exil* ('Songs from Exile'). These poems, together with the cycle *Hiob oder Die vier Spiegel*, are considered to be some of the most significant examples of lyric poetry written by German authors forced into exile during the Nazi period.

Karl Wolfskehl died on 30 June 1948 and was buried in Auckland's Waikumete Cemetery. In accordance with his wishes, his gravestone bears only his name (in Hebrew and Roman lettering) and, beneath that, the Latin inscription 'Exul Poeta' ('Poet in Exile'). A cypress tree behind the grave was planted by friends as a sign of mourning and a symbol of the Mediterranean.

Karl Wolfskehl's grave at Waikumete Cemetery, Auckland, reflecting the cypress tree behind it. *(Rochelle Gebbie)*

1   Wolfskehl's major book publications up to 1938 were: *Gesammelte Dichtungen* (1903), *Der Umkreis. Gedichte und dramatische Dichtungen* (1927), *Bild und Gesetz. Gesammelte Abhandlungen* (1930), and *Die Stimme spricht* (1934).

2   Paul Hoffmann, 'Karl Wolfskehl 1869–1948: A German poet in New Zealand', *Landfall*, vol. 23 (1969), p. 388.

3   Wolfskehl had only a very scant knowledge of New Zealand, its geography, and its political and social structure. The most valuable information he received only a few months before his arrival from Gerda Eichbaum (later Gerda Bell). She was a friend of his niece Marie Luise Wolfskehl, and had already emigrated to New Zealand (in 1936), where she had been working as a teacher of foreign languages. Cf. Gerda Bell, 'Letters from Karl Wolfskehl, written during his time of exile', *AUMLA*, vol. 37 (1972), pp. 57–72.

4 Letter to J.W. Schülein of 2 August 1946, in Karl Wolfskehl, *Zehn Jahre Exil. Briefe aus Neuseeland*, ed. Margot Ruben (Heidelberg & Darmstadt, 1959), pp. 278f.

5 Cf. Jane Sydenham, 'Stopover in exile: Karl Wolfskehl and Australia', in Johannes H. Voigt (ed.), *New Beginnings: The Germans in New South Wales and Queensland* (Stuttgart, 1983), pp. 233–45.

6 In 1936, Wolfskehl had sold his famous library to the publisher Salman Schocken for the sum of 20,000 marks. Part of the money went to Wolfskehl's two daughters, and the remainder was used to provide a monthly pension of around £20 for Wolfskehl himself for the rest of his life.

7 A version of the poem appeared under the title 'Feigenbaum' together with a parallel English translation by Margot Ruben, in *Meanjin Papers*, vol. 5 (1946), p. 155. The German text of the poem as it is cited here follows the version as given in Wolfskehl's *Gesammelte Werke* (Hamburg, 1960), vol. 1, p. 179.

8 Wolfskehl had first befriended the Steinhofs in Auckland. Caesar Steinhof (1909–54), a pupil of the German–Jewish religious philosopher and noted Zionist, Martin Buber, had come to New Zealand with his family from Hamburg in 1938. After settling initially in Auckland, the Steinhofs moved to Dunedin towards the end of 1939, where Caesar later worked for the Hebrew congregation as a teacher and prayer leader.

9 Wolfskehl and Margot Ruben already knew the Binswangers from Germany. Paul Binswanger had lost his academic position in Berlin because of his Jewish background. He and his wife emigrated first to Italy in 1933 and then to New Zealand in 1939. Otti Binswanger (née Lilienthal) published a collection of 'Stories of New Zealand', which appeared under the title *And How Do You Like This Country?* (Christchurch, 1945).

10 Margot Ruben, '*Karl Wolfskehl. Exul Immeritus. Erinnerungen an Neuseeland*', in Paul Gerhard Klussmann (ed.), *Karl Wolfskehl Kolloquium. Vorträge—Berichte—Dokumente* (Amsterdam, 1983), p. 52.

11 Cf. Frank Sargeson, *More Than Enough: A Memoir* (Auckland, 1975), pp. 102–15, and Michael King, *Frank Sargeson: A Life* (Auckland, 1995), pp. 222–8.

12 Hoffmann had come from Austria, where he had done some work towards a doctorate before he and his family were forced to flee because of their Jewish background. In 1939 they came to New Zealand. Hoffmann completed a doctorate in Vienna after the war and returned to New Zealand, where he became Lecturer and then Professor of German at Victoria University in Wellington; from 1970, he was Professor of German at Tübingen.

13 Pia Richards was a highly educated woman and the daughter of the English novelist Maurice Henry Hewlett, through whom she also had contacts with the Bloomsbury group.

14 Alice and Wolf Strauss had come to New Zealand from Czechoslovakia in 1941 and soon got to know Wolfskehl and Margot Ruben. After the war, Alice Strauss taught for many years as a lecturer in the Department of Germanic Languages and Literature at the University of Auckland.

15 Letter to Faber du Faur of 27 September 1946, in Karl Wolfskehl, *Briefwechsel aus Neuseeland 1938–1948*, ed. Cornelia Blasberg, with introduction by Paul Hoffmann (Darmstadt, 1988), vol. 1, p. 107.

11

Maria Dronke

PETER VERE-JONES

At the outbreak of World War II, the Germans began sinking their own freighters to avoid enemy capture. On board one of these, and destined for New Zealand, were the sole possessions of John and Maria Dronke. The couple and their two children, Peter and Marei, were already safely in New Zealand. It was the final humiliation and rejection from a country in which Maria had achieved recognition as a major theatrical talent and her husband John as a distinguished judge.

Born into a German–Jewish family in Berlin on 17 July 1904, Maria Dronke died a Roman Catholic in Lower Hutt on 28 August 1987. Her inherited Jewish blood and later conversion to Catholicism were two critical factors in her life—the former bringing exile from her homeland, and the latter an intense interest in religious poetry and drama. Maria spent forty-eight years in New Zealand and greatly influenced a generation of actors, writers, and musicians. She was a beautiful and commanding presence and a woman of diverse talents. She had a history and affinity with leading European artists of the day, as well as a deep understanding of the great playwrights and poets of the past. Vocally gifted and theatrically intuitive, she was a brilliant student and fine teacher. As so often happened during the late pre-war years, Germany's loss was mirrored by another country's immeasurable gain.

Maria's parents, Dr Salomon Kronfeld, a barrister, and Laura Liebman, were respectable middle-class Berliners of comfortable means. Maria was the only daughter, and the last-born, of their four children. Although her parents were not devoutly Jewish, it was not until their death in 1928 that Maria became a Catholic. She had been receiving instruction in Vienna in the 'Schottisches Kloster' and was received into the church by the Reverend P. Blaha.

Educated at the Dorotheen Lyceum in Berlin, Maria was top student in her final examinations and went on to study philosophy and modern literature at the University of Berlin. On one momentous day at the age of 17, she borrowed a fox fur in an attempt to make herself appear a little older and presented herself to the celebrated voice teacher Professor Daniel, director of the Berlin Conservatory of Music. Not only did he accept her as a student, thereby making, as Maria wrote, 'my small voice an instrument obeying every thought and mood and feeling',[1] but he was also to offer her the place of assistant teacher in voice production and recitation.

Left: Maria Dronke,
Berlin, 1929. *(Marei
Webster Collection)*

Right: Maria Dronke,
Wellington, 1940. *(Marei
Webster Collection)*

During Maria's teenage years, she rubbed shoulders with a dazzling array of musical and literary talent. She regularly attended the Beethoven-Saal and the Berlin Philharmonic, where she met the singers Joseph Schwartz and Sigrid Onegin, the violinist Fritz Kreisler, the pianist Edwin Fischer, and the conductors Bruno Walter and Arthur Nikisch. Privately, she was acquainted with Einstein, discoursed with the theologian Paul Tillich, and listened to Bertolt Brecht singing his own songs at a party attended by the producer Erich Engel, who 'misbehaved towards me that night'.[2]

Maria gave her own first public recital in the Berlin Meistersaal in December 1924. It was the start of her stage career. After a provincial engagement playing eighteen leading roles in nine months, she moved to the Burgtheater in Vienna and, two years later, the Berliner Theater under Max Reinhardt. Within seven years she had adopted the stage name Maria Korten and played many of the great roles: Juliet, Ophelia, Portia, Olivia, Titania, Gretchen and Helena in *Faust* I and II, Minna in *Minna von Barnhelm*, and Elizabeth in *Don Carlos*. She performed Shaw, Hauptmann, and Strindberg, and she was also asked to read Rilke's work at his memorial service, held in Vienna when he died in 1926.

Watching passengers board a steamer at one of its European ports of call, a young district court judge named John Adolf Dronke noticed a young woman wearing a headscarf who looked a little like a young gipsy, and was bemused to find her placed at his table for dinner. It was table 7, Maria's fateful number, and they were married in 1931. John Dronke, son of Ernst Dronke, chief justice of Frankfurt, was a district court judge in Hamburg at that time and a talented amateur musician. (In 1946 in New Zealand he was to become an inaugural member of the Symphony Orchestra, or 'National Orchestra' as it was then known, playing the double bass.)

They settled in Cologne, where John continued his legal career and Maria began raising their two children, Peter (Ernst Peter Michael, born in 1934), and Marei (Maria Gabriele, born in 1935). Having left the theatre to devote more time to her children, Maria directed theatrical pieces for various Catholic organisations and gave lectures on modern Catholic poets and Catholic literature, as well as working with theological groups at the Katholischer Akademiker-Verband, where she presented a number of papers.

Fleeing the Nazi Party's repression of Jewish people, and helped by members of her church, Maria left Cologne in 1938. 'My last impressions of Germany were very sad … There was a young blackshirt … not more than 22 years old … we had to leave everything … I do not like to think about it. … [But] even to have lost everything is better than that my husband should have to fight for Hitler.'[3]

Given refuge in England by the Sisters of the Sacred Heart at their teachers college convent, Newcastle-on-Tyne, Maria taught and assisted in the library. She searched for a country where the family might settle. New Zealand's open and politically progressive society appealed, but its doors appeared closed. While seriously considering a job as cook for a family in South America, there was a change of heart from the New Zealand Government. Perhaps this was just as well, for cooking was never Maria's strong point. She left that task initially to her lifelong companion, Lölein, Maria's governess, theatre dresser and nanny to the children, and later to John, who was, as Maria said, 'So much better at synchronising the fires.'[4]

Maria was joined in England by John, Lölein, and the two children, and they sailed for Australia on the *Strathallan* on 9 June 1939. From Sydney they completed their journey to Wellington on the *Wanganella*, arriving on 2 August. They were safe but unknown and without possessions; a new life had to be built. John's legal training and German degrees were worthless in New Zealand, and there was little call for a 35-year-old actress with a European accent. Moving from one miserable accommodation to another, the family finally settled in Hay Street, Oriental Bay. It was not the most salubrious of dwellings but offered one good room where Maria was able to set up a studio for teaching. Before that, an advertisement in a 1939 Wellington newspaper offered 'Drama, Voice Production and Voice Restoring', from Maria Dronke at room 403, DIC Building.[5] John found poorly paid work at the Rehabilitation League, making artificial limbs for returned servicemen, and the first two pupils arrived for vocal tuition with 'Madam Dronke', as she was to become known—a figure whose European bearing and theatrical aura were sometimes a little intimidating to the locals.

Maria's theatrical talent also had to find opportunities for expression. Her first New Zealand performance was in 1940 as Sister Gracia in her own production of *The Kingdom of God* by Sierra in an English translation by the Granville-Barkers. One reviewer commented: 'It was certainly a bold thing to produce a play of this nature in a country where the reticence of the Catholic people is enhanced by the inherent Puritanism of its less pagan inhabitants and the blatant "modernity" of its non church-going people.'[6] Of Maria's performance, another reviewer remarked: 'In the role of Sister Gracia

Maria Dronke as Sister
Gracia in *The Kingdom of
God*, Wellington, 1940.
(Marei Webster Collection)

Madam Dronke acted with restraint and a sensitive grace that carried full conviction. Her performance dominated the play and made it memorable.'[7]

Good reviews followed for her performance as Phaedra in Euripides' *Hippolytus*. Maria produced this play in aid of the Red Cross Society, which benefited from her next production as well, *Shakespeare's Women*, at the Wellington Concert Chamber. This also received great critical acclaim, although one reviewer seemed deaf to the fine verse-speaking: 'Maria Dronke made an introductory appearance in a three-quarter length coat of black taffeta, with shaded underskirt, and later appeared in a number of beautiful costumes.'[8]

Maria was to direct some twenty-five plays, including works by Ibsen, Shaw, Shakespeare, and particularly T.S. Eliot. Her love for Eliot was life-long, and her production of *Murder in the Cathedral* in Wellington's Old St Paul's Cathedral, in 1947, was probably her most memorable.

Poetry readings, talks, and lectures on verse, drama, and acting technique were given around New Zealand. The Workers Educational Association, articles in journals, and broadcasts for the New Zealand Broadcasting Service, all helped her to become known to the public. The presentation, and subsequent tours, of many of her productions and recitals were often under the umbrella of her early New Zealand friend, manager, and entrepreneur, D.D. (Dan) O'Connor. O'Connor was well aware of her enormous talent and the importance of bringing works of a more intellectual and classical nature to a culture-starved New Zealand. The *New Zealand Observer* of 16 February 1944 raved: 'It is probably unique in the history of Auckland that all seats for a poetry recital should have been sold out days before the event. It *can* happen here. It *did* happen with Maria Dronke's poetry recital last Friday night.'

It would be difficult to decide whether Maria's greatest love was for poetry or drama. She rejoiced when they came together in the plays of Eliot and Shakespeare, but I think she saw the drama in all verse. Her son, Peter, was to inherit her love of medieval lyrics, devoting his career to their study. She was equally at home with Elizabethan or contemporary works, and was instrumental in introducing many New Zealanders to their own poets. Included in her recitals were works by James K. Baxter, Ursula Bethell, Allen Curnow, A.R.D. Fairburn, Denis Glover, R.A.K. Mason, and Louis Johnson.

Many New Zealand poets were to form part of a group that was to enjoy the frequent soirées held in John and Maria's tiny cottage on Muritai Road, in Eastbourne. They moved there in 1951, the property having been bought with money received as compensation paid to victims of Nazi persecution. Its warm, dark, book-lined interior was a rare haven in which local artists could partake of and enjoy lively and good-humoured debate on music, poetry, and drama. Different disciplines were united from such meetings, as when Maria requested composer Douglas Lilburn to write a piece for Allen Curnow's poem, 'The Changeling', together with two classical works, and form 'Three Poems of the Sea', which she performed with the Alex Lindsay String Orchestra in 1960.

As well as being the year in which the Dronkes moved to Eastbourne, 1951 was when Maria opened her large studio on Lambton Quay, a place where she was to hold workshops on plays, present recitals, and, for many years, teach a succession of would-be professional actors the skills of voice production and dramatic art. This was a privileged group, for there has not been a teacher in New Zealand since who has combined teaching skills learned from one of the greatest European masters and such an enormous personal talent. Many of her students have gone on to become leading professional actors both in New Zealand and abroad.

In 1957 Maria retired from teaching, and devoted her time to further academic study. From Victoria University, Wellington, she obtained MA degrees with honours in both English and German, and commenced work on a doctorate on one of her favourite German authors, Heinrich von Kleist. She was awarded an OBE in 1979 for services to the performing arts.

Maria Dronke died at the age of 83 at the Kairangi Medical and Convalescent Home in Lower Hutt, on 28 August 1987. Her greatest champion, devoted friend, and constant staff and guide, John Dronke, the man who helped to 'synchronise her fires', had died five years before.

1   Autobiographical notes of Maria Dronke, held by her family.
2   Ibid.
3   *New Zealand Listener*, 9 February 1940.
4   Personal recollection of the author; this was a phrase Maria Dronke used on a number of occasions.
5   The advertisement, unidentified apart from the year 1939, is among Maria Dronke's personal papers.
6   *New Zealand Tablet* vol. 67, no. 7, 14 February 1940.
7   *Zealandia*, vol. 6, no. 22, 15 February 1940.
8   From an unidentified newspaper cutting, Wellington 1941 or 1942, held among Maria Dronke's personal papers.

12

Marie Vandewart Blaschke

MAJA BEUTLER AND KATHRYN SMITS

July 1996. Party at the Blaschkes. No fuss, but a momentous occasion nevertheless. Marie is eighty-five, Alfons ninety, and for good measure they celebrate their fiftieth wedding anniversary as well. The two of us come in through the back yard. A jumble of vines. Flower pots. Gardening gloves in the porch. The open door leads into an old-time kitchen. What could be more welcoming, more *New Zealand*? The house is full of friends: artists, musicians, neighbours past and present, former university colleagues, new friends (like Maja) or friends from way back. The grandchildren put bits of paper in our hands, drawings, their own work of course: admission tickets to Grandma's concert. In this house one is surrounded by silent instruments: harpsichords and clavichords built by Alfons, cellos and violas da gamba on the walls, and by pictures waiting to be looked at. Beyond the throng of guests the winter sun comes streaming in through huge windows, revealing an unexpected vista across leafy Remuera to the Waitemata Harbour and to the city, now dominated by the all too blatant Sky Tower. They could have asked us, grumbles Alfons, it ruins our view.

Marie and friends play Haydn quartets. Relaxed and professional, she is at one with the younger players. Theirs is a true musicians' blend of eagerness and concentration. It conveys that music-making is an exhilarating business.

An hour later: a curious contrast. We stand around with our glasses and listen as Marie, leaning in the doorway, says a word or two, dispassionate, as though putting her life under the microscope. The first seven years, in Wellington, she had spent alone. Alfons was stuck in England because of the war. Those years, she tells us, are a sun-filled sequence in her memory, like a never-ending holiday. At times she had to shake herself as a reminder that this was for real. Last year, however, she had found her old diaries and read a different story there: one of unhappiness and agonising worry, a record of her sense of loss and loneliness, her fear for her parents back in Germany from whom she received no word. Standing there, white-haired in her flowing Indian dress and her black sneakers, looking bemused, Marie tells us that she is at a loss to explain how human nature is capable of experiencing, simultaneously, two such diametrically opposed emotions. Anyway, she says, wiping away the contradiction with a gesture of the hand: I have good memories, and … oh yes, Alfons and I are at home in New Zealand.

January 1997. Marie and Maja, alone now with the house and the garden, talk about the past. What follows is based on this interview.

Marie Vandewart was born in Berlin in 1911, the eldest of three sisters. Both parents were of Jewish origin and came from Bavaria, her mother from Ansbach, her father from Nuremberg. Chamber music was part of Marie's

Marie Vandewart
Blaschke and Alfrons
Blaschke, late 1960s.
(Anthony Henry)

home life. She remembers her pride as a 12-year-old, playing with her mother and father: Haydn trios whose cello parts are relatively easy.

MAJA: Did you grow up in the Jewish tradition?

MARIE: No. Both my parents came from a Jewish background. But especially my father was very anti-Semitic, as were so many Jews. He had very little to do with his own family. But we did go to our grandparents on summer holidays, we did pay family visits. A sort of tribute. I was especially fond of my maternal grandparents in Ansbach.

She studied the cello at the Hochschule für Musik in Berlin. When Hitler came to power in 1933, she was not yet 22. Recording technology was in its infancy then, and musicians were engaged for live radio broadcasts.

MAJA: Did you get any work in Berlin?

MARIE: No, of course not, of course not! Because ... I think I played for Berlin radio twice, but restrictions were becoming more stringent all the time, and that was the end of broadcasting for me, and of playing in any non-Jewish context. And in the end we were even forbidden to attend concerts.

The Jewish community started an orchestra, and the Jüdischer Kulturbund played a big part in the life of the remaining Jews. So I was in that orchestra for a while and did quite a bit—ah well, *some* teaching.

MAJA: Jewish children?

MARIE: Yes. Yes, they must all have been Jewish children. There are one or two who got in touch with me later, when I was in New Zealand … A Wolfgang Zuckermann. Alfons and I ordered a kit set for making a harpsichord. I ordered it under my maiden name. When it arrived there was a letter attached: 'You must be the Marie Vandewart who taught me the cello in Berlin.' Through the cello he had become interested in Baroque music, and through that in harpsichords, and then he founded this big workshop in America, the first to produce kit set harpsichords. The ones that my husband built, harpsichords and clavichords, are all from Zuckermann kit sets. Well, with him we are still in contact.

MAJA: I wonder what it must have been like in Berlin in the thirties. I mean: if you've never been to Synagogue before, and all of a sudden you have to stick together to the last …

MARIE: Well, I had no Jewish background at all. I was totally ignorant of Jewish customs, too, as were so many who were classed 'non-Aryan'.

Unlike several of their Nuremberg cousins, Marie and her sisters did not leave Germany until 1939. Her father, not grasping the desperate nature of the situation, refused to let the family break up. His motto was 'Hitlers come and Hitlers go'. He did not give Marie his blessing until he himself had been detained in a concentration camp for a while. (As a specialist engineer in the ship-building industry, he was important to Germany's war effort, and his employers had managed to get him released.) Marie was engaged to Alfons Blaschke. As a pacifist and trained social worker, he himself was regarded with suspicion by the Nazis. How their relationship survived between 1935 and 1939—that of an 'Aryan' man with a 'non-Aryan' woman under the Hitler regime, which strictly forbade such associations—is a saga in itself. The risks they ran are barely imaginable today.

In 1939 Alfons, through his long-standing connections in England, managed to find a New Zealand sponsor and guarantor for Marie—the *sine qua non* for her being granted an entry permit. He was a Hawke's Bay farmer, an uncharacteristic member of the notoriously flamboyant English Mitford family. The Blaschkes remember him with gratitude for his role in the saga of Marie's emigration to New Zealand. Once Alfons knew that Marie could leave Germany, in early 1939, he engineered his own escape from Berlin, only weeks before his impending conscription into Hitler's Wehrmacht. He went to England and briefly met Marie there before she sailed to the other side of the world. His own plans to follow her were thwarted by the outbreak of war. Alfons remained in England, officially classed as a 'refugee from Nazi oppression'. For seven years they were separated and could communicate by letter only (and that, of course, meant surface mail), not even able to write in their own language. They used English, because of censorship.

All subsequent efforts to get Marie's parents out of Germany through the Red Cross failed: Marie's father knew too much and had seen too much. Years later, after the war, Marie and her sisters learned in a roundabout way that their father and mother, faced with deportation to a death camp, had taken their own lives in Berlin.

Marie found herself alone in New Zealand. Her entry permit classed her as a 'domestic'. Strictly speaking, she should have been employed by her sponsor, but she never went to his farm. Releasing her from this obligation, he urged her to stay in the city, well aware that a musician should not be stuck out in the country. She did, however, feel morally obliged to fulfil the conditions of her entry permit, more so because there was a great demand for domestic workers. She did jobs of all kinds, meeting people, making friends. Yet it seemed to Marie at this stage that, with an as yet inadequate command of English, she was living in an unreal world. Virtual strangers made plans for her and 'handed her around'.

MARIE: I was to go to this lady in Dunedin and meanwhile was staying with her cousin in Wellington for a bit. And this cousin had a piano teacher and took me to meet her. We played together. And the piano teacher introduced me to other musicians, and somebody said: 'You must go to Broadcasting and play for them.' So I played. And when I had finished, one of the men listening behind the studio window said, 'Thank you, but I'm afraid …' and I thought: that's the end of it. But he said: '… I'm afraid we cannot offer you anything next week, only the week after.'

For a long time, Marie did not quite overcome her fear of persecution, which had become ingrained during the Nazi years. But friendships were forged and consolidated through music, above all with the Beaglehole family[1] and through them with others such as May and Walt Long[2] and Fred and Joan Wood.[3]

Soon the music grapevine started buzzing. Marie played for Broadcasting and became part of the music scene in Wellington, making more friends, teaching, forming a trio with Dorothy Davies[4] and Erika Schorss,[5] becoming a seminal influence in New Zealand's chamber music tradition. The years went by, the war came to an end. In 1946 she sailed to join Alfons, who by now had a good position and was settled. They got married, the first of their two sons was born. They lived in England for four years, then started the laborious immigration process all over again and, with the help of New Zealand friends, came to this country, Alfons for the first time.

MAJA: But why did you come a second time?

MARIE: I was very homesick for New Zealand. Once shipping became easier, many of my New Zealand friends came over to England, some of them making delayed trips 'Home', others taking up scholarships—that sort of thing. They came and visited. Alfons now had a job in a Barnardo's institution in the Midlands. We lived between the rural and the industrial areas, in a small town. It was pleasant enough, but … life was difficult. Where we lived we did not have many friends. But New Zealanders came and stayed with us, and they helped us to come back to New Zealand.

MAJA: What were you homesick for, mainly?

MARIE: Maybe it was the landscape, maybe it was the atmosphere, the people … My many friends …

For ten years, from 1951, Marie and Alfons lived and worked in Wellington. Marie joined the Alex Lindsay String Orchestra,[6] later the New

Zealand Opera Company as well, touring frequently, looking after their two children, greatly supported by Alfons.

MARIE: It had been Ruth Pearl[7] who persuaded me to join the Lindsay Orchestra. I played with them until I left Wellington. We played a lot. The members were either women with children like myself or they were front-desk players from the National Orchestra. So one couldn't do anything before four, half past four in the afternoon. It was absolutely crazy, really. We'd go up to Wanganui, play a concert there and come back the same night. The fact is: that was accepted, that was how one operated.

MAJA: So Alfons looked after the children.

MARIE: Well, he had to ... I suppose ...

In 1962, Marie and Alfons moved north. Marie had been appointed to the Auckland University School of Music, where she taught the cello until her retirement in 1977. Over the years, she has made a significant contribution to music in New Zealand through her teaching and in what became her special interest: Baroque and Early music. Her love of playing is unabated. Alfons and Marie's shared love of New Zealand has long found expression in active support of the visual arts and conservation in this country.

MARIE: Once you have lived here it is difficult to live somewhere else.

MAJA: But why? Why exactly?

MARIE: For me it is ... the bush ... the coastline ... the clouds ... our garden ... our house ... And the children, of course ... Oh yes, Alfons and I are at home in New Zealand.

1　The Beagleholes: John C. Beaglehole (historian and Captain Cook scholar, also instrumental in the formation of the Chamber Music Society of New Zealand, the Arts Council, and the Historic Places Trust), his wife Elsie, his brother Ernest (who held the Chair of Psychology at what was then Victoria University College), and Ernest's wife Pam (an anthropologist).

2　Walter Long (a Wellington manufacturer) and his wife May were Marie's closest friends. She looked after their children when May was at university as a part-time student and part-time tutor. Marie lived with the Longs for several years until her departure for England in 1946. The Longs were also enormously helpful in making it possible for her to return to New Zealand, with Alfons and their firstborn child, and to settle in Wellington.

3　The Woods had moved to Wellington in 1935 when Fred Wood, a graduate of Sydney and Oxford universities, was appointed to the Chair of History at Victoria University College. Joan Wood, in 1941, became one of the founders of the New Zealand playcentre movement. For a time, from the late 1960s, Joan Wood was an executant tutor in singing at Victoria University. In the later 1930s, Fred Wood was a prominent advocate of a more liberal government immigration policy. Both were active in the sponsorship of refugees.

4　Dorothy Davies: a well-known New Zealand pianist and chamber music player. Around the time when Marie came to New Zealand, Davies had returned from an extended period of study and performing experience overseas, including study with Artur Schnabel. She became an influential teacher in this country.

5　Erika Schorss: a violinist who also hailed from Berlin and who had arrived in New Zealand about the same time as Marie. She became a founding member of the National Orchestra.

6　The Lindsay Orchestra was started in 1948 by Alex Lindsay, a New Zealand violinist who had gained valuable orchestral experience in London. He later became leader of the New Zealand Symphony Orchestra. Lindsay was particularly interested in promoting contemporary New Zealand composers.

7　Ruth Pearl: an English violinist, leader of the well-known Jacques Orchestra in London, where Marie had met her. Having come to New Zealand, Pearl became leader of the Lindsay Orchestra in Wellington.

13

Margot Philips

MARGARET SUTHERLAND

Without the contribution of the works of Margot Philips, the history of art in the Waikato would look quite different. During her thirty years of painting in her adopted homeland, she presented us with an entirely new and unique perspective of the landscape, one that was exclusively her own.

Margot Leonie Louisa Philips was born on 5 April 1902 in Duisburg-Ruhrort, Germany, as the fifth and youngest child of Selma and Julius Philips. Her father was a grain merchant by trade, and Margot's early years, at least, were spent in relative comfort in a household with two or three maids. Described by her father as 'deutsche Staatsbürger jüdischen Glaubens' ('German citizens of Jewish faith'), hers was a family with a strong sense of its Jewish background, although liberal in outlook.[1] Young Margot was educated as one of the few Jewish pupils at the strict Kaiserin Augusta Viktoria Schule (Empress Augusta Viktoria School), where she claimed that art instruction was 'unimpressive' and did not extend beyond the linen-covered sketch books into which the girls were supposed to copy things. She said: 'I don't think I was a star.'[2] With World War I came a change in the family's fortunes, brought about by the collapse of the business and by the death of her father.

The Philips family, c. 1915 (left to right): Kurt, Richard, Mr and Mrs Philips, Margot. *(Fay Foreman Collection)*

In 1920, the family moved to Cologne, where Margot initially stayed at home to assist her mother with the running of the household. She was then encouraged to train as a shorthand typist and was employed in the main office of Tietz, a large chain of department stores, from 1929 until 1934. As the Nuremberg Laws excluding Jews from the workforce took effect, the Jewish owner of the business was divested of his job, and the stores were gradually purged of Jewish employees. The staff in Margot's division were among the last to be dismissed.

The worsening situation prompted Margot and her four siblings to consider leaving Germany. Eventually all of them were successful. In 1935, she departed on a nerve-racking journey by train and boat to Britain, where she first worked illegally as a governess for a Polish Jewish family before obtaining a work permit for six months and then a year. During this time, she approached New Zealand House in England on behalf of her brother Kurt and his wife, who were still in Germany, about the possibility of their emigrating to New Zealand. Permission was duly granted by the New Zealand authorities. Once settled in Hamilton, Kurt was then in a position to sponsor Margot, and on 16 January 1938 she embarked on the *Tainui*, reaching Wellington two months later.

Her arrival in the Waikato was a 'terrific emotional onslaught' for her,[3] and her early years in the middle-sized rural town were difficult, both physically and emotionally. Her time was primarily occupied with serving, and later cooking, in the Vienna Café, which Kurt, a qualified wine, champagne, and coffee specialist, had bought and transformed into the town's first café soon after his arrival. Here this tiny, warm, strong, and dignified woman was able to cajole dairy farmers into new ways of eating, offering such unfamiliar fare as real coffee, eel, goulash, potato salad, and the chocolate truffles for which she became famous. The café was a haven of otherness in an arch-conservative society, and the Philips' cultured German background was demonstrated by their displaying pictures by various local artists on the walls. Their aesthetic awareness was also manifested in their modern, functional, Bauhaus-like furniture, which Kurt had made especially for the café.[4] This interest in elegant, well-proportioned, contemporary design was shared by Margot, who possessed an innate feeling for shape and a subtle sense of colour long before she became a painter.[5] She attributed her later involvement in art to her interest in interior decoration in the mid 1940s.[6] Also important in this regard were undoubtedly some of the many contacts she made socially and through the café—people who would encourage her in her artistic endeavours. Janet Paul, for example, invited her to sit as a model for her Friday evening drawing group, and although Margot had not attempted drawing or painting by then, the experience no doubt showed her that it could be done.[7]

Margot's entry into the art world began comparatively late in her life when she was about 48. In Germany she had always taken a lively interest in it, regularly visiting the Wallraf-Richartz Gallery in Cologne, as well as a gallery of modern art on Sunday mornings for group tours led by the curator. She was also an avid reader of art books, but it was not until she heard from a client of the café about drawing classes offered at the Hamilton

Technical School that she took her first tentative steps. Her initial enthusiasm was quickly dampened by her discovery that she had little aptitude for drawing.[8] Her resilience and determination are revealed, however, in her decision to persevere. She joined the WEA[9] art classes run by Geoffrey Fairburn on Saturday mornings, and in 1949 and 1950 enrolled for summer schools run by Arthur Hipwell at Ardmore Teachers' Training College; in 1951, she also attended the first of nine consecutive summer schools instigated by the director of the Auckland City Art Gallery, Eric Westbrook. One of the teachers was Colin McCahon, and after an inauspicious start with two other tutors, Margot asked for permission to study with him. A man not always noted for his tolerance towards aspiring artists, he appreciated her for her personality, humour, and aesthetic sense, and recognised in her an ability he thought worth fostering. She attributed her success as a painter entirely to his unusual, non-interventionist approach, and said of him: 'He gave me encouragement. He gave me no teaching, he left me completely alone. He built up my confidence.'[10] It was he who helped her to lose her fear of failure and who taught her how to look and observe. These classes and an evening course in linocuts by Campbell Smith at Fairfield College in the 1960s were the only formal instruction she received.

Despite her strong impulse to paint and what she called her 'tremendous urge to create',[11] painting remained an intensely difficult task for her. In her meticulous, orderly fashion, she would complete her housework before devoting herself to several hours at her easel each day, using tiny number 4 brushes, which she later employed as stakes for her garden![12] She painstakingly built up her painting, beginning in the top right-hand corner and moving along and slowly downwards in a process that has been likened to knitting.[13] Her pictures evolved as she worked on them and, in contrast to

Margot Philips, early 1960s. *(Fay Foreman Collection)*

many trained artists who paint a particular image, she never had a preconceived idea of how her painting might ultimately look until she had reached the bottom of the canvas. Her precision, resulting in almost invisible brushwork, meant that she was only able to complete three or four paintings a year.

Described at various times as 'naive, primitive [or] visionary',[14] her paintings were predominantly inspired by the Waikato landscape, which intrigued and excited her with its sense of movement and angularity. However, her works are seldom of specifically recognisable places, but are usually composites from her memory—distillations of a myriad of impressions, which found their way into her subconscious and which nevertheless capture, with their distinctive shapes and variety of greens and browns, the quintessence of the Waikato. Tim Walker says of them: 'There's something about Margot's work that makes you see things in the landscape you hadn't consciously noticed before.'[15] It often depicts empty, expansive areas, devoid of human beings or their edifices[16]—characteristics also common to her series of paintings inspired by the Coromandel coast, the South Island, and Northland. Hers are pictures that demand one's time and invite one to wander through them.

Above left:
Margot Philips, *Hilly Landscape*, 1962. Oil on canvasboard. *(Waikato Museum of Art and History)*

Above right:
Margot Philips, *Coromandel Coast*, 1969. Oil on canvasboard. *(Waikato Museum of Art and History)*

A trip in 1965 to Britain, Italy, and Israel gave rise to her Lake District, Italian, and Negev Desert series, the latter, like her South Island ones, using a different palette, mainly in tones of browns and greys. Some of these works, along with a number of her monoprints, were included in Margot's first solo exhibition organised in 1966 by Kees Hos, the owner of the New Vision Gallery in Auckland and opened by Colin McCahon. A second similar exhibition took place in 1972.[17]

After thirty years of working as an artist, Margot gave up painting in 1980 because of deteriorating health. This situation seemed almost presaged in her paintings from 1976 onwards, with their distinctive, often lowering skies, which were in marked contrast to many of the neutral ones of earlier works. Her final painting, *The Homestead* (1980), with its two small, grey-roofed houses tucked modestly into the countryside, reintroduces motifs from some of her first pictures,[18] and seems like a metaphor and reflection of her own circumstances—a lone woman isolated in a large, empty, and, for her, foreign landscape.[19]

In 1983 the Waikato Art Museum honoured her by mounting a retrospective of seventy-eight works, and in October 1987 her valuable contribution to art in the Waikato was acknowledged with an exhibition entitled 'Margot Philips—Her Own World' to mark the opening of the new Waikato Museum of Art and History. Margot Philips died on 30 December 1988.

Like many refugees of her era, Margot wanted to give back something to the country that had taken her in. She did so not just through her paintings, many of which she left to the Waikato Museum of Art and History, but through a generous bequest to the museum and the Waikato Society of Arts so that future generations might benefit. It is particularly fitting that some of it goes towards a biennial Margot Philips Children's Art Exhibition to encourage young artists, for although having no children of her own, she was always able to bridge the generation gap, acting as an honorary aunt to the children of many of her friends as well as supporting the Save the Children Fund.[20]

Margot Philips, *Lighthouse*, 1967. Oil on canvasboard. *(Waikato Museum of Art and History)*

1 *Margot Philips—Her Own World* (Hamilton, 1987), p. 9.
2 Ibid.
3 Shenagh Gleeson, 'Paintings show reward of struggle', *Waikato Times*, 26 March 1983.
4 Architect Aubrey de Lisle designed the furniture (interview with Aubrey and Mary de Lisle, 31 August 1996).
5 Interviews with Beryl de Jong, 30 November 1996, and Janet Paul, 18 April 1996.
6 Gleeson [note 3].
7 Interview with Janet Paul, 18 April 1996.
8 Beryl de Jong reports Margot's dismay at being unable to draw a cake tin at her first drawing class (interview, 30 November 1996).
9   The Workers' Educational Association (or WEA) was an adult education movement whose aim was to provide instruction in a wide range of skills and disciplines for mainly working-class people who had received limited formal schooling. Originally founded in England early in the twentieth century, the WEA was first established in New Zealand in 1915.
10 Gleeson [note 3].
11 *Margot Philips—Her Own World* [note 1], p. 7.
12 Interview with Enid Claris, 12 February 1996.
13 Interview with Tim Walker, 7 February 1996.
14 Janet Paul, 'Margot Philips', *Art New Zealand* 46 (Autumn, 1988), p. 85.
15 *Margot Philips—Her Own World* [note 1]. p. 58.
16 Some notable exceptions are *Takapuna Beach* (1956–57), *Landscape* (c. 1955), and *The Homestead* (1980).
17 Her paintings also appeared in at least twenty-five exhibitions between 1961 and 1980.
18 See *Landscape* (c. 1955). Interview with Tim Walker, 7 February 1996, who likens the two houses to Margot and her sister Helene, who emigrated to Hamilton in later life.
19 Interview with Janet Paul, 18 April 1996.
20 Interview with Anne Opie, 7 November 1996. In addition to the people mentioned in footnotes, I also wish to thank Ruth and Lester Davey, Jean and Geoff Fairburn, Fay and Mary Foreman, Phyllis Gant, Rob and Eve Gardiner, Lois Luke, Cecilie McShane, Campbell Smith, Pam Thompson, Jeanette Ward, and Shirley Whittlestone for their generosity in speaking about Margot and providing invaluable information about her life and works. I am also extremely grateful for the wonderful assistance of Lara Strongman and Kay Greed of the Waikato Museum of Art and History.

14

Friedensreich Hundertwasser

HANSGERD DELBRÜCK

Friedensreich
Hundertwasser, 1986.
(Steven Young)

Friedensreich Hundertwasser was born in Vienna on 15 December 1928 under the name of Friedrich Stowasser. His Austrian father died in 1929, and he was brought up, an only child, by his Jewish mother. In 1943, sixty-nine members of his mother's family, including his grandmother and aunt, were deported and killed, and that experience of Nazi terror left him scarred for life.

During the winter of 1949–50, he changed the first syllable of his family name to 'Hundert', a literal translation from the Slavic word *sto*, meaning 'hundred'. This transformation of his last name into the more poetic 'Hundertwasser' reflects his well-known love of water. The change of his first name came about during a visit to Japan in the early 1960s, where his name 'Friedrich' was transcribed into Japanese script using the characters for 'peace' ('Friede' in German) and 'realm' ('Reich'), which he then combined into 'Friedensreich'. The two names now contained thirteen letters each—a magic number, which Hundertwasser believes brings good fortune. Indeed, Hundertwasser has since become a world-famous and controversial painter, architect, and environmentalist who exhibits and travels widely around the world.

After having fallen in love with New Zealand on his first visit here, a touring exhibition in 1973, which went to the main centres of both islands, he applied for and was granted permanent residence in New Zealand in 1974, and in 1988 his New Zealand citizenship application was approved.[1] An artist whose reputation as a painter stems to a large extent from the richness of his colours, he was therefore thrilled to be able to live in a country that enjoys an abundance of rain, particularly in winter: 'On a rainy day, colours begin to glow; that's why a cloudy, rainy day is the kind I like best. That's the kind of day when I can work. When it rains, I'm happy. And when it rains, I know my day is beginning.'[2]

Although he wished to remain an Austrian citizen, based in Vienna, and to live and work regularly for part of the year in Venice, he decided to live for three to six months every year on a farm that he bought in the Bay of Islands, in the far north of the North Island. There, in the Kaurinui Valley, Hundertwasser can live 'as though in a landscape painting, with trees which he has planted, not painted, with a Böcklin pond which he has dammed up himself, with valleys named after Brueghel, Klimt, Schiele, and Sonnenstern: He has also named valleys after his mother "Elsa"'.[3] On the 455 hectares of his dairy farm, he has planted some 60,000 trees, and practises his concept of the grass-roofed house with solar panels to generate electricity for the interior lighting and the hot water cylinder. He has also built a guest house there with walls consisting of coloured glass bottles embedded in cement and sawdust. Having been attracted to New Zealand for environmental reasons, Hundertwasser is thus able to indulge in that famous luscious green of the New Zealand bush and farmland—a green that he has not found anywhere else in the world. On a muddy tidal creek nearby, 'Hundertwasser keeps a dinghy, which at high tide can navigate to the harbour at Opua, and *Regentag*, now moored there'.[4]

As a painter, Hundertwasser created an immediate interest among New Zealanders: the 25,000 catalogues printed for his 1973 tour were soon sold out. From 1973, a large number of the paintings of this prolific artist, who always gives the exact dates and places of origin of his works, have been promoting New Zealand, as have photo reports, published in European magazines, on the lifestyle of Hundertwasser on his Bay of Islands property. The New Zealand authorities have recognised that the country has profited from the public relations value of the painter's status, so they have sometimes gone out of their way to accommodate his often eccentric wishes. In 1985, for instance, Hundertwasser applied for permission to be buried on his own land amid his own trees in order to practise his ideas of recycling the dead; the application was subsequently approved by the Minister of Health.

The interest created by his paintings among the general public of New Zealand, however, has been superseded increasingly by an interest in his work as an environmentalist and architect. Whereas pertinent comments were written about his paintings in journals and papers like the *New Zealand Listener* and the *Dominion* in 1974,[5] later on, his art work was usually mentioned only in passing. However, the 'outspoken Austrian artist'[6] has taken every opportunity to influence the development of New Zealand's architecture and environmental policy, and thus ordinary New Zealanders have often been more intrigued—and sometimes irritated—by Hundertwasser's views on architecture and issues of national identity than by his visual art.

In the late 1980s, for instance, he denounced the high-rise buildings of Wellington as inhumane and brutal—'High Reich' architecture that Hitler would have loved.[7] In letters to the editor of the *New Zealand Listener*, one local reader counterattacked, saying that Hundertwasser's claims were 'not just eccentric but wildly inaccurate, and that the Nazis would probably have loved Hundertwasser's ideas on architecture'.[8] Hundertwasser in turn presented the Wellington City Council with a free design of a new waterfront National Museum, in which he wanted to combine both the square European or Pakeha style of architecture and the spiral-inspired style of architecture found on Maori pa.[9] His design was rejected, however, as was his design for a Whangarei art gallery, which was to be built by transforming a post office into a grass-roofed building.[10]

In an article by Martyn Evans, published in autumn 1993 in a New Zealand architecture journal along with a good number of photos of the spectacular Vienna Hundertwasser House,[11] such failures were not mentioned. Indeed, Hundertwasser was characterised in more general terms as one of those 'non-professional' persons who, with their new concepts, evoke 'disbelief and often ridicule from the profession concerned'.[12] There certainly seemed to be no trace of disbelief in the mind of the article's author. He quoted without reservation from Hundertwasser's well-known manifestos, which state that 'modern architecture is totalitarian, alienated from nature and the longings of man', that the ruler's straight line is 'imitative and not creative, engendering emptiness and the downfall of our civilisation', and that optical pollution is 'the worst environmental poison because prevailing ugliness kills our soul'.[13] The article finished with an acknowledgment of New Zealand's debt to Hundertwasser for 'opening doors to the possibilities of humane and sustainable architecture'.[14] The new acceptability and even trendiness of Hundertwasser's ideas as an architect are further attested to by a number of other articles published in the same journal, which deal with issues close to Hundertwasser's heart. At the end of the article 'Green means go', for instance, a list of recommended reading includes Hundertwasser's 1985 publication, *Das Haus*.[15]

Hundertwasser's views on matters of national identity—the second major issue with which he has confronted New Zealanders—inevitably touch on questions of nationalism, but the form of nationalism that came through in his public comments on this subject could not be accused of being comparable in any way to that form of nationalism that manifested itself in National Socialism. Hundertwasser did not wish to establish the roots of the New Zealand nation in either the Pakeha or the Maori past, but found them instead in a time before even the Maori came to New Zealand, that is, in the natural heritage of New Zealand.[16] Indeed, he refused to see his own nationality defined merely by the bureaucratic act of the authorities conferring it, and insisted that he was a New Zealander long before he ever came to New Zealand; thus, his promotion of the idea that New Zealand should have an identity all its own went together well with his claim that, in spite of his dual nationality, he was used to being regarded as a foreigner and an outsider in whatever country he lived in.[17]

In 1983, Hundertwasser designed a flag that was meant to capture New Zealand's singular identity as he saw it. While his 1986 flag design for Australia does not seem to have impressed many Australians, his New Zealand flag created a lively and often animated debate. He wanted to satisfy the need for a flag that 'was genuinely and indigenously New Zealand and which couldn't be mistaken for that of other countries', and he tried to achieve this objective with 'the coiled fern, or koru, design in the natural green of the New Zealand bush, on a long white cloud background ... a curved diagonal shape which stands out from right-angled flags'.[18] When the flag was first publicised, the design was 'variously described as looking like an Irish snail, a sexist symbol and a flag more befitting of a banana republic'.[19]

On 1 July 1986, the Christchurch *Star* reported that an informal survey conducted at the Auckland City Art Gallery had shown some public support, and on 18 July 1986 it was reported in the same paper that 'Several Arts of Colombo St', Christchurch, was flying Hundertwasser's flag as 'a possible alternative to the present New Zealand flag'. However, an opinion poll pub-

lished in October 1986 showed that 86 per cent of people questioned wanted to keep the New Zealand ensign as it was.[20] This confirmed an assump-
tion voiced two months earlier by the Minister of Internal Affairs, Dr Peter
Tapsell, who was certain New Zealanders did not want to change the present flag, because 'it's the flag that we have been to two world wars with'.[21]
Hundertwasser, however, reacted to negative polls by saying that 'the question should not have been about changing the New Zealand flag but
whether New Zealanders would like a distinctive alternative to fly in tan-
dem with the ensign', and he reported that the Bay of Islands County
Council was already flying his design alongside the approved flag outside its
Kawakawa offices. Hundertwasser added: 'The official ensign should remain
because it represents the European history of the country, even though the
southern cross is not unique to New Zealand. My flag represents the grown-
up confidence of the country.'[22]

Hundertwasser's koru
flag designed for New
Zealand in 1983. *(A Flag
of Our Own Committee
leaflet)*

For some years, Hundertwasser was the single best promoter of the flag,
but he was soon assisted by the 'Flag of Our Own Committee', based in
Wellington. The committee promoted the flag with poetry-driven slogans.
However, its spokesperson and Hundertwasser were reported as being
'adamant that they don't want to replace the current national flag. The duo
talk of the fern koru being an "alternative design", a "second flag" for the
country. In time, however, they have a take-over in mind'.[23]
Between 1986 and November 1989, Hundertwasser sold 5,600 copies of
his flag.[24] In 1989, the koru ensign also became available as a lapel badge and
as an artist's sticker, and in 1990 the koru flag was available at some twenty
outlets scattered from the Bay of Islands to Dunedin. In 1990, the Wellington
Sesquicentennial Trust chose Hundertwasser's koru flag design as its logo. As
planned by Hundertwasser, the koru ensign is seen as symbolising New
Zealand's commitment to a wholesome planetary environment.

1 *New Zealand Herald*, 2 March 1989.
2 Friedensreich Hundertwasser, *Regentag. Rainy Day. Jour de pluie* (Munich, 1972), p. 36.
3 Hans Brockstedt (ed.), *Aotearoa. Insel der verlorenen Wünsche. Island of Lost Desires. Ile des desirs perdus: Hundertwasser in New Zealand* (Hamburg, 1979), p. 64.
4 Harry Rand, *Hundertwasser* (Cologne, 1991), p. 157. *Regentag* (lit. 'rainy day') is the name of an old wooden sailing ship that Hundertwasser bought and renovated to sail the Atlantic and the Pacific.
5 Cf. *New Zealand Listener*, 3 August 1974; *Dominion*, 30 November 1974.
6 *Dominion*, 9 May 1990.
7 Interview with Hundertwasser broadcast by Television New Zealand on 17 June 1988. See also Mark Abernethy, 'Designer declares war on "visual pollution", ' *Dominion*, 12 May 1990. In an article in the *Evening Post* of 30 December 1996, Hundertwasser is reported to have said that Austria, birthplace of Adolf Hitler, was not particularly anti-Semitic: 'I see what happened as a very bad sickness that overcomes humanity from time to time.'
8 *New Zealand Listener*, 9 July 1990. The writer of the letter was Dr Alex Scobie, Reader in Classics at Victoria University of Wellington. He is the author of *Hitler's State Architecture: The Impact of Classical Antiquity* (University Park, Penn., 1990).
9 See Abernethy [note 7].
10 Hundertwasser's design for the Whangarei art gallery was rejected for engineering reasons. See *Northern Advocate*, 3 April 1993.
11 Martyn Evans, 'Organic practitioner', *Architecture New Zealand*, September/October 1993, pp. 68–71.
12 Evans [note 11], p. 69.
13 Ibid.
14 Evans [note 11], p. 71.
15 See *Architecture New Zealand*, September/October 1993, p. 84.
16 Interview with Hundertwasser broadcast by Television New Zealand on 2 December 1990.
17 Ibid.
18 'The "genuine" article is unfurled', *New Zealand Herald*, 1 July 1986.
19 Ron Palenski, 'Flag's designer still unperturbed', *Dominion*, 22 October 1986.
20 *Dominion*, 22 October 1986.
21 'NZ flag booklet published', *Dominion*, 14 August 1986.
22 Ibid.
23 'Furled again', *New Zealand Listener*, 20 November 1989.
24 *New Zealand Listener*, 20 November 1989.

Part 3

The academic world

Introduction

JAMES N. BADE

One of the areas in which German-speaking immigrants have made their mark, particularly since the end of World War II, is in research and higher education. Practically every tertiary institution in this country has German-speaking immigrants on its teaching staff, and they are too numerous to mention here. Indeed, it was a very difficult task to decide which academics should be featured in the following chapters. Those who do feature are among the better known, but it must be emphasised that their inclusion is representative of many others in their own and allied fields who could not be incorporated into this section for reasons of space. To do them all justice would require a book in itself.

George von Zedlitz is an important case not only because of his academic status as Professor of Modern Languages at Victoria University College but also because the treatment he received from misguided politicians typified the anti-German hysteria to which German immigrants were exposed during World War I. The fact that the University College Council was forced to dismiss von Zedlitz through an act of parliament is a shameful page in New Zealand's history. The Nelson School of Music managed to hold on to its principal, Julius Lemmer, despite similar calls for his resignation. The situation after World War II was not much better. Dr Fritz Gallas was threatened with dismissal from his position as physical instructor at Wellington Technical College in July 1945 because of his status as 'enemy alien', but fortunately the dismissal motion was lost at a meeting of the Board of Governors.[1]

The *New Zealand Truth* of 18 July 1945 printed 'draft regulations' supposedly under consideration by the government, which would have forced all aliens to vacate certain employment and business activities. Luckily, a deputation from prominent people in support of refugees met the Prime Minister on 28 August 1945 and helped dissuade the government from passing these regulations. By the end of the year, the naturalisation process for refugees had been restored to the situation that prevailed before the war.[2]

Given such hostility, it is all the more remarkable that refugees from Nazi Europe made the impact that they did in New Zealand academic circles, particularly during the war years and in the immediate post-war period. Most of the academics featured here came to New Zealand to escape from political or racial persecution or both, and it is ironical that two of them—Werner Droescher and Gerda Bell—were subject to a certain amount of persecution here also. Werner Droescher, who had emigrated from Germany for political reasons, suffered considerable harassment during the war years and was not allowed to continue as a Civil Defence paramedic because of his German nationality. Yet he managed to graduate MA from Auckland University and became a popular lecturer in German at Auckland University, initially in a part-time capacity (1946–48) and later as a full-time senior lecturer (1961–75).[3] Gerda Bell, who had emigrated on account of her Jewish background (although she was a baptised Lutheran), was dismissed from her teaching position at Woodford House in 1940 on account of her 'enemy alien' status, but, after some years as a librarian, went on to lecture in German at Victoria University (1964–71).

As Nelson Wattie points out, emigration of the racially and politically oppressed from Germany and Austria under Hitler brought an intellectual and cultural impoverishment to both those countries; the intellectual and cultural lives of the countries in which they settled, however, were greatly enriched. Karl Popper (later Sir Karl) emigrated from his native Austria in 1935 for political reasons and spent the war years in New Zealand as a lecturer in philosophy at Canterbury University College, but left in 1945 to take up a position at the London School of Economics. Paul Hoffmann, who like Gerda Bell had emigrated (from Austria) on account of his Jewish family connection, although—as was also the case with Gerda Bell—he had a Christian upbringing, graduated MA from Auckland in 1947, and after eight years in Austria (1951–59), returned to New Zealand to take up a lectureship in German at Victoria University of Wellington, later to become Victoria's first Professor of German. Wolfgang Rosenberg left Germany because of political and racial persecution, and studied during the war years at Victoria University of Wellington before embarking on a remarkable academic career in economics at Canterbury University College. Peter Munz's family fled Germany and then Italy to escape the persecution of the Jews and, on their arrival in Christchurch in 1940, Munz enrolled at Canterbury University College, graduating an MA in history in 1943. After four years at Cambridge University, he took up an appointment at Victoria University College in 1948, where his distinguished academic career spanned more than four decades.

1   'Dismissal move fails', *Dominion*, 31 July 1945. For calls to have 'enemy aliens' returned to the countries of origin, see introduction to part 4.

2   'Report of deputation to Prime Minister concerning the future status of refugees in New Zealand' (undated) by J. Meltzer (convenor), and cyclostyled letter dated 10 October 1945 from J. Meltzer to all those concerned with the deputation, kindly made available by Mrs Ilse Jacoby of Wellington.

3   See Sean D. Lovich, *German and Swedish at Auckland: A History of Germanic Languages and Literature at the University*, Auckland, Department of Germanic Languages and Literature, University of Auckland 1983, pp. 15 and 39.

15

George von Zedlitz

NELSON WATTIE

The case of Baron George von Zedlitz is a curious one, revealing much about New Zealand attitudes to Germans in wartime, although the person at the centre of the storm need not necessarily be seen as a German. Certainly he was born in Germany, in Hermannswaldau near Liegnitz, Silesia, in 1876, and certainly he was deeply interested in the history of his Prussian family, but his upbringing and the view of life that resulted from it are best described as cosmopolitan. Today, he would probably be classified as 'stateless'—or rather, he would rush to be naturalised in his country of residence to avoid such a classification—but in the years before World War I, it was possible to travel all over Europe without a passport and to enter New Zealand and take up work without evidence of nationality. For von Zedlitz, such formalities were a matter of little concern, and he simply never bothered to apply for British citizenship.

The volume entitled *The Search for a Country*, which was published in 1963 as his 'autobiography', but which is really a memoir addressed to his children and not intended for publication,[1] does in fact tell us a great deal about his family history and his childhood, but little enough about the matters that make his name significant to us today. It was possible for von Zedlitz to find traces of his ancestors in the Liegnitz region from the thirteenth and fourteenth centuries. The main ancestral line was one of small but independent landowners, able, like many others, to use the title 'Baron'. The closest English equivalent is 'squire'. Of a remote relative from another line, he says:

The most distinguished member of this branch was Minister of Education under Frederick the Great. He laid the foundations of the modern German educational system, found time when he was minister to follow Kant's lectures given at Königsberg, and had *The Critique of Pure Reason* dedicated to him. The minister Zedlitz was an honest man too, and lost office for reasons that do him credit, as you will find if you look in Carlyle's *Frederick the Great*.[2]

Considering his own career, it is not surprising that von Zedlitz chose to draw attention to this particular figure in his family past.

Despite these deep roots in German history, and because his parents were divorced, George von Zedlitz was brought up in an English-speaking family environment. At the same time, the social world around him was using German, French, Italian, or English, and he became familiar with all of these.

At an early age, he tells us, he refused to speak to an aunt in any language but English: 'I must have learned German quite young from Agnes [his nurse], though I can remember being teased long afterwards about my blunders in German and Anglicisms.'[3]

His mother was English, her European father having been naturalised before her birth, and she was always proud of it. Her family name was Wolff, but had apparently been Wolff von Sandau at an earlier time. It was not clear to von Zedlitz whether they were Jewish, nor whether they had originated in Germany or in Holland. In any case, the family of her former husband supported her and their son in a kind of modest gentility. Von Zedlitz's earliest childhood memories were of Dresden, but even then there were many trips to places near and far.

When he was 8, his mother moved to England and Guernsey, partly for her health, partly to avoid her former husband's creditors. Later they returned to the continent, and the Baroness von Zedlitz and her son lived in modest *pensions* in Italy, Switzerland, France, and Germany, often accompanied by a maid and an English tutor for George. For von Zedlitz, one feature of the life he would later lead in Wellington in the years immediately after the turn of the century was that it brought more stability than he could remember ever having had before:

22 March 1919

This day seventeen years ago I landed in Wellington from the *Monowai*. And a queer place I thought it then. A solid slice of life three or four times as long as ever before I spent in one place. Five years in Dresden from 3 to 8. Five or so at Loretto [Scotland] from 1896 to 1901, four at Oxford, three at Wellington College [in Berkshire], the rest all ones or less. How many hundred beds have I slept in, I wonder? Looked through how many thousand windows? Spoken to how many thousands of human beings? How many hundreds of trains, how many dozens of steamers?[4]

At the age of 15, von Zedlitz was sent to school to achieve a more formal conclusion to his education. He was a boarder at Wellington College in Berkshire (near London) and distinguished himself scholastically, although not in sport. The climax of his scholastic career was the award of a scholarship to Oxford. At Trinity College he distinguished himself, among other things, for his skill in oratory, and was a prominent member of the Oxford Union. His main opponent was Hilaire Belloc, and these two 'half-Englishmen' would astonish the others with the wit and intensity of their arguments.

During his school and university years, von Zedlitz continued to travel widely in Britain and in Europe. By not returning to Germany for his military service, he effectively let his nationality lapse, but he saw no urgent need to take on another. After completing his Oxford degree, he spent several years as a school teacher and private tutor, finally settling down at Loretto in Scotland as a school master. After the death of his mother in 1897, he felt free to leave Britain, and indeed wanted to do so—partly because he had always felt uneasy at British attitudes towards someone without a clearly defined position in the social hierarchy.

I have been brought up entirely in that atmosphere from childhood, of living among people who disliked and despised anything 'foreign'; of being afraid to give my name to strangers; of feeling an air of suspicion and hostility about me, even when none was. …

But in New Zealand I found an utterly different atmosphere, and that had much to do with my affection for this country. … You must not suppose I was ashamed of my birth, exactly. But I did rejoice at having found a community that did not make me feel uncomfortable about it ….You can perhaps hardly imagine a time when a German name was no drawback in New Zealand,[5] and you can also guess how I felt at being plunged, worse than ever, into the old nightmare feeling, which now must remain with me as long as I live.[6]

George William Edward Ernst von Zedlitz arrived in Wellington in early 1902 to take up the first chair of Modern Languages at Victoria University College. His diary records that he received a 'welcome incomparably cordial and pleasant',[7] and the next twelve years were to be the happiest of his life. He married a local woman, had three children, and found affection and respect among his students, who liked to call him 'Von'. J.C. Beaglehole writes that 'Von Zedlitz brought the college something it badly needed. … [H]e had inherited, to an extraordinary degree, the civilized mind of Europe'.[8]

In those pre-war years, a sense of peace and harmony, which von Zedlitz found comforting, was tempered by outbursts of militarism. The student paper *Spike* called it an 'epidemic', and in 1909 an Officers' Training Corps was instituted at the college. The pacifist von Zedlitz, with some of his professorial colleagues, responded by joining up, to encourage self-discipline and public spirit in the students. The students responded satirically:

> Beside [Kirk] strides, with features grimly set,
> Hung down in front his trusty bayonet,
> That foreign god, von Zedlitz. By and by
> They'll trust in him and keep their powder dry.
> His duty, too, when airships come and go,
> To analyse their language here below.[9]

The Professorial Board, Victoria University College, 1904. Left to right, back row: M.W. Richmond, C.E. Adams, D. Ritchie, Professor Maclaurin. Front row: Professor von Zedlitz, Professor Mackenzie, Professor Brown, Professor Easterfield. (Evening Post *Collection, Alexander Turnbull Library, Ref. no. F-123689-1/2*)

There are all too few such glimpses of von Zedlitz during his happiest years, but we find him again supporting the Heretics' Club, set up at the college in opposition to the Christian Union. '[T]hey would found a tradition of freedom and "go gallivanting down the Avenues of Posterity" (the phrase was Von's). ... [The club] protested against those who sought to obstruct all research and investigation, it proclaimed a doctrine of freedom of thought and speech for all.'[10]

This attitude ties the Heretics' Club in with the University Reform Movement, of which von Zedlitz was a prominent member. He hoped it would turn the University College into something less like a night school, reduce the importance of examinations, and encourage originality and research. Again von Zedlitz applied his eloquence at public meetings, and in 1911 he and his colleagues, Thomas Hunter and William Laby, published a pamphlet called *University Reform in New Zealand*.

The outbreak of war in Europe in 1914 brought unexpected changes to von Zedlitz's life. When war was declared between Russia and Germany, he applied at the German Consulate in Wellington for humanitarian work on the German side. Within days, Germany and Britain were at war, and at once he decided that his loyalties were with the British, but his first impulsive gesture was to be held against him later.

Anti-German feeling was suddenly rife in New Zealand, and to bear a German name, no matter how one's life had been lived, was to be suspected of 'enemy activity'. In Wanganui and elsewhere shop windows were broken—in hindsight a dreadful, if provincial, parallel to Nazi attacks on Jewish shops twenty years later. 'Patriotic Societies' flourished, and nationalistic hysteria could be sensed in newspaper columns. 'So von Zedlitz, the honourable, the civilized, the humane, became the target of every uncivilized fool in the country who could write an anonymous letter to a newspaper.'[11] Like D.H. Lawrence and his German wife in Cornwall at that very time, von Zedlitz was accused of spying. '[B]y implication, he was responsible for the invasion of Belgium and the sinking of the *Lusitania* and the whole host of atrocities which became one of the staples of anti-German propaganda.'[12]

In the weeks and months that followed, the campaign against von Zedlitz grew in intensity and hysteria. The government could not withstand such popular turmoil. Apart from von Zedlitz himself, who never lost his civilised dignity, only the university authorities, from today's point of view, emerge from the affair with honour. They refused to accept the resignation he offered on the day Britain joined the war against Germany (4 August 1914). However, other 'unnaturalised Germans' were interned on Somes Island, and 'patriotic' voices demanded that he be interned too. Both the government and the University Council were subjected to enormous popular pressure, partly from the parents of students, who feared their offspring would be corrupted. The students themselves, who, unlike their parents, knew the man in question, defended him unanimously.

On 25 August 1915, the opposition asked Prime Minister Massey in parliament whether the government would treat von Zedlitz like other 'alien enemies', and his reply was curiously self-contradictory, mixing an assurance that people 'whose known character precludes suspicion' would not be pursued with a final statement that if the council did not remove him from their employ, the government would introduce legislation to do so.[13] And indeed, some three weeks later, on 14 September, Massey introduced the Alien Enemies Teachers Bill, whose clauses affected only von Zedlitz: 'enemy subjects' were disqualified from teaching in publicly funded institutions.

Von Zedlitz again submitted his resignation, but the council stated that he was acting involuntarily, under duress, and on 17 September presented a petition against the Bill to both houses of parliament. In what Beaglehole calls 'a sort of patriotic moral orgy',[14] the Bill was passed in early October 1915, and the council had no choice but to accept von Zedlitz's resignation, praising him highly as it did so and exercising its option of granting him a year's salary. As a final act, the council published, later that year, the pamphlet entitled *Report of the Victoria University College Council concerning the case of Professor von Zedlitz*.

Some excerpts from the college's petition to the government[15] suggest the atmosphere of the time and the reputation of von Zedlitz:

[A]s an educational institution … [Victoria College's] success has been largely due to the teaching and good influence of the said George William von Zedlitz. … [A]nything which approaches an abandonment of principle at the dictation of prejudice, hatred, fear or the like is antagonistic to all the best influences of education, and your Petitioner believes that it is impossible to gauge the reaction for evil that such a course may have on the youth of this Dominion.

Von Zedlitz was never to return to the university, but rather ran his own University Tutorial College with the moral support of his former colleagues. Before his death in 1947, he became a well-known and respected book reviewer, broadcaster, and public speaker. This chapter has been written in the von Zedlitz Building of Victoria University, which houses some of the academic disciplines once identified with him.

1 *The Search for a Country: The Autobiography of G. W. von Zedlitz* ([Hamilton], 1963).
2 Von Zedlitz [note 1], p. 50.
3 Von Zedlitz [note 1], p. 65.
4 Von Zedlitz [note 1], pp. 70–1.
5 This was addressed to his children in 1919. At least one of them chose to use their mother's name, Fitzherbert.
6 Von Zedlitz [note 1], pp. 83–4.
7 Quoted in D.H.'s introduction to the memoir (von Zedlitz [note 1], p. 10). 'D.H.' has been identified as von Zedlitz's son-in-law, Professor D.O.W. Hall.
8 J.C. Beaglehole, *Victoria University College: An Essay Towards a History* (Wellington, 1949), p. 56.
9 General de Bility (pseudonym), 'Inaugural Ode on the V.C. Officers' Training Corps', *The Spike, or, Victoria College Review*, vol. 8, no. 2 (October 1909), p. 75.
10 Beaglehole [note 8], p. 123.
11 Beaglehole [note 8], p. 163.
12 Ibid.
13 Beaglehole [note 8], pp. 166–8. Cf. *New Zealand Parliamentary Debates*, vol. 173, 25 August 1915, pp. 144f.
14 Beaglehole [note 8], p. 170.
15 Printed in its entirety in Beaglehole [note 8], pp. 298–302.

16

Paul Hoffmann

HANSGERD DELBRÜCK

Paul Hoffmann,
Tübingen, 1996. *(Selwyn Hoffmann)*

Paul Hoffmann was born on 5 April 1917 in the Austrian village of Willendorf on the Danube, in the wine-growing Wachau district[1] where 'north and south, west and east blend'.[2] His Viennese father, from a wealthy, liberal Jewish family, opted for a life on the land and took a degree in agricultural science with the intention of becoming an independent farmer. His mother, a native of Slovakia (then a province of Hungary), was a schoolteacher and a devout Catholic. They had three sons and eventually worked a small mixed farm of their own at Willendorf.

Paul, the oldest son, spent his first four grammar school years as a boarder at the renowned school attached to the ancient Benedictine abbey of Kremsmünster, where he received a solid grounding in Latin and Greek. He then attended a similar type of state school in nearby Krems. His lifelong love of Latin dates back to childhood when he served at mass as an altar boy. His early fascination with the sound and rhythm of the Latin language had a lasting impact on his sensitivity for poetry, which became his lifelong preoccupation. Endowed with an extraordinary memory, he was able to recall poems with apparent ease. All his life he described them as a 'reliable source of spiritual nourishment, which served [him] well in times when other resources failed'.[3]

In 1935, Hoffmann enrolled at Vienna University, with history and *Germanistik* (i.e. the study of German language and literature) as his main subjects. The latter proved a disappointment to him because it neglected to study individual texts closely and disregarded the specific quality and cognitive content of the poetic form. Hoffmann was prevented from submitting his already completed doctoral thesis on the famous Austrian dramatist Franz Grillparzer by Hitler's invasion of Austria in March 1938—an event that put an abrupt end to the young academic's accustomed way of life and all his immediate plans. Although he had experienced some anti-Semitism since childhood, he was now stigmatised as a Jewish half-caste ('*Mischling ersten Grades*'). The intensity that anti-Semitism had reached by 1938 was seen by Hoffmann as 'its obscene grimace in unrestrained beastliness'.[4]

The Hoffmann family emigrated to New Zealand and took up dairy-farming. After a spell in the back-blocks and a season spent as share-milkers in the Waikato, they moved to Karaka county, south of Auckland. Carl, the youngest boy, went to school and then Training College, and Hoffmann senior ran a farm with his two older sons, Paul and Frank; initially it was leased, but after ten years they were able to purchase it. While Frank had considerable specialist knowledge and remarkable technical skill at his command from the start, Paul was completely unprepared for the job and, in his own view, was 'the least gifted for manual work', having been 'a clumsy bookish boy'.[5] But under Frank's guidance he succeeded in mastering the various tasks of a dairy-farmer. It was continuous hard work. In addition to routine farm work, eighty cows had to be milked daily, taking an average of seven hours.

After adjusting to the new work, Paul felt the need to exercise his mind, so he enrolled at the University of Auckland as an external student, studying Latin and English. Able to devote a maximum of four hours a day to study, he had to make do with only four hours' sleep for several years. Of great help to him was his personal acquaintance with Professor Arthur Sewell, head of the English Department at Auckland, a noted Shakespeare and Milton scholar and widely known as a playwright, public speaker, and a lively and imaginative mainstay of the New Zealand intellectual Left. He stayed on the Hoffmann farm a number of times, and would often discuss English literature with Paul as they worked together out in the paddocks.

However, the all-important event in Paul Hoffmann's formative years in Auckland occurred in June 1940 when he met the German–Jewish poet Karl Wolfskehl.[6] He stood in awe of Wolfskehl's overwhelming command of the German language—a command he thought he could never match. On his one day off each week, he used to visit the poet, and in order to arrive at about 9 a.m., he had to set off on a 47-kilometre bicycle ride from Runciman very early in the morning; later, however, he was able to afford to take the bus.

As Wolfskehl was nearly blind, books had to be read to him, and the poems that he scribbled in his diaries at night had to be deciphered the next morning by his devoted companion Margot Ruben and by Paul Hoffmann. The latter also read Wolfskehl his mail and books from overseas, such as Ernst Morwitz's English translation of the works of Stefan George, which Wolfskehl commented on in detail.[7] The poet's familiarity with English poetry had so far extended mainly to what was in vogue at the turn of the century or what had been translated by Stefan George. Wolfskehl knew nothing of Eliot or Pound, or of the nineteenth-century poet Gerard Manley Hopkins, and thus he also asked to hear the English poetry that Hoffmann was reading at university. Wolfskehl's enthusiastic and original comments were an inspiration to the young student of literature, who acknowledges that Wolfskehl taught him 'what constitutes a poetical line' and what causes verse to stand out from common language and from other literary genres.[8] Such knowledge was to prove extremely valuable to Hoffmann when his interests later shifted from writing poetry to translating it[9] and in his university career as a literary scholar specialising in poetry.

Wolfskehl was sometimes visited by the poets A.R.D. Fairburn and R.A.K. Mason. He held both in high regard, but it was Frank Sargeson whom Paul Hoffmann used to meet regularly at Wolfskehl's home. In particular, Hoffmann recalls a period of three consecutive months when his youngest brother stood in for him on the farm, thus allowing him to live and work in Auckland in the Reizenstein bakery so that he could visit Wolfskehl more often. At that time, Sargeson, who used to see Wolfskehl twice a week, asked Hoffmann many questions about Wolfskehl and about German literature in general, in which Sargeson showed a keen interest. Later, however, when Sargeson abruptly stopped visiting Wolfskehl, because he felt overwhelmed by the latter's erudition, he also lost touch with Hoffmann.[10]

Paul and Eva Hoffmann working hay at Runciman (near Auckland), 1948. *(P. Hoffmann Collection)*

In 1947 Paul Hoffmann graduated with an MA, and the following year, he married Eva Bichler, his Austrian childhood friend. (Also in 1948, Karl Wolfskehl died.) In 1951, Hoffmann returned to Vienna with Eva and their two small children. He enrolled at Vienna University and spent the next few years working towards a PhD, during which time he earned his living as a freelance radio writer, before graduating in 1957 with a thesis on Karl Wolfskehl's late poetry on religious themes, that is, the works written during his exile in New Zealand.

In 1959, Hoffmann took up a lectureship in German at Victoria University of Wellington[11] and in 1964 was appointed Victoria's first Professor of German.[12] His objectives, which he pursued passionately and highly effectively, were to attract students and at the same time raise the academic level of the study of German; to work towards interdisciplinary integration; to promote spoken German by introducing oral exams at every level; and to integrate the teaching of the language into the teaching of literature. He befriended Dr (later Professor) Peter Munz of the History Department and closely cooperated with two eminent colleagues from the English Department, Professor James Bertram and Dr Don McKenzie (the latter was later appointed to a chair at Oxford).[13] Hoffmann was instrumental in the introduction of comparative studies at Stage III, with teaching contributions from the English, German, French, and Russian departments. He gave public lectures on German and English Romanticism, contributed lectures on the Don Juan theme in literature to the university's Luncheon Series, and took part in the annual German drama productions. Together with Lisl Hilton and Douglas Fraser (the latter of whom was later to become Chancellor of the university), he founded, under the motto 'Humanitati', the Wellington Goethe Society and gave it a strong literary focus. He organised visits of German National Fellows to Victoria and worked ceaselessly to attract scholarships from Germany, Austria, and Switzerland for his students. In many areas, he worked in close cooperation with the embassies of the German-speaking countries.

In 1970, Hoffmann was appointed Professor of German at Tübingen University, one of the oldest and most highly regarded universities in Europe, where he continued his distinguished career as a teacher and researcher. At the time of widespread student demonstrations, when the study of literature was confronted with many challenges from both inside and outside German universities, his softly voiced but determined views had considerable influence on students and colleagues. His teaching and writing included such diverse subjects as Weimar Classicism, comparative studies of German and English literature, the reception of English literature in Germany, German–Jewish poetry, Nietzsche, Thomas Mann, Grillparzer, Robert Musil, and the problems of translation of poetry. Even today, in his very active retirement, Hoffmann regularly offers new courses on poetry,[14] which rank among the most popular courses offered by any lecturer at Tübingen, and he is still one of the most successful supervisors of PhD theses. For more than ten years, he has been inviting poets from all over Germany (including the former East Germany) and from many other countries as well to give public readings in the world-famous Hölderlin Tower in Tübingen and to take part in discussions afterwards with his students.[15] In 1978, Paul Hoffmann was awarded the Queen's Service Medal for his achievements in the country in which he had spent twenty-two years of his life. He has always kept in touch with New Zealand. Since his arrival in Germany, he and his wife Eva have had many visitors from New Zealand, and for many years they have looked after students who come to Tübingen from Wellington on scholarships. Paul Hoffmann made a return visit to Auckland as a guest professor in 1979, and in 1993 he gave lectures in Wellington and a paper at the Grillparzer Symposium in Dunedin, thus renewing old acquaintances and establishing new ones on both occasions.[16]

Whereas Paul Hoffmann's older son lives in New Zealand, his daughter and younger son live in Germany. As for the other two Hoffmann brothers who found shelter and a new home in New Zealand in 1939, Frank, a model farmer, has remained on the original property, where he and his wife have brought up eight children, while Carl, a distinguished Waldorf school teacher, has returned to New Zealand after holding posts in Germany, England, and the USA, and now lives in Henderson in active retirement, lecturing and writing.

1 The Wachau is renowned also for its prehistoric statuette, the so-called 'Venus of Willendorf'.
2 Much of the information contained in this chapter was obtained in an interview with Paul Hoffmann in Tübingen in January 1996.
3 Interview with Paul Hoffmann [note 2].
4 Ibid.
5 Ibid.
6 Paul Hoffmann has written of Wolfskehl's exile years in Auckland in his article, 'A German poet in New Zealand', *Landfall*, vol. 23 (1969), pp. 381–91; a more detailed description by Hoffmann of Wolfskehl's life in Auckland can be found in his introduction to *Karl Wolfskehls Briefwechsel aus Neuseeland 1938–1948*, ed. Cornelia Blasberg (Darmstadt, 1988), pp. 13–44.
7 Wolfskehl's comments, written up by Paul Hoffmann, were sent to Morwitz and resulted in considerable improvements in Morwitz's second rendering of George's verse into English. See Paul Hoffmann, 'Vom Dichterischen. Erfahrungen und Erkenntnisse', in Hansgerd Delbrück (ed.), *Dem Dichter des Lesens. Von Ilse Aichinger bis Zhang Zao. Für Paul Hoffmann zum 80. Geburtstag* (Tübingen, 1997), p. 208.
8 Interview with Paul Hoffmann [note 2].
9 Paul Hoffmann still writes poems occasionally himself (interview [note 2]).
10 Before this, Sargeson had visited Hoffmann and his father several times on their farm. Shortly before Sargeson's death, on a visit by Hoffmann from Germany to Auckland, the two had a moving last reunion in Sargeson's famous bach in Takapuna.
11 Before this, Hoffmann had already been offered a lectureship at the University of Auckland by Dr (later Professor) John Asher, who, having travelled to Vienna, tried in vain to persuade Hoffmann to suspend his PhD and lecture at Auckland instead (interview [note 2]).
12 Hoffmann's Inaugural Address was published under the title *The Metamorphosis of Humanism in German Literature* (Wellington, 1964). As head of German, Hoffmann was supported by his colleagues at the German Department, Dr Gerda Bell, David Carrad, and Lisl Hilton.
13 Together with Don McKenzie, Hoffmann founded the journal *Words*, which accepted contributions from all philologies, including Classics. All three scholars, together with other colleagues from Victoria, contributed articles to a collection of essays in honour of Hoffmann in 1987 (*Sinnlichkeit in Bild und Klang. Festschrift für Paul Hoffmann*, ed. Hansgerd Delbrück, Stuttgart, 1987). (Most contributions came from Germany.)
14 Paul Hoffmann's book *Symbolismus* (Munich, 1987) has become a standard work.
15 In 1997 the poets thanked Paul Hoffmann by contributing poems to the anthology *Dem Dichter des Lesens*, published in his honour on the occasion of his eightieth birthday (see note 7 above).
16 It seems fitting that *Dem Dichter des Lesens* includes poems contributed by five New Zealand poets: Lauris Edmond, Koenraad Kuiper, Bill Manhire, Vincent O'Sullivan, and Alex Scobie.

17

Gerda Bell

RENATE KOCH

The year is 1933, the place is Mainz, Germany. Gertrud Eichbaum (later to be known as Dr Gerda Bell) is confronted with a political situation that requires a grave decision: Hitler has come to power, and she is of Jewish ancestry. Although she had been confirmed in 1917 in the Christus-Kirche in Mainz and is a Christian by upbringing, she knows she will still be considered a Jew by the new regime.

Her life until then had been that of the daughter of a well-to-do manufacturer, Jewish by descent but baptised as a Lutheran, whose wife had seen to it that Gerda and her two brothers grew up in a household befitting their standing in the community. Much of our information about her early youth stems from the recollections of an old schoolfriend of hers, Dr Trude Klein, who is now aged 94 but remains bright and vivacious and still possesses a remarkable memory.[1] Dr Klein remembers:[2]

Gerda spent her childhood and youth with her family in Mainz. They lived in a beautiful home directly overlooking the Rhine. Her father was a shoe manufacturer, a quiet and agreeable gentleman. Her mother was artistically inclined and had many interests. She loved the theatre and going to concerts. Thus Gerda was already stimulated early in life. She occupied herself more with books on art than with children's books. In school she stood out with her knowledge, and she learned easily. German was her favourite subject. Students as well as teachers liked her. Starting in 1919, after the return of young teachers from service in the military or confinement as prisoners of war, new ideas were introduced into the schools that led to debate about the future.

Gerda Bell, 1921. *(R. Koch Collection)*

Literary circles were formed which met at her parents' house. When the weather was good, we all used to look down on the Rhine from the balcony and discuss the situation. This was the time when Gerda first began to put her ideas into writing. Articles of hers appeared in the *Mainzer Anzeiger*, but they appeared under a pseudonym and she kept total silence about them.[3]

Toward the end of our school years, the French occupation [of the Rhineland] caused problems for us pupils. During the celebration of her obtaining her *Abitur* [University Entrance] in 1923, she and I sang a duet, and her mother sang as a soprano soloist.[4] After obtaining our *Abitur*, we all pursued our own plans. Gerda went on to study German. Her uncle on her mother's side invited her to Prague, and she went to the university there. It was ten years before we met again. She seemed to be very agitated because she had not been accepted into the German school system as a teacher despite her excellent exam results and academic qualifications. The reason was simple: she was Jewish.

Gerda Bell, 1923.
(Eichbaum Collection, São Paulo)

Having been educated between the wars and before the rise of National Socialism in Germany, it came as a shock to her to be called a '*dreckiges Judemädche*' ('filthy Jewish girl').[5] Religion had never been discussed much at home and did not play an important part in her daily life. Her father had volunteered for service in World War I and had seen combat at the front. He, like most assimilated German Jews, felt totally integrated and saw himself as a German. This was one of the bitter ironies of Hitler's anti-Semitism: many officially designated as 'Jews' never thought of themselves as Jews, and had grown up as Catholics or Lutherans. It was only when the notorious 'Nuremberg Laws' of 1935 came into force did they find out that they were technically regarded as Jews.[6]

Gerda Eichbaum's academic career was just beginning. A curriculum vitae she submitted with her doctoral thesis[7] in 1929 summarises her academic achievements up to that point:

I, G.E. Eichbaum, of Lutheran faith, was born on 20 October 1903 in Mainz as the daughter of factory owner Adolf Eichbaum and his wife Else, née Altschul … From 1910 to 1920 I was a student at the Höhere Töchterschule [Higher Girls' School] in Mainz, and from 1920 to 1923 at the Studienanstalt [Institute of Studies] where I took my *Abitur* on 23 February 1923 … In 1924 I commenced my studies at the University of Heidelberg where I studied German, English, and Art History, and attended lectures given by Professors Gundolf, Hedicke, Hoops, Jaspers, Neumann, Panzer, von Waldberg (Heidelberg), Gierach, Grünwald … , Sauer (Prague) Clemen … , Rauch, Viëtor (Giessen) …

I passed my PhD oral examination on 23 June 1928 … then the examination for the Höheres Lehramt [graduate diploma in teaching] … I asked for temporary dispensation from the teaching profession and took the position of Private Assistant where I am still working at this time.

After finishing her doctorate in 1928, she first worked in Giessen with Professor Hermann Aubin for about two years and then went back to Mainz. She remembered these times sixty-one years later:[8]

From 1924 to 1928 I studied in Heidelberg, Bonn, Prague (at the German University), Giessen, and at summer school in Oxford, taking such subjects as German, English, and Art History. I graduated summa cum laude under Professor Viëtor in Giessen and finished my teaching diploma with an 'A'. Then I became assistant to Hermann Aubin, Professor of History in Giessen and Breslau. In 1932 I started my unpleasant final year as a *Referendarin* [teaching assistant] in Mainz.

Unpleasant it certainly was. She was transferred from one school to another, and between the beginning of October and mid December 1932 she taught English for a total of three weeks, German for two weeks, and history for one month—some of these concurrently. Then came a letter from the Ministry of Education, Darmstadt, dated 12 December 1932, which said that they were forwarding to her school her document of termination of her probationary year, effective from 18 December, because 'Fräulein Eichbaum [not *Dr* Eichbaum], by order of the school authority, has left the school'.[9] What it really meant, of course, was that she had been dismissed.

Her Jewish background clearly had a tremendous impact on her immediate situation, and this in turn had consequences that would affect her life long after 1933. She did not feel Jewish and resented it very much when she was called a Jewess in school. She seems to have been deeply hurt by it, and this might well explain why, later in life, she seldom acknowledged her Jewish background and even changed her name from Eichbaum to Bell.[10] The mystery as to why she chose the name 'Bell', however, now seems to have been solved. Gerda herself said that she took it because it sounded English and was short, but there also seems to have been a deeper symbolic reason. Dr Klein says:

During her secondary school days there was a teacher named Dr Bell. Gerda was in love with him. It was so obvious that the whole class giggled about it. That was just after 1918. He was rather left-wing politically, and brought new ideas into class. These were probably the inspiration for the articles in the Mainz newspaper. I think she took the name 'Bell' in deference to and in admiration of her former teacher.[11]

This view is shared by a later acquaintance, Frau Ursula Bell-Köhler from the Deutscher Akademischer Austauschdienst (German Academic Exchange Service), who now lives in Mainz. Gerda met her there after the war to discuss Gerda's proposal for a programme to be run by the DAAD called Studienaufenthalte ausländischer Wissenschaftler (Studies Abroad for Foreign Academics). They remained in touch for many years, not only because of the name Bell.[12]

But back in Mainz in 1932, Gerda had seen what was coming and what her future would be. Once she made her decision, action soon followed. In July 1933 she left for Italy and took a position as tutor with an aristocratic Italian family. During her stay in Italy, Gerda happened to read an advertisement that a girls' school in New Zealand was looking for a language teacher. She addressed her application simply to 'Woodford House, New Zealand'— the only part of the address she could remember—and somehow it arrived. She was offered the position, and came to New Zealand in 1936. At Woodford House she taught German, Latin, French, Italian, and the history of the English language, before being forced to resign as an 'enemy alien' in 1940, as indeed were many other German refugees in New Zealand, regardless of whether they were Jewish or not. Mary Varnham comments in the school's centenary publication *Beyond Blue Hills: One Hundred Years of Woodford House*:

Gerda Eichbaum (later changing her name to Gerda Bell) also went on to make a mark in her adopted land, first as a librarian, and then as a distinguished scholar at Victoria University … Following her departure from Woodford, she became a family cook. Erika Schorss, who visited her, would 'never forget the sight of Gerda, the high brainy person [*sic*], in someone's kitchen with an apron and a cooking spoon. We both laughed, it was so absurd'.[13]

But as Gerda later said herself, she bore New Zealand no grudge: it was 'nobody's fault, just politics'.[14] She wrote a booklet called *German for New Zealanders*, a handbook of German for the soldiers in the occupation forces in Germany, but was not permitted to put her name to it.

What was happening to her family around this time is best told in her own words:

Before the annexation of Czechoslovakia, my parents moved from Mainz to Prague (the home town of my mother) in the naive belief that they could escape persecution. But after the invasion of Czechoslovakia by Hitler, my mother and my brother were sent to the concentration camp in Theresienstadt, where all my Prague relatives ended up. My brother was shot 'while attempting to escape'. Only my father survived all the horrors, and spent his twilight years with my brother, a medical doctor who lived in Brazil … I have, as you can understand, from time to time a bad conscience that I did not do anything for the survival of my family but under the circumstances at that time, it was impossible.[15]

After the war, Gerda worked for seventeen years as a librarian in the Department of Education. C.E. Beeby, director of the department for thirteen of them, remembers that she introduced many new things, one of which was the periodical *Nga Pukapuka*, which appeared for many years.[16] During this period she also made a trip to Brazil to visit her remaining family—her widowed sister-in-law, who lived in São Paulo with her son Jan and daughter Katia.

Gerda Bell's academic career resumed when she was appointed to a post in Italian at Victoria University in 1962. In 1964, when the new German Department was formed, she was appointed lecturer in German and became senior lecturer in 1970, before retiring the following year. Gerda was one of the first members of the Wellington Goethe Society, which was founded in 1960, and was a regular guest speaker there for many years, giving talks on such subjects as Franz Marc and 'The Image of Easter in Art'.

She led a very active intellectual life, pursuing her literary and musical interests, and teaching German, Italian, and French; after her retirement, she also tutored students at her home at all hours of the day, charging low fees that everyone could afford. She published a number of articles and books throughout her life, but her biography of Ernst Dieffenbach[17] occupied her the most. She always felt it was her greatest achievement. Before its publication in 1976, she had already published several articles and essays about this man—an explorer, medical doctor, and natural scientist from Giessen who had been a political refugee in England before coming to New Zealand in 1839 as a naturalist for the New Zealand Company. She must have felt a certain kinship with him—as a refugee, a resident of Giessen, and as an academic, philosopher, and writer. There were so many parallels to explore.

Her knowledge of literature and her appreciation of art were extensive, and her various publications on Dürer, Petrarch, von Heiseler, Büchner, and Rodin bear testimony to her wide range of interests. In the twenty-one years that I knew her, I never found her to be short of an informed answer. She started a German conversation group that came to be known as 'the Gerda Group' and still exists today. We all marvelled at her knowledge of the Renaissance. She seldom spoke about day-to-day matters and never about money. Her disdain for anything to do with numbers[18] once led to a remark by one of the group's members: 'Gerda, you know everything, but nothing about money.' We all believed that, because she lived so frugally. We were therefore very surprised to learn after her death that she had left an estate of more than a million Marks. It seems to have been German restitution money for her father's property, which might be why she was reluctant to use it. Dr Klein, on the other hand, with whom she stayed during her first trip back in Germany, had the impression that Gerda was well off, as she paid for all their concert and theatre tickets, and gave her a necklace in appreciation when she left.[19]

It is idle to speculate about the fate of Gerda Bell had the events of 1933 not taken place. She might have become a famous scholar or a distinguished teacher. She still achieved both to a degree. It was always her vast knowledge, her earnestness in mental pursuits, and her dedicated teaching that impressed her friends and acquaintances. Year after year, her students would come back to see her, just to visit. Correspondence with her friends also went on for many years, as Gerda was a prolific letterwriter. She loved to have guests, and entertained at home well into her eighties, yet she liked it just as much to be invited to a party at the German or Italian embassies. Even in her final illness, she enjoyed receiving visitors daily in hospital. With her mental faculties sharp to the last minute, she resisted pain and made her usual humorous remarks right to the end.

To show her thanks to and appreciation of the German Department of Victoria University in particular, and to young New Zealanders in the higher pursuit of German culture and literature in general, she made provision in her will for a scholarship of $10,000 to be awarded annually for ten years. It is to be called the Dr Gerda Bell Scholarship. In keeping with her lifelong interest in German literature and music, the scholarship is to be awarded to 'New Zealand-born or New Zealand naturalized students of German at Victoria University of Wellington of good character who, in order to complete their BA Honours Degree, submit a research essay on a topic of German Language or Literature or on German literature as a component of Comparative Literature or Music'.[20]

The Federal Republic of Germany had recognised her promotion of things German by awarding her the German Bundesverdienstkreuz (Order of Merit) First Class in 1982 in recognition of the cultural ties she forged between the two countries. Gerda Bell, who died in 1992, had always inspired young New Zealanders to learn German and thus encouraged links between the two peoples. She was proud of New Zealand, and New Zealand can be proud of her.

Gerda Bell at German *Bundesverdienstkreuz* investiture, 1982. (*R. Koch Collection*)

1 Another important source of information is a letter written by Gerda to Oberstudienrat Reinhard Frenzel, who is now at the Frauenlob Gymnasium (grammar school) in Mainz, the former Höhere Töchterschule (Higher Girls' School) at which Gerda was a pupil. The school was celebrating its centenary, and he was carrying out some research on former students; in this connection, Gerda had been asked to provide some information about herself. Herr Frenzel graciously made her correspondence available to me.

2 Information from Dr Klein, which will be referred to throughout this chapter, is taken from correspondence from February to July 1996, as well as from an interview conducted in Freiburg on 30 August 1996.

3 Only during a visit to Germany after the war did she confess to Dr Klein that she had actually written them herself.

4 Frau Eichbaum was an accomplished singer who sang first soprano in the Mainzer Liedertafel, a professional singing group.

5 Letter to Reinhard Frenzel [note 1].

6 These laws required that every German must have an *Ahnenpass*, a certificate of ancestry to the fourth generation, which had to be produced by everybody in any dealings with officialdom—registering births, enrolling at school, obtaining a marriage licence, making job applications—to prove an Aryan heritage.

7 The thesis was dedicated to her grandparents, Theodore and Ottilie Altschul.

8 Letter to Reinhard Frenzel [note 1].

9 Communication from the Ministerium für Kultus und Bildungswesen, Darmstadt, dated 12 December 1932.

10 She changed her name in 1959.

11 See note 2.

12 Correspondence with U. Bell-Köhler from February to May 1996.

13 Mary Varnham, *Beyond Blue Hills: One Hundred Years of Woodford House* (Havelock North, 1994), p. 104. Erika Schorss was a fellow German–Jewish refugee and one-time colleague of Gerda Eichbaum at Woodford House; she had taught music there briefly before being dismissed around the same time as Gerda. Schorss became a foundation member of the National Orchestra in 1947.

14 Unpublished interview between Gerda Bell and historian Ann Beaglehole, quoted in Varnham [note 13], p. 104.

15 Letter to Reinhard Frenzel [note 1].

16 Forty years later, I met students at her place who had been introduced to a library while under her tutelage and who never forgot the experience.

17 *Ernest Dieffenbach: Rebel and Humanist* (Palmerston North, 1976).

18 Commenting on Gerda's aversion to figures, Dr Klein (see note 2) relates how once, during an oral examination, a question concerning circles arose, and Gerda dismissed this with the remark 'Mathematik interessiert mich nicht' ('Maths does not interest me').

19 See note 2.

20 Will of Gerda Bell (May 1988), and codicils sections 1–5 (1988–92).

18

Werner Droescher

NORMAN FRANKE

In *Odyssee eines Lehrers*, Werner Droescher's autobiography written at the Wilderland community on the Coromandel Peninsula shortly before his death, the parallels between his adventurous life and the first hero of Western literature become apparent. Werner Droescher's whole life was a search for a place of harmony: harmony between human beings and nature as well as among humans. He was looking for a place where individual freedom and solidarity could be realised.

Werner Droescher.
(M. Sutton Collection)

The most important stations of this modern-day Ulysses' journeys around the world were New Zealand, Germany, Spain, England, and Australia. Like the ancient hero of literature, Werner was not only driven by the historical events of his time, he also shaped them. In many ways the story of his life is typical of that of a critical intellectual of his generation. In his autobiography he grants us important insights into his concept of self and into the epoch in which he lived. In this biographical sketch, derived from his autobiography and interviews with his friends and colleagues, I have set out to reconstruct Werner's life anti-chronologically with the emphasis on his time in New Zealand.

At the time he built his own house in the commune of Wilderland, Werner was still 'half a member of the Establishment'. His move to Wilderland nonetheless marks his disillusionment with big-city life and his Establishment role as an Auckland University academic. The community seemed to be the place where a true partnership with others and an ecological life in harmony with nature could be realised. It also enabled Werner to leave behind the ruthless competitiveness and material orientation of the metropolis. Of the political and academic establishment, Werner wrote: 'No one questioned whether society and the state were still any good. There was some talk about the ecological self-annihilation of the human race, but not enough was done to stop this madness. ... The whole complex of government and administration is involved. The whole range of political decisions contradicts reason. Is there any alternative?'[1]

Typically, his own reaction was to live his life in a manner consistent with his fundamental critique of society—an early example of the now-popular slogan: think globally, act locally. This attitude also became apparent during his time as a lecturer in German at the University of Auckland. A large number of his students and colleagues admired Werner for living up to his principles. Not only did he teach the traditional canon of German literature, he also endeavoured to draw students' attention to (then) new and controversial authors like Bachmann and Enzensberger. Departmental conflict soon emerged over his teaching methods and style. Fluent in five languages, Werner dismissed the outdated word-by-word translation technique. He organised highly popular drama productions in which everything from the auditions to the ticket sales was done in German. His pedagogics were based on his student years at the Pädagogische Hochschule Altona, in Hamburg, in the early 1930s. Students were to be treated as partners. They had to define their own interests and learning strategies. The ultimate test for acquired knowledge was life. With his revolutionary teaching methods, Werner influenced a whole generation of New Zealand German teachers and Germanists, among them Martin Sutton, Alan Kirkness, and Stan Jones. Werner was also an accomplished linguist. His dialectological study of the German-speaking colony of Puhoi is still unsurpassed.

Towards the end of the 1960s, international student protest reached Auckland University. Young lecturers in the Department of Germanic Languages and Literature found themselves in opposition to the head of the department, whose achievements in establishing the department were unquestioned. Werner described the conflict as a typical example of a generation conflict. Although of the older generation himself, he supported his younger colleagues. He argued that the patriarchal system, although possibly well intended, was ultimately bad for the development of young colleagues and students. He saw clear parallels to the political situation in post-war Germany, where superficial success and sheer power was often put before self-reflection and partnership. Advancing arguments of the Frankfurt School,[2] Werner increasingly viewed universities as agencies of the state. His health deteriorated because of the conflict, so Werner decided to redirect his energies towards other important areas of social commitment. He worked with Polynesian immigrants in Auckland and taught German and Spanish at Paremoremo prison near Auckland.

Werner's time at Auckland and Wilderland represent his second period in New Zealand. His first (1940–48) was spent here with his first wife, Greville Texidor, who was born in England. They met during the Spanish Civil War. Before she met Werner, Greville had worked as a film actor, a dancer in a chorus line, and a contortionist's assistant. Her great beauty won her the attention of painters like Mark Gertler and Augustus John. Unfortunately, her great talent as a poet went unrecognised. A collection of her short stories, *In Fifteen Minutes You Can Say a Lot*, which matches Hemingway's prose in language and content, was not published until 1987.

With the help of her mother, Editha Greville Prideaux, and their Quaker friends, Werner and Greville managed to leave war-torn Europe. The refugees' first years in New Zealand were marked by economic hardship, but the practical-minded Werner enjoyed working as a gardener and share-milker and later as a carpenter. He was dismissed as a paramedic from the Civil Defence Service because he held a German passport. However, he was admitted to the then Auckland University College, where he eventually graduated with an MA.

The 1940s saw Greville and Werner in the centre of a group of artists and reformers with many links to the North Shore Circle.[3] When still in Paparoa they were introduced to Frank Sargeson by Len Salter. Sargeson and Greville became friends for life. In his autobiography Sargeson remembered the harassment to which Greville and Werner were subjected simply because they both held German citizenship: 'I saw the bedroom window that looked towards the harbour and because of Greville Texidor's German husband the local cop had one night hidden himself in the fern outside, just in case light signals were made to enemy craft at sea ...'[4] Sargeson describes Werner as very communicative. 'He told me about his young life in Germany—until Hitler. And then his serious and troubling decision ... to cut himself off from the destinies of the German people.'[5] Unlike Werner, the sensitive Greville found it almost impossible to come to terms with the psychological and social consequences of the war. Sargeson recalls an afternoon when they took a stroll along the beach and it became obvious to him that Greville lived close to the brink. She ended her life by suicide in Australia in 1964, many years after she and Werner had separated.

Towards the beginning of the war, Werner and his friend Ian Hamilton made plans for the foundation of a school based on modern pedagogic principles. Although the land had already been acquired when Hamilton was detained for his pacifism, the project came to an abrupt end. Werner became a teacher at Takapuna Grammar School, where Mr Dellow, the headmaster, made a great impression on him. Working as a language and sports teacher, Werner made a lot of innovations. He also received his first teaching jobs at Auckland University College. In 1946 he was naturalised as a New Zealand citizen. Yet, despite great improvements in their living conditions, Greville and Werner were overcome by wanderlust and moved to Australia. The years in Australia were Werner's 'black years'. He worked in a camp for refugees and later became a teacher, but his involvement with the trade unions subjected him to harassment. In the 1950s he also spent some time in London as a chauffeur and in Spain as a travel guide and as a lecturer at Barcelona University. Living in Spain during the Franco dictatorship was risky, because Werner feared the discovery of his involvement in the Spanish Civil War.

Werner had left Nazi Germany in 1933 and had gone to Tossa de Mar because he was a strong opponent of the *Gleichschaltung*[6] of the education system in his home country. Together with Greville, he fought on the side of the Anarcho-Syndicalists against the Fascists at the Aragon front, where they experienced the first systematic air raids by the German Condor Legion. They endorsed and lived the principles of philosophical anarchism: self-determination, solidarity, and spontaneity. From the front, Werner and Greville made trips to London where, together with their American Quaker friend Alfred Jacob, they organised food supplies for starving children in Spain. They also became directors of a home for orphans from Madrid. In an interview, given many years later in New Zealand, Werner described their time in the Spanish Civil War thus:

We realized that [anarcho-syndicalists] were people who really lived up to their ... ideas, that is, their behaviour toward each other was real social behaviour and ... that was a great discovery. ... At the end of the war ... I was really physically and emotionally quite done ... because [a free society] had been the great utopia. ... We felt let down by all the democratic—so-called democratic—governments in Europe, because we very rightly said, we are also fighting the fascism in Germany and Italy, we are fighting your battle against that ...[7]

When the Spanish Civil War was over, Werner went back to Germany. He was interrogated by the Gestapo but was able to conceal his activities in Spain. For a short while he taught languages at the Berlitz School in Hamburg. But during the Munich Crisis he escaped to England where he worked with the Movement for the Care of Children from Germany. In Ipswich he became the director of Barnham House, a home for Jewish children who had escaped the terror in Germany. When World War II started he was sent to an internment camp. As bad luck would have it, he ended up in a building where supporters of the Nazis were detained. This alone was reason for many 'left-wingers' in the camp to shun him. Werner, on the other hand, made an extra effort to listen to individuals' stories and reflected on the strange need of so many people to categorise and qualify others.

Where did the strength that enabled Werner to oppose the labelling of people in an age of ideologies come from? How did he manage to keep his pedagogic optimism? In *Odyssee eines Lehrers* he tells us about his own years as a student in Hamburg, which inspired him for the rest of his life. The Pädagogische Hochschule was one of the few democratic teachers' colleges that maintained the spirit of the young Weimar Republic. More specifically, Werner fondly remembered individual teachers who became his role models. Finally, he maintained that it is the opportunities for cooperation, debate, and friendship that distinguish an educational institution.

In the process of the autobiographical reconstruction of his life in Wilderland, Werner recalls the years in authoritarian schools of his own youth as well as brief respites from them on hiking tours along the rivers Main and Neckar. He remembers his longing for living together harmoniously with other people and a simple life close to nature. In Wilderland he particularly enjoyed gardening. Images of the vineyards and fruit trees of his south German childhood years mingle with those of the citrus trees and the tree ferns in Wilderland, which display similar patterns to the stars visible on a clear night sky over the Coromandel.

1   Werner Droescher, *Odyssee eines Lehrers* (Munich, 1976), p. 140 (my translation).
2   Frankfurt School: a philosophical school based on the writings of Theodor Adorno (1903–69). Closed by the Nazis, it was reopened after the war, and later influenced the 1968 student movement.
3   The North Shore Circle was a loose association of artists and intellectuals, based on Auckland's North Shore, who developed and promoted the arts in a characteristically New Zealand way.
4   Frank Sargeson, *Sargeson* (Auckland, 1981), p. 347.
5   Sargeson [note 4], p. 347.
6   *Gleichschaltung*: the various political and legal measures taken by the National Socialists in Germany to suppress political opponents and freedom of the press. Under these measures, the education system was reorganised to function as an agent of fascist ideology.
7   Werner Droescher, taking part in a 1977 Auckland University seminar (02.102) entitled 'Experiences and Assessments of the Civil War'.

19

Sir Karl Popper

NELSON WATTIE

Although less well known among non-specialists than Albert Einstein, Ludwig Wittgenstein, or Bertrand Russell, Sir Karl Popper was, in fact, comparable with them: he was one of the greatest and most influential thinkers of the twentieth century. His term of residence in New Zealand was relatively short—some eight years—but it covered the time when he was writing some of his finest work, and it left a lasting legacy in the country.

Born in 1902, Karl Raimund Popper was of a slightly later generation than the astonishing wealth of geniuses who made Vienna the birthplace of the twentieth century, but he grew up in their shadow and in a stimulating environment where the Vienna Circle of logical positivists provided a trying ground for his ideas. They were, however, fundamentally different from theirs. Otto Neurath, a member of the circle, called him 'the official opposition'.[1] His father's library, well stocked with law books, Greek and Latin texts, and a selection of the world's greatest philosophers, as well as 'the standard authors of German, French, English, Russian, and Scandinavian literature',[2] was the main source of his education. Marx, Engels, Lassalle, and other social analysts as well as some great pacifist thinkers were included in the boy's reading. Popper's father, a lawyer, historian, and poet, encouraged his intellectual interests while his mother stimulated his love of music; composition was to be one of his later accomplishments.

As a youth, Popper was first a Marxist and then joined the Social Democrat Party. In more mature years, he was allied to no party, but much of his writing, especially on social themes, was coloured by the debates on morality and strategy that occupied his youth. The difficulty of formulating the scientific method and defining scientific thought also occupied him, and even here his solutions can be interpreted as anti-dictatorial, because they avoid imposing one thinker's concepts on another. Critical thinking, applied to all ideas, even the most firmly established and revered, is at the core of his work. His book *Logik der Forschung* (1934), which was opposed to the dogmatism of the Vienna Circle, was greeted with some astonishment, and remains provocative today. Not until a quarter of a century later, in 1959, did it appear in English, when it was called *The Logic of Scientific Discovery*, but before then many New Zealanders had had the good fortune to learn of its ideas through the lectures Popper gave while living in Christchurch.

Popper could see that the Nazis would soon be virtually unopposed in his native Austria, and determined to leave before they took power—a decision that no doubt saved his life. In 1935 he moved to Oxford, where he conversed with Schrödinger, Russell and, notoriously, Wittgenstein, who would later threaten him with a poker (or merely wave it to emphasise a point, depending on who is reporting the incident) during a heated discussion between the two at Cambridge in October 1946.[3] However, Popper then accepted a position at Canterbury University College in Christchurch. Even in England, he found that there was no real understanding of the threat Hitler presented, and in New Zealand this was even more clearly the case: 'There was no harm in the people: like the British they were decent, friendly, and well disposed. But the continent of Europe was infinitely remote. … I had the impression that New Zealand was the best-governed country in the world, and the most easily governed.'[4]

Popper always had pleasant memories of the people he met in New Zealand, some of whom became lifelong friends, but he had a sterner view of academic values and the administration of the university. Friends he records include[5] Hugh Parton, Frederick White, Bob Allan, Colin Simkin, Alan Reed, George Roth, Margaret Dalziel, John Findlay, and John Eccles; a chemist, a physicist, a geologist, an economist, a lawyer, a radiation physicist, a classicist, a philosopher, and a neurophysiologist respectively, all of whom benefited from his conversation as he did from theirs. This in itself gives some sense of the range of Popper's interests and the intense activity of his mind.

One colleague he found less likeable was the head of his own department, Sutherland, who, although Professor of Philosophy, was more interested in social psychology. Long before, Popper had studied under the great psychologist and linguist Karl Bühler, who supervised his doctoral dissertation, but he had rejected such studies in favour of broader accounts of the nature of the world. 'Despite tension in the department, Popper's impact on the academic life of the college was greater than that of any other academic person before or since.'[6] He seems to have paid little attention to the prescribed syllabus, narrowly focused on Aristotelian logic as it was, and to have lectured on the topics nearest to his own interests. Popper's opening talk to his first seminar in New Zealand was later published in *Mind* (1940), and is now chapter 15 of *Conjectures and Refutations* (1963).[7] The result was that students came in from all faculties, not to learn for their examinations but 'for enlightenment and the sheer intellectual joy of exploring the unknown with him'.[8] I have met several of the students who crowded his lectures; their later lives were spent in a variety of occupations, but all remembered with affection and even excitement the stimulus they had received from Popper. It can be assumed that his influence was felt in many situations and at various social levels at least for a generation of New Zealand life—indirectly, perhaps, much longer. One of his students, for example, was Peter Munz, who, as Professor of History at Victoria University of Wellington, was to influence more generations of students.

More specifically, his presence stimulated awareness of the need for resources and effort to be expended on research in universities. It might seem obvious that universities carry on research, but the careers of both Popper and von Zedlitz (discussed in chapter 15) demonstrate that it was

Karl Popper (right) with Mrs Popper and Henry Dan Broadhead at a waterfall, Akaroa, 1941. *(Alexander Turnbull Library, Ref. no. F-139835-1/2)*

not. Thirty-four years after von Zedlitz collaborated with colleagues on a pamphlet calling for a research culture in the university, Popper and a group of reformers at Canterbury (as well as Eccles at Otago and Forder at Auckland) published a pamphlet entitled *Research and the University* (1945) pointing out the community's need for the university to be a research institution and the steps that should be taken to reach that end. 'For the first time there was an appreciation of the proposition that the real business of a university is with the borders of the unknown and that the community should support the men who crossed them.'[9] Popper's recollection of his personal situation was painful:

I had a desperately heavy teaching load, and the University authorities not only were unhelpful, but tried actively to make difficulties for me. I was told that I should be well advised not to publish anything while in New Zealand, and that any time spent on research was a theft from the working time as a lecturer for which I was being paid. The situation was such that without the moral support of my friends in New Zealand I could hardly have survived.[10]

Even today, anti-intellectual and anti-academic attitudes are widespread in New Zealand and colour the universities' decision to fund work by student numbers with scant attention to research. A glance at the careers of von Zedlitz and Popper shows that throughout the twentieth century these hostile attitudes to academic research have been typical, and Popper's words can be salutary, even today. In this respect, too, his influence might continue.

Despite these disadvantages and the huge lecturing programme Popper took on outside the university, it was in New Zealand, in fact, that he wrote two of the books most readily associated with his name: *The Open Society and Its Enemies* (1945) and *The Poverty of Historicism* (1957, based on articles written much earlier). The concept of 'historicism' is basic to both. Any of the many theories, such as those of Plato, Hegel, and Marx, which suggest that the course of history is predetermined and/or inevitable, is anathema to Popper, partly because the free exercise of the critical mind seems stifled by such theories and partly because they conflict with the idea that is fundamental to all of Popper's work.

In an essay of 1937, he expressed this idea in the formula P1→TT→ EE →P2, where P1 is a problem to be solved, TT is a Tentative Trial towards its solution, EE is Error Elimination from the results of the trial, and P2 is the new problem, which can then be subjected to the same—consequently endless—process. In his early essays and in *Logik der Forschung*, this concept is applied to the progress of scientific thought. Such progress is not inductive, as the Vienna Circle and most practising scientists believed—many still do—but rather deductive, following a leap of the mind that suggests a solution, which must then be rigorously tested by ruthlessly critical thought: error elimination.[11]

Rather than develop constantly new theories, Popper spent much of his intellectual life applying this basic insight to more and more fields of human thought and activity, as well as to animal behaviour and the evolution of life itself. In the books written in New Zealand—which Popper called his 'war effort'—the basic idea is applied to social and political history. Not by a gradual departure from an idea (as Plato suggests) nor by approaching a goal (such as that of Marx), nor yet under the power of a guiding 'Spirit' (such as Hegel's) but rather by trial and the elimination of recognised error can human societies evolve.

A picture of Popper in New Zealand is provided by his friend and Nobel Prize winner Sir John Eccles in the latter's article, 'My living dialogue with Popper'.[12] Eccles arrived in Dunedin in 1944 to be Professor of Physiology and 'heard marvellous stories … about the academic stir that was being made by a philosopher, Karl Popper, in Canterbury University College at Christchurch. … It was a great and welcome surprise, as I had regarded my New Zealand venture as an academic exile after my many years at Oxford'. Eccles invited Popper to Dunedin:

It seems incredible today that one could make such an invitation with an offer only of private hospitality (at my home) and a second-class railway fare for an intensive course of five lectures! … The train was very late, so the lecture perforce had to start about thirty minutes late to a crowded audience of at least five hundred in the largest lecture theatre of the University. It was a unique occasion for the University, so remote and in wartime. … I was an immediate convert to the Popperian message. … I fully appreciated the devastating attack by Popper on the inductive method of science, in which up till then I had naively believed. … The aftermath of that intensive week was that between

Karl and me there arose an intimate and devoted friendship that has shone on us without cloud ever since. … I delighted in the prominence given to creative imagination. Science had become an exciting adventure and not a routine collection of facts with cautious hypotheses. … After that memorable visit of May 1945 there was an enormous correspondence between us. … In addition we met in Christchurch on the occasions when I was passing through on the way to conferences in Wellington. Karl would meet me on arrival at Christchurch station and travel with me to the harbour at Lyttelton, whence I would depart by ship with conversation continued as long as possible from ship to shore! I particularly remember one such occasion when we were deep in discussion until the ship departed beyond shouting distance. Two days later, when the ship arrived at 6:30 am at Lyttelton, I was amazed to find Karl on the wharf for a renewal of the conversation that continued on the drive to his lovely home in the Cashmere Hills for breakfast and so to the train departing from Christchurch to Dunedin.

The 'Body–Mind Problem' was one of Popper's major philosophical concerns, and dialogue with Eccles, a world authority on brain structure and functioning, was very fruitful for him. Years later, Popper and Eccles published their large collaborative book, *The Self and Its Brain* (1977).

The emigration of Jews from Germany and Austria under Hitler brought an intellectual and cultural impoverishment to both of those countries as well as much pain to individuals. But there was an up-side as well: the intellectual and cultural lives of other countries, notably the United States, were greatly enriched. Through Popper and several other remarkable and charismatic figures, this enrichment also occurred in New Zealand.

1 Quoted in Bryan Magee, *Popper* (London, 1973), p. 11.

2 Karl Popper, *Unended Quest: An Intellectual Autobiography* (London, 1976), p. 11.

3 An account of this incident can be found in Popper [note 2], pp. 122f.

4 Popper [note 2], p. 112.

5 Ibid.

6 W. J. Gardner et al., *A History of the University of Canterbury 1873–1973* (Christchurch, 1973), p. 262.

7 Popper [note 2], p. 222, n. 166.

8 Gardner et al. [note 6], p. 263.

9 Gardner et al. [note 6], p. 307.

10 Popper [note 2], p. 119.

11 The 1937 essay was revised to become 'What is dialectic?', i.e. chapter 15 of *Conjectures and Refutations: The Growth of Scientific Knowledge* (London, 1963). For general accounts of the theory, see Popper [note 2], pp. 132–5; his *Objective Knowledge: An Evolutionary Approach* (Oxford, 1972), pp. 174–7; and Douglas E. Williams, *Truth, Hope and Power: The Thought of Karl Popper* (Toronto, 1989), p. 61. A collection of Popper's essays applying it to many fields is *The Myth of the Framework: In Defence of Science and Rationality*, edited by M.A. Notturno (London & New York, 1994).

12 Paul Levinson (ed.), *In Pursuit of Truth: Essays in Honour of Karl Popper's 80th Birthday* (Atlantic Highlands, NJ, & Sussex, 1982), pp. 221–36. The following works were also used as sources in the writing of this chapter: Robert John Ackerman, *The Philosophy of Karl Popper* (Amherst, MA, 1976); T.E. Burke, *The Philosophy of Popper* (Manchester, 1983); Gregory Currie and Alan Musgrave (ed.), *Popper and the Human Sciences* (Dordrecht, 1985); Robert D'Amico, *Historicism and Knowledge* (New York & London, 1989); Anthony O'Hear, *Karl Popper* (London & Boston, 1980); and Colin Simkin, *Popper's Views on Natural and Social Science* (Leiden & New York, 1993).

20

Wolfgang Rosenberg

GERHARD TRÄBING

When he retired in 1980 as Reader in Economics at the University of Canterbury in Christchurch, Wolfgang Rosenberg was honoured with a collection of essays by colleagues and fellow academics.[1] In his foreword to this *Festschrift*, Bill (later Sir Wallace) Rowling, Prime Minister of New Zealand from 1974 to 1975, and a student at Canterbury himself after his return from war service in 1947, credited Rosenberg with having exerted a 'singular influence on the development of New Zealand economic policy. His contribution has always been vigorous, independent, and above all, related to his personal concern for the wellbeing of people'.[2] The fundamentals of Rosenberg's beliefs, and in particular his concern for the welfare of others, were something he had brought with him from Europe to New Zealand— a land he had once seen described, before his arrival here in 1937, as an experiment in 'Socialism in the South Seas'.[3]

Wolfgang Rosenberg was born in Berlin on 4 January 1915. He was still a baby when his father, a lawyer by profession, was engaged after a period of active service in the German army to act as a German–French interpreter at a prisoner-of-war camp near Darmstadt in 1918.[4] At the age of 5, Wolfgang was sent to the Französisches Gymnasium (French College) at Berlin, where his older brother Gerhard was also a pupil. Founded in the late seventeenth century by exiled French Huguenots, the school already looked back on a long and distinguished history, and enjoyed a special character all of its own—a character that persists to this day. French was the language of instruction in the upper forms, and at the time the young Wolfgang was a pupil there, Latin and Greek were also taught to pupils from the ages of 12 and 14 respectively. English was available as an option during the last two years.

Having been admitted to preparatory classes as a 5-year-old, Wolfgang was able to advance to the equivalent of form 1 at the age of 8 and to matriculate at the age of 17—always a year ahead of his peers. Highly motivated, he was able to cope, while still only 15 and 16 years old, with extracurricular courses that included, among other things, an introduction to Hegelian thought as well as seminars on Goethe's *Faust*. He also enjoyed rowing and, through this pastime, forged a close friendship with three classmates, all of whom, like him, later had to emigrate for political or racial reasons and then went on to become eminent academics in their chosen fields. They were Peter Franck, who became a professor of economics, first in the

United States and then in Beirut; Albert Hirschman, now an economic sociologist based in Princeton; and Helmut Mühsam, professor of demography at the University of Jerusalem.[5] It was around this time, while Wolfgang was still at school, that he joined the Sozialistische Arbeiter Jugend (Socialist Workers' Youth Movement) or SAJ.

Germany, at this time, was in a state of economic and political chaos. The economy, still reeling from the hyper-inflation of the 1920s, was now feeling the disastrous consequences of the Great Depression, and supporters of opposing political parties were locked in irreconcilably bitter (and often violent) conflict with one another. Having gained the German equivalent of University Entrance, Rosenberg was initially apprenticed to the largest state-owned bank in Berlin, but was removed from this, his first position, in 1934 for racial reasons, the Nazis having come to power the year before. Despite this setback, however, this free-thinking son of Jewish parents managed to finish his apprenticeship at a small private bank, and later joined the staff of M.M. Warburg & Co., international bankers of Hamburg and Berlin.

It was here, as he was compiling the daily news summary for the firm, that his attention was caught by an item under the heading 'Socialism in the South Seas', which described the economic and social reforms being introduced by New Zealand's first Labour government.[6] This was not the first time that Rosenberg had heard of this distant land in the South Pacific. Some years earlier, in 1923, his family had received a postcard with the comment 'This is a country without beggars' from a schoolfriend of his mother who had married a New Zealander and settled in Wellington.[7] The then 8-year-old Wolfgang had promptly made up his mind to travel to New Zealand, and the bulletin that he happened to read more than a decade later served only to strengthen his resolve to leave the Fatherland and realise his boyhood ambition. More than forty years later, Rosenberg would make the

Wolfgang Rosenberg (left) with Helmut Mühsam, Albert Hirschman, and Peter Franck, 1931. *(Rosenberg Collection)*

following observation about the enormous contrasts that he noticed on his arrival in New Zealand:

When I arrived in New Zealand—on the 28th June, 1937—from Hitler Germany, I was struck by the contrast between a nation (which I had left) drunk with nationalist fervour and one which looked at Great Britain as the mother country, the monarchy as its inspiration and events in Europe as its main pre-occupation. At that time, this was a wonderful relief. New Zealanders seemed to be able to look at themselves as part of the world rather than as its centre, and consequently there was a wonderful atmosphere of relaxation.

There was another wonderful contrast which I perceived. In Germany there had been six million unemployed when I left—some of them by 1937 re-employed in the fury of re-armament. ... [U]nemployment here was overcome ... The country was at work—there was optimism and pride around me.[8]

Friends of the family helped to find him a job with the Alliance Finance Company (the hire purchase finance arm of the Ford Motor Company), but as the post office experienced the utmost difficulty in deciphering his handwriting, he was subsequently advised, politely but firmly, to leave.[9] Over the following months and indeed for a few years to come, he held a variety of jobs, which included work for a wire importer, a job in a radio factory, and even milking cows in the country at Pahiatua.[10]

He combined all these occupations with part-time studies in economics and accountancy at Victoria University College in Wellington, where he was elected to the Students' Association executive and served as its honorary treasurer for two years, and eventually graduated Master of Commerce with first-class honours in 1943. One of his fellow members of the executive was his wife-to-be, Ann Eichelbaum.[11] Following the example of fellow refugee Henry Lang, Rosenberg applied and was permitted to join the Royal New Zealand Air Force in 1944 and served as a member of its ground staff.[12] When demobilised, he married Ann Eichelbaum, and soon after was appointed Lecturer in Economics at Canterbury University College in Christchurch.[13] Promotions to senior lecturer and reader followed, and by the time he retired in 1980, Wolfgang Rosenberg was regarded as one of the best-known academics in New Zealand.

While Rosenberg's first publication—'The evolution of central banking during the crisis' (1938)[14]—was directed at a select few, many of his subsequent publications were written more with a wider political audience in mind than a purely academic one. In the period 1947–51—the early years of the Cold War—Rosenberg sought, in his weekly contributions to the Labour Party's *Standard*, to counter 'the tendentious propaganda that was spreading throughout the Western world'.[15] These articles, written under the pseudonym of 'Criticus', incurred the wrath of the then Prime Minister, Peter Fraser, and led to much pressure being applied—unsuccessfully, as it happened—on the paper's editor to suppress his outspoken contributor.[16]

In 1950, after the Chancellor of the University of New Zealand, Sir David Smith, had spoken at a meeting of Senate on the question of who should and should not be appointed to academic positions, Rosenberg was moved to publish an article in reply in *Landfall* entitled 'Freedom in the university'.[17] Although intended as a response to what he saw as an attack on academic freedom of thought and speech, Rosenberg's essay is notable for the way it reveals his idea of a university's function, the qualities that should be encouraged in its research students, and of the role of the university teacher.[18] 'To exclude men from the universities who are critical of our existing social and moral institutions could mean a threat to good teaching', he wrote.

Good academic teaching is calculated to rouse a desire to probe into the very foundations of knowledge. Having learned from his teacher how to search for truth, the student is encouraged to set out for research. This means that successful instruction in the method of scientific thought will stimulate the student to go over the field of learning again and to try and see for himself, independently, how false or true the theories are which have been handed on to him. In this process of research the student will bring out not only new or hitherto unknown facts, but new interpretations, and some of these (particularly if they lie in the realm of the social sciences) may be shocking and distasteful to the public at large.[19]

The essay, which received national acclaim (and some criticism), helped Rosenberg to become known as a defender of academic freedom and independence in this country, and just a few years later, he would become one of the people instrumental in founding the Canterbury Council for Civil Liberties.

In the years that followed, Rosenberg became known as a prolific writer of articles and reviews, a progressive economist, and an adviser on trade union matters. Study leaves abroad widened his own horizons and, indirectly, those of his students and readers. He enrolled at the London School of Economics for a term when on study leave in 1952, and worked at the Bank for International Settlements at Basel under Per Jacobsson, who later became managing director of the International Monetary Fund. He also attended the Vienna Congress of the International Peace Council as a private observer.[20]

Towards the end of the 1950s, Rosenberg initiated and developed a plan to establish an independent journal to replace the Auckland periodical *Here and Now*. The fruit of this idea was *New Zealand Monthly Review*, which came into being in 1960. H. Winston Rhodes was its editor, but Rosenberg was acknowledged as 'the chief guiding force behind it'[21] and remained so for many years until the journal eventually ceased publication in 1996. The *Review* published numerous articles and contributions written by Rosenberg, and his series of monographs on economic matters entitled *What Every New Zealander Should Know* was published by or in conjunction with the New Zealand Monthly Review Society.[22]

Growing up in Berlin in the 1920s and being close to young working-class members of socialist youth groups had provided a balance to Rosenberg's predominantly conservative education. Having seen mass unemployment at first hand, he brought with him to New Zealand the belief in the necessity of employment for all and expressed this conviction in his first book, *Full Employment* (1960), which sought to answer the question raised in the book's subtitle, namely: 'Can the New Zealand economic miracle last?' In this book Rosenberg predicted that with the abolition of import controls, the structurally weak, import-thirsty New Zealand economy would have to revert to the conventional form of capitalist economy with its fluctuating levels of mass unemployment.

In 1961, when it was announced by the new National Minister of Finance, Harry Lake, that New Zealand would apply to join the International Monetary Fund, Rosenberg was alarmed at what he saw as the resulting loss of the country's economic independence and published a warning against such a move. His pamphlet, *What Every New Zealander Should Know About the International Monetary Fund* (1961), became a best-seller. Some 14,000 copies were sold. Its contents were attacked in parliament by the then Minister of Labour, Tom Shand, but this only resulted in an outcry of criticism from one end of the country to the other against the intemperance of Shand's attack.[23] New Zealand did join the IMF, however, but borrowing from it did not begin until 1967–68. Full employment was maintained, but only until the period around 1967–68 when Harry Lake was succeeded by Robert Muldoon as Minster of Finance—and then the level of New Zealand's unemployed suddenly soared to 10,000. This marked, in Rosenberg's opinion, an abrupt turning point in the country's proud record of economic and social achievement: what followed was a period of decline into a 'state of depression, despair and rejection'.[24]

In the meantime, however, Rosenberg continued battling in books and letters for better alternatives and sought to enlighten New Zealanders on a variety of issues in a series of informative monographs, among which were: *What Every New Zealander Should Know About EEC* (1962), *What Every New Zealander Should Know About the Effects of Import Controls and Industrialization on New Zealand* (1965), *What Every New Zealander Should Know About Foreign Investment in New Zealand* (1966), *A Guidebook to New Zealand's Future* (1968), and *The Coming Depression and How to Overcome It* (1978). Further periods abroad in the 1960s and 1970s in countries such as the then German Democratic Republic (which he visited in 1978) served to strengthen his conviction that 'Socialism is the economic and social system of the future'.[25]

In 1975, while still teaching economics at the University of Canterbury, Wolfgang Rosenberg began studying law. Inspired by the efforts of one of his sons, George, who had established a thriving law practice in Wellington in the 1970s, Rosenberg recognised an opportunity 'not to retire at age 65 into abandonment of an active life, but to change professions'[26] and decided to enrol as a law student. Even in those days 'mature' students were still something of a rare sight—and senior staff sitting among young students even rarer. He recalls one particular occasion when he went from his study to the lecture theatre where law lectures were held and sat down with the other students, only to be asked by the person sitting next to him: 'Aren't you going to lecture us today?' It turns out that he had mistaken the time, and he was supposed to lecture on economic history at that hour. He quickly slipped back into the role of lecturer, but still looks back on this incident with much amusement.[27]

On his retirement in 1980 from his position as Reader in Economics, Rosenberg began an apprenticeship at his son George's law practice in Wellington, intending to establish a law firm George Rosenberg & Father

Wolfgang Rosenberg,
1974. *(Rosenberg
Collection)*

in the not too distant future. However, the transfer of George's activities to Hong Kong put an end to these plans, and Rosenberg senior returned to Christchurch, where he practised first as a barrister and solicitor, then as a barrister sole in criminal law, which he has pursued ever since.

In the intervening period, Rosenberg has continued to write, publish, and comment publicly on political decisions that he sees as responsible for damaging the economic and social climate of New Zealand. In his book *The Magic Square* (1986), for instance, he adopted the economic paradigm formulated by German economist Jürgen Kuczynski, arguing that the 'magic square' of equilibrium between full employment, the balance of external payments, economic growth, and price stability has to be achieved in order to arrive at the ideal economy, and that the brand of economic liberalisation introduced in New Zealand in the mid 1980s by then Minister of Finance Roger Douglas ('Rogernomics') would only lead to greater unemployment and poverty. As the National Government that replaced Labour in 1990 in many respects maintained the same economic policies, Rosenberg renewed his criticism of this continued process of economic reform in his book *New Zealand can be Different and Better* (1993).

The sum of his arguments is listed in the book's concluding chapter under the title 'A manifesto for social change'. Here, Rosenberg first reinforces the 'magic square' concept by advocating, among other things, international economic cooperation (provided it does not harm national economic sovereignty), foreign trade and exchange controls (a necessary but not sufficient condition for full employment), and 'social improvement in health and education, greater Maori self-determination and nature's conservation and enhancement',[28] before going on to outline other prerequisites for full employment. Many of the principles stated in this 'manifesto for social change' reflect beliefs expressed in the 'Manifesto of the Broad Left', submitted to and accepted unanimously by a meeting of the Economic Policy Network of the New Zealand Labour Party chaired by Jim Anderton in 1988.[29]

Wolfgang Rosenberg's writing on economic affairs continues unabated. In 1997, in collaboration with his son Bill, he wrote a contribution to a book dealing critically with the issue of foreign investment in New Zealand. Now in his eighties, Wolf Rosenberg maintains a lively interest in German *Kultur*. Not only does he lecture on aspects of Goethe's life and works at the Centre of Continuing Education of the University of Canterbury or at meetings of the Goethe Society in Christchurch, but also above all he upholds the political and social principles for which Büchner and Heine expatriated themselves from their homeland more than 150 years ago.

1　W.E. Wilmott (ed.), *New Zealand and the World: Essays in Honour of Wolfgang Rosenberg* (Christchurch, 1980).
2　Bill Rowling, 'Foreword', in Wilmott [note 1], p. 3.
3　H. Winston Rhodes, 'The making of a New Zealand economist', in Wilmott [note 1], pp. 11, 13.
4　Rhodes [note 3], p. 12.
5　Wolfgang Rosenberg in a letter to Gerhard Träbing of 10 December 1996.
6　Rhodes [note 3], pp. 12f.
7　Rhodes [note 3], p. 11.
8　Wolfgang Rosenberg, 'Forty years of joy and sorrow of a New Zealand economist', in Wilmott [note 1], p. 128.
9　Rhodes [note 3], p. 13.
10　Rhodes [note 3], pp. 13f.
11　Rhodes [note 3], pp. 14f; cf. letter to Gerhard Träbing of 10 December 1996. Ann Eichelbaum (now Rosenberg) was a second cousin of the present Chief Justice of New Zealand, Sir Thomas Eichelbaum (see chapter 31), who arrived in New Zealand in 1938, a year after Rosenberg.
12　Rhodes [note 3], p. 15; cf. letter to Gerhard Träbing of 10 December 1996. Austrian-born Henry Lang (1919–97) came to New Zealand in 1939 with his mother and stepfather, renowned archi- tect Ernst Plischke (see chapter 24), and later served as Secretary to Treasury (1968–76); he was awarded the Order of New Zealand in 1989.
13　Rhodes [note 3], p. 15.
14　*Economic Record*, vol. 14 (June 1938), pp. 93–8. Rosenberg's article was written in continuation of studies of central banking policies which he had done when working for M.M. Warburg & Co. (letter to Gerhard Träbing of 10 December 1996).
15　Rhodes [note 3], p. 15.
16　Ibid.
17　Rhodes [note 3], p. 16; cf. Wolfgang Rosenberg, 'Freedom in the university', *Landfall* vol. 4, no. 2 (1950), pp. 152–4.
18　Cf. Rhodes [note 3], p. 16.
19　Rosenberg [note 17], pp. 152f.
20　Rhodes [note 3], pp. 16f.
21　Rhodes [note 3], p. 17.
22　See the 'Bibliography of W. Rosenberg' in Wilmott [note 1], pp. 140f.
23　Rhodes [note 3], p. 17; cf. Rosenberg [note 8], p. 134.
24　Rosenberg [note 8], pp. 133f.
25　Rhodes [note 3], p. 18.
26　Letter to Gerhard Träbing of 10 December 1996.
27　Ibid.
28　Wolfgang Rosenberg, *New Zealand can be Different and Better: Why Deregulation does not Work* (Christchurch, 1993), p. 163.
29　Anderton, president of the New Zealand Labour Party (1979–84) and leader of the break-away NewLabour Party since 1989, contributed forewords to both *The Magic Square* and *New Zealand can be Different and Better*.

21

Peter Munz

DAVID VENABLES

The only thing certain in knowledge is uncertainty. Words similar to these were uttered by historian–philosopher Peter Munz during a lunch-time discussion with colleagues at Victoria University in the early 1980s. So apt were they as an expression of the philosophy of the then Professor of History that they were used as the title of a volume of tributes to Munz written in 1996.[1] This persistent scepticism and the effect it has had on the students he taught during his forty-two years at Victoria is perhaps part of Munz's lasting contribution to New Zealand academic life.[2]

Peter Munz, an expatriate German, has proved difficult to pin down as a scholar, moving between disciplines with apparent ease: history, social anthropology, religion, philosophy, psychology, the philosophy of science and, most recently, biology and evolutionary theory. These interests are reflected in 'the extraordinary prodigiousness and breadth of his writing'.[3] He has avoided, almost as a matter of principle, specialising either in one area of history or in one academic discipline, even to the extent of passing up overseas job opportunities that might have forced him to narrow his vision of inquiry.[4] Munz says he has been driven to range between subject areas by an irrepressible sense of curiosity, following his own interests throughout.[5] Among the few consistent threads discernible through his intellectual travels have been his tendency to reach strong and bold conclusions and his conviction that the only thing certain about his conclusions is that they are open to doubt.[6] One historian has described Munz as 'New Zealand's intellectual Man Alone'.[7]

Peter Munz began life in the eastern German city of Chemnitz on 12 May 1921, the son of Leo (an eye specialist) and Carlotta Munz. Leo died in 1927, leaving Carlotta with young Peter and his sister Eva. Carlotta moved the family to Berlin in 1930. The Munzes effectively commuted to Italy every six months during this period, moving to Florence permanently in 1933 as Adolf Hitler consolidated his hold on Germany. The family was Jewish, although non-practising.[8] Following the outbreak of World War II, Italy too became increasingly dangerous for Jews, leading Carlotta to seek refuge in New Zealand. New Zealand's progressive record and the assistance of the father of a pen-pal from Methven have been cited as reasons why Carlotta brought her children halfway across the world in January 1940.[9]

Peter Munz began his relationship with New Zealand's universities that same year, at Canterbury University College. Four years of study followed, including training at Christchurch Teachers' Training College (1941–42), before the young Munz completed his MA in history in 1943. Appointment to Victoria University College as a junior assistant followed in 1944, before Munz took up a travelling scholarship at St John's College, Cambridge, in 1946. He returned to Victoria with his PhD in 1948, and married one of his students, Anne Vickerman, in 1950.

The 1940s were formative years for the emerging historian. At Victoria, Munz taught under the then head of the History Department, Fred Wood, who was to hold a protective hand over him for more than two decades.[10] These years also saw Munz's introduction to the work of a fellow European refugee whose thinking was to profoundly affect his own thought. Austrian philosopher Karl Popper had arrived to teach at Canterbury in 1937, eventually spending some eight years at the college. Peter Munz counts Popper as 'a gigantic influence'. For two years he spent Saturday mornings at the master's proverbial feet engaged in private tutorials where he was free to ask questions.[11]

Popper was so impressed by the young Munz that he later praised him in his autobiography.[12] Later, there was a brief cooling of the relationship between the two men when Popper realised that Munz was not content to become 'a mere mouthpiece' of his mentor.[13] This did not, however, stop Munz expounding and developing Popper's ideas, particularly on the philosophy of history and the parallels between the theory of evolution and the growth of human knowledge. One writer has described Munz's work as resting 'firmly on Popperian pillars', with his 'real contribution' being to highlight Popper's move towards evolutionary theory.[14]

Popper left New Zealand at the end of 1945 and took up a post at the London School of Economics. At Cambridge (1946–48), Munz studied under Ludwig Wittgenstein, and once witnessed a rather animated debate between that philosopher and Popper, chaired by Bertrand Russell. Wittgenstein is said to have shaken an apparently red-hot poker in front of Popper before storming out. Munz later wrote that this event led him to see Popper and Wittgenstein as epitomising the choice between evolutionary 'biology-oriented philosophy' and anti-evolutionary, anti-historical 'sociologising philosophy' respectively. He himself came down firmly on the side of the former.[15]

At first sight, it seems a long way from Peter Munz's PhD thesis on the place of Richard Hooker in the history of thought (published as a book in 1952) to his most recent book, *Philosophical Darwinism* (1993). Yet his interest has always been in the philosophical aspect of history and knowledge. This interest led Munz to study religion and mythology in order to discover what truths, if any, these bodies of beliefs contained.[16] Examining Hooker's ideas also led Munz to the medieval period. He spent the late 1950s and the 1960s researching the Middle Ages, in the process perhaps becoming as close as he has ever come to being considered a historical specialist. One of his best known works of this period, *The Origin of the Carolingian Empire* (1960), reflected Munz's philosophical bent. Attacking the practice among medieval specialists of focusing on minute details, he exhorted historians to start with a theory that the facts could then test rather

Peter Munz, *c.* 1951.
(Carlotta Munz)

than trying to build a theory from the facts.[17] His belief in the importance of historical theories gained clearer philosophical expression through Munz's work in the 1970s and 1980s. In 1971, he wrote: 'There is no such thing as a "fact". Every single fact we can think of is infinitely sub-divisible.'[18] Historical events are also 'infinitely sub-divisible', constructions of smaller events.[19] Historians, therefore, cannot work without using theories to determine whether events are connected. Scepticism about historical certainty led Munz to agree with Popper in rejecting two schools of thought that had grown up in the eighteenth and nineteenth centuries: historicism and positivism. The former held that history progressed in stages, while the later suggested that history had culminated in scientific knowledge.[20] Munz saw the two theories together as producing 'one of the unholiest alliances in the history of thought'.[21] Munz, again reflecting Popper, applied to the history of science the same scepticism about facts that he had applied to medieval history. He wrote: 'In all cases, a philosophy of science must precede a history of science because the alleged empirical record is a construction and does not lie ready, waiting to be inspected by positivists.'[22]

Following the publication of Popper's *Objective Knowledge* in 1972, Peter Munz's interest took a major new turn: to examine the impact of biology and the theory of evolution on philosophy. This he did in two books: *Our Knowledge of the Growth of Knowledge* (1985) and *Philosophical Darwinism* (1993). He saw his arrival at Darwin's door as the logical result of tracing back through time to the Middle Ages and beyond in order to explain modern society.[23] Munz drew a parallel between Darwinian natural selection and Popper's ideas about how knowledge was acquired. Popper's view was that theories of knowledge were selected on the basis of how much they explained and whether they stood up to rigorous testing. This was 'selection by criticism'.[24] Central to Popper's 'biological model of knowledge' was the concept of 'falsificationism' whereby a good theory was one that could be tested and that stood up to testing.[25] Munz characterised Popper's overall view as the development of theories towards increasing universality whereby a theory becomes more truthful, or 'verisimilitudinous', as it becomes compatible with a greater part of the environment.[26]

For Munz, biological evolution helped with the age-old philosophical problem of establishing the existence of an objective reality in the world. 'The only positive evidence we can have for believing that there is a reality out there, and that we must have some knowledge of it, consists in the negative fact that it has brought about all those eliminations without which evolution could not have taken place.'[27] Elsewhere, he said that Popper's philosophy of knowledge showed there was an objective reality, which had allowed human evolution, and the world that had allowed it must be of a certain type or we would not be here.[28] Evolution also puts paid, in Munz's view, to Sartrean nausea and the view of humankind as an accident because now there is a biological explanation for why we are here.[29] Since evolution itself is a theory, both Munz and Popper characterise this realism as 'hypothetical realism'.[30]

Evolution also provides Munz with an argument to use against the current fashion for sociological relativism, which asserts that all knowledge is

Peter Munz, early 1980s.
(Carlotta Munz)

culturally based, with one culture's knowledge being equal to another's. Particularly galling for Munz is their contention that science is nothing more than a form of literature, the mythology of European men. He accuses relativists of being arrogant in analysing the theories of others in terms of class interest and other political considerations.[31] The greatest weakness of post-modern relativism, in Munz's view, is the idea that cultures are self-contained 'closed circles'. He says theorists such as Wittgenstein and Thomas Kuhn who follow this line, which Munz labels 'historism', are wrong because they are unable to show how cultures relate to one another or how they evolve.[32]

Munz is not entirely hostile to sociology and the related field of social anthropology, having incorporated their perspectives into his historical work for decades. In his view, historians need the work of sociologists as they construct their theories about what happened in the past. However, ignoring the importance of time leads to sociologists making exactly the error that the 'closed circle' school has made. 'The historian, without an appreciation of social relationships, is at the mercy of his written sources … And without the historian's time dimension, too many of the social anthropologist's descriptions of societies read like descriptions of permanent systems of static order.'[33]

Peter Munz has eschewed the line of most of his fellow New Zealand historians and has written little about New Zealand and the issues surrounding the Treaty of Waitangi, beyond a number of journal articles, and he is not about to change tack, preferring as always to follow his own nose. This is not to say that he will not write about his adopted country, but when he does so, it will be, as it has been in the past, by bringing the big picture of history to bear on New Zealand, not by pursuing narrow lines of inquiry.

As of writing, Munz was working on three books, all of them continuing to study his current passion, Darwinian evolution. Two of the books focus on the philosophy of psychology, while the third continues his battle against what Munz describes as the post-modern 'enemies of the Enlightenment'.[34] Perhaps it is his constant to-ing and fro-ing between grand theory and minute detail, his determination to scour far and wide in the pursuit of knowledge, and his commitment to 'relentless doubt' in the face of temptations to believe in certainties that are Peter Munz's greatest contributions to New Zealand scholarship.[35]

1 Miles Fairburn and Bill Oliver (ed.), *The Certainty of Doubt: Tributes to Peter Munz* (Wellington, 1996). The anecdote about Munz's use of the title's words can be found in Miles Fairburn's introduction to the volume (p. 9).

2 Munz himself is particularly proud of his role in arranging for Keith Sinclair and Bob Chapman to deliver the first lectures on New Zealand history at Victoria University in 1960 (interview with the author, 29 January 1997).

3 Fairburn [note 1], p. 9. Justin Cargill's record of Peter Munz's work in *The Certainty of Doubt* counts 189 items published 1940–95, including a dozen books, journal articles, reviews, and pieces on contemporary issues in daily newspapers (Fairburn and Oliver [note 1], pp. 352–65).

4 Interview with the author, 31 December 1996. Munz says that working in a larger history department, e.g. Reading, Sydney, or Melbourne, would have forced him to specialise and give up his self-driven lines of inquiry. A number of writers in *The Certainty of Doubt* (e.g. J.L. Roberts, p. 24) have asked why Munz has stayed in New Zealand, to which Munz replies that he loves its 'uncomplicated and unpopulated' aspect and that it allows him to work in a small history department (interview with the author, 31 December 1996). While he has remained based in this country, Peter Munz has also travelled, lectured, and researched in a number of countries, including Germany, Italy, Australia, India, Brazil, France, and England (interview with the author, 29 January 1997).

5 Interview with the author, 31 December 1996.

6 Interviews with the author, 31 December 1996 and 29 January 1997.

7 W.H. Oliver, in Fairburn and Oliver [note 1], p. 28.

8 Peter Munz describes himself as coming from 'a long line of Jewish non-believers' (interview with the author, 31 December 1996). The biographical details in this article come from the author's interviews and from articles in *The Certainty of Doubt* by John Roberts and Bill Oliver; see Fairburn and Oliver [note 1], pp. 20–7 and pp. 28–37 respectively.

9 J.L. Roberts in Fairburn and Oliver [note 1], pp. 21–2.

10 Peter Munz (ed.), *The Feel of Truth: Essays in New Zealand and Pacific History* (Wellington, 1969), pp. 12–13. Munz praised Wood for his open-mindedness and his capacity to doubt. He followed Wood as head of the History Department on the latter's retirement in 1968. Munz now refers to Wood as his 'patron saint' (interview with the author, 31 December 1996).

11 Interview with the author, 31 December 1996. In the preface to *Our Knowledge of the Growth of Knowledge* (London, 1985), Munz wrote that his involvement with Popper was an 'extraordinary accident', the full significance of which did not become apparent to him for decades (p. x).

12 Popper wrote: 'Before our move to Buckinghamshire [in 1950] my main work was on "natural deduction". I had started it in New Zealand, where one of the students in my logic class, Peter Munz, encouraged me much by his understanding and his excellent and independent development of an argument.' See 'Autobiography of Karl Popper' in P.A. Schilpp (ed.), *The Philosophy of Karl Popper* (La Salle, Ill., 1974), part 1, p. 100.

13 Interviews with the author, 31 December 1996 and 29 January 1997. Munz says his friendship with Popper soon recovered and continued until the latter's death in 1994, although he notes that Popper still criticised all his books.

14 Friedel Weinert in Fairburn and Oliver [note 1], pp. 244 and 263.

15 Munz [note 11], pp. 1–2 and 18–19. The debate took place at the Cambridge University Moral Sciences Club in October 1946. Munz continues to have a very low opinion of Wittgenstein.

In his interview with the author of 31 December 1996, he said: 'Wittgenstein I didn't get on at all with. Nobody gets on with Wittgenstein … dreadful man.'

16 Interview with the author, 29 January 1997. Munz's publications in this area include *Problems of Religious Knowledge* (London, 1959), *Relationship and Solitude* (London, 1964), and *When the Golden Bough Breaks: Structuralism or Typology* (London, 1973).

17 *The Origin of the Carolingian Empire* (Dunedin, 1960), p. ix.

18 'The purity of historical method: Some sceptical reflections on the current enthusiasm for the history of non-European societies', *New Zealand Journal of History*, April 1971, p. 19; quoted by Paul Hoffmann in his essay in Fairburn and Oliver [note 1], pp. 55–6.

19 Munz [note 11], pp. 87–9. Also see Munz's *The Shapes of Time: A New Look at the Philosophy of History* (Middletown, Conn., 1977).

20 Munz [note 11], pp. 3 and 10–11, and see also Peter Munz, *Philosophical Darwinism: On the Origin of Knowledge by Means of Natural Selection* (London, 1993), pp. 81–102.

21 Munz [note 20], p. 94.

22 Munz [note 20], p. 216. Popper saw scientific knowledge as based on 'guesswork controlled by criticism and experiment', quoted in Munz [note 20], pp. 1–2.

23 Munz [note 20], p. viii.

24 Munz [note 20], pp. 176–7, 182–3, 205–6, and 214, and Munz [note 11], pp. 14–15. For appraisal and criticism of Munz's philosophical Darwinism, see the essays by John Ziman, I.C. Jarvie, and Peter J. Wilson in Fairburn and Oliver [note 1], pp. 269–303, 304–15, and 316–35 respectively.

25 Munz [note 20], pp. 205–6, 214. Also see Munz [note 11], pp. 215–27 and 252. Munz notes that 'the primary importance of consciousness' in evolution is that it allows the production of both true and false theories, which compete, leading to the growth of knowledge (Munz [note 20], p. 166).

26 Munz [note 11], p. 252. For Munz and Popper, evolution has become the process of the acquisition of knowledge (ibid., p. 279).

27 Munz [note 20], p. 229.

28 Munz [note 11], p. 237.

29 Munz [note 20], pp. 187–91, and Munz [note 11], pp. 307–9.

30 Munz [note 20], pp. 182–3 and 229.

31 Munz [note 20], pp. 131 and 136; Munz [note 11], pp. 72–3; and interview with the author, 31 December 1996.

32 Munz [note 11], pp. 130–212, and Munz [note 20], pp. 133–4. Also see Alan Ward in Fairburn and Oliver [note 1], pp. 141–2, for a discussion of Maori tribal histories as historism.

33 Peter Munz, *Life in the Age of Charlemagne* (London, 1969). Munz has followed the sociological line in exploring the importance of myths and legends for the historian in *When the Golden Bough Breaks* [note 16]. In *Frederick Barbarossa: A Study in Medieval Politics* (London, 1969), Munz noted the value of folk tales for historians if they 'reflect contemporary popular beliefs and impressions' (p. 5). He even assigns value to false knowledge on the basis that it can act as a means of social bonding, which may be crucial in a particular culture; see Munz [note 11], pp. 283 and 303.

34 Interview with the author, 31 December 1996.

35 Interview with the author, 29 January 1997.

Part 4

The business and professional world

Introduction

JAMES N. BADE

The German contribution to business and professional life in New Zealand is a considerable one, both in the nineteenth and the twentieth centuries. From brewing to the manufacture of chemicals, from architecture to law, from photography to medicine, Germans and Austrians have left an indelible mark on New Zealand society. Again, the problem has been who to profile in the following chapters, as the immigrants who deserve to be mentioned in this context are legion. The Chief Justice, Sir Thomas Eichelbaum, was an obvious choice; but as far as the others are concerned, it must be emphasised once more that, although some of the personalities treated in this section are well known to average New Zealanders, the main criterion for inclusion was their representativeness.

Most New Zealanders associate Germany with wine[1] and beer, and the main German family to be associated in successive generations with brewing this century is the Kühtze (Coutts) family, featured in chapter 22, from Joseph Kühtze of Cologne, after whom the celebrated Dominion Breweries Joseph Kuhtze Exhibition Lager was named, through to his grandson Morton Coutts, who in 1996 was honoured with the New Zealand Distinguished Biotechnologist Award.[2]

Less well known is the contribution made by German-speaking immigrants to architecture in New Zealand. As Leonard Bell mentions in chapter 6, the contribution of German-speaking architects and town planners, such as Helmut Einhorn, Fritz Farrar, Ernst Gerson, Henry Kulka, Frederick Newman, Imre Porsolt, and Max Rosenfeld, merits a separate study. Ernst Plischke, profiled here, needed to escape from Nazi Austria in 1939 on account of his wife, who was Jewish. Once in New Zealand, Plischke put tremendous energy into his work for the Government Housing Department, and buildings and housing estates throughout the country testify to his imagination and common sense. New Zealand benefited inestimably from the quarter century that he devoted to architecture in this country.

Another group worthy of further study is the former German internees. As soon as war was declared in 1914, there were calls to intern all German nationals, and camps were set up on Motuihe and Somes Islands for this purpose. The Register of Aliens compiled in 1917 lists 234 Germans among the 277 internees held on these two islands.[3] During World War II Somes Island was once again used as an internment camp. Army files list seventy-six German internees as at 8 June 1942, of whom twenty-eight were from

Somes Island, 1938.
*(Evening Post Collection,
Alexander Turnbull Library,
Ref. no. C-23167)*

Samoa.[4] It is outside the scope of this book to look at the fairness of these internments, particularly the case of German Jews interned on Somes Island during World War II, which warrants investigation.[5] But it is certainly striking that, once released, many internees went on to make a major contribution to New Zealand. Gregory Riethmaier, who established himself as one of New Zealand's top photographers, is typical of this group.

Eight of the eleven immigrants profiled in this part of the book are Jewish or part-Jewish. Like the academics profiled in part 3, some refugees, having sought to escape persecution in Europe, were subjected to considerable abuse and discrimination—the sort of thing they thought they had left behind in Nazi Germany and Austria—on account of their 'enemy alien' status. Such discrimination peaked in July 1945, after Germany's defeat, when the Dominion Conference of the RSA passed a resolution that 'any person or persons who arrived in New Zealand from Germany, Austria, Hungary, or Italy since 1939 must return to their own countries within two years'.[6] This resolution provoked an outcry from responsible members of the community, including the Rev. Gladstone Hughes, who condemned it as 'un-British and unjust'.[7] Fortunately, common sense prevailed. One of the most effective protests was a poem entitled 'Alien Ways' by 'Whim Wham' (Allen Curnow), which appeared in the *New Zealand Listener* of 6 July 1945. The first verse reads as follows:

> Let's put the Alien in his Place.
> Let's show him Who's the Master Race.
> Hitler, alas, is dead and gone:
> But (Heil!) his Soul goes marching on.
> He wrecked their Homes, He bade them pack,
> He chased them here.—Let's chase them back!
> On with the Dance! It's none too soon:
> They know the Steps, They know the Tune!

What is perhaps most noticeable about many of the German-speaking immigrants who came to New Zealand was the contribution they made outside their immediate professions, and this is true of many of the immigrants profiled here. Willi Fels, from Halle, having married Bendix Hallenstein's eldest daughter Sara,[8] emigrated to Dunedin in 1888 and became closely involved with Hallenstein Brothers and the DIC. Fels is probably best known, however, for his association with the Otago Museum, which benefited enormously from his leadership and his philanthropy, as did, indirectly, the community at large, for services to which he was awarded the CMG in 1938. Peter Jacoby had a remarkable career as senior research officer in the Department of Education, but is probably better known as a scholar of international renown with his publications on Tönnies and Hobbes. Arthur Hilton was the respected managing director of CMC, but he and his wife Lisl are best known for their activities in the New Zealand Federation of Chamber Music Societies. Similarly, Denis Adam has certainly made his mark as an insurance broker, but his reputation in the wider community is based on the generosity shown by his active support of the arts through the Adam Foundation. Erich Geiringer's medical positions in New Zealand made him, as Dr George Salmond puts it, 'one of the most significant figures in public health' in the twentieth century. Yet in the general community he is probably best remembered as a very effective anti-nuclear campaigner. Georg Lemchen was a highly competent medical practitioner, but was just as well known in the Upper Hutt Valley for his activities with the Music Society, the Historical Society, and the Rotary Club.

On a personal note, I remember Dr Lemchen well as our family doctor. Always calm, and seemingly with all the time in the world, even when his waiting room was full, he was well versed in Freudian principles, and a leisurely chat with Dr Lemchen would often do his patients more good than any medicine he might prescribe. Upper Hutt owed a lot to Georg Lemchen, but his dedication was typical of the work that was being done up and down the country by a significant number of other medical practitioners who had, like him, come to New Zealand to escape the Nazi menace and had adopted a New Zealand community as their own.

1   Although some German pioneers experimented with wine production (see *The German Connection: New Zealand and German-speaking Europe in the Nineteenth Century*, ed. James N. Bade, Auckland, Oxford University Press, 1993, pp. 54, 58, 175ff.), the full-scale successful production of wine by German immigrants is a relatively recent phenomenon. For this reason, German winemakers are dealt with in part 5 of this volume.
2   The Ehrenfried and Myers families are dealt with in 'Louis Ehrenfried' by Bade [note 1], pp. 179–83.
3   New Zealand Department of Internal Affairs: Register of Aliens, 1917, held at National Archives, Wellington. My thanks to Val Burr for providing this information.
4   National Archives of New Zealand, Archive Reference AD 1 336/1/11 Vol. 3.
5   See National Archives of New Zealand, Archive Reference AD 1 336/1/6 Vol. 2.
6   *New Zealand Listener*, 6 July 1945, p. 5. Cf. chapter 3 of this book by Ann Beaglehole.
7   *Dominion*, 18 July 1945.
8   For more information on Bendix Hallenstein, see Roger Paulin, 'Bendix Hallenstein' in Bade [note 1], pp. 184–8.

22

Joseph Kühtze

AXEL LAURS

Dominion Breweries' launch in 1986 of a new lager to commemorate the pioneer New Zealand brewer, Joseph Kühtze, created a flurry of controversy. The Joseph Kuhtze Exhibition Lager Beer was promoted around the figure of Kühtze. The beer itself was billed as: 'No ordinary beer. A beer that, like the man it's named for, is far from ordinary.' From a promising start, celebrating a far from ordinary brewer, the initial publicity proceeded to sacrifice fact to sensationalism. It featured a man, purportedly Joseph Kühtze, behind prison bars, with the caption: 'His life wasn't always trouble-free.' Subsequent advertisements had Kühtze out from behind bars but sporting a black eye and clearly leading a life that was still far from trouble-free. Even allowing for the subliminal pun that the Joseph Kuhtze beer was about to be released and would be available behind bars throughout the country, the promotion gave offence to Kühtze's descendants. Some family members reportedly sold their Dominion Breweries shares.

Stripped of advertising hype, the story of Joseph Kühtze is in fact one of an innovative man of considerable character, who, in the face of continuous financial difficulties, typical for small brewers of the time, and a seemingly never-ending succession of disastrous fires, established some twelve breweries throughout the young colony. From all accounts, Kühtze emerges as an affable, well-liked family man, who occasionally infringed minor brewing regulations and might have been a little haphazard in his bookkeeping but was an excellent brewer.[1]

Kühtze set up his first brewery in Cromwell during the Otago gold rush and thus began one of the longest family associations with the brewing industry in this country. Over the next thirty years, other breweries followed in Dunedin, West Clive, Ormondville, and Palmerston North. On Kühtze's death in 1901, his son, William Joseph, became proprietor of the Standard Brewery at Palmerston North and went on to establish the Main Trunk Brewery at Taihape. In 1929 William Coutts, with his sons, founded the Waitemata Brewery in Otahuhu, which through mergers evolved to become the flagship of Dominion Breweries.

The founding father of the Coutts 'dynasty' was born Joseph Friedrich Kühtze in Cologne, Germany, on 8 April 1833, son of Carl Kühtze, a master joiner, and Caecilia Gierssen. At the age of 15, Joseph became an indentured pupil to a brewer in Cologne and learnt the trade thoroughly.[2] Two years later, in 1850, Kühtze was called up for military service but elected to join the German Maritime Marine as a cadet instead. Little is known of his movements during the next two decades. One source has Kühtze in Victoria, Australia, working as a brewmaster in the late 1850s.[3] The exact date of Kühtze's arrival in New Zealand is unknown. Family tradition suggests that he was wrecked north of Napier in the *Ida Ziegler*, which had come direct from Hamburg and was *en route* to a third destination. While the cargo of 6,000 wool bales floated out to sea, Joseph Kühtze swam ashore, saving the ship's cook, who could not swim.

In 1867, Kühtze surfaced in Dunedin, where it seems likely that he worked for the brewers Theyers & Beck. On 24 August 1870, he married Eleanor Turvey in the Baptist Chapel, Hanover Street, Dunedin.[4] Elizabeth Gretchen, born in Manuherikia on 25 July 1871, was the first of eleven children, the last of whom was born in Palmerston North in 1895. Kühtze was naturalised as a British subject in Alexandra on 19 July 1872, listing his occupation as brewer in the employ of Theyers & Beck.

In 1873, on the dissolution of the Swan Brewery partnership of A.H. Jaggar and J. Harding, the licence for premises in Hartley's Gully was granted to Joseph Kühtze. The Swan Brewery was situated about 300 metres from where gold was first discovered in the Clutha River. The Cromwell Argus of 15 September 1874 advertises the Swan brewery's 'unrivalled XXXX ALES in any quantity'. Along with his partner, Goodger, Kühtze had made extensive improvements and alterations, as recorded in *Mackay's Otago Goldfields Almanac Directory 1875*:

Joseph Friedrich Kühtze. *(Coutts Family Collection)*

Cromwell. Messrs Goodger and Kuhtze have erected an extensive malthouse and kiln at the Swan Brewery, filled with every recent improvement. They have also added the manufacture of cordials and aerated waters on a large scale, the machinery employed being unsurpassed in the colony for completeness and capacity. This enterprising firm are about to enlarge the brewery to an extent unequalled in the Province out of Dunedin.[5]

May 1875 saw the dissolution of the partnership with Goodger. By the end of the year, Kühtze was operating a new brewery, the North East Valley Brewery in Dunedin, guaranteeing 'to supply an article equal to the best in Dunedin'.[6] For a while things went well, but 1877 must have qualified as Kühtze's *annus horribilis*. Disaster followed disaster. Early one morning in May, a devastating fire destroyed almost the entire brewery and stock. The fire had not gained a very strong hold when first discovered, but owing to a strong wind and want of water, the fire could not be extinguished before the greater part of the building and property was destroyed. Kühtze and Smith, the partner who had discovered the blaze, both believed that the fire originated from a spark, falling on the roof of the brewery from the furnace fired to keep water boiling for brewing the next morning.[7]

Within weeks Kühtze had rebuilt the brewery 'on a far larger scale, and of more solid material than before', and was operating it with a capacity of eighty hogsheads (4,320 gallons) a week.[8] By this stage, however, with a bill of sale over the premises and his stock as collateral for a bank loan, financial problems were threatening to overwhelm him. The *Mercantile Gazette* of 13 October 1877 listed Kühtze as bankrupt. By November he applied for an order of discharge from bankruptcy. January 1878 saw him charged with fraudulent preference, favouring one creditor over others. At his trial in April he was found not guilty. Things scarcely improved, however. In September 1879 a new partnership with a bootmaker, Redmond Kirp Meliskey, was dissolved. His next partnership with a Mr Wootten ended with another fire that broke out early in the morning of 18 September 1880. Kühtze was reported to have been the last to leave the building before the fire. 'He had gone around the premises with a candle at 11 p.m. on the proceeding night to see that all was secure.'[9] The proprietors lost £150 over the sum insured, and the North East Valley Brewery ceased operating shortly thereafter.

To add to his woes, in December 1880, Kühtze was charged 'with neglecting to affix proper stamps to two casks of beer'. The case was dismissed on Kühtze's evidence that the said stamps were obliterated by 'rain, beer oozing, and children playing with the casks'.[10]

A move to Hawke's Bay followed. Kühtze ran the Edinburgh Brewery at West Clive for several years in the early 1880s before moving to Ormondville in 1885. At least twice in Clive he was to run foul of an overly scrupulous collector of customs. On one occasion, Kühtze was charged again with neglecting to affix and cancel a duty stamp on a cask of beer, and on another with a minor breach of the Beer Duty Act. In upholding the law, the magistrate was overwhelmingly supportive of the defendant, calling the first count 'one of great hardship' to Kühtze and urging him to apply to the government for relief.[11] On the second charge of brewing beer without a licence, 'His Worship considered the offence proved, but in consideration of the defendant being a foreigner, and not so likely to know what he was doing, he would inflict the lowest penalty—£10 and costs'.[12]

In 1884, following the horrific murder of the Edwards family, in which alcohol had played a part, the Settlers Arms Hotel in Ormondville was closed and the licence cancelled. With sly-grogging on the increase, Joseph Kühtze concluded that there was an opportunity for a brewery in the district. He moved from West Clive in 1885 to open Ormondville's first—and last—brewery about two kilometres from Ormondville. The raised driveway from the Ormondville–Norsewood road to the site of Kühtze's operation is still evident today.

Fire plagued this venture, too. The *Bush Advocate* of 1 November 1888 reports:

Mr Kuhtze began business, but a fire destroyed the fruits of his toil and he had to make another beginning. He rebuilt the brew house, which now stands on the site of the one destroyed by fire, and is now doing a very fair trade, and the business is expanding rapidly as the quality of the article supplied becomes known.

The reporter concludes a very full description of the brewing process with a product endorsement: '... A very clear and tempting beer is brewed here, but as I make it a rule never to taste beer when gleaning particulars such as those contained in these letters, I can only say that I am informed that the beer brewed here is excellent in quality as in appearance.' While the sober reporter was interviewing the brewer, 'six hogsheads of beer were sent away to customers along the line'. Over the next few years, Kühtze's beer was to be given further glowing testimonials in the *Bush Advocate*.[13]

Ormondville–Norsewood road showing raised driveway that formerly led to the Kühtze Brewery. *(Dorothy Ropiha)*

It is clear that Kühtze and his family were active and popular and made an impact on the local community. During his time in Ormondville, local lore tells of Kühtze driving his springcart around the block, a distance of 10 kilometres, with casks of beer 'to help the mix'.[14] Miriam, the couple's second daughter, taught at the Ormondville School. The headmaster's report on Miriam as pupil teacher for 1888 is fulsome in his praise of her contribution. Several other Kühtze children achieved creditably and were mentioned in dispatches as well.[15]

On 9 March 1888, the Norsewood correspondent of the *Hawke's Bay Weekly Courier* describes an annual ball for the young of the district 'given by Mr Kuhtze, the celebrated bush brewer, the genial, good-hearted "Bacchus ever fair and ever young", and I can tell you we had a gala time of it. … The party broke up … after one of the most enjoyable affairs given in the bush'.[16] Only days later, the devastating Norsewood fire, which destroyed more than thirty buildings and left forty families homeless, swept towards Ormondville before a fierce gale. This time, although his house and brewery caught fire twice, Kühtze with tremendous effort was lucky in saving his property.[17]

In June 1888, Kühtze made an appearance in the Ormondville court, charged with assault on Jans Christian Sorenson at his brewery. According to a witness, the parties (with the exception of Kühtze) were 'a little bit on', words were exchanged, and there was a fight of a 'rambling' kind, during which the defendant struck the plaintiff 'straight between the two [*sic*] eyes'. The plaintiff and all other witnesses being clearly intoxicated at the time in question, Kühtze's defence of provocation was upheld, and the case was dismissed without costs.[18]

A charge of having sold eight glasses of beer without having a retail licence on the same evening as the above assault was then brought against the brewer. Kühtze denied taking any money, saying that he gave beer to the men to get rid of them, 'as they were in liquor'. The prosecution rested on the evidence of the selfsame J.C. Sorenson, already proven to have both a grudge and a massive hangover. The counsel for the defence summed it up: 'We admit having supplied beer to these persons, but if your Worship is in the habit of visiting breweries, you will, no doubt, know that brewers are very generous in the way of giving a taste of the beer to visitors.' After all, Kühtze *had* wanted to get rid of these visitors. His Worship was of like mind and dismissed the case.[19]

In 1889, the Ormondville Brewery was sold, and the family, along with the vats and the brewing plant, returned to Clive. Three years later, following the opening of the Napier railway in 1891, on Anniversary Day 1892, Joseph Kühtze moved a final time to Palmerston North to set up the Palmerston North Brewery in Church Street. With his death on 21 November 1901 in Palmerston North, a remarkable chapter in the history of the New Zealand brewing industry came to a close.

Successive generations of the family, who changed their name to Coutts in 1918, a casualty to the anti-German feeling of the time, have carried on this proud tradition. Joseph's son William shifted brewing operations from Palmerston North to Taihape in 1908. After the success there of the Main Trunk Brewery, which became the Cascade Brewery under the brewing direction of Kühtze's grandson, Joseph T. Coutts, another move came with the foundation of the Waitemata Brewery in Otahuhu, a forerunner of Dominion Breweries. Although both breweries were operated using Joseph Kühtze's original methods, a pioneering innovativeness—a family trait—was also much in evidence.[20]

Nearly 130 years of distinguished family involvement in the New Zealand brewing industry, beginning with Joseph Friedrich Kühtze, culminated recently in the prestigious New Zealand Distinguished Biotechnologist Award 1996 to another grandson, Mr Morton Coutts, at the age of 93. The award recognised the international impact of Mr Coutts' invention of the first major innovation in brewing since the time of Henry VIII. Coutts' new continuous fermentation process, patented by Dominion Breweries in 1956, revolutionised beer production and gave New Zealand biotechnology a world first. By the 1960s, the Coutts method accounted for 85 per cent of all beer produced in New Zealand. Dominion Breweries, still using the continuous fermentation process today, has regularly won the world's most prestigious beer awards, including the World's Best Ale and the World's Best Lager trophies. Although retired from Dominion Breweries, Morton Coutts is still regarded in the industry as a 'living legend', an extraordinary brewer, following in the footsteps of Joseph Kühtze.

1   The very generous assistance, particularly of Dr John and Mrs Lois Coutts, Mr Morton Coutts, and Mrs Dorothy Ropiha, is gratefully acknowledged.

2   Throughout his career as brewer, Joseph Kühtze favoured a brewing method that was closer to English methods and quite different from the Munich/Bavarian method. Morton Coutts believes it was a method peculiar to the Cologne area. The method was still being used at the Taihape Brewery in the 1920s, where Morton was taught by his father. Yeast was stored in open tubs and had to be covered with an iron bar about 3–4 inches wide and $1/4$ inch thick. In the event of an electrical storm, it had to be earthed. The other important feature was that the mash was not boiled, and was not to go above 170°F in order to maintain the activity of the enzymes.

3 See J.E. Coutts' informative entry for Joseph Kühtze in the *Dictionary of New Zealand Biography*, vol. 2, 1870–1900 (Wellington, 1993), p. 261. There appear to be no records for this period, and Morton Coutts assumes that Joseph Kühtze was never actually in Australia.

4 Eleanor was the daughter of Mr Joseph Turvey, a theological student who founded the Benevolent Society, the first form of charitable aid organisation in Birmingham. He had died young, and Eleanor had come to New Zealand as a girl with her mother in 1867.

5 *Mackay's Otago Goldfields Almanac Directory 1875*, p. 45.

6 Otago *Daily Times*, 6 December 1875.

7 *New Zealand Illustrated Herald*, 29 May 1877.

8 Otago *Daily Times*, 2 July 1877.

9 Otago *Witness*, 25 September 1880.

10 Contained in information from Dominion Breweries Archives.

11 *Hawke's Bay Weekly Courier*, 26 August 1881.

12 *Hawke's Bay Weekly Courier*, 17 February 1882.

13 *Bush Advocate*, 30 October 1888: 'Mr Kuhtze, the popular Ormondville brewer, seems to be receiving good support in the district, and is sending out a large quantity of his famous brew to customers along the line.' *Bush Advocate*, 19 February 1889: 'We have to acknowledge the receipt of a dozen of bottled ale from Mr Kutzhe's Ormondville Brewery. Mr Kutzhe must have been reading the advertisements about "Wolfe Schnapps" lately and noticed it stated there that "newspaper men are about the best judges of a good drink." Hence that dozen which reached us the other day. Thanks, Mr Kutzhe, it was capital beer and a similar article should meet with extensive sale.'

14 Mrs Dorothy Ropiha provided background notes on Kühtze's time in the Ormondville area.

15 *Bush Advocate*, 15 December 1888.

16 *Hawke's Bay Weekly Courier*, 9 March 1888.

17 *Hawke's Bay Weekly Courier*, 23 March 1888.

18 *Hawke's Bay Weekly Courier*, 13 July 1888.

19 Ibid.

20 *Dictionary of New Zealand Biography* [note 3], p. 261.

23

Willi Fels

JAMES BRAUND

Willi Fels was born in the town of Halle on the Weser, in the Duchy of Brunswick, on 17 April 1858, and died in Dunedin, a city he had made his home for more than fifty years, on 29 June 1946.[1] While he achieved prominence in Dunedin and New Zealand business circles as a senior director of Hallenstein Brothers Ltd and the Drapery and General Importing Company of New Zealand Ltd (popularly known as the DIC), it is probably for his activities as a philanthropist that this German immigrant will be remembered best in his adoptive homeland.

The eldest of four children of the merchant Heinemann Wilhelm Fels and his wife Kätchen Hallenstein, the young Willi Fels attended a Jewish school run by a cousin of his father, Dr Albert Fels, and later went to a school near Hildesheim, where, under the influence of a gifted headmaster who taught physics, he renounced his religious beliefs. A talented and enthusiastic student of languages, particularly of Latin and Greek, Fels had hoped to study history and classics on the completion of his elementary schooling, but acceded to his father's wishes and entered the family's shoddy mill (shoddy is a kind of low-grade woollen cloth made partly from refuse rags) at Neuhaus near Paderborn, where he quickly became familiar with all the tasks involved in the running of such an enterprise.

In 1881, Fels's uncle Bendix Hallenstein, who had risen to prominence as a merchant and businessman in New Zealand, first in Central Otago and later in Dunedin, visited Germany with his wife and four daughters in the course of an extended European tour.[2] Fels and Hallenstein's eldest daughter, Sara Elizabeth, became engaged in July of that year and married some four months later, in November 1881. The couple spent the next six years in Neuhaus, during which time they began raising a family that would eventually number four children: Helene (who would later become the mother of poet Charles Brasch), Emily, Kate, and Harold. In 1887, however, their fortunes took an unexpected change of direction when the family's shoddy mill burned down. Fels was persuaded to emigrate to New Zealand, where his father-in-law, apparently motivated by the fact that he had no immediate male relatives to carry on the family business, was prepared to offer him a share in the running of Hallenstein Brothers Ltd. The Felses arrived in Dunedin in January 1888, and soon took up residence in the house bought for them by Hallenstein, opposite his own, on the corner of London and Victoria Streets (the latter now known as Haddon Place).[3]

On his arrival in Dunedin, Fels promptly joined his father-in-law at the head office of Hallenstein Brothers. With the latter's blessing, and aided by other associates and members of the extended Hallenstein family, Fels began to assume increasing responsibility for the day-to-day running of the firm and its sister company, the DIC, which had been established by Hallenstein in 1884.[4] Indeed, by 1895, the active management of all of Hallenstein's New Zealand concerns had been taken over from the ageing Bendix Hallenstein by his sons-in-law Willi Fels and Isidore de Beer, his nephews Emil and Percy Hallenstein, and his associate Hyam Hart—although they dutifully continued to consult him in all matters relating to the general welfare of the family's businesses.[5]

Willi and Sara Fels.
(Hocken Library)

Fels's primary duties included maintaining close contact with all Hallenstein branches and interests throughout New Zealand. Capable and energetic, he quickly established a reputation for himself as a tireless traveller for the firm[6] and, in the course of his travels around the country, came to acquire an intimate knowledge of both the main centres and the lesser provincial towns of his adoptive homeland. Although he did hold directorships in other firms from time to time, as well as serving as German consul in Dunedin for a number of years early in the twentieth century,[7] Fels's success and reputation in the world of business will probably remain most closely linked with his involvement in Hallenstein Brothers and the DIC, of which he was respectively managing director and chairman of directors for a number of years.[8] A partner in the former company from 1890,[9] Fels had become a director of the firm when it was incorporated as a limited liability company in 1906, and chairman of directors on the retirement of Hyam Hart in 1915; he would remain on its board until the year of his death.[10]

Fels, however, was by no means someone whose life was devoted entirely to the world of commerce. For all his adult life, he remained a man of extraordinarily wide and varied interests, many of which betokened a keen and inquiring mind possessed of a genuine enthusiasm for a diverse range of intellectual and artistic pursuits. Fels was extremely widely read, and over his life time amassed an impressive library containing books on subjects as varied as history, archaeology, biography, travel, and botany, but above all about Italy and the Renaissance, and the classical world—not to mention the great classical historians and philosophers themselves, as well as their latter-day commentators.[11] He was an enthusiastic member of the Dunedin Classical Association, whose meetings he regularly attended and occasionally lectured to, and for more than fifty years he also belonged to the Otago Institute (later known as the Otago branch of the Royal Society of New Zealand), serving on its council at various times as treasurer and vice-president, and counting among his acquaintances such eminent fellow members as the naturalist Augustus Hamilton, the biologist W.B. Benham, and the botanist J.E. Holloway. A keen gardener, and a member of the Dunedin Naturalists' Field Club as well, Fels was also fond of tramping, and in the course of many a holiday spent in inland Otago, he became intimately acquainted with the areas around Lakes Manapouri, Wakatipu, and Te Anau. Indeed, the Helena Falls (in Fiordland) and the Emily Pass (in south Westland) were named after his two eldest daughters.

The undisputed private focus of Fels's intellectual and artistic interests, however, was to be found in Manono, his magnificent red-brick home on the lower corner of London Street and Haddon Place in Dunedin, then surrounded by a sprawling but well-ordered garden adorned with marble copies of figures from classical mythology and enriched by plant specimens that he had gathered in the course of his travels throughout New Zealand and Europe.[12] Here at Manono Fels loved to entertain visitors, the most frequent of whom were his university friends, often academics from Otago University but occasionally some from further afield. Among the latter were such eminent scholars as Peter Buck and John Macmillan Brown.[13] Above all, however, Manono was home to Fels's extensive collections of coins, decorative art, and ethnographic material from all around the world.[14]

A born collector and connoisseur, Fels had developed a keen eye for items of historical and artistic value. His judgement in such matters was no doubt refined through a lifetime of collecting and an intimate knowledge, acquired over many years, of numerous museums, galleries, and dealers' shops in such places as London, Paris, Vienna, Rome, and Cairo. He had begun collecting coins and stamps as a boy and, soon after arriving in New Zealand, began to collect Maori and Pacific artefacts as well. A sizeable number of his Maori items were found in the course of his own archaeological prospecting along Otago beaches (Fels had mastered the technique of surface collecting). From the turn of the century onwards, he had also started collecting oriental arms, and, in time, acquired an impressive selection of *objets d'art* and similar items that included ceramics, glassware, early Italian books and rare first editions of contemporary English authors, illuminated medieval manuscripts, and a diverse range of ethnographic material from Persia, Tibet, India, Burma, and Japan. In later years, however, Fels disposed of his stamp collection and concentrated more on his vast coin collection, whose scope he widened from Roman and Greek coins to include papal and English coins and

Manono. *(Hocken Library)*

medals as well, while at the same time starting a small but impressive collection of plaques and medals by contemporary European die-makers.

Fels had originally intended that these collections would pass on to his only son, Harold, but after the latter was killed in action in October 1917, he decided that they should instead be given to the community for permanent safe-keeping. Fels chose the Otago Museum as the future guardian of his collections,[15] thus beginning a close relationship with the institution that would last for nearly thirty years. The Otago Museum had been inadequately funded since its establishment and treated with apparent indifference by the University of Otago, its governing body for the previous forty years. The arrival on the scene of someone such as Willi Fels, a man possessed of seemingly unflagging faith in the future of such an institution, would have seemed a welcome and, in some respects, long overdue event.[16]

His first significant contribution to the museum, albeit a somewhat indirect one, took place in 1918 with his offer to the University of Otago, made anonymously at first, to contribute £200 a year for five years to the salary of a specialist in Polynesian and Melanesian anthropology. This, together with a government subsidy, enabled H.D. Skinner, an Otago graduate who had recently obtained a degree from the University of Cambridge, to be appointed in December 1918 to the dual positions of Lecturer in Ethnology and Assistant Curator of the Otago Museum.[17] He served the museum with distinction for nearly forty years, the majority of those spent working in close collaboration with Fels.[18]

In 1920, Fels established an Ethnology Fund (now known as the Fels Fund), whose income was to be used to help extend the museum's newly established ethnological collections, and, with the gift of various oriental arms and Maori artefacts in 1924, he made the first of many transfers of items from his own collections to the museum.[19] As his donations of material to the museum had revealed a shortage of gallery space in which to display new exhibits, Fels, in mid 1925, helped to organise a Museum Extension Committee comprising influential Dunedin businessmen whose aim was to gather funds for both the building of a new South Wing on to the existing buildings (the old annexe had been demolished in 1923) and the establishment an endowment fund, which would assist the museum's future development.[20] Within a few years, the committee had raised some £31,000, which, together with a government subsidy of £25,000, enabled construction of the new wing to proceed.[21] Tenders were called in August 1928, and the successful tenderer was announced the following month.[22]

Once construction was under way, the suggestion was made by the Extension Committee, almost certainly at the instigation of Fels, that a board of management be established to exercise general control over the museum's affairs and advise the University Council on the expenditure of museum funds.[23] In May 1929, after some months hesitation, the University Council eventually agreed to implement the suggestion.[24] The proposed board of management, subsequently known as the Museum Committee, met for the first time on 17 October 1930 and elected Fels chairman—a gesture described as 'a fitting reward for one who had striven so earnestly over the previous decade to improve and enrich the Museum's collections and to establish a broad base upon which it could flourish'.[25] Two days earlier, the new extension had been opened and named, appropriately, the Fels Wing— a name it bears to this day.

For the remaining sixteen years of his life, Fels would retain a dominant position on the Museum Committee, whether as chairman or as a representative of the Association of Friends of the Museum.[26] Always a man of great foresight as far the future of the museum was concerned, Fels established a new Otago Museum Building Extension Fund in 1934 and in 1943 proposed the construction of a new wing as a means of permanently commemorating the upcoming centenary of Otago Province.[27] With the eventual completion of the Centennial Wing some years after his death, the museum's display area would be more than doubled.[28] Fels's involvement with the Otago Museum, however, was by no means restricted to purely administrative matters or to fundraising. In the museum itself, he remained an interested, critical, and yet cheerful visitor who made a point of getting to know every member of the museum staff,[29] and, in the course of his travels, whether in New Zealand or overseas, he often acted as a purchasing agent for the museum.[30] Indeed, in the final years of his life, Fels could even be found assisting with the arranging and cataloguing of the museum's coin collection.[31]

Willi Fels was awarded the CMG for his services to the community in 1936. Although he had first come to New Zealand to help manage his father-in-law's business interests, and indeed continued to run them until well into his own old age, this inveterate collector and would-be historian was to leave his most enduring mark in a different area of community life altogether: that of large-scale private philanthropy. A life-long student and admirer of the finest achievements of his native Europe, Fels came to acquire a similarly deep and abiding fascination for the indigenous culture of his adoptive homeland, and through his activities as a collector and philanthropist, he undoubtedly inspired those around him to appreciate and preserve both their own dual heritage and that of other peoples in the Asian and Pacific regions. The undisputed monument to Fels's appreciation for the history and material culture of different branches of humanity will of course remain the Otago Museum—an institution whose independence and worth as a community body he had always encouraged and whose displays he had personally enriched with generous monetary gifts and the donation of several thousand items from his own collections. He was, and remains today, the museum's greatest benefactor.

1   Unless stated otherwise, the biographical information used in this chapter is derived primarily from H.D. Skinner's monograph *Willi Fels, CMG 1858–1946* (Dunedin, 1946), as well as from the articles on Fels by G.M. Strathern in A.H. McLintock (ed.), *An Encyclopaedia of New Zealand* (Wellington, 1966), vol. 1, pp. 637f, and Dimitri Anson in *The Dictionary of New Zealand Biography*, vol. 3, 1901–20 (Auckland & Wellington, 1996), pp. 155f.

2   The Hallenstein entourage had left New Zealand in April 1880 and did not return until March 1882. See Louise K.Vickerman, 'A colonial capitalist: Bendix Hallenstein 1835–1905', BA Hons thesis, University of Otago, 1981, p. 46.

3   Vickerman [note 2], pp. 65f.

4   Vickerman [note 2], pp. 48 & 60.

5 Vickerman [note 2], p. 61.
6 Charles Brasch and C.R. Nicolson, *Hallensteins—The First Century: 1873–1973* (Dunedin, 1973), p. 39.
7 This was another business-related responsibility that Fels had taken over from his father-in-law. Bendix Hallenstein served as German consul in Dunedin from 1892 until his death in 1905, but during his absence from New Zealand on his third and final extended overseas trip (May 1900–March 1903), his consular responsibilities were taken over temporarily by Fels as acting consul. See the *Cyclopedia of New Zealand*, vol. 4 (Christchurch, 1905), p. 93, but in particular Vickerman [note 2], pp. 66, 67, & 71. Fels went on to succeed Hallenstein as German consul after the latter's death, but resigned shortly before the outbreak of World War I, apparently in anticipation of anti-German sentiment. Although he had been a naturalised British citizen since 1890, and had since acquired such respect among his fellow New Zealanders as to be above suspicion, Fels nevertheless thought it prudent to curtail his activities as a traveller for Hallensteins during the war years. See Charles Brasch, *Indirections: A Memoir 1909–1947* (Wellington, 1980), pp. 113f.
8 Brasch [note 7], p. 54.
9 Vickerman [note 2], p. 59.
10 Brasch and Nicolson [note 6], pp. 40f.
11 See Brasch [note 7], pp. 54f.
12 For descriptions of Manono and its garden, see Brasch [note 7], pp. 51–4, 116f, & 120. Fels's former home still stands today, although it has recently been turned into a homestay and the original property has since been subdivided, thus resulting in the loss of a large part of Fels's beloved garden. See Sarah Quigley, 'Manono secured a writer's peace', *New Zealand Historic Places*, no. 60 (September 1996), pp. 7f.
13 Brasch [note 7], pp. 116–19.
14 The following summary of Fels's activities and acquisitions as a collector is based primarily on information supplied by Skinner [note 1], but see also Brasch [note 7], pp. 53f & 114f.
15 A.D. McRobie, 'An administrative history of the Otago Museum', MA thesis, University of Otago, 1966, p. 63.
16 McRobie [note 15], pp. 50–61 *passim*, but see also W.P. Morrell, *The University of Otago: A Centennial History* (Dunedin 1969), pp. 141f.
17 McRobie [note 15], pp. 63f. Cf. Morrell [note 16], pp. 123f, and Brasch [note 7], p. 117.
18 Morrell [note 16], p. 124, but see also McRobie [note 15], pp. 75 & 212f, and in particular J.D. Freeman, 'Henry Devenish Skinner: A memoir' in J.D. Freeman and W.R. Geddes (ed.), *Anthropology in the South Seas: Essays presented to H.D. Skinner* (New Plymouth, NZ, 1959), pp. 9–27.
19 McRobie [note 15], p. 63.
20 McRobie [note 15], pp. 66f.
21 McRobie [note 15], p. 67.
22 Morrell [note 16], p. 142.
23 McRobie [note 15], pp. 68f.
24 McRobie [note 15], pp. 69f.
25 McRobie [note 15], pp. 72f.
26 McRobie [note 15], pp. 73–6.
27 McRobie [note 15], pp. 77f.
28 McRobie [note 15], p. 210.
29 Skinner [note 1], p. 12.
30 Cf. Brasch [note 7], pp. 118 & 269.
31 Skinner [note 1], pp. 9f.

24

Ernst Plischke

JANET PAUL

Wellington people were initially suspicious of Ernst Plischke when he arrived in their city from Austria in 1939.[1] A brilliant architect brought up in the Vienna of Mahler, Gropius, Wittgenstein, and Freud, he was already recognised in Europe as a second-generation leader of the Modern movement in architecture. His background was different, in nearly every way, from the experience of most New Zealanders, and he was initially perceived as an 'Austrian with very strange ideas'.[2] Although Plischke spoke fluent English (he had worked in New York for several months in 1929), the language of his thinking was unfamiliar. He spoke of 'care and love'[3] in town planning and in the design of individual buildings. He wanted an architecture that would be able to stand the test of 'this hard present reality',[4] not with boring routine conformity to current fashion or by looking backwards to the 'dolled up formalism of a bygone age',[5] but by new concepts of space and sculptural quality, which would evolve out of the tension between function and construction that 'makes a building alive and its architectural quality sensually appreciable'.[6] Ideas such as these permeated all his thinking and conversation, not to mention his publications. Plischke's own shock on arriving in this country, however, must have been to find that his outstanding professional qualifications and engineering experience were not recognised by the New Zealand Institute of Architects.

Portrait of Ernst Plischke by Greig Royle, Wellington, 1962. (On the Human Aspect in Modern Architecture, *Vienna, 1969*)

Hitler's invasion of Austria in March 1938 had impelled this man to emigrate with his Jewish wife and one stepson. They arrived in Wellington in May 1939. Because Plischke was himself not classed as a political refugee, he had to be guaranteed work before being admitted as an immigrant. A fellow Austrian, Dr Otto Frankel, who was then working in Christchurch as a DSIR soil scientist, helped find a job for him in the newly formed Government Housing Department. However, as Plischke's wages just covered his rent, he was obliged to supplement his income. Through new-found contacts in Wellington he managed to find additional work assisting with preparations for the Centennial Exhibition, due to be held in Wellington in 1940 to celebrate the first hundred years of British settlement in New Zealand.

Plischke, who would have expected little from a small and remote English-speaking country, must have been very surprised to learn that some understanding of the Modern revolution in architecture—as one possible style among many—had already reached New Zealand. He must have been especially surprised to learn that the director of the Housing Department, Gordon Wilson, already knew of some of his work, particularly his Employment Office Building (*Arbeitsamt*) in Liesing, Vienna, from Alberto Sartoris's influential text *Gli Elementi dell'Architettura Funzionale* (1935), a copy of which Wilson kept in his office.[7] Without accreditation as an architect, however, Plischke was employed merely as a draughtsman, and was initially set to draw details for the back porches of state houses, but was soon moved to his own office and assigned to plan semi-detached units for a government housing development in Auckland.

Two perspective drawings of his, entitled 'Multi-unit houses with living terraces' and signed 'EAP', were exhibited in the Centennial Exhibition in Wellington.[8] However, the units eventually built in Kupe Road, Orakei, differed noticeably from his original conception: the flat roof was replaced by a low-pitched one; the large sky-lights which were to provide light to the southern rooms were dispensed with; his open sun balconies on the top floors were roofed over; and a heavy wall was intrusively added, which separated the front entrances. As a result of these changes, Plischke's original well-considered, sun-oriented design had now become 'tame and mundane'.[9]

In private conversation, Plischke later related how, since these houses were to be lived in by Maori families, he had tried to find out the future residents' specific preferences: these were for communal kitchens where all meals were prepared and eaten, as well as for the well-used deep verandas such as were commonly found in Maori meeting houses. In his initial design, Plischke had altered the small separate spaces of the kitchen, the tiny dining area, and the sitting room of the typical state house to make instead one large kitchen/living room, which opened on to a sheltered sun terrace. The sketch went up through the Housing Department as far as a final arbiter—the Prime Minister, Peter Fraser—who then rejected it on the grounds that 'our Maoris deserve the same housing as is made for Pakeha New Zealanders'.[10] That was pretty much the story of Plischke's designs for housing projects during the eight years he worked for the government: the escalator of bureaucracy took each plan, altering it at every stage until it emerged watered down, mediocre, and acceptable under the signature of the government architect.[11] However, the department had seen from the Kupe Road units at Orakei that semi-detached housing could be humanised.

Later, in 1943, Plischke would be given a brief to design a ten-storey block of flats in downtown Wellington for city-dwelling couples and senior citizens with no children: there were to be fifty flats on a sloping site in Dixon Street, the largest high-density government housing design since the government architect Gordon Wilson's pioneering multiple units, which had been built in Grey Street, Auckland, in 1936. In her study of Plischke's architecture in New Zealand, Linda Tyler makes the following assessment of the completed project: 'In the Dixon Street flats, Plischke's concern for efficient planning is paramount, and results in a composition which is convincingly modern in all aspects. ... Dixon Street is Plischke's only major Housing Department design to be built largely according to his conception; it was altered only slightly with flowerboxes being provided for each unit.'[12]

Meanwhile, in 1942, the New Zealand and Dutch governments were preparing to celebrate the three-hundredth anniversary of the arrival of Abel Janszoon Tasman in New Zealand waters. Since Tasman's expedition had made no landing on New Zealand soil, the site chosen to commemorate the event was Tarakohe, as the nearest point east of Golden Bay to his only anchorage. J.C. Beaglehole, in his position as historical adviser to the Department of Internal Affairs, suggested to the under-secretary of the department, Joseph Heenan, that Plischke be asked to design a Tasman tercentennial memorial. After making several initial sketches, Plischke decided on a tall column and table on a cliff top. The original column still stands today on its magnificent site, although the original concept and relationships of elements have been altered somewhat: the seven marble panels of inscription, its text composed by Beaglehole, lettering designed by Janet Wilkinson and incised by the stone cutter at Karori Cemetery, are no longer held on a table top but have since been relocated to serve as a kind of edging fence.

Plischke's experience of the 'art of total design' as taught by Peter Behrens, his professor in the Master School of Architecture at the Vienna Academy from 1921, gave substance to his wish to transfer to the Town Planning Section of the Ministry of Works.[13] From November 1942 to March 1943 he worked on a plan to establish an independent community of 10,000 people in 2,500 houses at Naenae in the Hutt Valley, the objective of which was to build a modern ideal community with an exciting point of focus: the civic centre. Much later, in an article that appeared in the *Dominion* in April 1963, George Porter, a senior and well-respected architect and town planner in Wellington, would ponder the discrepancy between Plischke's numerous designs and what was eventually built. He summed up the Naenae project as follows:

This scheme must have been the cause of many battles, most of which were lost. In fact, the only recognisable feature remaining of his original layout is the pedestrian shopping court, the most successful feature of the centre.

His layout for Naenae was a beautiful scheme—and practical as well as beautiful. Its shopping courts were enclosed for shelter, unlike the open wind-tunnel of the present scheme. The buildings were unified and not the disjointed blocks they are today. There was ample parking everywhere. The local shopkeepers would not have complained, as they do today, about a parking problem.

He had the foresight and skill of a master, but New Zealand was not big enough to accept what he offered [my italics].[14]

The planning of towns such as Kaingaroa and Mangakino, which were intended to serve forestry and hydro-electricity projects, would later offer Plischke a rare opportunity to work without interference. He had to accept modification of design—sometimes from lack of funding—in subsequent plans for housing estates in Epuni (1945), Taita (1946), Mount Roskill (1946), Trentham (1946), and Tamaki (1947). However, in communities such as these some of the ideas for urban town planning that Plischke gleaned from Le Corbusier's *Urbanisme* (1925; known in English under the title *The City of Tomorrow and Its Planning*) were left in this country.

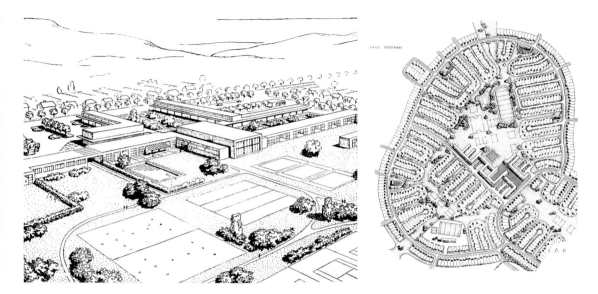

By 1943, Plischke had made other friends and contacts, and his design influence and ideas for living had now spread beyond the Ministry of Works. One of his contacts was with a group of lively intellectuals who lived in Wellington and ran the Army Education Welfare Service, and who were concerned to use the armed services' magazine, *Korero*, to make soldiers think about their own history and future. George Gabites, the editor of the magazine, asked Plischke to provide ideas in modern house design and town planning for group discussions. His suggestions, in the form of a bulletin, were sent to New Zealand army study groups in the Pacific, and eventually resulted in a whole text and drawings, published under the title *Design and Living* (1947).[15]

Beginning in 1943, and in subsequent years too, Plischke also gave lectures in the history of modern architecture in Europe, and in the history of modern art in general, to honours history students at Victoria University College—something that was all very stimulating at a time when Victoria had no department of music or art history. (The lectures were subsequently taken over by the Workers Educational Association and continued with wide public enthusiasm after the publication of Plischke's book.) Here Plischke's ideas on house design and town planning had the most widespread influence, and would later bring him clients when he set up in private practice.

Something of a turning point in Plischke's New Zealand period occurred in 1947—and in more ways than one. Having become a naturalised citizen, Plischke could officially call New Zealand his home. His professional career, however, witnessed a rather more abrupt change of direction. He had applied for the position of Professor of Design at Auckland University's School of Architecture, but was then controversially passed over for an English architect.[16] (On his return from Auckland he stayed in Hamilton and took up Blackwood Paul's request that he redesign the narrow family book

Above left:
Proposal for Mount Roskill community centre. (Design and Living, *Wellington, 1947*)

Above right:
Proposal for Trentham, 1946. (On the Human Aspect in Modern Architecture, *Vienna, 1969*)

Design concept for
Massey House,
Wellington, 1952. (On
the Human Aspect in
Modern Architecture,
Vienna, 1969)

shop in Victoria Street.)[17] By the end of the year, Plischke had had enough of his work in the public service[18] and resigned his town planning position to go into private practice with Cedric Firth, a New Zealand–registered architect, in Wellington. The new firm's one major building was Massey House (completed in 1957) on Lambton Quay.[19] This was Wellington's first modern post-war office block, which George Porter described in 1963 as

> ... still the best-designed office building in the city. It illustrates not only his skill as a designer but also his overall skill as an architect. He has thought primarily of the build-ing in its setting. He has realised that it has to live with its neighbours and future neigh-bours yet unbuilt. And so it is designed to be lived with. It is not aggressive, but quiet, dignified and simple. With the loving care of a true architect, he has lavished thought on every detail. Everything in the building down to the last door-knob has had full and care-ful study.
>
> It must have been a bitter pill for him to swallow when he saw the drawings for the new building now under way on the adjoining site. Here we shall have the ultimate in contrasts ... the perfect lesson for all to see. ...
>
> Massey House and its new neighbour illustrate not only the need for good manners in architecture but also the tragic lack of civic guidance in the rebuilding of our city cen-tres—one building crowding out the other, blocking its light, air and view, making the street fronts into solid walls of building ... Massey House has a positive and human qual-ity that will endure.[20]

Porter's praise for Plischke's achievements as an architect in New Zealand, of which Massey House was but one example, is matched only by his criti-cism of the New Zealand Institute of Architects' failure, up to that time, to give any real public credit to the Austrian, a man whose professional cre-dentials and experience, it should be remembered, the institute had refused to recognise for the entire twenty-four years he worked in this country. The lack of publicity given to Plischke's work by the institute, Porter writes, 'is one disadvantage of professional protectionism'.[21]

Plischke's belief in the relevance of good design for good living probably found most expression and widest impact in his domestic architecture.[22] Like-minded people approached him to design or modify living spaces. In every case he gave them beauty and proportion, seemliness and order in design, thus providing a sun-oriented, logical shape to their daily life. From the first house he designed in New Zealand, a commission for Otto and Margaret Frankel at Opawa, Christchurch (designed 1939), to his domestic *chef d'oeuvre* (and perhaps New Zealand's most precious mid-twentieth-century architectural treasure), the house for Bill Sutch and Shirley Smith in Brooklyn, Wellington (designed 1953–56), Plischke took the utmost care in all his domestic projects to make the best use of sunlight, shelter, views, and privacy, while at the same time taking careful notice of the individual needs and wishes of each client. He would easily flout convention if these require-ments meant, for instance, that small kitchen and laundry windows faced the street.

From the first, he favoured an L-shaped, flat-roofed house, with an increasingly light framework, and an infilling of large glass windows and slid-ing doors, which intimately connected interior and exterior living. Flat roofs overhung to protect the interior from the strongest of summer sun, but combined with stone or brick paving to allow winter sun to penetrate and hold warmth. Sometimes his detailed forethought gave his clients greater satisfaction with the completed design than they had expected; and his sense of harmony with nature, his proportioning of space, and a finesse of detail have left some—after forty years—still living with enduring pleasure.

Plischke's satisfied clients were not necessarily able to afford steel framework or sumptuous materials: he sometimes undertook work for clients with very limited finances. When Plischke made an alteration to an existing house for John and Beatrice Ashton (in 1948), for instance, he used a glass partition between kitchen and living spaces, and redesigned the house so that, instead of facing south, it now looked north towards the sun and a sheltered courtyard. Beatrice Ashton's magazine article about the completed alterations to their house tells us something about the human face of Plischke's work: 'Sunlight poured in all winter, and whenever the sun shone we managed without a heater. What is more, the courtyard that we both secretly regarded as a concession to art and architecture suddenly became the most pleasant place in our lives. We hadn't expected it to create so much privacy …'[23]

Every house Plischke designed was a new challenge in his pursuit of greater lightness and openness; and in his aim to make inside and outside environments harmonious, he was greatly helped by the partnership of his wife Anna, who, as a trained landscape gardener, would plan the planting of each garden. Most of their houses were in Wellington itself or up the Kapiti coast at Raumati or Waikanae, although one was built as far south as Alexandra: this was the house Plischke designed for Russell and Barbara Henderson (completed 1950)—the only domestic commission in his New Zealand period to be made of stone. Some of his houses are still lived in, unaltered. And some clients still treasure examples of the exquisite cups and bowls of Plischke's student friend, the Viennese potter Lucie Rie. It was through his influence that her work was sold in Stockton's pottery shop, in Wellington's Woodward Street, in the 1940s. Her fine, sophisticated porcelain bowls provided an elegant contrast to the more earthy influence of works by Bernard Leach and to the Japanese pottery also on sale there.

During the late 1940s and throughout the 1950s, Plischke continued to accept domestic commissions, but he also turned his taste and consummate ability to design other types of buildings. A notable example was the Cashmere Community Centre at Khandallah in Wellington (1948), which had been commissioned by a Methodist church group. Here Plischke amply demonstrated his ability to plan for the multiple demands of usage within a confined space, his original brief having been to design a building in which people could work, play, worship, and run a kindergarten.[24]

When, in 1963, Plischke was offered (and accepted) a professorship at Europe's most distinguished post-graduate school of architecture, the Master School of Architecture in the Vienna Academy, he left here two further completed church buildings: St Mary's Catholic Church in Taihape and St Martin's Presbyterian Church in Christchurch (both completed in 1954).[25] Had he been made Professor of Design in New Zealand's only School of

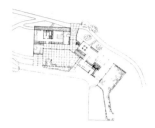

Design for Sutch house, Wellington. (On the Human Aspect in Modern Architecture, *Vienna, 1969*)

Sutch house, Wellington. (On the Human Aspect in Modern Architecture, *Vienna, 1969*)

Architecture, he might have left, in Wellington, a campus designed to match one of the world's most beautiful university sites, as well as a generation of New Zealanders trained to make their own contribution to organic building. In Vienna's Academy, Ernst Plischke was an inspiring and much-loved teacher, and the Master School of Architecture there became a lively laboratory, which so fully occupied his life that he personally undertook only two private commissions for houses.

Plischke's work received special international acknowledgment through his investiture as an honorary fellow of the American Institute of Architects on 15 May 1988. Ernst Plischke, the architect who always put great emphasis on the human aspect in architecture, died in Vienna, 18 May 1992.

1 The primary source of information used in this chapter is Linda Tyler, 'The architecture of E.A. Plischke in New Zealand: 1939–1962', MA thesis, University of Canterbury, 1986.

2 John Saker, 'Rediscovering Ernst Plischke', *Wellington City Magazine* (September 1985), p. 59; cf. Tyler [note 1], p. 39.

3 Ernst Plischke, *Vom Menschlichen im neuen Bauen—On the Human Aspect in Modern Architecture* (Vienna, 1969), p. 10.

4 Ibid.

5 Ibid.

6 Plischke [note 3], p. 13.

7 Tyler [note 1], pp. 23, 41.

8 The drawings are now held in the Plischke Archive in Vienna.

9 Ernst Plischke, interview with Linda Tyler, April 1984 (Tyler [note 1], p. 43).

10 Ernst Plischke in conversation with the author, 1942–43.

11 Ibid.

12 Tyler [note 1], pp. 48, 49.

13 Tyler [note 1], pp. 10f & 54f; cf. also Ernst Plischke, 'Gedanken zu Peter Behrens', *Bauforum*, vol. 5, no. 6 (1968), pp. 15–17.

14 D.G. Porter, 'Exile brought fresh vision to NZ architecture', *Dominion*, 6 April 1963.

15 Plischke's book, published by the Department of Internal Affairs, quickly became something of a bestseller; see *Parson's Packet*, July/August 1947, p. 1; quoted in Tyler [note 1], pp. 76ff.

16 See Keith Sinclair, *A History of the University of Auckland, 1883–1983* (Auckland, 1983), pp. 210f.

17 In 1958, Plischke also transformed an old factory space in High Street, Auckland, into a fine bookshop for Pauls with a vividly modern design of which no trace now remains.

18 Henry Lang in communication to the author, November 1996.

19 See Tyler [note 1], pp. 164–79.

20 Porter [note 14].

21 Ibid.

22 A detailed discussion of some of the private houses designed by Ernst Plischke can be found in Tyler [note 1], pp. 65–129 passim.

23 Beatrice Ashton, 'Additions to a house', *Design Review*, vol. 3, no. 4 (1951), p. 93; cf. Tyler [note 1], p. 85.

24 See Tyler [note 1], pp. 130–40.

25 See Tyler [note 1], pp. 140–8, 149–58.

25

Georg Lemchen

DAVID SCHNELLENBERG

In 1934, Dr Georg Lemchen, a Jewish physician, decided to leave Germany. He had been working at a hospital in Berlin, where he had moved from the small German-speaking town of Czarnikow (at that time in the eastern Prussian province of Posen, now in Poland) to study medicine. Lemchen's work brought him into daily contact with the Jewish victims of increasing Nazi violence. More upsetting than the nature of their wounds was the fear in the eyes of the patients and their unwillingness to attribute blame for the injuries on the perpetrators. Broken bones were said to have been caused by 'a fall down stairs', a lacerated face by 'a stumble'.[1]

At a distance of more than sixty years, it can be tempting to compress the years from Hitler's rise to power until the German invasion of Poland and thus overlook the gradual nature of the Nazis' actions against the Jewish population. The increasing violence inflicted on the Jews did not occur overnight, but rather in a more steady fashion. Even after *Kristallnacht* on 9 and 10 November 1938,[2] it was not uncommon to hear Jews arguing that things could not get any worse and questioning the need to emigrate from Germany. In that context, the prescience of Georg Lemchen is most remarkable. Although approximately 37,000 Jews (or 7 per cent of the Jewish population of 503,000) fled Germany in the first year of National Socialism, followed by another 23,000 each year until 1938, the vast majority of Germany's Jews could not or would not leave.[3]

Lemchen, already experiencing discrimination as a Jewish doctor, could see no future for Jews in Germany. Nevertheless, the question remained of where to go. One possibility was to move with his family to the United States. This option was rejected as soon as Lemchen discovered that as his qualifications would not be accepted in America, he would be forced to give up medicine. In the end, the decision was made for him by former colleague and co-religionist Dr Alfred Sternberg.

Sternberg had begun his medical studies with Lemchen at the same hospital in Berlin. However, unlike Lemchen, Sternberg completed his qualifications at the medical school in Edinburgh. While working there, Sternberg made the acquaintance of a number of New Zealand medical students. Armed with a qualification from one of the few universities recognised by the New Zealand authorities, Sternberg set sail for the South Pacific in 1934. Sternberg remained in close contact with his friend. At the time Lemchen decided to leave Germany, Sternberg had made the acquaintance

Title page of Georg Lemchen's doctoral thesis, completed at the Friedrich-Wilhelms-Universität, Berlin, 1929. *(James N. Bade Collection)*

of a Mr Lavin from Upper Hutt. With the agreement of Lavin to act as a guarantor, Sternberg persuaded Lemchen to join him as a partner in his practice in Upper Hutt, at the time a town with a population of about 5,000.

Georg and his wife Ruth made their decision to emigrate. In spite of pressure from friends and family to remain in Germany, they left for New Zealand in early 1935, accompanied by their daughters Hannah and Susi. (A third daughter, Barbara, was born in Upper Hutt in 1938.) Still nervous that they had made the wrong decision, they arrived in Wellington in June, almost four months to the day before the Nazis announced the infamous Nuremberg Laws. At Sternberg's request, Lemchen brought with him medical equipment that was either too expensive to purchase in New Zealand or simply unobtainable. It included an examination table, a microscope, an X-ray machine, and an ultraviolet machine used to improve the health of patients during the dark European winters.

It was not long before Lemchen experienced his first disappointment. His medical qualification from Berlin was not accepted, and he was therefore issued with only a provisional certificate to practice until he had completed and passed the final year of medical school in Dunedin. (Ruth Lemchen, who was also a qualified general practitioner, never sought requalification as a result of having to look after the family.) Despite his competence and his greater experience than the other students, Lemchen struggled with the English language. He failed his exams, and although deeply humiliated, he remained in Dunedin for a further three months before successfully qualifying and returning to Upper Hutt as a general practitioner.

As the situation in Europe gradually deteriorated, the Lemchens realised that they had been right to emigrate. However, the task of securing safe passage to New Zealand of Lemchen and his wife's parents had now become more urgent. In 1938 Lemchen's parents arrived in New Zealand, followed by his wife's, a few months before the outbreak of war. The reunification of the family, however, caused severe financial burdens. As refugees, Georg and Ruth's parents were ineligible for New Zealand Government pensions. As Jews, there was nothing they could expect from the Nazis. Dependent solely on Lemchen's income to support the extended family, his mother and mother-in-law turned to selling crocheted gloves in a shop owned by a fellow member of the Jewish community.

As New Zealand went to war, the distinctions between a German national and a Jewish refugee from Germany were often too subtle for some New Zealanders to appreciate—both were suspect. For its part, the New Zealand Government initially classified all German nationals, including Jews, as 'enemy aliens'. Regulations were enacted forbidding possession by aliens, without police permission, of charts or large-scale maps, cameras, motor vehicles, sea-going craft, aircraft, military documents or more than three gallons of inflammable liquids, as well as any radio set capable of receiving beyond New Zealand or at most Australia. Aliens could not leave their registered homes for more than twenty-four hours or travel beyond a 20-kilometre distance without a permit, and they also had to pay a weekly visit to the police.[4] For most Jews in this category, these formalities were accepted as part of the price they had to pay for having the chance to survive.

As an enemy alien, Lemchen was denied membership of the New Zealand branch of the British Medical Association, without which he could not obtain insurance for his practice; faced with the choice of not practising medicine or working without insurance, Lemchen chose to work, luckily without incident. Of all the difficulties imposed on the Lemchen family, Georg's rejection by the BMA was the most ignominious, and one that he would never forgive, for it struck at the very core of his competence. After the war, Lemchen shunned all BMA social functions, and even refused the presidency of the local branch when it was offered to him in the 1960s.

As well as the official restrictions, there was also the fact that New Zealanders in general viewed with great suspicion the foreign-accented people in their midst. Individuals acting strangely were often reported to police. Lemchen's father-in-law, Uli Mai, a cousin of the artist Max Liebermann and a talented artist in his own right, was fond of painting the local scenery. On one occasion, he was reported to the police on the suspicion that he was making paintings of New Zealand's coastal defence positions for a German U-boat lurking off the coastline.

Before the war, Lemchen's German manner was viewed as exotic by some New Zealanders, for it was considered fashionable to consult a European doctor. But in response to the wartime suspicion, the Lemchen family shunned the speaking of German around New Zealanders and kept social contact to a minimum. Lemchen sought to instil in his family tolerance of the attitudes that confronted them. When a neighbouring family ceased contact with them following the death of a son on the battle front, Lemchen persuaded his family to understand that the pain the neighbours were feeling was not a personal affront.

However, the Lemchens opened their doors to fellow Jewish refugees. Many would travel from Wellington or Lower Hutt each Sunday morning to enjoy Ruth's home-made *Brötchen* and other German delicacies while the melodies of Beethoven and Mozart played on Lemchen's gramophone in the background. An island of European Jewish sophistication was thus recreated where German was spoken in a relaxed atmosphere without the fear of antagonising other New Zealanders.

Lemchen's parents were strictly observant Jews, while his wife's parents were not observant at all. However, as a new bride Ruth had promised Lemchen that she would keep a kosher home. Accordingly, she took on the burden of maintaining a kosher home in New Zealand, in which the sabbath and festivals were strictly observed. This meant that the non-religious members of the family had to adapt to religious requirements. Uli Mai, for example, gave up smoking on the sabbath. For Lemchen's parents, the significant distance they lived away from the main Jewish community in Wellington meant that, for most of the year, they were unable to go to the synagogue on the sabbath and on festivals when travel is forbidden according to Jewish law. Instead, Lemchen's parents would stay in a Wellington hotel for the holidays of the Jewish New Year, Rosh Hashana, and the Day of Atonement, Yom Kippur.[5]

In a country of only a few thousand Jews, most of whom were non-observant, the Lemchen household maintained their strong Jewish faith and

Ruth and Georg
Lemchen at Trentham
Racecourse, 1947. *(Susi
Williams Collection)*

practice. Many of the community would join the Lemchens for some of the
more joyous festivals such as Passover and Sukkot. Lemchen was deeply
committed to serving the needs, both religious and secular, of Wellington's
Jewish community. Noticing that the community lacked a *mikveh*, the ritual
bath considered, along with the synagogue, a focal point of a community, he
set about the task of raising both the funds and the motivation of the Jewish
community to have one built.

As soon as the war had ended, Lemchen sought to come in from the cold
and have himself and his family naturalised, which he achieved in 1947. Like
other immigrants, Lemchen was comfortable in the German culture, its language and music, but he was anxious to be thought of as a New Zealander.
Lemchen was also deeply conscious of the debt he felt he owed to New
Zealand. The Holocaust, once it became known in all its horror, served to
reinforce his drive to repay the community that had adopted him. As a 'new'
New Zealander, Lemchen reached out to the local community and overcame his reticence to socialise with non-Jewish New Zealanders.

In spite of the cosmopolitanism and European sophistication in which he
was raised, Lemchen was more at home in the role of a 'country GP' than
that of consulting physician in a larger city.[6] As an activist in Zionist youth
groups in Berlin, he had developed a strong socialist ethic committed to the
ideal of service to the community. Furthermore, as Sternberg had left the
partnership to move to Wellington, there was an enormous variety of tasks
for Lemchen to do. With much enthusiasm, he set to work healing, teaching, advising, leading, and acting as mentor to a number of diverse sporting,
service, and social groups in the Upper Hutt area. From being the official
doctor at the local horseraces, to allowing his scales to be used by the
boxing and rugby clubs for their annual weigh-ins, Lemchen was always
available to help. In return, his offers to assist were greeted with warmth. In
recognition of his standing in the community, clubs competed to have
Lemchen as their patron or vice-patron. In 1962, he was made president of
the Upper Hutt Rotary Club,[7] and in 1967 he became the first chairman of
the Upper Hutt Music Society.[8]

However, Lemchen's chief passion was to push for the establishment of a
free community ambulance service, a goal that was achieved in the late
1950s. His untiring support for Upper Hutt's St John's Ambulance Service
continued for many years, both as its instructor and patron. In 1963, his work
gained wider recognition when he was awarded the Officer Brother
(Associate)[9] of the Order of St John Medal from the Governor-General.
After his death, the local ambulance service acknowledged his contribution
by naming a room in its local headquarters after him.

A proud Jew and a proud adopted New Zealander, Georg Lemchen was
a remarkable man. Like many of his fellow refugees, Lemchen did not see
New Zealand as a disappointing choice, a poor contrast to the Europe he
had left behind. Rather, New Zealand not only offered sanctuary from the
Nazi horror, it also provided an opportunity for individuals of Georg
Lemchen's character to make a significant contribution to a developing
nation. After his death in August 1971, the Upper Hutt City Council named

a new block of pensioner apartments in his honour, in recognition of his almost forty years of service to the local community.

1   Interview with Georg Lemchen's daughters Susi Williams and Hannah Lemchen Templeton.
2   Often referred to in English as the 'Night of Broken Glass', i.e. the night of violence directed by Nazi followers against Jewish people and their properties, so called from the sea of broken glass left lying outside Jewish-owned businesses and synagogues vandalised and destroyed during the pogrom.
3   Leo Sievers, *Juden in Deutschland* (Gütersloh [n.d.]), pp. 272–74.
4   Nancy Taylor, *The Home Front* (Wellington, 1986), vol. 2, p. 881.
5   Hannah Lemchen Templeton, 'The Lemchen family', in Stephen Levine (ed.), *A Standard for the People: The 150th Anniversary of the Wellington Hebrew Congregation 1843–1993* (Christchurch, 1995), pp. 363ff.
6   Interview with Susi Williams and Hannah Lemchen Templeton.
7   J.A. Kelleher, *Upper Hutt—The History* (Upper Hutt, 1991), p. 285.
8   Kelleher [note 7], p. 295.
9   The term *Associate* is used for non-Christian members of the Order of St John.

Upper Hutt St John's Ambulance Brigade, 1964. Georg Lemchen is seated centre front between Brigade Superintendent Ted Menzies (left) and Senior Officer Charlie Hammond. *(Menzies Family Collection)*

26

Peter Jacoby

PETER RUSSELL

Eduard Georg Jacoby, known to his friends as Peter Jacoby, was born on 3 April 1904 in Breslau, Silesia, the youngest of three children of Dr Felix Jacoby, a lecturer in philology and classics at Breslau University who later became an eminent professor of classics at Kiel University and, from 1939, at Oxford University.[1] His mother Margarete (née von der Leyen) came from a Bremen family. Peter was educated in Kiel, studying law and economics there, as well as in Freiburg and Berlin, during which time he also spent a year as a research assistant to the eminent Kiel-based sociologist Ferdinand Tönnies (1855–1936). Jacoby maintained a lifelong interest in Tönnies and was later to publish extensively on his social philosophy.

After completing a doctorate in law in 1929 with a thesis on the economics and constitutional law of federal finance, and then taking his final professional examinations in 1930, Jacoby was appointed to a position as assistant secretary in the Ministry of Commerce and Trade in Berlin in 1931. With the accession of the Nazis to power in 1933, however, he was forced to resign, as he had Jewish ancestry on his father's side. For the next four years, he was manager of the foreign department of a small Jewish bank in Berlin, until further strictures against Jews forced the bank into liquidation. Fortunately, he had been making plans to emigrate to New Zealand, and the necessary permit was granted at just that time.

In 1935 Jacoby had become engaged to Ilse Moschel, the daughter of the company secretary of a chocolate factory in Magdeburg, who was then working as a typist in Berlin. As Nazi law prevented their marriage in Germany, they travelled separately to England in 1938 and were married in Oxford, embarking several days later at Southampton for New Zealand. They arrived in Auckland in July 1938 with fifteen fellow refugees—among them the young Thomas Eichelbaum, one day to become New Zealand's Chief Justice (see chapter 31).

Although an official of the New Zealand High Commission in London had put the Jacobys into contact with the New Zealand economist W.B. Sutch in Wellington, emigration to New Zealand was otherwise a venture into the unknown. The corrugated iron roofs of Auckland shocked them. They settled in Wellington, and Peter sought a position in a variety of departments in the public service where he might put his qualifications and experience in banking and foreign exchange control to use. All doors proved closed, however, and from 1939 to 1943 he was forced to work for the business firms of W. Hildreth & Sons and the Associated Bottlers Company, where he began by washing bottles and then kept accounts. After this, he spent five years as an accountant with the New Zealand Educational Institute. Ilse meanwhile found a position, first with the *New Zealand Agricultural Journal*, then with the New Zealand Council for Educational Research, where she began what was to be a long career as a secretary-typist and proofreader.

The outbreak of war brought 'enemy alien' status and police surveillance. The latter, however, was otherwise friendly; the policeman who had to check up on them once a week would invariably have a cup of tea with them.[2] Since their lodgings at Hataitai overlooked the harbour and were therefore thought by officialdom to allow enemy monitoring of shipping movements, the Jacobys were soon forced to move.[3] However, the move had a happy result: they found what was to be their beloved home on a Karori hillside—a place where they were to spend the remainder of their lives and where, over the years, they transformed a patch of clay and gorse into a superb garden of New Zealand native trees and shrubs.

Peter became a naturalised New Zealander in 1946, Ilse the following year. Although Peter was later offered the opportunity to return to Germany to a well-paid senior position in his former profession, he and Ilse decided to commit themselves to their adopted country. In the immediate post-war years Peter hoped that his qualifications and research record in social science might find him an academic position. This hope was not realised, but in 1948 he was appointed to the newly created position of research (later senior research) officer in the Department of Education—a post he occupied with distinction until his retirement in 1969.

Peter Jacoby, 1948. *(Ilse Jacoby Collection)*

The increasing birth-rates that began in the early 1940s meant that the previous two decades of static or even declining school populations would be followed by a period, unknown in duration, of explosive increases at all levels. Jacoby brought a new conceptual approach to the department's demographic planning. The forecasting techniques he devised and the information systems he created became the basis for all forward planning for the education system. The result of his work was published in 1949, 1958, and 1969 in three government forecasts of the size, composition, and regional distribution of school and university populations for the forthcoming decade. The last was notable for the inclusion of a technical appendix explaining the methodology and setting out the assumptions on which the forecasts were made. Peter's expertise was used by UNESCO as a model in educational planning.[4]

Peter Jacoby was awarded a Rockefeller fellowship in 1956–57, with which he and Ilse spent a year's leave chiefly at Princeton University in the United States. He also attended numerous overseas conferences as a New Zealand representative, including the UNESCO seminar on educational statistics in Tokyo in 1961, the United Nations world population conference in Belgrade in 1965, and a demographic conference in Sydney in 1967. While his work by its nature did not bring him into the public eye, brief celebrity did come to him when in 1959 the total number of pupils reported by New Zealand's 350 secondary schools (107,650) precisely replicated the figure he had estimated in April of the previous year—a feat that even earned him a place in the internationally syndicated newspaper column, Ripley's 'Believe it or not!'

While working for the Department of Education, Jacoby also maintained an active interest in academic sociology, officiating as chairman of the Social Sciences Section of the Wellington branch of the Royal Society in 1949, and publishing on aspects of New Zealand society and demography. After his retirement he energetically dedicated himself to scholarship in sociology and social philosophy. A private scholar in the liberal tradition, he combined an unfailing enthusiasm and zest for his subject with meticulous discipline, and his excellence gave him an international standing. He initially worked on Ferdinand Tönnies, amassing the most complete collection of printed and manuscript materials outside Kiel, publishing (in addition to several conference papers and articles) his full-length study *Die moderne Gesellschaft im sozialwissenschaftlichen Denken von Ferdinand Tönnies*,[5] and editing Tönnies' papers in *Ferdinand Tönnies: Studien zur Philosophie und Gesellschaftslehre im 17. Jahrhundert*.[6] Jacoby also provided an introduction to Tönnies for English-speaking readers by editing, translating, and annotating a selection from his major writings, which appeared in both hardback and paperback under the title *Ferdinand Tönnies: On Social Ideas and Ideologies*.[7]

Through Tönnies he had also come to the study of the English social philosopher Thomas Hobbes (1588–1679). Research into Hobbes increasingly absorbed Jacoby in his last years. Indeed, Hobbes became a constant companion peering over his shoulder, and his friends discovered that any conversation begun, on whatever subject, however mundane, mysteriously and rapidly developed into a conversation about Hobbes. A member of numerous learned societies, and in almost daily correspondence with scholars in places as distant and as different as New York, Paris, and Bradford, Jacoby published on Hobbes in scholarly journals, and at the time of his death in 1978 was engaged on a major entry on Hobbes for a Swiss encyclopaedic history of philosophy, Friedrich Ueberweg's *Grundriss der Geschichte der Philosophie*.[8]

Peter and Ilse explored every corner of New Zealand and came to know it intimately. The breadth and detail of Peter's knowledge are reflected in the scrupulously thorough, accurate, and balanced German guidebook to New Zealand, which he wrote for the *Mai's Weltführer* series in 1975.[9] There was no better guide to New Zealand flora than Ilse, whose reading in New Zealand history was also encyclopaedic. They were close friends of Elsie and John Beaglehole; Ilse helped the latter, New Zealand's celebrated authority on James Cook and Pacific exploration, to decipher the handwriting in Cook's journals.

Both also entered enthusiastically into the cultural life of Wellington. They were founding members of the Wellington Goethe Society, of which Peter was president in 1974, and privately did much to foster German language and culture, especially by offering hospitality, food, and conversation to university students of German. Their enormous contribution is commemorated in the Jacoby Prize, awarded annually to the best student in the Goethe Society's German Oral Competition for schools in the Wellington region.

Both passionate music-lovers, they were orchestra subscribers and founding members and mainstays of the Wellington Chamber Music Society. Through their kindness in ferrying musicians between airport, hotel, and concert chamber, and the hospitality they offered them, Peter and Ilse must have become known to almost every major quartet and trio in the world. The Turnbull Library in Wellington and the Victoria University Halls of Residence Foundation in addition received generous bequests in Peter's will.

Peter Jacoby, 1976. *(Ilse Jacoby Collection)*

With his sudden death in 1978 the scholarly world lost an expert on Thomas Hobbes, the philosopher who had famously declared the human condition to be one of war of everyone against everyone, and human life to be 'solitary, poor, nasty, brutish, and short'.[10] Jacoby's own life, however, decisively disproved Hobbes's dicta. For although a sceptic in temperament and of a sober, serious, and methodical nature, Jacoby was also an epicurean: a connoisseur of good food and wines, a lover of music, a concert-goer, a traveller, and a man who much enjoyed conversation and wit. The blue eyes that expressed such penetrating scepticism could equally sparkle with delighted merriment; he entertained women especially with teasing gallantry. He was a *bon vivant*, a lover of company, and unfailingly kind to his friends. He was also exceptionally fortunate in having a partner who not only helped him with his work, both inside and outside their home, but also provided her husband with steadfast moral support and companionship in what were often difficult times. Peter and Ilse Jacoby brought with them the best qualities of German culture, and both gave generously to their adopted country.

1   For this and the following biographical information I am indebted to Mrs Ilse Jacoby and her generous provision of documentation.

2   Under wartime regulations, the New Zealand police were obliged to investigate all refugees on behalf of the authorities charged with supervision of alien affairs. The resulting interviews with refugees, some of which were conducted at the local police station, others at the refugees' own residence, could, depending on the personality of the interviewing policeman, range from a most intimidating interrogation to a pleasant and informal chat. Further examples of refugees' experiences of police surveillance during wartime are given in Ann Beaglehole, *A Small Price to Pay: Refugees from Hitler in New Zealand, 1936–1946* (Wellington, 1988), pp. 99–104.

3   Under wartime regulations, the Minister of Justice had the power to restrict where aliens lived and could, in theory, prevent them from buying property 'in view of shipping or other places of military significance if investigations showed them to be suspicious'; see Beaglehole [note 2], p. 110. In practice, however, the then minister seems to have been most reluctant to invoke such powers, and in any event, most of the suspicion directed at the supposed 'monitoring' of shipping movements by refugees originated with the refugees' suspicious neighbours, who believed espionage to be afoot when in fact there was none; cf. Beaglehole [note 2], p. 162, n. 128, and pp. 110f.

4   For this information I am indebted to Dr W.L. Renwick, Director General of Education 1975–88.

5   Stuttgart, 1971.

6   Stuttgart-Bad Cannstatt, 1975.

7   New York, 1974.

8   Jacoby's contribution is to be found in *Die Philosophie des 17. Jahrhunderts*, Bd. 3: England, ed. Jean-Pierre Schobinger (Basel, 1988), pp. 93 ff.

9   Eduard Georg Jacoby, *Neuseeland: Reiseführer mit Landeskunde* (Mai's Weltführer no. 15), Buchenhain, 1975.

10 Thomas Hobbes, in *Leviathan* (1651), part 1, chapter 13.

27

Erich Geiringer

BEVAN BURGESS

Erich Geiringer was born to Jewish parents in Vienna on Schubert's birthday, 31 January, in 1917. With three siblings, all later distinguished in their fields, Erich grew up listening to socialist intellectual discussions in the Café Geiringer, run by his politically active socialist father.[1] (The building is still there but is now a Turkish laundromat.[2]) After attending *Realgymnasium*, he entered Vienna University as a medical student in 1936. Two years into his studies when Germany invaded Austria, Geiringer fled. He caught a train in the middle of Germany, as the safest way to throw the authorities off his scent. At the Belgian border, he paid someone helping refugees to show him where to cross the border at night and how to time it between border guard patrols. The man then picked him up on the other side and drove him to the nearest town.[3]

Erich lived hand to mouth in Belgium for six months, largely on potato chips, often all he could afford. His brother Alfred helped him get to England in October 1938, under the sponsorship of the World Student Service.[4] He obtained a job as a laboratory assistant in Birmingham until France fell in 1940. He was then interned for six months in four different camps across Britain.[5] At one, known as the 'University of Huyton' near Liverpool, he shared quarters with three of the four members of the Amadeus Quartet and other leading representatives of Vienna's former intelligentsia.[6]

Erich found work on release at Chislehurst County School for Boys as a science teacher. He sat external exams and was accepted as a student in medicine at the University of London,[7] but because of the war[8] trained at the extramural School of Medicine of the Royal Colleges at Surgeons' Hall, Edinburgh, qualifying in 1947.[9] He was a Whaitt scholar at the Gerontological Research Institute at Edinburgh University from 1947 to 1949; junior research fellow (1949–51) and senior research fellow (1951–53) at Edinburgh University; ran a National Health Service general practice[10] in the Stockbridge area of Edinburgh[11] (1948–53); and was a Fulbright scholar at Peter Bent Brigham Hospital, Boston, USA, for six months in 1953. By 1954, he had a doctorate of medicine from Edinburgh and a PhD from London University.[12] He became research pathologist at the Royal Hospital for Sick Children, Glasgow, from 1953 to 1956, and medical registrar, Whipscross Hospital, London, in 1957–58, managing 150 beds. Next, he travelled for eight months, visiting hospitals in Sudan and Ceylon, and leprosariums and medical schools in Colombo and Rangoon, and working as

Erich Geiringer.
*(Photograph by Vicki Ginn,
featured on cover of* Spuc
'em All, *Martinborough,
Alister Taylor, 1978.
Reproduced courtesy of
Alister Taylor)*

a house surgeon in Canada and as ship's surgeon on a Liverpool–Rangoon return voyage.[13]

All this time he published prolifically on an astonishing range of medical and sociomedical subjects. His bibliography lists twenty medical papers published between 1946 and 1959. His interest in medico-political matters and health service organisation began before he left Britain, with his publication of a paper called *Murder at the Crossroads*, about the deficiencies of the National Health Service.[14]

Geiringer came to New Zealand to take up an appointment as senior research officer to the Clinical Research Committee of the New Zealand Medical Research Council, Department of Medicine, Otago University, in Dunedin, in 1959.[15] In New Zealand medicine and medical training were controlled by a small, self-perpetuating oligarchy and were in disarray. There was a shortage of both GPs and specialists; there was only one medical school in the entire country; medical research was underfunded; hospital doctors were grossly underpaid; abortion laws were antiquated; and the Mental Hygiene Division of the Department of Health was run down. Moreover, at that time the government retained power to direct medical labour wherever it thought desirable.[16]

Ferociously intelligent, formidably erudite, Geiringer devoted himself with Rabelaisian gusto to scourging the hypocrites in Dunedin's medical temple. In speech or writing, like the pamphleteers of the sixteenth and seventeenth centuries, he knew how to position an argument with the precision of an acupuncture needle, then drive it home with the force of a meat-axe cleaving bone. He made enemies rapidly. He became, in response to the fury of the traditionalist local medical establishment, a medical politician almost overnight. His approach was non–party. He was close to a younger woman, the daughter of a leading Cabinet minister. But his medico-political meetings would ultimately cause a spectacular electoral upset in a government seat.

Overqualified and underemployed, Geiringer had time to teach, something he loved and excelled at. But his methods, modelled on overseas practice, were unconventional by local standards. In Dunedin, students were still subjected to learning by lecture.[17] Geiringer brought specialists in different disciplines together to discuss a case before the students. His evening sessions were enormously popular, to the outrage of other faculty members accustomed to more distant and frosty relationships. One of them got so cross one night that he doused the lights. In response, Geiringer held his subsequent sessions by candle-light. His Candlelight Symposia became a roaring success with the students, but further soured relations with a bigoted hierarchy.[18]

George Salmond, a former Director General of Health, recorded his memories of Erich: 'A student then, I remember him larger than life. His appearance on public occasions in a black cloak, and his silver open-topped Armstrong Sidley car, caused excitement wherever he went. He challenged social conventions and the established order, a catalyst for change, a sort of academic pied piper.'[19]

In 1962, Geiringer shocked conservative Dunedin by publishing a pamphlet advocating the lewd, unmentionable practice of smear-testing women for cervical cancer and tried to distribute it to doctors. The university authorities responded by banning medical students from helping to distribute it. The local police commander was advised it was obscene, but Erich said it would save lives. The commander had seen a close relative die of cervical cancer. 'Go ahead,' he said.[20]

Geiringer resigned at the end of his contract, before he could be dismissed.[21] After a few GP locums, he pawned his watch and sailed to Britain as a ship's doctor.[22] In the Shetlands, as a locum, where he once again became acquainted with Robert Burns, bawdy Scots songs and the even bawdier Scots jokes he had loved as a student. He came back to New Zealand at the end of 1962 (with a length of Scottish tweed which, tailored into a new cape, he subsequently wore for many years),[23] romantically in time for the graduation ceremony of his Cabinet minister's daughter, Carol Shand.[24] He and Carol married in 1964. They established a general practice in Wellington, which they ran together for more than thirty years. They built a strong, loyal practice serving New Zealanders from all walks of life. Erich, a sensitive and brilliant doctor with a deep and extraordinarily empathetic intelligence, delivered to his patients care and caring of exceptional and exemplary quality. I know. I was one of them.

He was blackballed from membership of the New Zealand branch of the British Medical Association for the accuracy and the savagery of his pamphleteering—ostensibly because he published under his own name, not anonymously. The *New Zealand Medical Journal* refused to print his articles.[25] Erich responded with typical bravura by forming his own rival New Zealand Medical Association. The name was a political master stroke.[26] All doctors got for paying their subscription was a magazine that Erich wrote and circulated free to every doctor in the country—yet in due course, a quarter of the doctors in New Zealand paid to join.[27]

That membership gave him the best medical intelligence service in the country. He used his magazine to make a full-frontal assault on the privilege and obscurantism typical of New Zealand medicine in those days. He used satire mercilessly to attack what he saw as ignorance, pomposity, and stupidity. 'If you want change in medicine, play the man, not the ball,' he said to me once, explaining the strategy he adopted in his magazine. 'Hit their egos so hard that they can't stand what they look like in the eyes of their neighbours or the shaving mirror.'

'Aren't you frightened of the cost of libel action?' I asked, after one issue advocated the dismissal of the Director of Mental Health on the grounds that he sat his psychiatry exams twice, failed both times, and had no qualifications to hold the job.

Erich shook his head. 'No one would take me to court. They would look too foolish. I have no money, and I know too much,' he said.

He shamelessly politicised his campaigns, for example, by making health the central election issue in selected government marginal seats. The more or less continuous establishment cry, 'Get Geiringer!' culminated in 1976 in the worst nightmare a doctor can face: an accusation of patient-rape. It was thrown out by the jury.

A tirelessly energetic promoter of reform, he organised an appeal for population control. He campaigned for measles vaccinations and abortion law reform and against rules outlawing the possession of injection needles (he planted needles in the pens of the inquiry panel to illustrate his point). He made submissions to Parliament and to royal commissions. He compiled medical papers and he wrote books. He had single-handedly, he would claim later, 'dragged New Zealand medicine forward into the nineteenth century'. His magazine and one or two of his books remain, writes colleague Dr Roger Ridley Smith, 'a very readable record of medicine in the 60s and 70s—a *tour de force* of publishing that we are unlikely to see again.'[28]

In the thick of these activities, between 1973 and 1984, he took time out to conduct a late-night radio show answering the questions of troubled listeners on socially taboo subjects in language that no one could misunderstand. Asked by one woman if masturbation was harmful, he replied: 'Absolutely not. In fact it has the advantage that if your partner is late home, you can start without him.'[29] He won a cult following, including some whose primary, if impossible, aim in life was to shock their talk-back host.

Erich had always found it amusing that he was quite free to say 'that fucking dog' in New Zealand, but if he said, making purer linguistic use of the term, 'that dog is fucking', people who used it in the same sense daily found it offensive. Occasionally, he used it on radio in its original sense, knowing that was how most Radio Windy listeners described in private what the middle classes refer to as 'intercourse'. The station put its foot down and demanded assurances. Erich wouldn't give them, so a decade unique in the annals of New Zealand medical broadcasting finally terminated.[30]

From 1985, with the publication of his anti-nuclear primer, *Malice in Blunderland*, Erich devoted himself almost entirely to campaigning for the global elimination of nuclear weapons. This became a passion that he pursued relentlessly and despite increasing disability to within a few days of his death.[31] It was retired judge Harold Evans of Christchurch who first suggested in an open letter to the prime ministers of New Zealand and Australia that the legality of nuclear weapons be challenged at the International Court of Justice. It was Erich Geiringer who, when governments would not help, persuaded the Nobel Peace Prize winners, International Physicians for Prevention of Nuclear War, to seek from the International Court of Justice, through the World Health Organisation, an advisory opinion on whether the use of nuclear weapons by a state in war or other armed conflict would breach its obligations under international law.[32]

The anti-nuclear weapons strategy Geiringer devised as international coordinator for the World Court Project of the International Physicians for Prevention of Nuclear War was typical of the man for whom dealing with controversy was second nature. He saw nuclear arsenals and the states that make and own them as stupid, man-made threats to life as we know it. In his view, the planet should be a better place than the one into which he was born.[33] Geiringer's view was that the World Court Project couldn't lose. If atomic weapons were legal, then Pakistan was entitled to them, and not even Caspar Weinberger could enjoy that prospect.[34]

Only organisations within the UN system can transmit such questions to the World Court. Geiringer travelled to New York, sent a tide of faxes, letters, and telephone calls, and built up a campaign aimed at getting first the World Health Organisation, then the UN General Assembly, to request an opinion from the court. The New Zealand authorities, in cahoots with American–British–French nuclear interests, refused to take up the issue, so he phoned doctors and officials in smaller countries to get the item on the agenda. It paid off. In 1993, WHO asked the court to rule on the legality of nuclear arms. Within a few months, the UN General Assembly endorsed the question.[35]

Erich Geiringer lost his battle with multiple myeloma, a form of blood cancer, on 24 August 1995. Two months after his death, the World Court case he had successfully sought against such odds began in the Hague on 31 October. Four days before he died, Erich was still working to persuade the New Zealand—and any other—Government that the best way to stop French nuclear testing in the Pacific was a direct approach to the Security Council under Sections 33–34 of the UN Charter to claim that the tests were a threat to the peace and security of the region. A message on his death notice requested, instead of flowers, donations to the IPPNW.

On 8 July 1996, the World Court ruled out the WHO request on technical grounds, but recommended in response to a companion request of the General Assembly that nuclear weapons be banned from warfare, provided national integrity is not at stake. Commenting on the court ruling, the leader of the Opposition in New Zealand, Helen Clark, said it was absolutely clear that if Geiringer, George Salmond, and others had not pushed WHO to take a stand, the issue would not have gathered the momentum required to reach the court.[36] New Zealand Prime Minister Jim Bolger said the most important aspect of the court's decision was its finding that there was an obligation on states to successfully negotiate nuclear disarmament. 'Hopefully the judgement will assist in getting a completed comprehensive test ban treaty. When negotiators resume, they face the court's direction that there should be comprehensive nuclear disarmament.'[37]

In an oration at Geiringer's funeral, Dr George Salmond, former Director General of Health and Geiringer's close colleague in IPPNW, concluded: 'History will I believe show Erich Geiringer to be one of the most significant figures in public health in New Zealand this century. He helped us, at times drove us, to confront issues, important issues, for our growth as a medical profession and as an independent Pacific nation. We have much to thank him and to thank Carol for.'

1 Fritz Spiegel, *Independent*, 8 September 1995.
2 Dr Carol Shand, letter to Fritz Spiegel, 3 September 1995.
3 Ibid.
4 Ibid.
5 CV supplied by Dr Carol Shand.
6 Spiegel [note 1].
7 See note 5.
8 Verbal communication, Dr Carol Shand.
9 See note 5.
10 Ibid.
11 Lawrence Dopson, *Scotsman*, 5 October 1995.
12 See note 5.
13 Ibid.
14 Ibid.
15 Ibid.
16 Spiegel [note 1].
17 Peter Kitchin, *Evening Post*, 31 August 1995.
18 Ibid.
19 Dr George Salmond, farewell tribute, Old St Paul's Cathedral, Wellington, 29 August 1995.
20 Kitchin [note 17].
21 Verbal communication from Dr Carol Shand to me.
22 Kitchin [note 17].
23 Ibid.
24 Verbal communication from Dr Carol Shand to me.
25 Spiegel [note 1].
26 See note 19.
27 Personal knowledge; I was at that time political correspondent for New Zealand Newspapers Ltd and pioneered the newspaper publication of materials from his magazine. It was not easy to be true to the spirit of the original without offending libel laws.
28 Dr Roger Ridley-Smith, *Capital Times*, 30 August 1995.
29 Jeremy Rose, *City Voice*, 31 August 1995.
30 Verbal communication from Dr Carol Shand to me.
31 See note 19.
32 New Zealand Press Association report, *Evening Post*, 6 July 1996.
33 Kitchin [note 17].
34 Dr Peter Munz, draft for funeral oration, provided by Dr Carol Shand.
35 Dr George Salmond, 27 September 1995 draft for an obituary in the *New Zealand Medical Journal*, provided by Dr Carol Shand.
36 New Zealand Press Association Report, *Evening Post*, 10 July 1996.
37 Ibid.

28

Arthur and Lisl Hilton

MARGARET SUTHERLAND

One of four children, Arthur Hirschbein was born on 19 August 1909 in Vienna, where he grew up and received his education.[1] His study of chemical engineering at Vienna University enabled him to enter the field of oil refining, first in his home city and then in Bratislava, where his compulsory military service had unexpectedly taken him. He was surprised to discover that, because his father had been born in an area that happened to become part of Czechoslovakia in 1918, he himself was considered Czech by the military authorities, although he had never lived on Czech soil and was unable to speak the language. The proximity of Bratislava to Vienna, with its opera, theatres, and rich cultural life, allowed him to foster the passion for music he had acquired in childhood. His thorough knowledge of many operas led to an invitation to join the claque, 'an organised group of knowledgeable people who at each performance of an opera gave the lead to the audience as to when to applaud'.[2]

In Bratislava he met Elisabeth Kohn, daughter of a Viennese mother and Hungarian father, whom he married in 1936. She, too, was steeped in European culture, having enjoyed weekly visits to the theatres of Vienna with her parents and two sisters from an early age,[3] and she also shared her husband's love of sport. New Zealand was to benefit positively from their expertise and enthusiasm obtained in their native Europe.

The frightening prospect of a German invasion of Czechoslovakia made the couple decide to emigrate in 1939, and they opted for New Zealand, the first country to respond to their inquiries. (They also applied to Canada and Australia.)[4] With the aid of Sir Oswald Michael Williams, an English friend, Arthur, his brother, Otto Hilton, and Theo Ranov set off, on the day Hitler crossed the Czech border, on a harrowing journey across Europe to Britain. From there they sailed for New Zealand on the *Strathmore*, disembarking in Wellington in June.[5] Their temporary permits were eventually transformed into permanent ones by H.R.G. Mason, the Minister of Justice, who recognised the men's potential value to the country. Lisl Hilton reached New Zealand via Britain in November 1939.

The early years here were tough and demanding, but the Hiltons made a conscious decision to put something back into the country that had taken them in.[6] Their commitment to New Zealand was evident when they were naturalised in the 1940s, and they each immersed themselves in activities that directly or indirectly touched and enriched the lives of innumerable people. Lisl Hilton already had a fine arts degree from the University of Bratislava, but in Wellington she studied German literature at Victoria University. Professor Conlon, Professor of Modern Languages, invited her to join the staff of the department in 1956, where she taught German. She remained there throughout the years of Paul Hoffmann's headship, retiring in the 1970s. Her vivacity and exuberance proved an inspiration to many young students of German grammar and literature. In addition to teaching, she directed the annual German student drama and was the initiator of the weekly *Kaffeestunde* where, with coffee and cake, students were enticed to speak German in a social and convivial atmosphere. She was also a founding member of the Wellington Goethe Society, formed to promote German language and culture. The Hilton house, too, was an oasis of Europeanness enjoyed by students as well as visiting German-speaking authors and musicians.

Arthur Hilton. *(Hilton Collection)*

The Hilton brothers and Theo Ranov used their knowledge of the petrochemical industry to set up a chemical firm. (Later Hugo Halberstam joined the firm to replace Ranov.) They started out in an old house on Thorndon Quay, where they experimented with the manufacture of lubricating grease in a tin billy over a gas ring—a modest beginning to what was to become the Chemicals Manufacturing Company Ltd. A fortuitous coincidence focused attention on the immigrants. HMS *Ramilles*, in Wellington to escort troops to Egypt, had depleted its supply of grease because of its extended period at sea. Failure to locate any in New Zealand resulted in an approach to the immigrants, who created a product of similar quality. They got a contract to supply the New Zealand Railways with side-rod grease, and in 1941 shifted to bigger premises in the old bacon factory at Ngauranga. CMC was declared an essential war industry.[7] They diversified into other car-care products and established a re-refining plant for used crankcase oil, long before New Zealand became conservation-conscious.[8] From Ngauranga they moved to Seaview. CMC became one of our main industrial chemical industries, and was taken over by BP (NZ) Ltd in 1970, with Arthur Hilton as managing director until his retirement in 1975.

The contribution made by CMC is outstanding in its own right, but is only one of three areas in which Arthur Hilton left an indelible mark on this country. His devotion to sport induced him to become involved in soccer at all levels—a game much less familiar to New Zealanders than rugby at the time of his arrival. He coached young players, served on the committee and later as chairman of the Petone Football Club, was chairman of the National League Club of Wellington, and served on the Executive and Council of the New Zealand Football Association. His involvement is commemorated by the Hilton Cup, which he and his brother donated.

It is arguably in the field of music, however, that this somewhat shy, decisive, and charming man made his most significant impact, and it was certainly the area that he acknowledged brought him the greatest pleasure.[9] From the time of its foundation in 1945, the Hiltons were closely associated with the Wellington Chamber Music Society. Arthur Hilton served on the executive from 1950 until 1965 and was chairman from 1959 until 1966. His genius for organisation, his vision, and his entrepreneurial spirit, however, really came to the fore during his twenty-one-year reign as president of the New Zealand Federation of Chamber Music Societies, a position which he held from 1961 until 1982.[10]

The federation had been founded in 1950 as a means of coordinating the six different chamber music societies in existence at the time and of forming a touring network. This enabled audiences in even relatively small centres to hear high-quality music at a price within their means—something that many visiting musicians noted was unique to New Zealand. Gradually more societies joined the federation, so that, by 1960, twenty centres were on the circuit, hearing six concerts a year.[11]

In 1961, a year after the resignation of Fred Turnovsky as president, Arthur Hilton took over the reins. Under his guidance the already highly successful organisation went from strength to strength. The superb calibre of many of the musicians, such as the Vlach and Juilliard Quartets, the Beaux Arts Trio, and the Amadeus Quartet, to which the music-loving public was treated was only one indicator of his many achievements. This chapter can only touch on others and in no way do them justice.[12] His recognition of the importance of flexibility and the necessity to adapt to the needs of the market were important elements in his success, as were his frugality and financial astuteness.[13] One example of the latter was his establishment of the Music Federation Foundation in 1976, a fund designed to provide the federation with a capital base, so that it had some independent income and could more effectively weather the onslaught of devaluations and other financial hardships. He constantly sought to attract the interest of new audiences and to foster contemporary and New Zealand music. By the end of his period as president, about half of the performers involved in concerts arranged by the federation were New Zealand residents. His role in the federation has been summed up as follows: 'Arthur Hilton's flow of innovative ideas seemed inexhaustible. Like some sort of musical blotting paper, he absorbed ideas from all directions to involve them imaginatively in the work of the Music Federation.'[14]

Particularly dear to his heart was the musical education of the younger generation, who he recognised would, with the right encouragement, become the musicians and the audience of the future, just as young soccer players would be tomorrow's players and spectators. He was a foundation member and on the board of the Wellington Youth Orchestra. In 1965, he instigated the School Chamber Music Contest, initially linked to a design contest for programme covers,[15] with the aim of encouraging young musicians at local and district levels. The best eight groups then progressed to the national finals. After the first year, he approached his own bank, the then Bank of New South Wales, for sponsorship. Since its inception, the contest, now known as the Westpac School Music Contest, has fostered some remarkable musical talent, including Michael Houston, who participated in a group from Timaru Boys' High School. There were also awards for composition and works commissioned by young and mature composers. By 1982, the competition, which had originally had 300 entrants, attracted more than 2,000 competitors.[16]

On 27 August 1973, Arthur Hilton was awarded the Austrian Cross of Honour for Arts and Sciences, First Class, by the Austrian Government. He felt especially honoured that it was presented by the country of his birth for his services to music in his adopted country, and most particularly as an acknowledgement of his work in fostering young musicians. For three years from 1973, he also found time to serve as a member of the Queen Elizabeth II Arts Council. In 1974, he was appointed the Honorary Consul for Austria, and in 1979 Honorary Consul General for Austria in New Zealand.

Arthur Hilton died on 27 February 1982. Since his death, New Zealanders have continued to benefit from his contributions. The Westpac School Contest remains an annual event on the musical calendar, and in recognition of his remarkable services to music, the federation established the Arthur Hilton Memorial Prize, which provides a cash prize for the winning group in the small instrumental section of the School Music Contest.[17]

Lisl Hilton. *(Hilton Collection)*

1 Arthur Hirschbein changed his name to Hilton after coming to New Zealand (R.H.Thomson, 'A transplant that took', *Evening Post*, 18 January 1975). I wish to thank Mrs Lisl Hilton for her generous assistance with information and kind permission to allow the use of her photograph. My thanks also to Miss Elisabeth Airey, Miss Joan Kerr, Mr Robert Lithgow, and Dr John Mansfield Thomson for their excellent information.

2 R.H.Thomson [note 1].

3 Interview with Lisl Hilton, 25 May 1996.

4 R.H.Thomson [note 1].

5 Their sponsor was accountant Gilbert Clark.

6 Interview with Elisabeth Airey, 6 November 1996.

7 Ann Beaglehole, *A Small Price to Pay: Refugees from Hitler in New Zealand, 1936–1946* (Wellington, 1988), p. 77.

8 Interview with Robert Lithgow, 13 November 1996.

9 See Arthur Hilton's acceptance speech for his Austrian Cross of Honour, in J.M.Thomson, *Into a New Key: The Origins and History of the Music Federation of New Zealand 1950–1982* (Wellington, 1985), p. 154.

10 The New Zealand Federation of Chamber Music Societies changed its name three times over the years, first to the Chamber Music Federation of New Zealand, then the Music Federation of New Zealand, then to Chamber Music New Zealand Inc. (interview with Elisabeth Airey, 6 November 1996).

11 J.M.Thomson [note 9], p. 84.

12 J.M.Thomson [note 9] provides a detailed discussion of Arthur Hilton's achievements in the music field.

13 Interview with Joan Kerr, 15 November 1996.

14 Owen Jensen, 'A tribute to Arthur Hilton', *Evening Post*, 6 March 1982.

15 Discontinued in 1975.

16 See Bruce Mason, 'Tribute to Arthur Hilton', *Evening Post*, 6 March 1982.

17 This prize initially paid tuition fees for the same group to attend the annual Cambridge Summer School of Music, which now no longer takes place.

29

Gregory Riethmaier

JAMES N. BADE

Gregory Riethmaier in his Government Tourist Bureau dark room, c. 1975. *(G. Riethmaier Collection)*

When Gregory Riethmaier left Hamburg in 1937 on a round-the-world cruise with his boyhood hero, Count Felix von Luckner, no one would ever have guessed, least of all Riethmaier himself, that he would be leaving Germany for good. Ten months later, his childhood dream of a voyage with von Luckner had turned into a nightmare. Von Luckner left Auckland without him. Yet Riethmaier was always determined to make the most of every situation. After a number of setbacks not of his own making, including a lengthy internment on Somes Island, he embarked on a successful career in photography, which saw him become one of the most prominent professional photographers in the country.

Gregory Riethmaier was born in 1913 in Munich. His parents, devout Roman Catholics like most Bavarians, ran a small pub ('Schnappsbude') in Lindwurmstrasse. With the outbreak of World War I, Riethmaier's father was conscripted into the army and served as a sergeant on the Western Front until he was killed in action in 1918. Riethmaier's father twice came home on leave—one such visit resulted in the birth of his sister in 1917—but Riethmaier remembers nothing of him at all.[1] After the war, his mother sold the family business, but by the time the deal was completed, the German inflation of the 1920s rendered the proceeds practically worthless. Consequently Riethmaier's memories of childhood are characterised by poverty and the seemingly unfair punishments handed out by a young war widow scarcely able to cope with life.

When his mother became seriously ill, her parents looked after him and his sister, and his godmother arranged for him to spend a year attending school in the Swiss town of Dietikon. When he returned to Munich, his mother, now recovered, had moved to an apartment in the Nymphenburg Palace on the outskirts of Munich, the former summer residence of the Bavarian royal family. Prince Ludwig Ferdinand still occupied part of the main building. Riethmaier attended nearby schools, but did not do particularly well, justifying his lack of effort with the example of Count von Luckner, who had always been bottom of the class and then left school altogether at the age of 13. In 1927 Riethmaier took up an apprenticeship in cabinet-making, but two years later the firm he worked for fell victim to the worldwide depression, as did so many others at that time, and had to close its doors. Thanks to the intervention of Prince Ludwig Ferdinand, Riethmaier was able to complete his apprenticeship at a piano factory.

Spurred on by the lessons in positive thinking and practical psychology that he had received from his membership of Oscar Schellbach's 'Großdeutscher Erfolgsring',[2] Riethmaier successfully applied for a job as part of a new post and telegraph initiative in the post office, where he worked for the next few years. Once the Nazis gained power in 1933, however, Riethmaier's unit became part of a new type of 'post police' and was issued with a new 'Postschutz' uniform complete with a pistol in a holster. Before long the political reasons for this Postschutz unit became clear. Every time Hitler made a broadcast, the Postschutz unit was ordered to patrol the whole distance of the cable between the radio station in central Munich and the transmitter 25 kilometres away on the Erdinger Moor. The Postschutz were also asked to collect special bags of mail from every express train arriving from the north, deliver it to party headquarters, and return it to the central sorting office. It was only later that Riethmaier realised that this mail was being opened and checked by party officials before being delivered. Riethmaier felt that he, like many Germans at the time, was quite naive when it came to politics: 'Generally speaking, the German public was far less involved in politics than is the case out here in New Zealand; I would even say we were naive "Spießbürger" ("dullards") many of us. The vast majority, including me, were not only law-abiding and obedient, but excessively so, and we were quite prepared to leave it to Hitler.'[3]

Riethmaier had long been an admirer of Count von Luckner, having read his book *Seeteufel* as a schoolboy (see chapter 4). When von Luckner visited Munich as part of a lecture tour, Riethmaier attended his lectures, and when he heard that von Luckner was to set sail again on a world tour to promote better understanding among the peoples of the world, he decided then and there that he must be one of the crew. Riethmaier approached von Luckner in Munich and kept up a regular correspondence with him for some time, enclosing references, one of them from Prince Ludwig Ferdinand. Finally he was chosen. In a letter dated 18 April 1936, von Luckner wrote to him that there would be only six crew members and that he needed to familiarise himself with the cutter *Seeteufel* before they set sail, adding: 'You will be able to see what no mortal in this country would be able to experience.'[4] Riethmaier wasted no time in resigning from the post office and left for Hamburg.

Once in Hamburg, Riethmaier helped prepare the *Seeteufel* for the long voyage, but before he could depart, he had to do two months' military training. When told that Riethmaier was required to stay on for NCO training, von Luckner intervened, having him sent instead to the navigation college in Blankenese to study for a wireless operator's certificate. Some in the navigation college cautioned Riethmaier against sailing with von Luckner because of alleged unresolved grievances against him on earlier voyages. At one stage, Riethmaier says, he actually decided not to go on the voyage, but von Luckner persuaded him otherwise by threatening to bring in the Gestapo and use his influential top-ranking Nazi 'friends' to cancel Riethmaier's wireless operator's certificate and ruin his future. Riethmaier passed his exams on 2 April 1937, and ten days later the *Seeteufel* sailed from Stettin in Germany for Malmö in Sweden. There were eight crew, not

Above left:
Gregory Riethmaier as wireless operator on board the *Seeteufel*, 1937. *(G. Riethmaier Collection)*

Above right:
Gregory Riethmaier (left) with Holm Winter and Otto Katschke at Tahiti, 1937. *(G. Riethmaier Collection)*

including Count Felix von Luckner and his wife Ingeborg, comprising Krause (first officer), Kunert (engineer), Riethmaier (wireless operator/secretary), Müller (bosun), Thiele (seaman), Katschke (seaman), Winter (cook), and Oesterreich (film cameraman).

Originally, Riethmaier was intended to be cameraman, but this function was taken over by Oesterreich, who was a late addition to the crew. Once they had left Europe, serious problems started to emerge. Disagreements with crew members, and the Count and the Countess in particular, and resentment over what seemed to be unfair apportionment of resources, created difficulties. Riethmaier discovered that the electricity generators interfered with radio communications, thus greatly restricting wireless operations. After a ten-month voyage via the Azores, Saba Island in the West Indies, Puerto Rico, the Panama Canal, Balboa, Cocos Island (where Riethmaier impressed the Count and Countess by shooting three ducks in a row), the Galapagos Islands (where a shark was caught that contained forty-four baby sharks), Tahiti (where they had their lifeboat repaired and took on fresh provisions), Mopelia Island (where they saw the remains of von Luckner's previous vessel, the *Seeadler*, but did not land), and Samoa (where the reception was so friendly that Riethmaier vowed he would return some day), the *Seeteufel* arrived in Auckland on 20 February 1938.

The *Seeteufel* docked at Freemans Bay, and Riethmaier, still wearing a lava-lava from the islands, was looking for the post office to collect mail when a motorist stopped and offered him a lift. This was, Riethmaier says, one of his first encounters 'with the friendly New Zealanders'.[5] Newspaper and radio reporters interviewed all on board. The crew was overwhelmed with hospitality, and Riethmaier was invited home by many amateur radio operators. The German consul, Dr Walter Hellenthal, came up from Wellington, and the crew used this opportunity to air various complaints, the principal one being that their wages had not been lodged in Germany as had previously been agreed. The consul considered that they had a strong case, but that the Reich would not condone their quitting the *Seeteufel* in Auckland because of the bad publicity that would result. After the meeting, Riethmaier talked to the consul privately and asked whether he could sign off in Auckland if he managed to do so quietly, to which the consul replied that he would do what he could to assist. Riethmaier composed a letter to von Luckner outlining his grievances and sent it care of the German consulate in Wellington, as the Count and Countess were touring New Zealand on their lecture tour. In the letter, Riethmaier asks for his discharge and says, among other things:

I should like to point out in the first place that (as you are no doubt aware) before I came aboard at Hamburg I desired to withdraw, but was forced to abandon my decision through your insolent threats (such as arrest by the Gestapo, reports to your influential friends, and cancellation of my transmitting licence). At that time I still believed in all these fairytales.[6]

On his return, two days before their scheduled departure from Auckland, von Luckner treated Riethmaier as if he had never received the letter; when pressed, however, he said he had received the letter and that he had spoken to the consul, who said he must stay on the *Seeteufel*. On hearing this, Riethmaier threatened to release his letter to the press. Von Luckner responded that if Riethmaier decided to stay in Auckland, he would make it impossible for him ever to return to Germany.[7]

Riethmaier realised that the next step was up to him. He had only two days to satisfy the Immigration Department's requirements—he needed two guarantors, a cash deposit of £10, and employment. Luckily the contacts he had already made in New Zealand came to his rescue. A businessman, 'Tiki' Roberts, arranged for him to get a job as a waiter at the Glendowie Country Club. Riethmaier's place on the *Seeteufel* was taken by Colin Moore and Michael Hutt, two 1ZB radio announcers, and von Luckner left without him.

The owner of the Glendowie Country Club, Don Higgins, treated Riethmaier well, and he thoroughly enjoyed working there, although the occasional incident indicated that anti-German feeling still lingered from World War I.[8] Riethmaier's residence permit was renewed for two years. After ten months at the Glendowie Country Club, Riethmaier took on a job at the Dominion Brewery at Otahuhu, and at the same time he had started part-time studies towards a Bachelor of Commerce degree at Auckland University College. With the outbreak of war, the *New Zealand Truth* newspaper embarked on a series of articles accusing Count von Luckner of spying activities during his time here. A *Truth* reporter came to the brewery, but Riethmaier said that he could not comment because of the war situation. The result was a banner headline: 'German spy's ex-wireless operator works at Dominion Brewery.' Riethmaier considered it advisable to leave, and his landlady helped him to find a new job, at Tanner Trailers Ltd in Penrose.

Riethmaier had only been working at Tanner Trailers two months when he returned home one evening to find two detectives waiting for him. One of them read out a warrant for his internment. He was taken to the central police station by car, where he met six further Germans. They were driven to Papakura Military Camp, and on 23 December 1939 were put on the express train to Wellington, where they were to spend most of the remain-

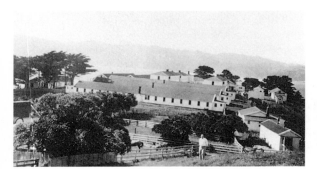

Above left:
Somes Island internment
camp, 1942. *(G.
Riethmaier Collection)*

Above right:
Group of Germans and
Samoan Germans on
Somes Island, 1939.
(G. Riethmaier Collection)

ing war years as civil internees on Somes Island. A small group of fifteen
Samoan Germans had preceded them; gradually the numbers grew until 300
'enemy aliens' of many different nationalities were interned on the island.
Riethmaier was one of the younger internees and was not overly worried
about his situation. It was, he said, much more difficult for married men
'such as those with a wife and children left behind to struggle for their existence in war-time'.[9] Riethmaier was put in charge of the internees' workshop and helped with the camp carpentry. As was his right under the Geneva
Convention, he was allowed to continue his studies at Victoria University
College, passing two papers in 1942 and three more in 1943. Finally, after
the war had ended, Riethmaier was released on 10 October 1945.

In spite of calls from some quarters[10] to 'throw the German internees out
of the Dominion',[11] no Germans who had been interned on Somes Island
were forced to return to Germany, and through his friends in Auckland,
Riethmaier managed to get a job as a waiter at Terraces Hotel in Taupo. Two
years later, he moved back to Auckland and worked for a while at Atwaters
piano firm until he got a job as a travelling photographer at Mansford
Photography. This proved to be a decisive change that determined the future
direction of Riethmaier's professional life. He joined Christopher Bede
Photography in 1948 as a portrait photographer and, at the suggestion of his
employers, who thought New Zealanders would not be able to manage his
surname, started to call himself 'Mr Gregory'. He became so well known
under this name that he decided in 1953 to branch out into his own photography business, and two years later he became a naturalised New Zealander.
His flourishing photography business continued until 1959, when he was
appointed senior photographer (based in Auckland) for the National
Publicity Studios. The twenty years that followed were, he says, 'the best,
most pleasant and most interesting years of my life'.[12]

This job took him all around the upper half of the North Island. In 1964
Riethmaier produced a tourist brochure on Rotorua featuring local identity Rebecca Faulkner. Further collaboration between the two resulted in
the pictorial volume *Rebecca and the Maoris*, published in 1964 by Reed,
which set out to show everyday Maori life in Rotorua. This was the first of
four pictorial volumes produced by Riethmaier: in 1968 *Auckland: Gateway
to New Zealand* appeared, followed five years later by *Auckland: Town and
Around*, and *Samoa ma le fa'a Samoa*.[13] The volume on Samoa gave

Riethmaier the opportunity to visit the country he had last seen in 1938 with von Luckner on the *Seeteufel*. He was delighted to find some of his former fellow German internees living there.[14]

Von Luckner might have brought him to New Zealand, and Oscar Schellbach might have taught him a great deal about positive attitudes and faith in oneself, but it was Gregory Riethmaier's own personal qualities—his congenial nature, his courteous manner, his insistence on high standards—that appealed to those New Zealanders who assisted him in his career, a career that saw his photographs appear on postage stamps, telephone books, in international journals, and magazines and newspapers, apart from his own publications. Now, in active retirement with his wife Elsie in their Northcote home, designed by Christopher Alberts,[15] he can observe the tuis and the woodpigeons and enjoy the company of his children and grandchildren. As he looks back on a varied life lived to the full, he has every right to call himself a 'happy immigrant in the land of the kiwi'.[16]

Advertisement for Gregory photography business (1953–59). *(G. Riethmaier Collection)*

1 The first section of this chapter, concerned with Riethmaier's life from 1913 to 1945, is based on Gregory Riethmaier's autobiography, 'A German immigrant remembers, Part 1: On Count Luckner's *Seeteufel* to New Zealand' (unpublished MS, Auckland, 1997). My thanks to Mr Riethmaier for the many interesting discussions we had in 1996 and 1997 about topics in the present volume, and for making available his memoirs and other material, particularly photographs.

2 'Großdeutscher Erfolgsring' could be translated as 'Pan-German Success League'. Oscar Schellbach appears to have been an early German example of an expert in the field of personal motivation and practical psychology.

3 Riethmaier [note 1], pp. 29f. Riethmaier felt that many Germans were of the opinion that Hitler had done well in improving the economy and reducing unemployment (letter to author, 30 August 1997).

4 Riethmaier [note 1], p. 40.

5 Riethmaier [note 1], p. 85.

6 A copy of this letter is held in the National Archives, ref. no. AAAR 493/66, J 1941/50/864 (National Archives Head Office, Wellington). Cf. Norbert von Frankenstein, *'Seeteufel' Felix Graf Luckner: Wahrheit und Legende* (Hamburg, 1997), pp. 189 and 193.

7 Riethmaier [note 1], p. 90.

8 Riethmaier [note 1], p. 97.

9 Riethmaier [note 1], p. 108.

10 This section of the chapter, dealing with Riethmaier's life after the war, is based on the German version of the second part of his autobiography, *Von Schloß Nymphenburg mit Seeteufel Graf Luckner nach Neuseeland, zweiter Teil* (unpublished MS, Auckland, 1996).

11 Reithmaier [note 10], pp. 191f.

12 Riethmaier [note 10], p. 242.

13 Gregory Riethmaier, *Rebecca and the Maoris* (Wellington/Auckland/Sydney, 1964); G. Riethmaier and R.L. Bacon, *Auckland: Gateway to New Zealand* (Auckland & London, 1968); Gregory Riethmaier and R.L. Bacon, *Auckland: Town & Around* (Auckland & London, 1973); *Samoa ma le fa'a Samoa*, photography by Gregory Riethmaier, text by Richard A. Goodman (Auckland & London, 1973).

14 *Samoa ma le fa'a Samoa* [note 13], p. 4; cf. Riethmaier [note 10], pp. 296–9.

15 Christopher Alberts, formerly an assistant of Third Reich architect Albert Speer, had worked for the New Zealand Government on state house design until he was interned on Somes Island. After the war he established his own architectural practice in Auckland (Riethmaier [note 10], pp. 215 & 227).

16 Riethmaier [note 10], p. 335.

30

Denis Adam

PETER RUSSELL

Denis Frederick Adam OBE, New Zealand businessman and patron of the arts, was born Dietrich Fritz Otto Werner Adam in Berlin in 1924, the fourth of four children of a German Jewish upper-middle-class family.[1] The family, in which both parents were Jewish, looked back on a long tradition in Germany and was socially and culturally thoroughly assimilated. On his mother's side, Denis Adam's ancestors included a supplier of horses to the court of Frederick the Great of Prussia and a great-great-grandfather who had been one of Prussia's more successful bankers, as well as a grandfather who practised medicine in Berlin, bore duelling scars from his student days, and was a major in the German army.[2] On his father's side, the family's rise to the middle class was more recent. A great-grandfather had been a tailor, and in the late nineteenth century his son, Saul Adam, had built the tailoring business into a conglomerate with its head office in Berlin, consisting of manufacturing, wholesaling, and retail divisions. Saul Adam had financed cousins and nephews into retail establishments all over Germany, thus laying the foundations of what became a prosperous family business.[3]

Denis Adam's father Fritz Adam was one of ten children. In common with his four brothers he did compulsory military service, and he fought in World War I as first lieutenant in a venerable Prussian regiment, winning the Iron Cross Second Class and First Class.[4] In common with other Jews, he was to find that this record of service to the fatherland counted for little when the Nazis came to power in 1933. When the implications of the Nazi policy of persecution of the Jews made themselves felt, Denis's brother Peter went to university in England, and Denis and his brother Ken were sent to boarding school in Edinburgh. In 1934 their parents also emigrated to London. They were permitted to take only their household effects with them. There his father died of a heart attack in 1936 at the age of 56, and his mother, to make ends meet, opened a guest-house. Denis continued his education in London, matriculating at London University at an unusually early age and studying accountancy while also working part-time for an insurance broking firm.[5] Volunteering at 16 for aircrew service with the RAF, he trained as a pilot in Rhodesia and saw service in the invasion of Europe in the last stages of the war.[6]

When the war ended in August 1945, Denis Adam was still only 21. In the RAF he had met many New Zealanders with whom he had become friends; this experience, and the desire to live in a young and developing

Above left:
Denis Adam's grandfather
Martin Saalfeld (centre)
in the uniform of a
Prussian Army major
(medical officer) with his
brothers-in-law Eddy
(left) and Paul, c. 1912.
(D. Adam Collection)

Above right:
Denis Adam's father,
Fritz Adam, in the
uniform of the Zieten
Hussars.
(D. Adam Collection)

country that would offer greater opportunities than the overcrowded UK,
persuaded him to emigrate to New Zealand in 1946. A cousin offered him
a job as a trainee cutter in his rainwear factory in Wellington, where he
arrived in January 1947 with £6 in his pocket.[7] This marked the beginning
of an exceptionally successful business career that was also to provide the
means for private patronage and promotion of the arts on a scale this
country has seldom seen.

Denis Adam had always been keenly interested in the arts, and there was
artistic talent in the family; his older brother Ken became one of the leading art directors of films of his time. Denis's happy Sunday morning visits
to the museums of Berlin with his father had been followed by his own
exploration of the museums and galleries of London and by frequent
concert-going; the family had several leading musicians among their friends.
The cultural scene in Wellington in the immediate post-war years was bleak
by comparison, yet generated its own excitement as a grassroots base of
interest in the arts developed, in part through a stream of immigrants from
Europe who brought with them the cultural traditions and expectations of
their countries of origin.

Lili Kraus, an excellent pianist and pupil of Artur Schnabel, made her
home in New Zealand for a number of years; the Czech-born immigrants
Fred Turnovsky and Arthur Hilton were promoting a chamber music organ-
isation that would bring outstanding chamber music soloists and groups to
New Zealand; in 1947 the New Zealand National Orchestra gave its first
concert; and in the 1950s both the New Zealand Opera Company and the
New Zealand Ballet Company were founded, and the Alex Lindsay String
Orchestra was giving concerts of high standard. In Wellington the Unity
Theatre, an outstanding amateur theatre, became the training ground for
many of the actors, directors, and designers who later established professional

theatre in New Zealand. New Zealand painters and craftspeople were also beginning to find a language of their own.

Having initially found his friends chiefly among people who had been in the British services during the war, Denis Adam soon began to move too in artistic circles and to find friends among musicians, painters, and actors. This was facilitated by the development of a coffee house culture in Wellington, fostered by such entrepreneurs as the Hamburg-born Harry Seresin.[8] However, Denis Adam's most important encounter of those years was with Verna Finlayson, an intelligent, strikingly attractive young woman from Canterbury who was working in Wellington as a private secretary. She and Denis married in London in January 1953 and, after a honeymoon in Europe, returned to Wellington to live.[9]

Denis Adam's business skills were evident early: promoted to positions of increasing responsibility in the rainwear factory, by the time he married he was enjoying a high income, part of which he invested in property. Eager to embark on an independent business career of his own, after an interim as a service station owner he turned his attention to insurance broking, of which he had had some experience in London, but which was a profession almost unknown in New Zealand at the time. In 1960 the firm of Adam & Adam Ltd came into being, with offices in Lambton Quay. The second 'Adam' was a ruse designed to provide the firm with a cachet of commercial respectability: predicted inquiries as to who the second Adam was enabled Denis to refer to his brother Peter, a director of a merchant bank and an underwriting member of Lloyd's![10]

Denis Adam brought to his brokerage practice an ebullient, positive, and engaging personality, a dedication to service for his clients, a huge energy and, not least, a genius for detecting where developments in the market were leading and finding innovative ways of meeting them. By the 1970s, he was annually visiting insurance markets in the USA, the UK, and Europe to attend to the placement of his clients' risks, and his firm had become by far the largest locally based insurance broker in New Zealand, with offices in Wellington, Auckland, Christchurch, Rotorua, and Melbourne. An association with the multinational insurance broker Stenhouse Reed Shaw resulted in 1980 in an amalgamation of the two companies, whose combined strengths enabled them to secure the broking contracts of such large companies as New Zealand Rail and other state-owned enterprises.

At the age of 65 Denis Adam retired from the firm he had founded—only to embark on a new career in partnership with a friend in a niche professional liabilities underwriting insurance company. At the same time, as the elder statesman of New Zealand insurance brokers, his advice is much sought after, and he also runs a small consultancy company.[11] He is, however, an equally familiar sight in concert halls and galleries. For it is not Denis Adam's business success that justifies his inclusion in this volume but the uses to which he has put the wealth thereby acquired. This began with art purchases. In the early 1960s Verna and he perspicaciously began buying New Zealand paintings of the twentieth century, particularly contemporary works. They decided to establish a charitable trust that would own the collection, and in early 1976 the Adam Foundation was formed.[12] It is one

Denis Adam. *(D. Adam Collection)*

of the most significant private collections anywhere of modern New Zealand painting, and it is intended that it will one day be available to the citizens of Wellington.

Then, as their financial resources increased, Denis and Verna decided that they would like to encourage New Zealand artists by sponsoring competitions in various artistic fields. The initial commitment was to fund competitions at two-year intervals, which were to alternate between the visual arts and literature; during the 'fallow' years in between the intention was to sponsor some activity in the field of music.[13] Thus began a career of private artistic patronage, which since 1988 has seen more than a million dollars contributed to the arts, and which in its generous far-sightedness, in an era of government parsimony, stands as a pioneering act whose significance might only become fully clear in retrospect.

The first competition funded was a visual arts competition in 1988 for young New Zealand artists, with a first prize of $10,000, won by Christine Hellyer. At the same period the School of Music at Victoria University, lacking the funds to provide a concert room in its planned new building, was the fortunate recipient of a generous grant from the Adam Foundation enabling the superb concert room to be built, which bears its donors' name.[14] A literature competition in 1990 with a first prize of $10,000 was won by historian James Belich for his book, *I Shall Not Die: Titokowaru's War*,

New Zealand, 1868–9, with runners-up Janet Frame, Owen Marshall, and
John Cranna.[15] Early in 1991 the foundation co-hosted a film seminar at the
Newtown Film Production Village, at which Denis Adam's brother Ken gave
a presentation and at which almost the entire New Zealand film industry
was represented.[16] In the same year, the Adam Violin Competition attracted
widespread attention throughout New Zealand. Its first prize of $10,000 was
won by Sarah McClelland.[17] In 1992 the inauguration of a New Zealand
Portrait Gallery, modelled on the National Portrait Gallery in London,
brought a competition in portraiture funded by the Adam Foundation, won
by Jo L'Estrange.[18]

The pattern thus established has continued and expanded. Indeed a
perusal of projects completed or planned reveals that no area of creative or
performing endeavour in New Zealand remains untouched by the Adam
Foundation: they have included a playwright's award, a film art award, several music commissions, sponsorship of exhibitions, of opera, of chamber
music summer schools and festivals, of artists studying overseas.[19] The most
prestigious competition funded so far by the foundation has been the
International Cello Competition, held together with a Cello Festival in July
1995 in Christchurch—a genuinely international event with five leading
international cellists as judges and a field of forty candidates from all around
the world.[20] It was held with success again in 1997.

Each of these ventures has been characterised not only by the generosity
of the donors but also by their personal engagement. Denis and Verna Adam
are not desk philanthropists; they are committed to the success of what they
support and are there on the spot to see it happening. In Denis Adam,
Germany's loss has been his adopted country's great gain.

1 This and all following factual information is taken from Denis Adam's *Profile of a New New
   Zealander: The Autobiography of Denis Adam* (Wellington, 1996). I am also grateful to Mr Adam for
   his unstinting assistance with information and documentation.
2 Adam [note 1], pp. 9f.
3 Adam [note 1], p. 10.
4 Ibid.
5 Adam [note 1], pp. 17–25.
6 Adam [note 1], pp. 29–43.
7 Adam [note 1], pp. 51f.
8 Adam [note 1], pp. 45, 54–60.
9 Adam [note 1], pp. 61–3.
10 Adam [note 1], pp. 67–71.
11 Adam [note 1], pp. 71–99.
12 Adam [note 1], pp. 101–4.
13 Adam [note 1], p. 109.
14 Adam [note 1], pp. 109f.
15 Adam [note 1], pp. 110f.
16 Adam [note 1], pp. 111f.
17 Adam [note 1], pp. 112f.
18 Adam [note 1], pp. 113f, 116.
19 See e.g. Adam [note 1], pp. 116–23.
20 Adam [note 1], pp. 119f.

31

Sir Thomas Eichelbaum

BILL SEWELL

With the possible exception of those whose business is literature or philosophy, no occupational group is more concerned with language and words than lawyers. Their work presupposes an understanding of the subtleties of a particular language that is denied even to all but a minority of native speakers. It is all the more remarkable, then, that two of New Zealand's most prominent jurists have had non-English-speaking backgrounds. One is O. T. J. Alpers (1867–1927), who was of Danish stock. The other is the current Chief Justice of New Zealand, Sir Thomas Eichelbaum, who was born on 17 May 1931 in Königsberg (then part of Germany and now part of Russia), and who emigrated to New Zealand in 1938 at the age of seven.

Königsberg was razed to the ground during World War II, and Eichelbaum has never returned to what would now be an unrecognisable home town. But he has positive early memories, which include going to the fishing villages of Nidden or Schwarzort on the sand spit enclosing the Kurisches Haff in summer, while in winter he enjoyed ice-skating and tobogganing. As the only child of a Jewish father, however, he was made painfully aware of the anti-Semitic fever then sweeping Germany when he was one day pelted with snowballs by a group of schoolchildren, before being attacked with fists. An adult came to his rescue but, clearly overcome by ambivalence, abused the young Eichelbaum by calling him 'a bloody Jew'.[1]

When Eichelbaum's parents made the decision to emigrate, and he discovered that their destination, New Zealand, was on the other side of the globe, he was alarmed by the thought that its inhabitants might have to walk upside down. The family journeyed to New Zealand via Canada, sailing across the Pacific on the ill-fated *Niagara*.[2] A principal reason influencing their choice of New Zealand was that a branch of the family was long established in Wellington: that of his father's cousin, Siegfried Eichelbaum, a prominent businessman who had qualified as a lawyer but never practised.

The early years after immigrating cannot have been easy for Eichelbaum and his parents. Not all New Zealanders were able or willing to grasp the distinction between a Nazi sympathiser and a refugee from Germany, especially during the war—a time that Eichelbaum spent in the unforgiving environment of school. In addition, his father, Dr Walter Eichelbaum, who had been a lawyer in Germany, had to content himself initially with work as a labourer in the Wright Stephenson woolstore near the Wellington railway yards. He made light of it, saying that he had attained a high position—'about three bales high'—but it was many years before he managed to secure legal employment, in the public service.

Walter was not a practising Jew, and the family did not associate exclusively with the German Jewish refugee community, although Thomas's mother, Frieda, a nurse, did set up a business baking rye bread, which was unobtainable in New Zealand in those days and particularly appreciated by refugee friends. But from the start, the Eichelbaums were determined to become assimilated within the wider New Zealand community. As Eichelbaum himself has put it, 'I came to appreciate that so far as my father and I were concerned, emigrating to New Zealand had meant survival, and I always tended to look forward to such future as New Zealand held, rather than backward to a lost childhood in Germany.'[3]

This attitude has coloured his approach to life ever since. One consequence was to turn his back on his German background. Another, and perhaps more significant, consequence is that he decided early on to make the most of the opportunities that egalitarian New Zealand had to offer. Unlike many New Zealand High Court judges, Eichelbaum was educated not at a private school but at a state one—Hutt Valley High School. And early on, too, he chose a legal career, little realising how far it would take him.

Law was, of course, in the family; but he would have to find his own way into the profession. There would have been one particular advantage to taking up the law: the lectures were timetabled so that after his first year at Victoria University of Wellington in 1949, Eichelbaum was able to work in a law office and study before and after work. This he did from the age of 18 until he graduated with an LLB in 1954. Any further legal education was gained not in postgraduate study overseas but in practice—as he progressed from law clerk to solicitor to partner to barrister sole to Queen's Counsel to High Court judge. He did, however, encounter some outstanding teachers at Victoria, in what was then regarded as the leading law faculty in New Zealand. They included Professors Ian Campbell and Robert McGechan, as well as George Barton and Sir John Marshall, who was to become a respected political figure and Prime Minister. Later, Eichelbaum himself was to lecture at Victoria for some six years, on civil procedure.

His association with the firm he joined as a law clerk spanned an unbroken period of twenty-eight years. The firm was Chapman Tripp & Co., now Chapman Tripp Sheffield Young, one of New Zealand's largest law firms. It has the distinction of having produced several High Court judges and two of the last seven chief justices. Eichelbaum, however, started at the bottom, putting away files and filing documents in the Supreme Court and Magistrate's Court (now renamed the High Court and District Court respectively). Gradually, he acquired a familiarity with legal documents, with other law offices and, perhaps most importantly, with colleagues in the profession. He joined the common law department of Chapman Tripp as a litigator, coming into contact there with such well-known names as W.P. Shorland and Ian Macarthur (both of whom became Supreme Court judges), as well as with Robin Cooke, later to become Lord Cooke of Thorndon,[4] who was then embarking on his distinguished career. The work

Sir Thomas Eichelbaum.
(Ralph Anderson)

in litigation began modestly, with minor appearances in the Magistrate's Court, in both civil and criminal matters. Much of the civil work involved personal injury cases—for those were the days before the establishment of the Accident Compensation Corporation—as well as negligence, insurance claims, and workers' compensation. It was, however, work without significant intellectual challenge, and it was not until the 1960s that Eichelbaum was able to exploit fully the development of commercial litigation.

But it was not the courtroom alone, and preparation for appearances there, that occupied Eichelbaum during his years at Chapman Tripp. He was made a partner as early as 1958, and a decade later he was the senior common law partner. This engaged him heavily in administration, but, as if that was not enough, he also became active in New Zealand Law Society affairs, an activity that culminated in his election as president of the society from 1980 to 1982. All this demonstrates his capacity for hard work and his devotion to duty; but work did not take up the whole of his life. In 1956 he married his wife Vida (Franz), with whom he was to have three sons, and he also became no mean tennis player, representing Hutt Valley for some years.

As a barrister, and then as a Queen's Counsel, Eichelbaum gained a reputation as not only hard-working and well-prepared but also determined and clear-thinking. Among his most challenging briefs were those as counsel in a number of commissions of enquiry. These included such high-profile matters as the proposed raising of Lake Manapouri in 1970 and the Marginal Lands affair in 1980, which concerned the propriety of loans granted to relatives of a Cabinet minister. He was able to put his court experience to good use as editor-in-chief of the New Zealand edition of the textbook *Mauet's Fundamentals of Trial Techniques*.

Appointment to the High Court bench in 1982 can be seen as something of an inevitability, given his career path. He was 51: hardly precocious, but still young enough to be able to make something of a mark. As a member of the judiciary, he would have to become a 'generalist'. No longer would he be able to confine himself to civil and commercial proceedings; he would have to confront some of the less savoury aspects of the criminal jurisdiction and sentence accordingly. He appears to have taken it all in his stride and, indeed, has since acquired an expertise in criminal law, now presiding in the Criminal Appeal Division of the Court of Appeal. Once again, he also immersed himself in administrative matters. From 1969 to 1980 he had been a member of the Rules Committee of the High Court, and shortly after becoming a judge he resumed his place there. This was only one of a number of bodies that he joined, including those largely responsible for beginning a process of modernisation of the New Zealand judiciary and courts system, which is still in train.

Eichelbaum's effectiveness both on the bench and in administration would have contributed greatly to his selection in 1989 as Chief Justice. But there are other qualities that do not appear on a curriculum vitae and are just as compelling. His strong and decisive personality; his ability to consult and seek advice; his setting of and meeting high standards; his capacity for hard work: all of these characteristics are relevant. Beyond these, however, is the fact that he is universally liked—for his modesty, his approachability, and his sense of humour. The last quality is not apparent in his public speaking, where he comes across as somewhat dry and guarded; but he is said to put a sense of humour to good use in his chairmanship of committees, where it is allied with firmness and the consistency that distinguishes everything he undertakes.

During his term as Chief Justice Eichelbaum has not become a household name, not possessing the high profile of an 'activist' judge like Lord Cooke of Thorndon. Eichelbaum's judgments, for instance, are written with economy and precision, rather than with flair. But it would be fair to say that Eichelbaum does not seek a high profile, although he is the spokesperson for the New Zealand judiciary. He has been aptly described as 'a liberal, moderately reformist CJ [Chief Justice]', who 'moves carefully and is unwilling to get too far ahead of the troops. But he does eventually move'.[5]

His cautiousness has expressed itself in a number of ways. He has been criticised for being slow to fully appreciate the vulnerability in court of the victims of sexual crimes (yet he was responsible for initiating the current Gender Equity programme for judges in 1994). Although he regards the abolition of the right of appeal to the Privy Council as 'inevitable', he has never been an abolitionist.[6] Indeed, he holds the view 'that there is not a lot wrong with our basic Court structure'.[7] Finally, he sees appointment to the bench as a duty that cannot be lightly relinquished, rather than 'as a bus on which lawyers may take a short trip in the course of their journey through professional life',[8] and he is a strong defender of the traditional notion of judicial independence.[9]

Yet since his appointment he has presided over significant changes in the New Zealand courts, which he himself has either initiated or facilitated. He has on a number of public occasions stressed the importance of change, showing at the same time a sensitivity to the often negative public perception of the law, the judiciary, and the courts. For instance, speaking at the admission of the first graduates from the Waikato Law School in May 1994, he said:

Like other institutions the legal profession needs constant stimulus towards change, towards adaptation to a modern and rapidly changing scene, and so equally do the Courts and the very law itself … The challenge for both of us is to maintain the traditional ethos of the profession, and the judiciary, while at the same time moulding and developing these institutions so that they keep in touch with and fulfil the needs of the modern community in which they have to operate.[10]

It is interesting to consider briefly some of the recent developments. There are now four female High Court judges, whereas before 1993 there were none. The large and cumbersome Department of Justice has been restructured, and an autonomous Department for Courts has been split off from it, a body whose main reason for existence is to service the courts and the judiciary. At the same time, judges have taken on an increased role in administration and case flow management, a role for which Eichelbaum campaigned vigorously, unwilling as he was to accept the notion of a 'cuckoo clock judiciary' that simply heard cases and wrote judgments.[11] No longer do barristers and High Court judges have to put up with the prickly and rather absurd horsehair wigs. Finally, judicial education is being taken seriously, and the first moves are being made towards a more 'visible, systematic and accountable'[12] appointment procedure for judges.

Eichelbaum is a modest, even shy, man and would be unlikely to claim full credit for these achievements. Many of them can, of course, be attributed partly to the teams he has built around him. But building the right teams is a considerable achievement in itself. He would also be unlikely to consider it as a remarkable accomplishment to have risen to the position of Chief Justice in spite of a non-English-speaking background and in spite of not having had the social and educational advantages of so many of New Zealand's High Court judges.

As for his German origins, he gives little outward sign of them, and although he still speaks German, he cultivates no special links with either Germans or Germany. Yet he now concedes, 'I could hardly shake off [my] heritage, and as I have grown older I think I have simply accepted as a fact that I have certain German and Jewish characteristics which have played a part in making me whatever I am.'[13] He adds that 'the German characteristics of being methodical and orderly are things that have been helpful to a legal career'. Helpful, perhaps, but only in combination with hard work, a devotion to duty, an acute intelligence, and an uncommon ability to get on with and motivate those around him.

1 Information provided by Sir Thomas Eichelbaum, 15 July 1996. Much of the information on his earlier years derives from these notes. Other biographical information derives from 'Chief Justice: Interview with Mr Justice Eichelbaum on 12 January 1989', *New Zealand Law Journal* (February 1989), p. 47.
2 The *Niagara* sank in the Hauraki Gulf on 19 June 1940 after hitting one of the mines laid by the German raider *Orion*. See chapter 1.
3 Information provided by Sir Thomas Eichelbaum [note 1].
4 Sir Robin Cooke, president of the New Zealand Court of Appeal, was appointed to a life peerage in late 1995 in recognition of his outstanding contribution to the law in the British Commonwealth.
5 Anthony Hubbard, 'A view from the bench', *Listener*, 4 May 1996.
6 Interview, 'Chief Justice at the Privy Council', *New Zealand Law Journal* (March 1994), p. 88.
7 Interview [note 1], p. 52.
8 Interview [note 6], p. 90.
9 See 'Political influences in the legal profession: Judicial independence—fact or fiction?', *New Zealand Law Conference Papers* (Wellington, 1993), p. 120.
10 *New Zealand Law Journal* (July 1994), p. 255.
11 'Winds of change in the courthouse', *Australian Law Journal*, 61 (1987), p. 454.
12 Eichelbaum, 'The swearing-in of Dame Silvia Cartwright as a judge of the High Court', *New Zealand Law Journal* (September, 1993), p. 335.
13 Information provided by Sir Thomas Eichelbaum [note 1].

Part 5

The present–day German connection

Introduction

JAMES N. BADE

Relations between Germany and New Zealand have arguably never been better than in the 1990s. The close political, economic, and cultural ties are epitomised in the official visits to New Zealand of President Scheel in 1978, President von Weizsäcker and Foreign Minister Klaus Kinkel in 1993, and Chancellor Helmut Kohl in 1997. Michael McBryde documents the political and economic links between the two countries, revealing that Germany is New Zealand's fifth largest source of imports and ninth largest export market (fifth largest export market if 'EU—destination unknown' statistics are taken into account). These facts obviously influenced the decision of the Trade Development Board (Tradenz) to establish its European headquarters in Hamburg. Michael McBryde also mentions German tourism as a major earner of foreign exchange: indeed, the number of German tourists coming to New Zealand in the 1990s has exceeded 50,000 per year, as a result of promotional efforts and the favourable image of New Zealand among Germans. New Zealand's image in Germany is taken up by Gisela Holfter, who examines some of the background factors influencing this image.

Up to 1914, the Germans were the second largest immigrant group in New Zealand after the British. For reasons explored elsewhere in this volume, German immigration came to a virtual standstill, apart from taking in refugees, for a number of decades after World War I, and only in the 1990s are the numbers of German immigrants, at present the second largest non-English-speaking European ethnic group in New Zealand,[1] once again reaching significant levels. Unlike the earlier German immigrants, who were motivated by poverty or political persecution, many of the present-day immigrants appear to have come here first as tourists.[2] The reasons for Germans staying here permanently, however, differ from the reasons for coming as tourists. New Zealand society is, it seems, regarded as less restricting and more egalitarian than that of Germany, and there is more room for individualism. For many immigrants, New Zealand is the result of a search for individual freedom.[3]

Where the tourist and immigrant images of New Zealand intersect is in the 'green settlers', whose concern for the environment was their principal motivation in coming to this country. This type of immigrant is Raymond Miller's primary concern in his chapter on German immigrants and New Zealand politics, which investigates the influence of German environmentalists on New Zealand's Green Party and Green Society, and the involvement of some German Green activists in the campaign for the adoption of the German mixed member proportional electoral system (MMP). Rod Fisher investigates a further aspect of recent German immigration: the impact of German immigrants on the wine scene in New Zealand. In this sphere, the new immigrants have taken up a tradition started by their predecessors in the nineteenth century.

However, in the second half of the twentieth century it is not the German immigrants who are the primary guardians of German language and culture in New Zealand. That is the privilege of teachers of and researchers in German studies at schools, colleges of education, institutes of technology, and universities. As Peter Oettli explains, Victoria, Auckland, Canterbury, and Otago Universities appointed full-time lecturers in German in the immediate post-war period, while Massey and Waikato Universities taught German from the time they were constituted. Professorial chairs in German were established at Auckland, Victoria, Canterbury, Otago, and Waikato Universities in the 1960s, although only two of these chairs (at Auckland and Victoria) remain today. The increase in German graduates led in turn to a growth in the teaching of German at schools, fostered by the university German departments and associated Goethe Societies, and in particular by the arrival of the Goethe Institut in Wellington, established in 1980. Student exchange schemes and intergovernment agreements have led to a big increase in New Zealanders studying in Germany and German students coming here. While the number of students taking German now has levelled off somewhat, teachers of German are responding to the challenging new educational environment by incorporating into their curricula courses that will appeal to a broader range of students interested in—for instance—international business, media studies, and social history. A flexible approach will ensure the healthy survival of German studies in future.

1   Information from Statistics New Zealand. From 1991 to 1994, the Germans were (apart from the British) the largest group of immigrants from Western Europe, followed by the Swiss and the Irish. Cf. *Immigration and National Identity in New Zealand: One People, Two Peoples, Many Peoples?* edited by Stuart William Greif (Palmerston North, 1995), p. 93.

2   A study undertaken by Manfred Cramer and Almut Kraft of the Munich Fachhochschule based on more than a hundred interviews with new German immigrants to New Zealand between 1990 and 1996 postulates a close connection between tourism and immigration.

3   Cramer and Kraft (see note 2) found that many German immigrants regard New Zealand as a less restrictive and more liberal social environment than Germany.

32

Political and economic links since World War II

MICHAEL McBRYDE

Few German politicians of the postwar period attracted more controversy than Franz-Josef Strauss. As federal Minister of Defence in the early 1960s, and as political party leader and folk hero in his native Bavaria, he appeared frequently in the headlines. But it was his final act that gave him a footnote in the history of modern links between Germany and New Zealand. In October 1988, he died suddenly while on a hunting trip. At that moment, Chancellor Helmut Kohl was on his way to New Zealand, on what was planned to be the first-ever visit of a German head of government. When the news of Strauss's death came through, the Chancellor's aircraft turned around, and he returned to Germany for the funeral. Kohl went on to ensure a place in history for himself as the Chancellor of German unity, but the visit to New Zealand was not rescheduled until 1997, nearly nine years later. By this time most Western democracies would have changed their leadership, some several times, but Kohl's position through the 1980s and the 1990s seemed impregnable. By a strange coincidence, while the Chancellor was in Wellington, the news came through that Strauss's successor as Defence Minister in the 1960s, Kai-Uwe von Hassel, had just died. But von Hassel did not have the continuing significance that Strauss had still enjoyed in the 1980s, and this time the Kohl visit continued uninterrupted.

President Richard von Weizsäcker visits Lincoln University, September 1993. *(Bunderbildstelle, Bonn)*

Those engaged in the conduct of foreign policy tend to attach considerable importance to high-level contact, to the meetings of ministers, heads of government, and heads of state. They add lustre to the everyday routine of business between states. Even when no pressing issues are on the agenda, visits provide the icing on the cake, particularly when a senior visitor from the larger country travels to the smaller one. In the case of German contact with New Zealand, the level of interest has been sporadic. In 1978 the first contact at head of state level took place, when federal President Walter Scheel made a state visit. Given the very limited powers of the German presidency, it was not a visit for delving into major policy issues. It did nevertheless provide an opportunity for putting the formal seal on an agreement between the two countries to cooperate in science and technology, an agreement that flourished in the succeeding decades.

Fifteen years later, in 1993, President Richard von Weizsäcker visited New Zealand. In the same year, Foreign Minister Klaus Kinkel also paid a visit, the first-ever by a German foreign minister. Kinkel's long-serving predecessor, Hans-Dietrich Genscher, had been on record as commenting that,

President Walter Scheel in New Zealand, October 1978, with the first four New Zealand ambassadors to the Federal Republic of Germany (left to right): Reuel Lochore, Dr Mildred Scheel, Mrs Lochore, German Ambassador Doering (obscured), the President, Doug Zohrab, Basil Bolt, Mrs Zohrab, Hunter Wade, Mrs Wade.
(Bundesbildstelle, Bonn)

despite his reputation as an inveterate traveller, he had never in the course of his eighteen years as Foreign Minister been to New Zealand. Genscher did not intend the observation as an insult. Indeed he added that because no problems existed between the two countries, there had been no need for him to make a visit.[1] Kinkel, on the other hand, took a more active and forward-looking approach. Under his stewardship the German Government developed a strategy for intensifying its political and economic relations with Asia–Pacific states, and he believed in making personal contacts with them himself. Chancellor Kohl had a similar motivation in making his 1997 visit. He had no major problems to resolve nor treaties to sign, but he judged it worthwhile to reinforce political and economic links with a friendly country and to learn something of New Zealand's economic reforms.

While visits back and forth might be the icing on the cake, they are not the cake itself. In building up relations with another state, each nation naturally pursues an agenda based on its own perceived interests. In the case of New Zealand's approach to Germany, those interests remained fairly dormant until the 1960s. A bilateral trade agreement entered into force in 1959, only eight years after the official termination of the state of war between the two countries. In the 1950s it tended to be the cities of London, Paris, and Brussels that provided New Zealand with its window on Western Europe and on what was then the European Economic Community (EEC). Not until 1966 did the government under Prime Minister Keith Holyoake decide to establish an embassy in Bonn. Holyoake's announcement noted that, despite the growing importance of Asia and the Pacific to New Zealand, 'we remain closely concerned with Europe. This is true not only as far as political matters are concerned but especially in the field of trade'.[2] Holyoake had in mind specifically the looming prospect of British membership of the EEC. At a time when the future of New Zealand's agricultural exports was uncertain, the government believed it was important for New Zealand's views to be kept before the government of Germany, a country that imported large quantities of food and raw materials. He went on to note that New Zealand exported mutton and lamb to Germany, and if difficulties with the application of Common Market rules could be overcome, there would be scope for an increase in these exports.

So the new embassy had the task of enlisting German support for safeguarding New Zealand's trading interests with Britain in the period of forthcoming negotiations over British entry to the Community and the secondary objective of boosting exports to Germany itself. The first of these objectives consumed a substantial amount of time and energy for more than twenty years, not only in the period before British entry into the Community in 1974 but also afterwards, in terms of maintaining New Zealand trading access against the constant efforts of some members of the Community to limit it. The German approach to New Zealand's difficulties tended to be a conciliatory one, as Germany itself did not produce large quantities of either sheepmeat or dairy products, and had a more relaxed approach to New Zealand exports than that demonstrated by France or (later) Ireland and Greece as well.

New Zealand's first diplomatic mission in Germany opened for business on 15 August 1966, in a modest free-standing house in the Bonn suburb of Bad Godesberg. It remained there for three years before moving to a new high-rise block nearer central Bonn. The first ambassador, Dr Reuel Lochore, had transferred from Jakarta, where he had been deputy head of mission at the legation there. For Lochore it was like coming home. In the Department of External Affairs in the 1960s there could have been few people as well qualified for the job of establishing a New Zealand diplomatic presence in Germany. He had studied at Berlin and Bonn Universities in the 1930s and had completed a doctorate at Bonn in 1935. He had witnessed at first hand the accession to power of the National Socialists, and legend has it that he had some regard for their organisational abilities. In the early 1930s, when Germany was emerging from the chaos of the Weimar period, such a view would not have been unusual, and it did not count against him thirty-one years later, when Holyoake's statement announcing his appointment referred to his 'professional skill of a high order combined with outstanding linguistic ability'.[3] Michael King's 1991 profile of Lochore demonstrates fairly conclusively that, while he was a tortured and eccentric character, Lochore did not in fact sympathise with Hitler.[4]

German President Richard von Weizsäcker meets Prime Minister Jim Bolger in Wellington, August 1993. *(Bundesbildstelle, Bonn)*

One of Holyoake's successors as prime minister, Robert Muldoon, coined the phrase: 'New Zealand's foreign policy is trade'. Like most aphorisms, it was an oversimplification, but in the case of New Zealand's relations with the EEC (later the EU) and with its individual members, the maintenance of access for agricultural exports did represent the highest priority for a long period. In this context Muldoon himself visited Bonn on three occasions (1977, 1981, and 1982), his successor David Lange went there in 1986, and Jim Bolger visited in 1992. In the late 1980s and early 1990s the focus moved from lobbying the Community to negotiating a lasting liberalisation of international trade in farm products under the General Agreement on Tariffs and Trade (GATT). Despite a natural inclination to protect the interests of its own small and inefficient farmers, Germany generally supported moves towards a liberal outcome on agriculture in the Uruguay Round.

New Zealand looked to Germany to exert influence on its partner France, for which agriculture represented a much larger proportion of GDP than it did for Germany.

Once the Uruguay Round had been completed successfully and new trading rules had been formalised under the auspices of the World Trading Organisation, New Zealand's trading relations with the member states of the EU moved on to a more equal footing. The regular visits of ministers and Producer Board delegations to Bonn were no longer devoted to lobbying or special pleading but to more wide-ranging and relaxed discussions of market prospects and further developments in the multilateral trading system. This did not mean that all problems disappeared. Contentious issues over trade still cropped up, over veterinary issues or labelling requirements, for instance, or perceptions that the competitive pricing of New Zealand products was depressing returns to local producers. But overall the playing field became much more level for New Zealand trading interests in the 1990s than it had been before.

The importance of Germany to New Zealand as a market for high-quality products was recognised by the Trade Development Board (Tradenz) when it decided to establish its European headquarters in the city of Hamburg. Trade promotion staff responsible for the German market had previously operated out of the embassy in Bonn. The new office in Hamburg was formally opened by the Trade Negotiations Minister Philip Burdon in 1992. Bilateral trade had become substantial. In 1996 Germany was New Zealand's fifth largest source of imports (principally machinery, electrical goods, and motor vehicles) and our ninth largest export market (mainly meat, fruit, wool, and fish). Tradenz calculated that if New Zealand's exports shown in the official statistics as 'EU destination unknown' exports were broken down and allocated to EU member states in accordance with the import statistics published by those states, Germany would move from ninth to fifth place on New Zealand's list of top ten export destinations. Although the principal exports to Germany were in the primary produce area, the market for high-quality manufactured products in certain niches had grown substantially. New Zealand-made radios for use in the freight business, and precision weighing and measuring equipment for use on farms, were among the specialised products that did well on the German market.

The economic relationship did not confine itself to visible trade. In the years when the New Zealand Government borrowed heavily on international markets, Germany became a major source of funds. A relationship between the Treasury and the Commerzbank of Frankfurt developed over this period, and successive ministers of finance included Frankfurt in their itineraries. Even after the period of large-scale borrowing had ended, the relationship with the banks continued. In more recent years they showed considerable interest in New Zealand's economic reform programme. In the area of intellectual property, an important example of German expertise being taken up in both Australia and New Zealand was the Blohm und Voss design for the ANZAC frigates, which were constructed for the naval forces of the two countries.

According to the records of the Auckland-based New Zealand–German Business Association, about fifty German companies had subsidiaries in New Zealand in the mid 1990s. These included the expected large players (BASF, Bayer, BMW, Bosch, and Siemens) as well as a respectable number of firms belonging to the *Mittelstand*, the medium-sized business structure on which German industry is largely based. The number of New Zealand companies represented in Germany was naturally much smaller. Several of the Producer Boards (notably the Dairy and Wool Boards) maintained German subsidiaries, but otherwise only a handful of companies that had sought and occupied a profitable niche in the large and diversified German market were in a position to accept the high cost and challenge of establishing a permanent presence.

The affluence of German citizens, their entitlement to long holidays, and their interest in overseas travel opened up new avenues for tourism as a major strand in the economic relationship between the two countries. A formal agreement on the mutual abolition of the requirement for visas between New Zealand and Germany as a means of facilitating travel was signed as early as 1972, but it was not until Air New Zealand began a direct service between Auckland and Frankfurt, as a consequence of the signing of an Air Transport Agreement in 1987, that tourist numbers began to climb steeply. The promotional efforts of Air New Zealand, the favourable image of New Zealand among Germans, and their readiness to travel great distances in search of new holiday experiences meant that German tourist arrivals doubled between 1990 and 1995 before levelling off. As tourism had become by then a major earner of foreign exchange for New Zealand, and as German visitors tended both to stay longer than other nationalities and to include the most remote corners of the country in their itineraries, their contribution to the GDP was substantial.

Civil aviation links bring benefits in both directions, and Air New Zealand did its part in promoting Germany as a destination for New Zealanders. The German national airline Lufthansa did not, however, choose to exercise its rights to fly between Frankfurt and Auckland. In addition, Lufthansa resisted efforts by Air New Zealand to expand services between the two countries, on the grounds that the route flown by Air New Zealand, via Los Angeles, enabled it to carry passengers between the United States and Germany, using so-called 'fifth freedom rights'. These rights diminished Lufthansa's returns, even in a small way, in a fiercely competitive market. Difficulties over civil aviation represented one of the very few clouds over the relationship between New Zealand and Germany in the 1990s.

The economic and political relationship between New Zealand and the other German-speaking countries has been less intense than with Germany. In 1991 the New Zealand Embassy in Austria was closed as an economy measure. Its principal purpose had been to facilitate the growth of economic relations with the countries of Central and Eastern Europe, but the economic conditions prevalent in these states both before and after the fall of communism prevented the realisation of these hopes. The ambassador in Vienna had also been accredited to the government of the former German Democratic Republic. The first New Zealand ambassador to East Berlin,

Tony Small, had the unusual experience, shortly after arriving to present his credentials, of seeing his own name in lights when he stepped into the street in East Berlin.[5] Such was the priority attached by the East German authorities to securing maximum international recognition for their state that a newly arrived ambassador, even from a small and distant state, received highly ostentatious treatment. Since the closure of the Vienna embassy, New Zealand's ambassador in Bonn has been accredited to both Austria and Switzerland.

In terms of the New Zealand–German relationship in the 1990s, two particular themes tended to lead to an increased public awareness of each country in the other. For their part, New Zealanders became more aware of Germany as a result of the choice made in the referendum of 1993 to adopt the mixed member proportional system (MMP) as a replacement for the Westminster-style, first-past-the-post electoral system. Officials, politicians, and journalists turned to Germany for lessons in how the new system would work in practice, as the system followed the German model very closely. Visits to Bonn specifically for the purpose of examining the methods and structures of the electoral system itself, and of the political and parliamentary processes flowing from it, became more frequent in the mid 1990s.

For Germans, who had thought of New Zealand principally as a pleasant tourist destination, New Zealand's economic reform programme sparked considerable interest at a time when Germany was grappling with its own economic restructuring as a means of maintaining international competitiveness and reducing the role of the state in the economy. During the course of 1996 alone, virtually every major German newspaper and periodical carried analyses of New Zealand's economic experiment. Some of these were quite explicit in suggesting that Germany could learn from New Zealand. The mass-market magazine *Stern*, with a readership of more than seven million, headlined a feature article: 'Have you ever been to New Zealand, Mr Waigel?'[6] and couched the whole piece in terms of a challenge to the German Finance Minister. Whether the New Zealand economic revolution could in fact be replicated in a society with much more complex constitutional structures remained open to question, but the publicity certainly increased understanding and admiration for New Zealand among the German public.

1   *Der Spiegel*, no. 19 (1992), p. 318.
2   *New Zealand External Affairs Review*, vol. 16, no. 3 (March 1966), pp. 18–19.
3   *New Zealand External Affairs Review*, vol. 16, no. 4 (April 1966), p. 17.
4   Michael King, 'The strange story of Reuel Anson Lochore', *Metro* (March 1991), pp. 114–25.
5   Conversation with the author, 1991.
6   *Stern*, no. 38 (1996), pp. 138–42.

33

The image of New Zealand in German-speaking Europe

GISELA HOLFTER

'Kiwis, sheep, ozone hole, beautiful nature, far away'—associations like these are the most common ones when someone first mentions New Zealand in a conversation in German-speaking countries.[1] How do these associations relate to the actual image of New Zealand? And what exactly is an image? Literature about this last point is fairly extensive,[2] and it is advisable here to adopt a working definition. In this article, I will follow Johannsen's definition, also used by Messerschmidt in her study of the image of New Zealand and its success in terms of marketing: an image is the entirety of all attitudes, insights, experiences, dreams, and feelings connected with a special object—or country, in this case.[3] In order to provide greater focus, it is useful to categorise these elements further: the experiences, the emotional (feelings, dreams, idealisation), and the factual side. None of these interrelated factors exist without a history (the influence of Tacitus), and while today New Zealand on the whole seems to enjoy a positive image in German-speaking countries, especially Germany and Switzerland, it is interesting to examine the development of this image.

In 1996, the New Zealand Tourist Board found that New Zealand possesses an 'underlying competitive advantage known as emotional closeness' as a result of a national identity based on European civilisation.[4] There was obviously no such emotional closeness affecting the first European explorers who reached New Zealand. The first impressions available to a German-speaking audience appeared more than 200 years ago in the form of translations of travel descriptions by Abel Tasman[5] and of James Cook's journeys. In particular, Georg Forster's itinerary, *Reise um die Welt* (1778–80), gives a detailed account of Cook's second journey and proved to be a very influential travel document.[6] While Tasman portrayed the Maori as warlike and unpredictable, Forster tried to give an objective and understanding account of these people, whom he regarded and portrayed largely as equals. He saw cannibalism more as something 'unusual' rather than some cruel act of barbarism; instead, he questioned the European value system that allowed and accepted wars instigated by ambition or simply the follies of the ruling classes.[7]

Generally it can be said that the initial view of New Zealand was of something exotic and ambiguous. In the beginning, people were not as enthusiastic as in their descriptions of Tahiti or other 'paradise' islands, but not as negative as in descriptions of the Australian Aborigines.[8] It was also

A typical image of New Zealand: the waterfall amid exotic bush.
(Caroline Schweder)

A typical image of New Zealand: the rugged romantic beach. *(Caroline Schweder)*

clearly influenced by ideas of the Enlightenment. And although the Europeans who were able to make this trip were very small in number indeed, interest in reading about the newly discovered countries, Australia and New Zealand, was very high, as is proved by the speedy translations of English travel accounts into German.

Two hundred years on, New Zealand is no longer a destination that only a select few are able to see. The number of German visitors has easily exceeded 50,000 per year in the 1990s. After a peak in 1994, with nearly 60,000 visitors, the number declined again in 1995 and dropped to 53,041 visitors for the twelve months ending in March 1996. In explanation, the New Zealand Tourist Board points to the current economic insecurity in Germany, yet it has had to face the same phenomenon with Swiss visitor numbers (while, interestingly, visitor numbers from the Netherlands have increased significantly). Still, from the point of view of the New Zealand Tourist Board, the German (and Swiss) tourists are especially desirable because of their high expenditure, an average of NZ$3,893 per trip[9] (compared to an all-nationalities average expenditure per visitor of NZ$2,776[10]— only Japanese tourists spend more than the Germans).[11] So the questions remain: who are the visitors coming to New Zealand, and what motivates them to spend that amount of money and to undertake such a long journey?

In terms of 'consumer profiles', the New Zealand Tourist Board distinguishes between two main target groups among the German visitors: 'culture seekers' and 'foreign adventurers'. Both are characterised as having 'high household income' and being well travelled. The 'culture seekers', in the age group 40–68, seem to prefer package tours that include as many things to do and see as possible, especially in the cultural sector. In contrast, the German 'foreign adventurers', aged 18–34, prefer free independent arrangements, which are generally more of interest to Swiss tourists as well.[12] In the view of the New Zealand Tourist Board, the main difference between German and Swiss visitors in New Zealand is that the 'Swiss are less concerned with culture and the background of the country they are visiting'. Instead, they get much more out of enjoying the natural features and the scenery in terms of 'mental and physical relaxation'.[13] Messerschmidt's study of the image of New Zealand and its success in terms of marketing suggests that the main attraction for the German visitors is also found in the country's unique nature—the variety, unspoilt character, and contrasts.[14] These results are reflected in newspaper articles with headlines like 'Pure nature in the Land of the Long White Cloud'[15] or the growing number of slide shows on New Zealand, which have appeared since the 1980s. One German travel handbook opens with this introduction: 'Fascinating New Zealand—never was I more spellbound by a country than by the green islands in the remoteness of the South Pacific. The breathtaking scenery and people whose natural, open and warm personalities surprise us Europeans has always attracted me—a country with two cultures, familiar and excitingly exotic at the same time.'[16]

Typical poster of travelling slide-show on New Zealand–'Green Pearl in the South Pacific'. *(D. & R. Bade)*

Nature is the dominating factor, but friendly people and the Maori culture should be added to the list of attractions for visitors from the northern hemisphere. The mixture of a foreign culture and a familiar one (the 'emotional closeness' described by the Tourist Board) seems to give visitors a feeling of safety while experiencing something new and unique. This can be conveyed to an extent by the impression that nature makes. Generally, the variety of landscapes, from the Southern Alps (which give the Swiss visitors in particular a feeling of familiarity) to Ninety Mile Beach, makes an impact on the visitors: 'Beaches and bays as they are on the Algarve, green hills as in the Scottish Highlands, mountains and glaciers like the Alps'— so begins the blurb on the back of another German travel guide on New Zealand.[17] Here again we find a wide variety of landscapes, the combination leading to a sense of uniqueness. But even more—in contrast to the named

New Zealand, the land of many sheep. *(Caroline Schweder)*

Rich dairying country against a rugged mountain backdrop. *(National Publicity Studios)*

European landscapes, or the main competitors for the 'green image', such as Ireland, Scotland, and Scandinavia[18]—it is far away, 'the [most beautiful, as the Tourist Board slogan goes] end of the world'. Not only the geographical distance plays a role in this; remoteness, to be 'far away from the crowd', is easier to achieve on an island. In the opinion of Bitterli, the geographical status of an island (or many islands, as in New Zealand) has always led to higher expectations and desires for a better world. Even in ancient times, island and paradise concepts were closely connected.[19]

With this thought we are already straight into the next image: New Zealand as a dream destination. The 'far away' factor is vital in encouraging dreams, as it is quite difficult to discover the truth about the reality of life in a far-off country. So what fascinates many of those who cannot afford the journey to an extent that they continue to dream about New Zealand as a kind of paradise? An article in the popular travel magazine *Merian* (August 1996) by the well-known German author Sten Nadolny describes a journey in New Zealand where he meets several German immigrants and, more importantly for my purposes, admits that he himself dreamt as a 19-year-old of leaving Germany and going to New Zealand for good.[20] His expression of a long-kept dream is vicarious for many, to whom New Zealand is, or was at least at some point in their life, an equivalent of a new start, a dream of a better world, a better life. Again, an important part of these dreams is nature, while the friendliness of the inhabitants is not as often an association with New Zealand for dreamers as it is for the actual travellers.[21]

Parts of the image also consist of facts such as economic matters. New Zealand is not economically important to any German-speaking country in Europe. However, products like kiwifruit and (to a lesser extent) sheepskins are generally associated with New Zealand. Apples from New Zealand also are imported and seen in German supermarkets in increasing numbers. All these items raise New Zealand's profile abroad.

General interest in New Zealand has also grown in the 1990s because of the popularity of New Zealand films and interest in books by authors such as Janet Frame and Keri Hulme—both included in the *Merian* publication mentioned above, either as contributors or as the main focus of an article.

Another event that put New Zealand in the headlines of German newspapers was the French nuclear tests at Muroroa. The New Zealand point of view on such testing received a large measure of sympathy, and the general attitude of having a nuclear-free zone in the whole country fits very well with the image of a clean and unspoilt environment.

Another fairly recent development should also be mentioned. The same economic problems in Germany that are given as the cause for a slight decrease in visitor numbers are also a reason to look around for ways out of the associated depression. And one example of comparatively good recent economic performance outside Germany has been found in New Zealand. Conservative commentators in particular see the decrease in the power of unions and the social reforms in New Zealand during the 1990s as a positive example to follow.[22] The very same developments, however, are seen very critically by others. The cuts in social welfare and

Fertile pasture land with snow-clad Mount Egmont (Taranaki) in the background. (National Publicity Studios)

the growing distinction between rich and poor provoked one travel guide writer to complain that 'the Sweden of the South Pacific threatens to become a copy of American society'.[23] But on the whole, his account of New Zealand remains extremely positive, his concern being more about a well-loved place in danger. Still, his views are a sign that, although associations with New Zealand are generally very positive, it would be wrong to assume that there are no complaints or negative aspects at all. Long distance and expense were named as main obstacles to going to New Zealand. Less important factors mentioned were unreliable weather and fear that there is already too much tourism.[24] Also cited, and even more serious for the tourism industry in the long run, as it might damage the image of the unspoilt, clean, and safe country, is the recent awareness of a growing ozone hole and the resulting dangers, such as a high incidence of skin cancer. Publications and documentaries portraying images of sunburnt sheep and recommending factor-20 sun lotion as a minimum show that not all is well in Paradise.

Such recent developments, however, only dent slightly the predominant image of New Zealand. Whether as an economic ideal, a place to experience a country with unspoilt and fascinating nature, or a dream of a better world, New Zealand manages to capture the imagination of many in German-speaking countries (and of course not only there!) and almost always in a positive way. The impact of largely emotional factors would suggest that this fascination is likely to continue well into the future.

1   Although this chapter aims to deal with German-speaking Europe, information on the image of New Zealand in Austria proved scarce. The New Zealand Tourist Board announced in 1996 that it would focus primarily on the German-speaking countries, Germany, Switzerland, and Austria (New Zealand Tourist Board, *Central Europe—Market Brief*, July 1996, p. 5). However, Austria is hardly mentioned afterwards, and no visitor numbers, consumer profiles, or information on expenditures are given. Instead, the markets in the Netherlands, Italy, and France are discussed in detail. Likewise, most German-language information on the Internet relating to New Zealand is from Swiss or German sources. Austria does not seem to be represented in the new media or in tourism research. How is this phenomenon to be explained—complete lack of interest from the Austrian side? The only explanation given by the New Zealand Tourist Board office in Frankfurt was that Austria is a secondary market. Visitor numbers vary around 5,000 and decreased in the previous year as well.

2   See, for example, Walter Lippmann, *Public Opinion* (New York 1922); Kenneth Boulding, *The Image* (Ann Arbor 1956); Peter Boerner (ed.), *Concepts of National Identity: An Interdisciplinary Dialogue* (Baden-Baden 1986); Bundeszentrale für politische Bildung (ed.), *Völker und Nationen im Spiegel der Medien* (Bonn 1989); Günter Trautmann (ed.), *Die häßlichen Deutschen* (Darmstadt 1991); Harald Husemann (ed.), *As Others See Us* (Frankfurt & New York 1994).

3   Ute Messerschmidt, *Die praktische Erfolgskontrolle: Am Beispiel einer Imageanalyse für Neuseeland* (Heilbronn 1991), pp. 5–6.

4   New Zealand Tourist Board [note 1], pp. 6, 9–10. Especially the British similarities, such as language, tradition, and customs, seem to ensure a feeling of safety 'whilst exploring the exotic elements of New Zealand' (p. 6).

5   See J.J. Schwabe, *Allgemeine Historie der Reisen zu Wasser und zu Lande; oder Sammlung aller Reisebeschreibungen, welche bis itzo in verschiedenen Sprachen von allen Völkern herausgegeben worden, und einen vollständigen Begriff von der neuen Erdbeschreibung und Geschichte machen. Zwölfter Band* (Leipzig, 1754).

6   See, for example, John A. Asher, 'Georg Forster' in James N. Bade (ed.), *The German Connection: New Zealand and German-speaking in the Nineteenth Century* (Auckland, 1993), pp. 126–33.

7   See Monika Klauck, *Die Reiseliteratur über Australien und Neuseeland 1750–1810* (Saarbrücker Beiträge zur Literaturwissenschaft, Bd. 28) (St Ingbert, 1992), p. 99.

8   See Klauck [note 8], p. 23.

9   New Zealand Tourist Board [note 1], p. 8.

10 New Zealand Tourist Board, *Tourism in New Zealand—Strategy and Progress 1996*, p. 4.

11 New Zealand Tourist Board [note 10], p. 5.

12 New Zealand Tourist Board [note 1], p. 16.

13 New Zealand Tourist Board [note 1], p. 7.

14 See Messerschmidt [note 3], pp. 105–6.

15 Peter Hinze, 'Natur pur im Land der langen weißen Wolke', *Bergische Landeszeitung*, 8 December 1991.

16 Ulrich Strobel, *Neuseeland: Das Reisehandbuch zum schönsten Ende der Welt* (Rappweiler, 1994), introduction (p. 5). This and all other translations are my own.

17 Hella Tarara, *Neuseeland* (Frankfurt & Berlin, 1991).

18 See Messerschmidt [note 3], p. 99.

19 Urs Bitterli, 'Die exotische Insel' in H.-J. König (ed.), *Der europäische Beobachter außereuropäischer Kulturen: Zur Problematik der Wirklichkeitswahrnehmung* (Berlin, 1989), pp. 65–82.

20 Sten Nadolny, 'Vom Glück der Müdigkeit' in *Merian* (August 1996), pp. 68–73.

21 See Messerschmidt [note 3], who mentions that friendly inhabitants were associated with New Zealand by 19.3 per cent of visitors, but only 2 per cent of those who were interested in but had not been to New Zealand (p. 85).

22 See, for example, Alfred Zänker, 'Ende einer Ära', *Die Welt*, 19 June 1996.

23 Joachim Fischer, *Neuseeland* (Cologne 1993), p. 14.

24 See Messerschmidt [note 3], p. 107.

34

The German winemakers

ROD FISHER

Links between German immigrants and winemaking in New Zealand go back almost to the arrival of the first immigrants from Germany. Among the crops introduced by the Kelling brothers in the second expedition to Nelson in 1844 was the grape-vine, despite the fact that the swampy, flood-prone land allotted to earlier German settlers at Moutere had proved too great a challenge.[1] Although the original estates are obviously not identical to modern vineyards in the area, it is worth noting that 150 years after the first settlements, Neudorf Vineyards, in the vicinity of Upper Moutere, produced a 1991 vintage voted the 'Best Chardonnay in the World' by the British magazine, *Wine*.[2] A neighbouring winemaker in Upper Moutere, Hermann Seifried, although sporting the Austrian eagle on his Seifried label, graduated in wine technology in Germany and won three gold medals for his wines in 1992. At the other end of the modern wine market, the label 'Wohnsiedler' on a less sophisticated range of wines commemorates a German immigrant who arrived around 1900 and pioneered winemaking in the Gisborne area after animosity during World War I ruined his small-goods business. Although his vineyards in Waihirere were not extensive on his death in 1956, Montana's efforts to popularise the name Wohnsiedler (including, in early advertising, a guide to pronunciation for the New Zealand public, which was at best misleading), suggest that there might be as much to be gained from German-sounding wine labels as there is from German names for beer. Another German winemaker in the Hokianga, Heinrich Breidecker, is commemorated in the name of a grape produced by crossing Müller Thurgau with a white hybrid Seibel 7053.[3]

The process of sophistication and export-led expansion in New Zealand wines began in the 1970s. Whereas many of the early winemakers were of necessity amateurs or hobby viticulturists, to be successful in modern markets requires highly specialised knowledge and experience. The renowned Geisenheim Institute in Germany has provided training for recent winemakers Almuth Lorenz of Merlen wines in Marlborough, Norbert Seibel in Henderson, Chris Lintz in Martinborough (whose vineyards are managed organically), and for Dr Rainer Eschenbruch, who after several years in South Africa initially took charge of wine-making research at Te Kauwhata before establishing his own winery, Rongopai Wines, with Tom van Dam. Another with experience in Europe, South Africa, and Australia is Daniel Schuster, who in the 1970s was employed in grape trials at Lincoln

University and is now a wine-growing consultant as well as a producer.

Of course, there has also been a natural flow of expertise from Germany because of the popularity and success of German grapes in the New Zealand climate. The best known of these is the Rhine Riesling, which was originally not widely planted but experienced a burst of interest between 1983 and 1989. The cooler regions of Canterbury and Central Otago promise the best results for Rhine Riesling, whereas Müller Thurgau is particularly strong in Poverty Bay, Hawke's Bay, and Marlborough. After a poor start in the 1950s, the more difficult Gewürztraminer is also becoming more widely established. The German influence is particularly evident in the newer vineyards of the South Island, where the long dry autumns and colder winters present a different challenge from the rainier Henderson region and the east coast of the North Island. Apart from grape varieties and expertise, Germany has naturally enough also continued to provide much equipment such as presses, bottling machines, and oak barrels.

Almuth Lorenz's Merlen wines are a typical example of the application of German experience to New Zealand conditions.[4] Lorenz was brought up in Rheinhessen and helped on her parents' vineyard of eight hectares before studying for four years at the Geisenheim Institute. It was assumed that she would eventually take over wine-making on the family's ancestral property, but a working holiday in New Zealand in 1981 led to employment as wine-maker at Hunters in Marlborough between 1982 and 1986, followed by a short period marketing under the Lorenz name. Her estate of five hectares was founded under the name Merlen, producing Chardonnay, Gewürztraminer, Sauvignon Blanc, Semillon, and Morio-Muskat from her own and local growers' grapes. A particular success was a Riesling 1991, which won a gold medal. These and other notable vintages helped to persuade Lorenz that her wine-making future lay in New Zealand rather than Germany, where there would not be the same opportunities to experiment or establish individual styles as there are in the relatively unfettered local industry.

Contributing to New Zealand's success with Rieslings and Gewürztraminer is another German immigrant, Norbert Seibel, who arrived about the same time as Lorenz, and who likewise appreciates the opportunity for individual attention that producing one's own wines in New Zealand affords.[5] Seibel was born in Mainz, graduated in wine-making at the Geisenheim Institute, and gained practical experience in the 1970s in South Africa. Like Lorenz, he first worked for an established winery, Corbans, and was then a consultant winemaker before producing his own wines in 1987. The larger-scale production of wine in established firms did not allow him to devote himself either to perfecting individual styles or to developing less well-known varieties. It is obvious that there is a niche for the smaller-scale producer with knowledge of German-style wines and of technology such as barrel fermentation; since 1993 Seibel and his wife have taken on an older winery in Henderson and have been successful with Gewürztraminer and Riesling grapes purchased from the North Island's east coast and from Marlborough. Their output is relatively modest even by New Zealand standards (about 2,500 cases) but is characterised by an individuality and complexity in almost all his range of varieties. With the freedom of their own

Norbert Seibel (fore-
ground) working in a
vineyard in front of St
Katharina Church near
Oppenheim, c. 1961.
(Norbert Seibel Collection)

winery they intend to venture into lesser known varieties such as Scheurebe,
Morio-Muskat, and Bacchus.

The recently discovered potential of New Zealand red wines, on the
other hand, has attracted the attention of Daniel Schuster in the South
Island.[6] After his apprenticeship in Europe and elsewhere and his work at
Lincoln University, Schuster served as winemaker at St Helena winery from
1980 to 1985, where he pioneered the production of high-quality Pinot
Noirs. Unlike some larger firms, which have preferred to produce Cabernet
Sauvignon, sometimes blended with Merlot, Schuster intends to remain
faithful to Pinot Noir, which he now produces at the Omihi Hills vineyard.

Canterbury has been the scene of another German success story, the
Giesen winery based at Burnham.[7] The Giesens are perhaps the most
'German' of winemakers, not only in their presentation of the product at
their wine-shop but also, more importantly, in their style of production, having made a conscious decision to make wines as they had at home. Their first
commercial production was in 1984. Giesen 1989 Riesling Dry Reserve
won a gold medal in London in 1991, and their Botrytised Riesling 1990
was overall champion in the 1991 Royal Easter Wine Show in Auckland.
More recently they have won awards with Pinot Noir and Chardonnay as
well. This is all the more remarkable considering that the Giesens have been
in New Zealand only since 1979 and that they did not come here with the
intention of making wine as a business. Their home was Neustadt an der
Weinstrasse, where the family made wine as a hobby, growing Riesling and
some Sylvaner grapes. The brothers Theo and Alexander arrived in 1979;
Marcel and their parents Kurt and Gudrun arrived in 1983. Theo and
Alexander came as monumental stone masons but, after drinking the local
wine, realised that there were commercial possibilities beyond the conve-
nience of a small-scale operation for private consumption.

They were impressed by the relative simplicity of getting started in New
Zealand, compared with the bureaucracy of Europe. The atmosphere here,

Norbert Seibel sharing
his wine with his family
at Seibel Wines,
Henderson, 1997.
(Rowena Baines)

Norbert Seibel in the
wine cellar at Seibel
Wines, Henderson, 1997.
(Rowena Baines)

The Giesen brothers—(left to right) Marcel, Theo, and Alex—at the Giesen Wine Estate, Burnham. *(Giesen Wine Estate)*

they feel, encourages free spirit and private enterprise. They began by looking at the growers already in the region and at results at Lincoln, drawing the conclusion (which Theo now calls perhaps naive) that if grapes grew in Lincoln they would grow at Burnham. They are now convinced that there are still many thousands of hectares stretching north suitable for winemaking. Advice from Lincoln persuaded them to avoid the risk of severe frost further inland and the rainfall and herbicide problems of Banks Peninsula. Their initial attention focused on Riesling grapes, but with changes in fashion and popularity they have since concentrated in Burnham on Pinot Noir, Chardonnay, and some Riesling, with the first two dominating. About half of their grapes they grow themselves.

Like the wine industry generally, their own production will continue to be market-driven. New Zealand's reputation in the mid 1980s as the best producer of Müller Thurgau in the world no longer ensures the popularity of the grape; the market has seen a swing to the more sophisticated Chardonnay and, in the South Island, to Sauvignon Blanc as well. The Giesens anticipate that New Zealand is ideally placed to continue to increase its exports, because of its climate, the quality of the wines, and the flexibility of the growers, whereas in Germany conservatism, tradition, and bureaucracy restrict both change and growth. To add to their diversification, the Giesens have recently ventured into sparkling wine, for example, using the traditional method, as well as Pinot Noir and Chardonnay, the grape varieties they already have.

Although recent years have seen ample evidence of such diversification, and the spread of winemaking south from the traditional regions, the Giesens believe that the full potential has still to be tapped. They recently visited a trade fair in Germany and made contact with an importer there who turned out to be from their home town of Neustadt. They are now in the happy position of exporting their New Zealand product back to

Germany, where New Zealand has a good image. With New Zealand's modest population and consumption, the potential for major growth must lie in export; of the Giesens' current production of between 400,000 and 500,000 bottles, 10 per cent is exported, with Australia the biggest market. They are exploring contacts in England and the United States. Of course, it is not only one-way business; because of the size of the wine industry in Germany and its technical know-how, the Giesens are dependent on German manufacturers for such equipment as presses and bottling machinery, which cannot be bought here. The Giesens have no major regrets about their professional decisions, nor have there been any major setbacks, beyond the vagaries of the weather to which all growers are prone.

Wine vats at the Giesen Wine Estate, Burnham. *(Giesen Wine Estate)*

There is a sense of a common goal among the German winemakers, who are all conscious of the need to push New Zealand wines abroad. Although they are all obviously in competition to sell bottles, the market is such that they can openly exchange views and mix professionally and socially without conflict. It is a happy circumstance for the flexibility and viability of the industry in New Zealand that each winemaker can bring his or her own philosophy and style on to the market. Almost invariably, German immigrants active in the industry stress the comparative lack of regulation and the freedom from the weight of tradition as major factors in their preference for wine-making here; they are able to devote their time and their expertise to the individual barrel, if necessary, and experiment according to their tastes without undue interference by bureaucrats. The best features of small-scale production have thus been linked to professionalism (training, equipment, quality control, marketing) in a way that is not possible in Germany. If there is to be even greater contact between the German winemakers here and the market in Germany, the challenge must be to educate German customers in the regional characteristics, particularly for those wines that are less well known in Germany.

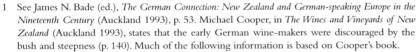

1   See James N. Bade (ed.), *The German Connection: New Zealand and German-speaking Europe in the Nineteenth Century* (Auckland 1993), p. 53. Michael Cooper, in *The Wines and Vineyards of New Zealand* (Auckland 1993), states that the early German wine-makers were discouraged by the bush and steepness (p. 140). Much of the following information is based on Cooper's book.

2   Ralph Talmont, *New Zealand Wineries and Vineyards: A Wine Trail Guide* (Auckland 1994), p. 80.

3   Cooper [note 1], p. 29.

4   See Cooper [note 1], p. 159.

5   Cooper [note 1], p. 72.

6   Cooper [note 1], p. 170.

7   For the following I am indebted to Theo and Marcel Giesen, who answered several questions in an interview in 1996.

35

German immigrants and
New Zealand politics

RAYMOND MILLER

The political relationship between New Zealand and Germany has fluctuated between the extremes of conflict and cooperation. In contrast to the first half of the twentieth century, when relations were dominated by political and military rivalry, New Zealand's growing independence, especially from Britain, has been reflected in the strengthening of its political, diplomatic, and trade associations with Germany.[1] This chapter will explore the German–New Zealand link with respect to two political developments, both of which contributed to a maturing of New Zealand's national self-image and involved members of the German immigrant community: the growing prominence of the environmental movement, including the formation of alternative green parties, and the successful campaign to replace the first-past-the-post electoral system with the German form of proportional representation, mixed member proportional (MMP).

Implicit in New Zealand's growing sense of nationhood has been a commitment to the protection of the natural environment, which entails guardianship of the country's 'clean-green' image, including its extensive coastline and territorial waters, as well as support for the decolonisation and environmental protection of the South Pacific. Few policies have symbolised the emerging sense of nationhood more powerfully than those on nuclear weapons. The opposition of both the Reagan Administration and the Thatcher Government to New Zealand's nuclear ship visits policy aroused the suspicion of many New Zealanders that Britain and the United States could no longer be trusted to protect our national and regional interests. Later, when New Zealand joined Australia and the rest of the Commonwealth in condemning French weapons testing at Muroroa Atoll, the British Prime Minister, John Major, sided with the government of the French President, Jacques Chirac. The New Zealand Government's anti-nuclear stand enjoyed strong public support, as well as alerting environmentalists to the importance of direct political action. This took several forms, including the formation of an electoral movement, the Green Party of Aotearoa–New Zealand, in 1990.

Following the election of the Labour Government in 1984, the Deputy Prime Minister, Geoffrey Palmer, questioned the appropriateness of New Zealand's first-past-the-post (FPP) electoral system, which had been borrowed from Britain by the young colony in the nineteenth century. In 1986 a royal commission recommended that New Zealand replace FPP with the

German mixed member proportional system. In the ensuing debate over the relative merits of the German system, several German immigrants became heavily involved in the pro–MMP campaign.

Environmental politics

It is not difficult to see why the environmental movement provided German immigrants with an immediate point of contact with New Zealand politics. Whereas the Values Party of New Zealand, which was formed in 1972, was the world's first national environmental party, the West German Green Party (Die Grünen), with forty-two seats in the Bundestag in 1987, was the most electorally successful. Beginning in the 1970s, leading members of these two green parties forged strong and enduring links. The fledgling German Green Party used Values' 1975 manifesto, *Beyond Tomorrow*, for guidance in preparing its own policy platform.[2] It shared Values' commitment to a range of green issues, including: opposition to nuclear energy and armaments; grassroots democracy, both in the community and in the workplace; limits on industrial and economic development; a liberal agenda on civil liberties; increased use of alternative forms of energy, such as wind and solar power; and an overriding concern for the national and global environments.

Several New Zealand environmentalists and anti-nuclear campaigners visited Germany, among them the University of Auckland's chaplain, Ray Galvin.[3] Following the German Green Party's twenty-seven-seat success at the 1983 national election, its most prominent personality, Petra Kelly, made a public speaking visit to New Zealand. Other visitors have included Juergen Trittin, the speaker of the Alliance 90 Greens in Bonn, who was a guest of the Green Party of Aotearoa–New Zealand in 1995.[4]

Perhaps more important than this periodic exchange of information and advice, however, has been the contribution to the New Zealand environmental movement of a small band of German immigrants. Whereas there is little evidence of earlier German immigrants being touched by environmental issues, a vast majority of those who arrived in the late 1970s and 1980s are said to have been associated with green politics in Germany (if not with the Green Party, then with citizens' initiatives).[5] Some viewed themselves as 'refugees' from what they believed to be the advanced state of environmental degradation, nuclear confrontation, and political instability in Europe. It is hardly surprising, therefore, that they arrived in New Zealand with 'green thoughts on their minds'.[6]

The success of the German Green Party has been attributed to 'the socioeconomic transformation of West German society during the post-war period, marked by an increase in the activities of the welfare state, a movement away from a production-based towards a service-sector-oriented economy and a general improvement in levels of education'.[7] Reflecting their largely postmaterialist values, supporters of green parties, whether in Germany or New Zealand, subscribe to the goals of the 'new politics' movement.[8] These are said to include 'personal and political freedom, participation, ... equality, tolerance of minorities and those holding different opinions, openness to new ideas and new life styles, environmental protection and concern over quality-of-life issues, self-indulgence and self-actualization'.[9]

As well as upholding shared postmaterialist values, the German 'refugees' who chose to settle in New Zealand manifested the same socioeconomic characteristics as their German Green Party counterparts. Studies of German Green Party members show them to be predominantly early middle-aged (aged 35 or older), highly educated, professionally trained, and relatively affluent.[10] A similar survey of Green Party activists in New Zealand found that those who came from Germany were overwhelmingly middle class and early middle-aged.[11] In their quest for an alternative lifestyle in New Zealand, a number reported having left successful professional careers in Germany. On arriving in New Zealand, their involvement in environmental matters tended to take the form of membership of one or more of the established environmental pressure groups, such as Greenpeace and the Forest and Bird Society, or grassroots action within the local community. Of the hundred or so German immigrants who have settled on Waiheke Island, for example, a vast majority are said to be environmental activists (in such areas as environmental planning, bio-architecture, alternative medicine, and organic farming).[12] Thus it was with a combination of environmental concern, experience of direct political action, and the resources to do something about it, that German immigrants became involved in party and/or interest group politics.

Shortly after arriving in New Zealand, one such immigrant, Klaus Bosselmann, helped to spearhead the move for a national green party. He took his message to environmental groups in various parts of the country. The Values Party had been beset by internal conflict, despite the strength of its appeal to young, middle-class voters (it gained 5 per cent of the vote in 1975). By the late 1970s, its core activists had largely abandoned electoral politics in favour of indirect lobbying. In 1989, buoyed by the election of a green candidate, Stephen Rainbow, to the Wellington City Council, a group of environmentalists met in Wellington to discuss the possibility of forming a green party to contest the 1990 general election.[13] Bosselmann summed up the mood of the meeting with his claim that, despite the success of the fourth Labour government in implementing its environmental agenda, its politicians suffered from an excess of talk and insufficient action.[14]

Having failed to persuade those in attendance at the first meeting, the advocates of direct action presented their arguments at a second conference, which was held at the beach resort of Kaiteriteri (near Nelson) in March 1990. Of the 150 people in attendance, some forty were German immigrants, mostly from the nearby German communities at Golden Bay.[15] Although he regarded himself merely as an observer,[16] Bosselmann played a major role in the debate. In a speech entitled 'Deep foundations—green principles', he expressed disappointment with the performances of both Labour and National and told delegates that they had 'the unique chance to tell the people in Aotearoa that this country desperately needs a national Green Party and that Green candidates will stand in the general election despite the undemocratic first-past-the-post voting system'.[17]

Klaus Bosselmann.
(Faculty of Law, Auckland University)

Bosselmann's endorsement of direct political action was widely reported in the New Zealand press. He was described as having an extensive background in environmental politics; he was a co-founder of the German Greens, a former MP (1981–82) of the parliament of Berlin, and a consultant to a number of environmental bodies, including the German Federal Environmental Agency and the United Nations Environmental Programme. In the absence of a readily identifiable New Zealand-born leader, Bosselmann was clearly regarded by the media as a necessary intellectual authority figure and leading personality of the pro-direct action group.

At the 1990 election, the fledgling Green Party of Aotearoa attracted 7 per cent of the vote (or an average of 9 per cent in the seventy-one seats it contested). Because of the disadvantages suffered by small parties under the first-past-the-post electoral system (the combined minor party vote in 1990 was 17.1 per cent, yet they received only one seat in the ninety-seven seat parliament),[18] in December 1991 the Green Party of Aotearoa entered into an informal electoral arrangement with three other minor parties (NewLabour, Mana Motuhake, and Democrat) with a view to putting up one candidate to contest a by-election in the Auckland seat of Tamaki.[19]

Despite almost winning the seat from National, the new four-party grouping (which adopted the name 'the Alliance') had its detractors, including several prominent Green Party activists. Taking up the theme of the latter party's ideological uniqueness, Bosselmann warned that, by joining up with 'mainstream political forces', the Green Party had sacrificed its overriding commitment to the principle of a 'sustainable environment'. In a statement that underlines the fundamental cleavage between materialist and postmaterialist values, he stated: 'Any compromising in whether "the environment" or "the society" or "the economy" or "jobs" should come first, automatically puts the identity of Greens at risk'.[20] Bosselmann compared the decision of the Green Party of Aotearoa with that of the German Green Party in the early 1980s. In their haste to sacrifice principle for 'the temptations of power', they reached an accommodation with the Social Democrats, which had put their own uniqueness at risk. Similarly, instead of offering a 'dark green' perspective and the politics of transformation to New Zealand voters, the Alliance Greens were offering no more than a 'light green' and mildly reformist perspective.[21] Bosselmann's argument was based on bitter experience. In 1991, he had been asked by Jim Anderton to help draft the NewLabour Party's environmental policy. The results were later dismissed by Anderton as being inconsistent with the fundamental principles of the labour movement.[22]

At the party's 1992 conference in Nelson, one delegate, Hans Grueber, warned that, if the Greens remained in the Alliance, the party would split and be challenged by a new green party. Although the Alliance had attracted many voters who were opposed to National and Labour, in Grueber's opinion there was 'nothing green about it'.[23] He advanced three main reasons why the Greens needed to leave the Alliance: the party's limited resources were being exhausted by the umbrella organisation; the dominating influence of the 'old-style politics' of the NewLabour Party and its leader, Jim

Anderton; and a failure to draw sufficient attention to the Green Party's distinctiveness and strong commitment to environmentalism.[24]

True to his word, in September 1994 Hans Grueber was instrumental in the formation of an alternative green party, the Green Society. Grueber had become involved in green issues shortly after his arrival from Hamburg, where he had practised law.[25] A former member of the German Social Democratic Party, he resigned over that party's involvement in the arms race. Disenchanted with the problems of industrial pollution and overcrowding in Europe, he emigrated to New Zealand with his family in 1984. After losing the battle to take the Green Party of Aotearoa out of the Alliance, Grueber organised a dinner party at an Auckland restaurant with the intention of convincing a group of ten environmentalists (including Gary Taylor, a local government politician, Guy Salmon of the Maruia Society, and Klaus Bosselmann) to join him in starting a new green party.[26] They failed to reach agreement. Taylor and Salmon later formed their own party, the Progressive Greens, which attempted to reconcile a commitment to environmentalism with faith in the free market.[27]

The Green Society began with a membership of fifteen (the minimum number legally required in order to register an incorporated body). All were former members of the Green Party of Aotearoa.[28] As well as being its founder, Grueber assumed the role of official spokesperson, although sensitivity to his immigrant status caused him to share this responsibility with several of the party's parliamentary candidates. Bosselmann's book, *When Two Worlds Collide: Society and Ecology* (1995), provided the new party with its intellectual *raison d'être* as well as its core principles and policies.[29] The Green Society prides itself in being the only party that opposes economic growth. Sustainability rather than growth would be the primary motivation of a Green Society government. The global environmental crisis can only be addressed, it reasons, through a transformation in the values on which industrial societies are based. New Zealand is regarded as being in the favoured position of being able to 'lead the way in the development of alternative, sustainable ways to live in harmony with ourselves and nature'.[30] Policies of the Green Society include a commitment to New Zealand's economic sovereignty, including ownership and control of its assets, strict anti-monopoly laws, support for a carbon tax, restoration and improvement of all natural habitats, a move from fossil fuels to alternative forms of energy, and support for the decolonisation of the South Pacific.[31]

Grueber proved to be an adept organiser, fundraiser, and publicist. Despite the party's modest beginnings, it enjoyed disproportionate attention from print journalists, who tended to focus on its distinctiveness *vis-à-vis* the other green parties, the Alliance and Progressive Greens. Grueber unsuccessfully challenged the right of the Green Party of Aotearoa to be registered with the Electoral Commission, on the grounds that it was undemocratic for it to be registered twice (the Alliance had already been granted registration).[32] He also drew publicity over the party's bid to attract the 500 members required for registration with the Electoral Commission and with his bold predictions about electoral prospects at the 1996 election (on one occasion he claimed that the Green Society would receive 5–10 per cent of the party list vote, which would have entitled it to between seven and twelve MPs).[33]

Despite its founder's optimism, at the 1996 election the Green Society attracted a mere 2,363 party list votes, or 0.11 per cent of the valid vote nation-wide. Apart from picking up modest support in the two Auckland electorates of North Shore and Auckland Central (which includes Waiheke Island), the party performed best in a handful of town and semi-rural North Island seats, notably Napier, Rodney, and Otaki. Any disappointment at the Green Society's poor showing, however, can be tempered with the knowledge that the more fancied Progressive Greens and the United Party (which had seven MPs in 1996) were also soundly rejected by the voters (0.26 per cent and 0.88 per cent respectively).

Electoral politics
In its 1986 report, *Towards a Better Democracy*, the Royal Commission on the Electoral System recommended the same MMP system used in the election of members of the German Bundestag, the federal lower house. Apart from its proportionality, the German system was favoured by the commission because it allowed for the retention of two long-established features of parliamentary representation in New Zealand: single-member constituencies and, through the use of nationwide lists, strong party organisations and government. The commission also recommended that New Zealand adopt an electoral threshold (although at 4,[34] not 5, per cent as in Germany), with a view to preventing the proliferation of small parliamentary parties, which, critics alleged, would result in political instability and the concentration of power in the hands of small parties.[35]

Hans Grueber.
(H. Grueber)

Part of the appeal of MMP to members of the commission was Germany's tradition of effective government. Responding to the claim of critics that coalition government is inherently unstable, the commission stated that 'West German governments have been extremely stable with early elections held on only two occasions since the war and changes in government occurring only in 1966, 1969 and 1982'.[36] To a second major criticism, that coalition governments are weak and indecisive, the commission responded that successive German governments 'have demonstrated their ability to act decisively when that has been necessary'.[37]

Far from being persuaded by these assurances, opponents warned that, under MMP, New Zealand could well become another Italy or Israel. The former, for example, was said to have a 'revolving-door, scandal-ridden type of governments [sic]',[38] and politically volatile Israel was described as having a form of MMP.[39] The Prime Minister, Jim Bolger, told parliament that 'people are marching in the streets in their tens of thousands in countries where MMP is in existence'.[40] He said that he would 'hate to think' that Germany's problems would ever be visited upon New Zealanders.[41] Besides, in the opinion of Warren Kyd, one of the Prime Minister's parliamentary colleagues, there was little point in attempting to follow a country whose much-vaunted economy was in decline.[42] Unmistakable parallels were drawn between the social disruption in the wake of German reunification and that of the Weimar Republic. Referring to then current events in

Germany, one government MP expressed the view that 'the potential replacement of that benign party, the Free Democrats, by the Republicans, which is a party that is anything but benign; and the recent fire-bombings and deaths—are an example that we do not want to follow'.[43]

Klaus Bosselmann and Hans Grueber reacted strongly to what they saw as a concerted effort on the part of some senior politicians to discredit the German electoral system. Grueber formed the MMP Campaign Committee in August 1992. With a budget of some $40,000, he and a small group of financial supporters made fifteen-second television commercials in support of MMP for screening each night during the final week of the 1992 electoral referendum campaign. As the only political advertisement to be televised by either side during the debate, it attracted considerable public attention.

Before it was screened, the advertisement was censored by the Television Commercial Approvals Bureau on the grounds that it infringed the Codes of Broadcasting Practice.[44] The bureau ruled that there was an 'unmistakable innuendo' in the words 'It's a two-party club. There's nothing to keep them honest'. It suggested that the words 'nothing to keep them honest' be replaced with 'nothing to keep them on their toes'. When the broadcaster Paul Holmes saw the uncut tapes he decided to screen them, along with the edited version, on his current affairs television show. According to Grueber, the sympathetic treatment given by Holmes only two days before the referendum vote was worth considerably more than the $40,000 invested in the advertising campaign.[45] Following the announcement of the referendum results (84.5 per cent of voters had voted for a change to the voting system, with 70.5 per cent choosing MMP), a Television New Zealand camera crew was despatched to Grueber's home to record the celebrations for their network news.

Conclusion

The influence of German immigrants on recent developments in New Zealand politics is impossible to gauge. However, it is fair to say that immigrants have been actively involved in two important developments: the pro-MMP campaign and, through the formation of alternative green parties, the gradual emergence of a more complex multiparty system. Both developments represent a major departure from the colonial Westminster system adopted from Britain. More broadly, by supporting environmental and anti-nuclear policies, which have helped to define New Zealand's national and regional interests, German immigrants can be said to be contributing to New Zealand's growing sense of nationhood and independence.

1   See, for example, S. Hoadley, *The New Zealand Foreign Affairs Handbook* (Auckland, 1989), pp. 1–25.

2   K. Bosselmann, 'Deep foundations—green principles' (speech to the Green Politics for 1990 and Beyond conference, held at Kaiteriteri, near Nelson, March 1990).

3   R. Galvin, telephone interview, 14 April 1997, Auckland.

4   *Greenweb,* September/October 1995 (official publication of the Green Party of Aotearoa–New Zealand), p. 1.

5   K. Bosselmann (personal interview), University of Auckland, 3 March 1997.

6   R. Miller, 'Postmaterialism and Green Party activists in New Zealand', *Political Science,* vol. 43, no. 2 (1991), p. 58.

7 T. Scharf in E. Kolinsky (ed.), *The Greens in West Germany: Organisation and Policy Making* (Berg, 1989), p. 160.

8 See, for example J.G. Andersen, '"Environmentalism", "new politics" and industrialism: Some theoretical perspectives', *Scandinavian Political Studies*, vol. 13, no. 2 (1990), pp. 101–18; and R. Eckersley, 'Green politics and the new class: Selfishness or virtue?', *Political Studies*, vol. 37 (1989), pp. 205–23.

9 S. Flanagan, 'Response to R. Inglehart's "Value change in industrial society"', *American Political Science Review*, vol. 81, no. 4 (1987), p. 1304.

10 G. Braunthal, *Parties and Politics in Modern Germany* (Boulder, 1996), pp. 95–6.

11 Miller [note 6], pp. 43–66.

12 Bosselmann [note 5].

13 *Auckland Star*, 10 November 1989.

14 *Sunday Star*, 10 December 1989.

15 Bosselmann [note 5].

16 'The German experience shared', *Nelson Evening Mail*, 31 March 1990.

17 Bosselmann [note 2].

18 R. Miller, 'The minor parties' in H. Gold (ed.), *New Zealand Politics in Perspective* (3rd edn, Auckland 1992), p. 312.

19 R. Miller and H. Catt, *Season of Discontent: By-elections and the Bolger Government* (Palmerston North, 1993), pp. 44–8.

20 K. Bosselmann, 'Green or not so Green? Thoughts on the identity crisis of the Green Party', *Greenweb*, September 1994, p. 13.

21 Ibid.

22 Bosselmann [note 5].

23 P. Lusk, 'Majority support Alliance but with safeguards', *Greenweb*, June 1992, p. 5.

24 H. Grueber, 'Alliance fever?', *Greenweb*, April 1992, pp. 13–14.

25 H. Grueber, personal interview, 25 February 1997.

26 Ibid.

27 R. Miller, 'Is there a blue-green electoral constituency in New Zealand?' (paper presented to the New Zealand Political Studies Association Conference, Victoria University of Wellington, 30 August–1 September 1995).

28 *New Zealand Herald*, 19 September 1994.

29 S. Rainbow and S. Sheppard, 'The minor parties' in R. Miller (ed.), *New Zealand Politics in Transition* (Auckland, 1997), p. 180.

30 Green Society, 'Towards a Green Society' (party manifesto), (Auckland, 1996).

31 Ibid.

32 *New Zealand Herald*, 12 May 1995.

33 *New Zealand Herald*, 19 September 1994.

34 When it legislated on the matter, the New Zealand parliament decided that a 4 per cent threshold was too low. In the Electoral Act (1993), the threshold was set at 5 per cent. Parliament also rejected the commission's recommendation that there should be no threshold for Maori parties.

35 Report of the Royal Commission on the Electoral System, *Towards a Better Democracy* (Wellington, 1986), pp. 66–7.

36 Royal Commission on the Electoral System [note 35], p. 57.

37 Royal Commission on the Electoral System [note 35], p. 58.

38 *New Zealand Parliamentary Debates (NZPD)*, vol. 537, 3 August 1993, p. 17208.

39 *NZPD* [note 38], p. 17209.

40 *NZPD*, vol. 532, 15 December 1992, p. 13165.

41 *NZPD* [note 38], p. 17104.

42 *NZPD* [note 38], p. 17134.

43 Ian Revell MP, *NZPD* [note 38], p. 17208.

44 Correspondence from W. Richards (executive director, Television Commercial Approvals Bureau) to H. Grueber, 7 September 1992.

45 Grueber [note 25].

36

German studies in New Zealand

PETER OETTLI

Professor Eric Herd.
(A. Obermayer)

The year 1996 saw the deaths of two New Zealand academics who can be regarded as the founding fathers of German studies in New Zealand: John Asher, Emeritus Professor of German at the University of Auckland, and Eric Herd, Emeritus Professor of German at the University of Otago in Dunedin. These two men contributed more to German studies in New Zealand than any other individuals, and this chapter is, among other things, a celebration of the achievements of the two founding fathers and their colleagues.

The concept of German studies can be interpreted in a number of ways. In the context of this chapter it means the study of German language, literature, and culture as defined in the syllabus for the School Certificate examination, for example, or in the prescriptions for 'German' in the calendars of New Zealand universities. In view of the global importance of German-speaking Europe, it is clear that New Zealand educational institutions that teach history, political science, economics, and other subjects offer courses in these disciplines with respect to Germany, while German music, mathematics, science, and philosophy form a significant part of any study of Western culture. Schools and universities will inevitably be the major focus of the discussion because that is where most German studies in New Zealand are carried out.

It might be expected that in a country that has a Haast Pass and a Franz Josef Glacier German studies would have flourished from the time when German scientists and explorers were in the country and described its fascinating geography, geology, flora, and fauna. This is not the case, although German settlement in New Zealand was early and numerous. The first settlers and missionaries, mainly from northern Germany, arrived in Nelson as early as 1843, and they were followed by further waves in 1861–67, 1872–86, and 1900–14. Before World War I, as one New Zealand geographer has pointed out: 'German born constituted the largest continental European population in New Zealand.'[1]

In spite of the scientific interest in New Zealand from German-speaking Europe, and in spite of comparatively large numbers of immigrants from that area to this country, interest in German studies in New Zealand was practically non-existent in the nineteenth and early twentieth centuries. It is true that German was offered as a teaching subject at Otago University in 1873, two years before French was introduced. Canterbury followed in 1875,

Auckland in 1883, and Victoria University of Wellington in 1899. But in all instances it was taught only sporadically to a very small number of students. Their teachers were often scantily qualified part-time lecturers who taught in the context of modern languages departments in which the teaching of French predominated. In most universities, with the possible exception of Victoria University College, there appear to have been many years up to the late 1940s in which German, although listed among the subjects offered, was either not taught at all or taught only reluctantly to the most enthusiastic and determined students, who at times had to cajole their teachers into fulfilling the obligations imposed on them by the offerings listed in the university calendar.[2]

This situation is not altogether surprising, and three major factors appear to be responsible for it. The first is that New Zealand is, after all, the furthest country from Germany, and its European orientation has always been firmly directed towards Britain, from where the overwhelming majority of its settlers came. In 1902, two local historians nicely overstated this orientation by saying: 'The stock from which the New Zealanders are sprung is not only British but the best of British.'[3] Quite apart from the fact that the Maori segment of the population is simply ignored by these authors, this is the blunt statement of a myth. It does, however, illustrate a strong Anglocentric attitude, which partly explains the reluctance of New Zealanders to study other European languages, particularly German. Since Britain joined the European Community, successive New Zealand governments have stated repeatedly that the future of this country lies in Asia and the Pacific rim, and that Asian languages should be studied. The effect of these pronouncements, which are certainly partly justified by geography and trade, will be considered later in this chapter.

A second factor militating against the rapid development of German studies in New Zealand is that Germany has been the enemy in two world wars. Peaceful cultural links were inhibited, and anti-German hysteria meant that the German settlers were prevented from maintaining their own cultural identity after the first war. Moreover, the chain of migration from Germany was broken. So although New Zealand did have German settlements before World War I, they have not, as for example in South Australia or Pennsylvania, had a major impact on any of the regions.

Finally, the New Zealand education system has, since its inception, been characterised by a severely utilitarian outlook, which had little use for subjects that did not impart what were perceived as immediately applicable useful skills. This is the case to some extent even today. A provincial North Island high school principal was sent a questionnaire by the New Zealand Language Teachers Association in the 1980s. Instead of answering detailed questions in which he was to give his assessment of the value of foreign language teaching in his school he wrote boldly across the page: 'If it doesn't grow wool, it's irrelevant!'

In spite of the hostile or at least indifferent climate, German studies began to grow and flourish in New Zealand in the 1950s and 1960s. In 1947 and 1948, Victoria University of Wellington and the University of Auckland appointed full-time lecturers (David Carrad and John Asher), while

Canterbury and Otago followed in 1949 and 1953. Three of the four appointees, John Asher in Auckland, Edward Carter in Canterbury (who had originally been employed to teach science German), and Eric Herd in Otago (who was the first German scholar to hold a chair of modern languages in New Zealand), were later to become the first professors of German at their universities. Thus the foundations were laid.

Two of these 'founding fathers', Eric Herd and Edward Carter, came to New Zealand with British training and qualifications and thus established an important link with British German studies. John Asher, on the other hand, was a New Zealander who, as a student, showed high motivation and tenacity combined with exceptional ability. In spite of being discouraged by his teachers at the Auckland University College, he became the first student at Auckland to take German for his MA and to gain first-class honours in French and German. Despite the fact that Germany lay in ruins at the end of World War II, John Asher was only slightly diverted, to German-speaking Switzerland, where he was the first foreign student after the war to complete a doctorate in German language and literature. After his appointment as lecturer in German in the Department of Modern Languages at the University of Auckland, John Asher set about fostering German with the same enthusiasm and drive with which he had pursued his studies.

It was with both these qualities, and creative leadership as well, that German studies began to grow in all four constituent colleges of what was then the University of New Zealand. Student numbers gradually increased, course offerings were expanded, and in the 1960s the first professorial chairs of German were established in New Zealand. Auckland led the way in 1962, followed by Victoria in 1964, where Paul Hoffmann, who had been the second lecturer in German since 1959, was appointed professor. In 1965, Canterbury established its chair, while Eric Herd at Otago, already Professor of Modern Languages since 1956, became Professor of German when a chair of French was established there in 1969 and the Department of Modern Languages was split into two separate departments of French and German.

Two new universities were established in New Zealand in 1964, and both decided to teach German from the very beginning. Massey University in Palmerston North and Waikato University in Hamilton both taught German from the time of their foundation as independent universities: Massey in a Department of Modern Languages, which still exists today, and Waikato in a separate German Department, which had its own chair from 1969 to 1992 when its incumbent, Hans-Werner Nieschmidt, who had been appointed from Germany, retired.

The expansion of German studies at university level was accompanied by a no less rapid expansion of the teaching of German language in secondary schools. Only one or two schools in major cities offered German as a subject in the late 1940s, with a mere handful of candidates presenting themselves for public examinations. In 1979, however, 1,155 students sat University Entrance German, 364 sat Entrance Bursary, and 74 took the subject for the Entrance Scholarship examination. While these numbers have dropped again in recent years, the proportion of students with University

Professor John Asher.
(M. Asher)

Entrance who continue German in the seventh form had risen significantly: from 38 per cent in 1979 to 75 per cent in 1995. There might be fewer students of German in New Zealand schools, for reasons that will be explained later, but the figures suggest that they are more highly motivated to continue with their studies. This is encouraging to anyone who considers German studies an important part of the school curriculum.

Figure 1, which plots secondary school enrolment figures for German, French, and Japanese over the decade 1987–96, shows that German has held its numbers between approximately 8,500 and 9,000, while Japanese has grown strongly, mainly at the expense of French. New Zealand's political and economic move away from Europe and towards an orientation to the Pacific Rim is clearly reflected in the languages its students choose to study. The figures for German suggest, however, that it has by now become firmly established in the school curriculum. In addition to the study of German at secondary schools, another 4,986 pupils are learning the language at primary schools. Many of them might not continue the language into secondary school, but the fact that German is offered at this level and is taken by a substantial number of pupils is again encouraging.

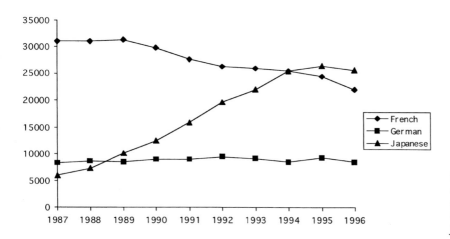

Figure 1: total number of secondary school students studying German, French, and Japanese 1987–96

The expansion of German studies in schools did not happen of its own accord. Vigorous promotion of the subject was undertaken by the newly founded university German departments and continues today. These vitally important promotional activities include competitions for students of German in schools, German 'Open Days' and 'Evenings', exhibitions (often in conjunction with German agencies), quiz evenings for school pupils, and countless addresses to Rotary Clubs, meetings of school careers advisers, business people, and virtually any group willing to be addressed on the topic of German language and culture.

More was needed than just enthusiasm, sound teaching, and research to achieve the situation now prevailing in our schools and universities. Two factors in particular were crucial if the teaching of German was to thrive. It needed first of all support from the community and then help from the countries whose language, literature, and culture were studied. The foundation members of our German departments were well aware of this and set out to promote interest in German studies in circles beyond their classrooms. As early as 1948, John Asher founded the Auckland Goethe Society, dedicated to the fostering and promulgation of German culture abroad. It was the first Goethe Society to be established anywhere in the world after World War II. Otago followed in 1953 and Wellington in 1960, although it had had a thriving German Language Society before this date. The Canterbury Goethe Society commenced activities a few years later, and the two new centres, Palmerston North and Hamilton, both had founded Goethe Societies by the late 1960s. These societies are not only an important link between the university and people particularly interested in German studies, they also bring other aspects of German culture to the community at large. The Waikato Goethe Society, for example, has participated in the National Sport and Recreation Fielddays, when aspects of German life, such as toys, popular music, and food, were presented to more than 10,000 people in a single weekend.

Another link with Germany is the fact that many young people travel abroad before they settle down. While the most favoured destinations are Australia, the United States, and Britain, a good proportion of these young New Zealand travellers, particularly those of European descent, also visit German-speaking Europe and thus establish informal links between the two parts of the world.

The second factor, support from German-speaking countries, has also been a tremendous help. A generous and enthusiastic response from the Federal Republic of Germany, Austria, and Switzerland to the efforts of the German departments has played a vital part in the development of German studies in New Zealand. The help and encouragement given by successive diplomatic representatives has been invaluable. Scholarship and cultural agencies, such as the German Academic Exchange Service, Inter Nationes, Pro Helvetia, and the Alexander von Humboldt Foundation, have provided generous support to an ever-growing number of students, teachers, and scholars who wish to further their studies by spending some time at a German university. It should be noted that some of these awards provide not only for travel to Europe and maintenance and other costs while there but also in some cases for return visits and continuous support once the recipient has returned from German-speaking Europe.

However, not only universities have benefited from support by the German Government. The teaching of German in our schools has been enriched and made more effective by the establishment of the German Adviser scheme. Since 1976, the scheme has provided for a support person sent from Germany for a period, and trained in language teaching methodology, to be available to teachers throughout New Zealand.

In 1978, a further measure was announced that was to foster German teaching in our schools and bring German culture to the wider community. During his visit to New Zealand in October of that year, the then President of the Federal Republic, Walter Scheel, also accepted an invitation

to the University of Auckland, where he was awarded an honorary doctorate. President Scheel paid tribute to the work of the German departments in our universities and announced that a Goethe Institut would be established in New Zealand in 1980. In October of that year, Dr Peter Hubrich arrived in Wellington, and eight months later the Institut was open for business. It now has five full-time staff members. Its rich and varied programme of visitors, exhibitions, and symposia has greatly contributed to the cultural life of New Zealand. In addition, the Institut is the only institution in New Zealand apart from some of the universities at which learners can continue their study of German to the level of the internationally recognised Zertifikat Deutsch als Fremdsprache (Diploma in German as a Foreign Language). About 220 students attend classes at the Institut in Wellington each year. A measure of the interest extended by the central administration in Germany to this furthest outpost of German culture in the world is demonstrated by the fact that since its inception, the Wellington Institut has been visited by all four leading figures of this world-wide foundation: the president, the general secretary, the assistant general secretary and the head of the foreign section.

The Goethe Institut programme that provides for teacher refresher courses in Germany is a further generous measure, which has vastly

German President Dr Scheel after his investiture as Honorary LLD at Auckland University in 1978. Standing in front: Acting Chancellor Mr H.H. Craig and President Walter Scheel. Immediately behind them (left to right): the Prime Minister, Mr R.D. Muldoon, Professor Asher, Dr Mildred Scheel, and the Vice-Chancellor, Dr C.J. Maiden. *(G. Boehnke)* enhanced German studies in our schools. Of the approximately 200 teachers of German in New Zealand, a large proportion have been to Germany to attend Goethe Institut courses. It is impossible to make precise statements about the value of these courses, but there can be no doubt that they provide tremendous enrichment to the individual teachers and therefore to the teaching of German in New Zealand schools.

The university German departments have, particularly since the 1960s, developed partly along different but complementary lines in their relations with overseas universities. While some have established valuable lines of communication with German departments in the English-speaking world, others have forged strong ties with German universities. In this way, it can be said that collectively the New Zealand universities' German departments have the best of both worlds. Overall, however, the New Zealand links with Germany and German universities have been very strong right from the beginning.

The strength of New Zealand contacts with German universities and German scholarship is demonstrated particularly in three areas: student exchange, formal and informal exchanges of scholars and artists, and the field of scholarly publications.

Student exchanges between New Zealand and Germany, particularly at senior secondary school level, have existed for several decades. The Society for New Zealand–German Student Exchange, funded mainly by German firms trading in New Zealand, has arranged for the exchange of about four candidates from each country for many years. A more recent initiative by the German Department of the University of Waikato provides for the exchange annually of a total of 230 secondary school pupils. Many New Zealanders who have been to Germany with the programme decide to continue with their studies of German as a result of the experience.

In addition to exchange visits, an increasing number of students from Germany choose to spend some time studying in New Zealand. An inter-

German students from Baden-Württemberg in New Zealand as part of the New Zealand–German Student Exchange organised by Waikato University. *(V. Knüfermann)*

German President Richard von Weizsäcker on a visit to Auckland University in 1993. *(G. Boehnke)*

government agreement means that German students at graduate level can study at New Zealand universities while paying the same fee as New Zealanders and not the considerably higher overseas students' fee. Special courses, such as papers in teaching German as a second language, and the possibility of working as tutors in German in New Zealand universities are further important factors that bring students from Germany to New Zealand. All these student contacts are valuable not only to the participants themselves but also to the people associated with and related to them. In this way, New Zealand–German relations are fostered at the personal level, and this can only be good for German studies in New Zealand.

The formal and informal exchange of scholars and artists is the second area of important contacts. The German National Fellowship scheme, established in 1955 and now administered by the New Zealand Vice-Chancellors' Committee, has enabled a number of German scholars, not only in the field of German studies but also in the natural and social sciences, to visit this country's universities for lecture tours. In 1963, on the initiative of John Asher, who had been appointed to New Zealand's first chair of German the previous year, a visiting professorship was established at the University of Auckland.[4] Distinguished scholars, mainly from Germany, came to teach in his department for a term almost every year until his retirement in 1986. The other universities also benefited from these visitors, who were only too willing to travel and give lectures at other centres. Later, Eric Herd at Otago extended these valuable links by organising a second visiting professorship, whereby the guest would be shared by the six universities that taught German. In 1986, the German Department at Waikato hosted a guest lecturer from what was then the German Democratic Republic. While these activities have declined since the late 1980s, there appears to have been an increase in the number of students who visit Germany either during or after the completion of their studies. Close relationships between individual colleagues in New Zealand and Germany have also continued on an informal basis, and they have contributed to teaching, research, and publications in both countries.

The visiting artists and exhibitions of works of German artists, most of whom have been brought out by the Goethe Institut, have not only supported the teaching of German literature and culture, they have also brought German studies to a much wider range of people than students of the subject. Musical groups, such as the Schubert Choir, writers like Hans Bender, Siegfried Lenz, or Hans Magnus Enzensberger, actors, for example Lilian Westphal, many of whom have visited New Zealand under the auspices of the Goethe Institut, have made a contribution to the cultural life of New Zealand as well as to academic work in the universities.

The final area of contact between New Zealand German departments and German universities is in scholarly publications. While there is a home-grown book series, the Otago German Studies, edited by August Obermayer at Otago University (who also has held editorial responsibility for part of the Canadian journal of Germanic studies, *Seminar*), it is nevertheless true that most of our publications appear in German periodicals and with German publishers. Editions by John Asher, Eric Herd, Kathryn Smits, and (most recently) Axel Vieregg, whose editions of the collected works of Peter Huchel and Günter Eich have been received very well, all appeared in Germany and Switzerland. Indeed, the large majority of publications by New Zealand German scholars are published in German-speaking Europe. Probably few students of *Germanistik* (German language and literature studies) in Germany who take these volumes from the shelves of their libraries suspect that they were produced by scholars from the other side of the world, in a country where the very concept of *Germanistik* was virtually unknown fifty years ago.

The concept of *Germanistik* has undergone considerable change in many of the New Zealand university German departments during the 1990s. While in the beginning all departments saw themselves as teaching mainly German language and literature, there has been a move to include the study of German 'culture' in the wider sense of German politics, economics, social, and political history. In addition, some German departments have entered into strategic alliances with other parts of their university to provide a language component to, for example, economics, management, or music.

Such moves are partly survival strategies in the face of increasing competition from Asian languages, a disinclination of students to choose courses in literature, and the government-imposed quest for 'efficiency' in universities, which is a threat to small departments. Another survival strategy that has been or is being adopted is the grouping of departments of German together with other departments in schools or departments of European languages or, as has happened at the University of Waikato, the formation of a Department of European and Hispanic Studies. While such moves might be seen as making a virtue of a necessity, the positive view is that such clusters can provide new opportunities for departments of German that are open to constructive change.

It is clear that the traditional study of German language and literature in New Zealand universities has passed its peak. While in the 1970s there were five professorial chairs in Dunedin, Christchurch, Wellington, Waikato, and Auckland, there are only two in the late 1990s, one each in Wellington and Auckland, and there seems to be little prospect of further chairs being established or re-established in the near future. The thirty full-time staff members who taught German in New Zealand universities in the 1970s and 1980s have shrunk to twenty-five, and numbers might decline further, with lecturers who resign or retire not being replaced. Most departments, however, report static or slightly rising student numbers since the mid 1990s. This means that German departments, like the university system as a whole, are becoming more 'efficient' at least in the sense that more students are being taught with fewer staff. It is a tribute to the dedication of the teaching staff that so far they have managed to maintain very high standards. New Zealand graduates continue to be able to find places for study in Germany and maintain their position alongside German students in their home institutions.

As a result of these high standards, some New Zealand graduates in German are now teaching or researching at universities such as Stirling, Cambridge, London, and Adelaide, and at *Gymnasien* (grammar schools) in Basel and Magdeburg. However, the employment prospects of graduates have spread much further than German studies. New Zealand graduates in German are active in many fields—in commerce and industry, journalism, travel and tourism, the diplomatic service, and in government departments. The senior official in Treasury responsible for many years for university funding was a graduate in German. The wide acceptability of graduates in German shows that, like most disciplines in the humanities, German studies provides a thorough but broad education that trains its students in how to think rather than in what to think, and produces adaptable workers who can make a contribution to the New Zealand workforce well beyond the specific language skills they have also acquired.

What about the future of German studies in New Zealand? The achievement of the last fifty years has been a record of progress due largely to the vision of the 'founding fathers' and the hard work, dedication, and support of their colleagues. The development has been from German within modern language departments to independent German departments, now increasingly grouped with other European languages in strategic clusters; from part-time lecturers to small but comparatively stable staff numbers; from antipathy and indifference in the community to Goethe Societies in six centres and the Goethe Institut in Wellington; from German in a few select schools to German in a large number of schools, complete with back-up services and overseas training possibilities for teachers. And all of this in fifty years!

In the time ahead there is both a threat and a promise. The threat is in the decline of the study of European languages at schools, which inevitably will also affect the universities. As we have seen, German has fared well in comparison with some other foreign languages, but there are very real pressures that threaten to entice students away from the study of any language towards the more vocationally oriented subjects. This trend, combined with a decline in resources available for German studies, both in this country and in Germany, will undoubtedly make our work harder. Funding cuts mean fewer staff, fewer scholarships, fewer exchange possibilities, and less current information. The climate for German studies is clearly not entirely favourable.

At the same time, there still is promise, and it is based particularly on three considerations. The first is the quality of the students who have graduated and who are continuing to graduate from our German departments. The future of German studies is assured because a promising new generation of New Zealand German scholars has been trained and is still being trained in our universities.

The second consideration is the development of new approaches to German studies. While German language, literature, and culture are, and always must be, the primary concern of any German department, it can also make a worthwhile contribution to course patterns in other faculties. First Waikato and then Victoria have introduced German into their management and commerce faculties to cater for the specific needs of these students, and Auckland has a German for business course taught within the German BA structure by a lecturer from the School of International Business. There are further possibilities in other areas, such as music, fine arts, architecture, and science, where German departments can provide a service and contribute to an expansion of the students' horizons beyond the English-speaking world.

The third consideration, and in many ways the most important, is the history of the establishment of German studies in New Zealand and thus the example of those who preceded the current generation of German scholars and teachers in New Zealand schools. Fifty years ago, they faced a climate that was incomparably more harsh than it is in the late 1990s. The difficulties they overcame were far greater than those that have to be faced in the late 1990s. They approached what appeared to be an impossible task with enthusiasm, energy, and dedication, and in that regard they are an inspiration to the generations that follow them.

German studies in New Zealand cannot escape the cold winds of educational reform currently sweeping the country. They are a challenge to the entire education system. At the same time, German studies are now established as a significant part of New Zealand education. A lot of generous help is available both inside and outside New Zealand, and a solid foundation has been laid by John Asher and Eric Herd and their generation. The challenges that German studies now face in New Zealand can be met, and if they are met, they will lead to new opportunities that will ensure the continuation of a flourishing tradition of German studies in this country.

1   I.H. Burnley, 'German immigration and settlement in New Zealand 1842–1914', *New Zealand Geographer*, 29 (1973), pp. 45–63.
2   For the situation at Auckland, see Sean D. Lovich, *German and Swedish at Auckland* (Auckland 1983), pp. 10–15.
3   See Keith Sinclair, *A History of New Zealand* (Harmondsworth 1959), p. 297.
4   Additional information kindly supplied by Mrs Monica Asher (Auckland).

Contributors

James N. Bade is Associate Professor of German at the University of Auckland, where he has taught since 1976. He studied at Victoria University of Wellington (MA Hons 1971) and the University of Zürich (Dr. phil. 1974). He has published widely on aspects of modern German literature, especially on the works of Thomas Mann, and more recently on the historical ties between New Zealand and German-speaking Europe. He is the editor of *The German Connection: New Zealand and German-speaking Europe in the Nineteenth Century* (Oxford University Press 1993), as well as its expanded German version, *Eine Welt für sich: Deutschsprachige Siedler und Reisende in Neuseeland im neunzehnten Jahrhundert* (1998).

Ann Beaglehole is a historian who came to New Zealand after the Hungarian uprising in 1956. In recent years, she has worked as a policy analyst at the Ethnic Affairs Service in Wellington. She is the author of three books dealing with the experience of Jewish people in New Zealand: *A Small Price to Pay* (1988), *Facing the Past* (1990), and *Far from the Promised Land* (1995).

Leonard Bell is Senior Lecturer in the Department of Art History at the University of Auckland. He has written extensively on aspects of New Zealand art, past and present. He is the author of *Colonial Constructs: European Images of Maori 1840–1914* (1992).

Maja Beutler is a prize-winning Swiss novelist, dramatist, and short story writer. She was born and grew up in Bern, and, after training in Zürich as a translator, studied in France, England, and Italy. Her most recent novel is *Die Stunde, da wir fliegen lernen* (1994).

James Braund studied German and classics at the University of Auckland, where he graduated with a PhD in German literature in 1994. Since 1995 he has worked as a research assistant in the Department of Germanic Languages and Literature at the University of Auckland. His research interests include the various literary and past scientific links between New Zealand and German-speaking Europe.

Bevan Burgess is a graduate of the University of Canterbury. After a decade spent as a political correspondent for NZ Newspapers Ltd, he taught as Senior Tutor in Journalism at Wellington Polytechnic before becoming a public relations consultant. In the mid 1980s he was communications adviser to the then Minister of Finance, Roger Douglas.

Hansgerd Delbrück is Professor of German and head of the School of European Languages at Victoria University of Wellington. He has written widely on aspects of German poetry and drama, especially the plays of Heinrich von Kleist and Gotthold Ephraim Lessing, and has also edited two collections of essays written in honour of his former colleague Paul Hoffmann.

275

Rod Fisher studied at the Universities of Auckland, Würzburg, and Cambridge, gaining his PhD in 1968. Since 1969, he has taught at the University of Canterbury, where he is head of the Department of German. He has published books and articles on aspects of modern and medieval German language and literature.

Norman Franke is Lecturer in the Department of Germanic and Hispanic Studies at Waikato University, having taught previously at the Universities of Hamburg (of which he is a graduate) and Reading. His research interests include early German Romanticism, German exile literature, and the literature of the former East Germany.

Gisela Holfter lectures in the Department of Languages and Cultural Studies at the University of Limerick (Ireland), where she is Director of the Centre for Irish–German Studies. She has also tutored at the University of Otago.

Graeme Horne completed his MA and is pursuing doctoral studies in the Department of Political Studies at the University of Auckland, where he works as a tutor. He is also vice-chairman of the Auckland branch of the New Zealand Institute of International Affairs.

Lauren Jackson has studied German and film, television, and media studies at the University of Auckland and the Konrad Wolf Institute for Film and Television, Potsdam-Babelsberg. She has been involved in the production of several New Zealand films, and played the lead role in the film *Alex* (dir.: Megan Simpson-Huberman 1993).

Jean King grew up in South Australia and moved to New Zealand in 1960. She has been deeply involved in the Lutheran Church of New Zealand since the mid 1960s, and is the author of a recent history of the Church, *The Lutheran Story* (1994).

Renate Koch was born in Czechoslovakia and has studied in Prague, Jena, Berlin, and George Washington University, Washington DC, where she completed a PhD in German literature in 1977. In addition to teaching at American universities, she has also lectured at Victoria University of Wellington and Wellington Polytechnic.

Axel Laurs studied at the University of Auckland, Victoria University of Wellington, and the University of Zürich, where he gained his Dr.phil. He is head of European Languages and European Studies in the School of Language Studies, Massey University, and specialises in film studies and nineteenth-century German literature.

Michael McBryde was born in Dunedin and grew up in the Cook Islands, Invercargill, Upper Hutt, and Christchurch. Postgraduate studies at the Universities of Stuttgart and Canterbury led to a PhD in German in 1976. Since then, he has worked for the Ministry of Foreign Affairs, serving at New Zealand diplomatic posts in Canberra, Apia, Rarotonga, and Bonn.

Ian McGibbon is a senior historian at the Historical Branch, Department of Internal Affairs, Wellington, specialising in the history of New Zealand's foreign policy and defence. His most recent publication is *New Zealand and the Korean War* (Vols I and II, Oxford University Press 1992 and 1996). He was made an Officer of the New Zealand Order of Merit in 1997 for services to historical research.

Raymond Miller is Lecturer in the Department of Political Studies at the University of Auckland, where he has taught since 1984. A regular media commentator on contemporary political developments in New Zealand, he is also the editor of *New Zealand Politics in Transition* (Oxford University Press 1997).

Peter Oettli was born in Switzerland and studied at the University of Auckland, where he completed his MA and PhD. He is Dean of the School of Humanities at Waikato University. His research interests include medieval German studies and the German missionaries who were active in New Zealand in the nineteenth century.

Janet Paul is well known in New Zealand literary and art circles for her contribution to art and typography but above all to publishing. With her late husband Blackwood (1908–65), she founded and ran Blackwood & Janet Paul, one of this country's best-known publishing houses, from 1945 to 1968. From 1971 to 1980 she was also Art Librarian at the Alexander Turnbull Library. She was created a Dame Companion of the New Zealand Order of Merit in 1997 in recognition of her long and outstanding services to publishing, letters, and the arts in New Zealand.

Peter Russell is Reader in German in the School of European Languages at Victoria University of Wellington. His research interests include aspects of modern German literature and German music, particularly the works of Gustav Mahler. He is the author of *The Divided Mind: A Portrait of Modern German Culture* (1988).

David Schnellenberg is a Jewish New Zealander whose father and paternal grandparents fled Nazi Germany for New Zealand in 1939. In 1990, the plight of David and his family was the subject of the television documentary *Star of David*, which linked David's New Zealand–Jewish experience to his German origins. David, his German-born wife Sarah, and three sons are regular visitors to Germany and its Jewish communities.

Bill Sewell worked as a senior research officer at the Law Commission in Wellington until early 1997. Before beginning law studies at Victoria University of Wellington in 1989, he taught for several years in the Department of German at the University of Otago, where he had also completed his PhD. He is the author of three books of poetry and has edited the volume *Sons of the Fathers* (1997).

Kathryn Smits was born in the Netherlands and studied at the Universities of Auckland and Freiburg. From 1966 she lectured in German at the University of Auckland, where she taught German language acquisition, medieval German studies, and contemporary German literature, retiring as Associate Professor of German in 1998. She has published extensively on aspects of medieval German literature and, in more recent years, on the Flemish writer Stijn Streuvels. She was awarded the Humboldt Medal (Bonn) in 1994.

Margaret Sutherland is Senior Lecturer in German at the School of European Languages at Victoria University of Wellington. She was born in Hamilton, studied languages at Waikato University (where she completed her DPhil), and has previously taught at Massey University. Her specialist field of research is in nineteenth-century German drama, especially the works of Christian Dietrich Grabbe.

John Mansfield Thomson, author of *The Oxford History of New Zealand Music* (Oxford University Press 1991), visited Darmstadt in 1962 and subsequently made contact with New Zealand composers such as Annea Lockwood and Robin Maconie, then studying in Cologne. With Janet Paul, he edited Frederick Page's *A Musician's Journal* (1986). They are now preparing a companion volume, *Musicians' Letters*, a selection of correspondence between Frederick Page and J.M. Thomson between 1959 and 1983.

Gerhard Träbing, formerly Associate Professor of German at Otago University, has long been interested in the German connection with New Zealand. Before his retirement he taught medieval and modern German literature and has several publications on German literature of the twentieth century.

David Venables was born in Wellington and studied history under Peter Munz at Victoria University of Wellington, where he graduated BA (Hons) in 1983. After training as a journalist, he worked for a number of daily and community newspapers, as well as for Radio New Zealand. He is Lecturer in Journalism at Wellington Polytechnic.

Peter Vere-Jones was born in England and educated at Muritai School, Eastbourne, and Hutt Valley High School. He attended Wellington Teachers' Training College before leaving in 1962 to become a professional actor. For many years he has also written professionally for a variety of media, ranging from children's radio adventure series to gardening columns and tourist documentaries for the Department of Conservation.

Friedrich Voit is Associate Professor of German at the University of Auckland, where he has taught since 1978. He studied at the Universities of Mannheim, Saarbrücken, and Bonn and has been a visiting lecturer in the United States and Germany. He has written widely on various aspects of eighteenth-, nineteenth-, and twentieth-century German literature, including such subjects as popular literature (almanacs), German–English literary influences, and exile literature.

Nelson Wattie studied at the University of Auckland, Victoria University of Wellington, and the University of Wuppertal. He has taught at the Universities of Riyadh (Saudi Arabia) and Cologne, and at present is lecturing in the Department of English at Victoria University. He co-edited *The Oxford Companion to New Zealand Literature* (Oxford University Press 1998).

Index

Names with *von* are indexed under the last name, e.g. Zedlitz, George von. Page numbers in italic, e.g. *227*, refer to illustrations.

Adam, Denis 179, 224–8, *227*
Adam, Fritz 224, *225*
Adam, Heinz 53
Adam, Ken 224, 225, 228
Adam, Peter 224, 226
Adam, Saul 224
Adam, Verna (née Finlayson) 226, 227, 228
Ahl 53, 54, 55
Aitutaki 38
Alberts, Christopher 223
Alexandra 181, 197
Allan, Bob 158
Allen, Sir James 41
Alpers, Antony 85
Alpers, O.T.J. 229
Anderton, Jim 167, 259, 260
Ansbach 118, 119
Apia 7
Arndt, Mina 63
Arnim, Count Henning von 78
Asher, John 86, 264, 265, 266, *266*, 268, *269*, 271, 272, 274
Ashton, Beatrice 197
Ashton, John 197
Aubin, Hermann 148
Auburn, Lore 69
Auburn, Walter 69–70
Auckland 8, 33, 39, 40, 41, 42, 45, 46, 66, 68, 69, 70, 101, 102, 107, 109, 110, *110*, 111, *111*, 126, 142, 143, 145, 154, 165, 193, 195, 204, 218, 220, 221, 222, 226, 243, 259, 260, 261, 273
Auckland Central (electorate) 261

Bach, Johann Sebastian 94

Bachmann, Ingeborg 154
Backhaus, Wilhelm 93
Bad Godesberg 241
Bad Soden 51, 52, 53, 54, 55
Bad Soden-Salmünster 54
Baden 106
Balling, Michael 90
Banks Peninsula 254
Barclay, Barry 101–2
Barta, Franz 68
Barton, George 230
Basel 92, 165, 273
Bavaria 71, 118, 239
Baxter, James K. 116
Bay of Islands 128, 129, 131
Bay of Plenty 8
Beaglehole family 121
Beaglehole, Elsie 206
Beaglehole, J.C. 139, 141, 194, 206
Beauchamp, Mary Annette 78
Becker, Jurek 82
Bedding, Major Geoffrey 4, 50–6, *54*
Beeby, C.E. 150
Beer, Isidore de 187
Beethoven, Ludwig von 93, 94, 201
Behrendt sisters *see* Brent sisters
Behrens, Peter 194
Belich, James 227
Bell, Gerda 135, 136, 147–52, *147*, *148*, *151*
Bell-Köhler, Ursula 149
Bella, Stefano della 70
Belloc, Hilaire 138
Bender, Hans 272
Benham, W.B. 187
Bensemann, Leo 109
Berendsen, Carl 6, 7
Berlin 60, 63, 71, 78, 95, 96, 101, 102, 106, 113, 114, 118, 119, 120, 121, 162, 163, 165, 169, 199, 200, 202, 204, 224, 225, 243, 244, 259

Bertram, James 77, 80, 144
Bethell, Ursula 116
Binswanger, Otti 109
Binswanger, Paul 109
Bitterli, Urs 248
Blacher, Boris 90
Blaha, Rev. P. 113
Blankenese 219
Blaschke, Alfons 118, *119*, 120, 121, 122
Blaschke, Marie Vandewart *29*, 60, 94,
    118–22, *119*
Bluff 83
Blumenburg, Hans 97, 98, 99
Blumenfeld family 110
Blythe, David 95
Bobrowski, Johannes 79
Böcklin, Arnold 128
Bolger, Jim 212, 241, *241*, 261
Bonn 148, 240, 241, 242, 244, 257
Bosselmann, Klaus 258, *258*, 259, 260,
    262
Bosshard, Kobi 73
Boulez, Pierre 90, 91, 92
Bourke, Captain 41
Brasch, Charles 77, 78, 79–80, *79*, 186
Bratislava 214
Brecht, Bertolt 102, 114
Breidecker, Heinrich 251
Bremen 71, 204
Brendler, Julia 103
Brent sisters 22
Breslau 148, 204
Britten, Benjamin 90
Brooklyn 69, 196
Brown, John Macmillan 188
Brown, Riwia 103
Brown, Vernon 66
Bruckner, Anton 93
Bruegel, Pieter 128
Brunswick, Duchy of 186
Büchner, Georg 150, 168
Buck, Sir Peter 188
Bühler, Karl 158
Burch-Korrodi, Meinrad 73
Burdon, Philip 242
Bürger, Gottfried August 81
Burnham 253, 254, *254*, *255*
Burns, Robert 210
Burt, Gordon 92
Bytinner, Inge 68

Cage, John 91
Callot, Jacques 70
Campbell, Ian 230

Campion, Jane 101, 103
Canterbury 226, 252, 253
Cape Colville 40, 41
Cape Egmont 8
Cape Farewell 8
Carlyle, Thomas 137
Carrad, David 265
Carter, Edward 266
Cashmere Hills 161
Castle, Len 70
Cavell, Edith 24
Central Otago 186, 252
Charters, Major David 51
Chatham Islands 8
Chemnitz 169
Chirac, Jacques 256
Christchurch *23*, 45, 64, 66, 109, 136,
    157, 158, 160, 161, 162, 164, 167, 168,
    192, 196, 197, 212, 226, 228, 273
Clark, Helen 212
Clemen, Professor 148
Clifton, Brigadier George 5, 16
Clive 182, 184
Clutha River 181
Cologne 12, 69, 92, 93, 115, 124, 177,
    180
Conlon, Professor 215
Cook Islands 38, 39
Cook, Captain James 80, 206, 245
Cooke, Sir Robin (Lord Cooke of
    Thorndon) 230, 232
Corinth, Lovis 63
Coromandel Peninsula 126, 153, 156
Correa-Hunt, Anna 70–1
Coutts, Joseph T. 184
Coutts, Morton 177, 184
Coutts, William 180, 184
Cox, Geoffrey 15
Cranna, John 228
Cromwell 180
Curnow, Allen 82, 109, 116, 178
Curtis Island 41
Czarnikow 199

Dachau 67
Dalziel, Margaret 158
Dam, Tom van 251
Daniel, Professor 113
Danube 142
Darmstadt 91, 92, 93, 94, 106, 111, 148,
    162
Darwin, Charles 171
Davies, Dorothy *29*, 121
Davin, Dan 15

Dawes, Frank 93
Decker, Franz-Paul 93
Dehmel, Richard 79
Dellow, K.J. 155
Devonport 39
Dieffenbach, Ernst 81, 150
Dietikon 218
Dittmer, Brigadier George 13
Dittmer, Wilhelm 62, 63, 71
Donaldson, Roger 100
Donaueschingen 91, 92, 94
Douglas, Roger 167
Downie, Paul 73
Dresden 37, 90, 138
Droescher, Werner 135, 136, 153–6, *153*
Dronke, Ernst 114
Dronke, John 113, 114, 115, 116, 117
Dronke, Marei 113, 115
Dronke, Maria 35, 60, 113–17, *114, 116*
Dronke, Peter 113, 115, 116
Duisburg-Ruhrort 123
Dunedin 64, 68, 72, 73, 109, 121, 131,
    145, 160, 161, 179, 180, 181, 186, 187,
    188, 189, 200, 209, 210, 264, 273
Dürer, Albrecht 150

East Cape 8
Eastbourne 116
Eccles, John 158, 159, 160, 161
Edwards family 182
Egk, Werner 90
Eich, Günter 79, 272
Eichbaum, Adolf 147, 148, 150
Eichbaum, Else (née Altschul) 147, 148,
    150
Eichbaum, Gerda/Gertrud *see* Bell,
    Gerda
Eichbaum, Jan 150
Eichbaum, Katia 150
Eichelbaum, Frieda 229, 230
Eichelbaum, Siegfried 229
Eichelbaum, Sir Thomas 177, 204,
    229–34, *231*
Eichelbaum, Vida (née Franz) 231
Eichelbaum, Walter 229, 230
Einhorn, Helmut 177
Einstein, Albert 114, 157
Einzinger, Erwin 84
Elgar, Edward 90
Eliot, T.S. 116, 143
Emile, Taungaroa 103
Emily Pass 187
Engel, Erich 114
Engels, Friedrich 157

Enzensberger, Hans Magnus 82, 154,
    272
Epuni 194
Erdinger Moor 219
Erdmann, Leading Seaman 39, 40
Eschenbruch, Rainer 251
Euripides 116
Evans, Harold 212
Evans, Martyn 129

Fairburn, A.R.D. 82, 109, 110, 116, 143
Fairburn, Geoffrey 125
Farrar, Fritz 177
Faulkner, Rebecca 222
Feldman, Morton 91
Fels, Albert 186
Fels, Emily 186, 187
Fels, Harold 186, 189
Fels, Heinemann Wilhelm 186
Fels, Helene 186, 187
Fels, Kate 186
Fels, Sara (née Hallenstein) 179, 186,
    187
Fels, Willi 179, 186–91, *187*
Fiji 8, 38, 39
Findlay, John 158
Fiordland 187
Firth, Cedric 195
Firth, Clifton 66
Fischer, Edwin 114
Fitt, A.B. 45
Focke, E. 21
Forder, H.G. 159
Forster, Georg 80, 245
Fortner, Wolfgang 90
Frame, Janet 78, 80, 228, 248
Francis, Captain 41
Franck, Peter 162, *163*
Frankel, Margaret 196
Frankel, Otto 192, 196
Frankfurt am Main 100, 114, 242, 243
Franz Josef Glacier 264
Fraser, Douglas 145
Fraser, Peter 34, 164, 193
Frederick the Great, King of Prussia
    137, 224
Freemans Bay 220
Freiburg im Breisgau 204
Freud, Sigmund 192
Freyberg, Major-General Bernard 13, 15
Fricker, Peter Racine 93

Gabites, George 195
Gallas, Fritz 135

Galvin, Ray 257
Gasteiger, Arno 73
Geiringer, Alfred 208
Geiringer, Erich 179, 208–13, *209*
Geissler, Julius 63
Genscher, Hans-Dietrich 239, 240
George V, King of England 5
George, Jack 97
George, Stefan 106, 143
Gerson, Ernst 177
Gertler, Mark 154
Gierach, Professor 148
Giesen family 253, 254, 255
Giesen, Alexander 253, *254*
Giesen, Gudrun 253
Giesen, Kurt 253
Giesen, Marcel 253, *254*
Giesen, Theo 253, 254, *254*
Giessen 70, 106, 148, 150
Gilmore, Lieutenant 42
Gisborne 22, *22*, 251
Glover, Denis 82, 109, 116
Godley, Major-General A. J. 6
Goethe, Johann Wolfgang von 79, 162, 168
Golden Bay 194, 258
Goldie, C.F. 71
Good, E.D. 25
Goodger, George 181
Gordon, Ian 85
Granville-Barker, Harley 115
Granville-Barker, Helen 115
Graz 67
Great Barrier Island 103
Grillparzer, Franz 142, 145
Grimm, Jacob 80
Grimm, Wilhelm 80
Gropius, Walter 192
Gross, Frank 64, 65
Grosz, Chris 69
Grueber, Hans 259, 260, *261*, 262
Grünwald, Professor 148
Gundolf, Professor 148

Haast Pass 264
Hadeln, Moritz de 96
Haedrich, Rolf 98
Halberstam, Hugo 215
Halcombe 23
Halle an der Saale 46
Halle an der Weser 179, 186
Hallenstein, Bendix 179, 186, 187, 190
Hallenstein, Emil 187
Hallenstein, Kätchen 186
Hallenstein, Percy 187

Hamburg 38, 71, 98, 101, 103, 114, 154, 156, 181, 218, 219, 221, 226, 237, 242, 260
Hamilton 22, 124, 195, 266, 268
Hamilton, Augustus 187
Hamilton, Ian 155
Harding, J. 181
Hart, Hyam 187
Hartley's Gully 181
Hartmann, Karl Amadeus 90
Hassel, Kai-Uwe von 239
Hataitai 204
Hauptmann, Gerhart 114
Hauraki Gulf 8
Hawke's Bay 120, 182, 252
Hedicke, Professor 148
Heenan, Joseph 194
Hegel, Friedrich 160
Heidelberg 78, 148
Heine, Heinrich 79, 168
Heinold, C. 23
Heinsen, Mr 21
Helena Falls 187
Hellenthal, Walter 220, 221
Hellyer, Christine 227
Hemingway, Ernest 154
Henck, Herbert 93–4
Henderson 145, 251, 252, *253*
Henderson, Barbara 197
Henderson, Russell 197
Henry VIII, King of England 184
Henze, Hans Werner 90
Herd, Eric 264, *264*, 266, 271, 274
Hermannswaldau 137
Herz, Max 62, 63, 74
Higgins, Don 221
Hildesheim 186
Hiles, Tony 103
Hill, Alfred 90–91
Hill, Sub-Inspector 39
Hilton, Arthur 179, 214–17, *215*, 225
Hilton, Lisl (née Kohn) 145, 179, 214, 215, *217*
Hilton, Otto 214, 215
Hindemith, Paul 90, 94
Hipwell, Arthur 125
Hirschbein, Arthur *see* Hilton, Arthur
Hirschman, Albert 163, *163*
Hitler, Adolf 7, 25, 44, 115, 119, 120, 129, 136, 142, 147, 148, 150, 155, 158, 161, 164, 169, 178, 192, 199, 214, 219, 241
Hobbes, Thomas 179, 206, 207
Hochstetter, Ferdinand von 81
Hof 101

Hoffmann family 142
Hoffmann, Carl 142, 145
Hoffmann, E.T.A. 78
Hoffmann, Eva (née Bichler) 144, *144*, 145
Hoffmann, Frank 142, 143, 145
Hoffmann, Paul 110, 136, 142–6, *142*, *144*, 215, 266
Hoffmann, Richard 91
Hofmann, Frank 66, 68
Hofmann, Hans 66
Hofmannsthal, Hugo von 106
Hokianga region 251
Hölderlin, Friedrich 79
Hollar, Wenceslaus 70
Holloway, J.E. 187
Holmes, Paul 261
Holst, Gustav 90
Holstein 37
Holyoake, Keith 240, 241
Hooker, Richard 170
Hoops, Professor 148
Hopkins, Gerard Manley 143
Hos, Kees 126
Houston, Michael 216
Hubrich, Peter 269
Huchel, Peter 79, 272
Hughes, Rev. Gladstone 178
Hulme, Keri 248
Humboldt, Alexander von 67
Hundertwasser, Friedensreich 59, 71, 128–32, *128*
Hunter, Thomas 140
Huth, Hanno 103
Hutt Valley 194, 231
Hutt, Michael 221

Ibsen, Henrik 116
Ikin, Bridget 100
Innsbruck 73
Ireland, Kevin 84

Jackson, Peter 103
Jacob, Alfred 155
Jacobsson, Per 165
Jacoby, Eduard Georg *see* Jacoby, Peter
Jacoby, Felix 204
Jacoby, Ilse (née Moschel) 204, 205, 206, 207
Jacoby, Margarete (née von der Leyen) 204
Jacoby, Peter 179, 204–7, *205*, *207*
Jaggar, A.H. 181
Jaspers, Karl 148
John, Augustus 154

Johnson, Louis 116
Jones, Stan 154

Kaa, Wi Kuki 102
Kaingaroa 194
Kaiteriteri 258
Kalkstein, Major 53
Kane, Lieutenant Pat 15
Kant, Immanuel 137
Kapiti Coast 197
Karaka County 142
Karori 204
Katschke, Otto *43*, 220, *220*
Kaurinui Valley 59, 128
Kawakawa 131
Kelling, Carl 251
Kelling, Fedor 251
Kelly, Petra 257
Kermadec Islands 8, 41
Kertész, André 66
Khandallah 197
Kiechlinsbergen 106
Kiel 204, 206
King, Michael 241
Kinkel, Klaus 237, 239, 240
Kippenberger, Major-General Howard 13
Kircheiss, Lieutenant 38, 39, *39*, 40, 42
Kirkness, Alan 154
Klebe, Giselher 90
Klein, Detlef 73
Klein, Trude 147, 149, 151
Kleist, Heinrich von 117
Klimt, Gustav 128
Kling, Lieutenant 38
Koenig, Gottfried Michael 93
Köglmeier, Siegfried 71–2
Kohl, Helmut 237, 239, 240
Königsberg 137, 229
Köpf, Gerhard 82–4, *83*
Körling, Herr 51, 55
Kraus, Lili 225
Krause, Paul *43*, 220
Kreisler, Fritz 114
Krems 142
Kremsmünster 142
Kronfeld, Laura (née Liebman) 113
Kronfeld, Salomon 113
Kuczynski, Jürgen 167
Kuhn, Thomas 172
Kühtze, Caecilia (née Gierssen) 180
Kühtze, Carl 180
Kühtze, Elizabeth Gretchen 181
Kühtze, Joseph Friedrich 177, 180–5, *181*

Kühtze, Miriam 183
Kühtze, William Joseph *see* Coutts, William
Kulka, Henry 177
Kunert, Günter 82
Kunert, Paul *43*, 220
Kurisches Haff 229
Kyd, Warren 261

L'Estrange, Jo 228
La Hood, Grant 103
Laby, William 140
Lake Manapouri 187, 231
Lake Te Anau 187
Lake Wakatipu 187
Lake, Harry 166
Lamsdorf 50
Lang, Henry 164, 192
Lang, May 121
Lang, Walt 121
Lange, David 23, 241
Lassalle, Ferdinand 157
Lavin, Mr 200
Lawrence, D.H. 79, 140
Le Corbusier, Charles-Édouard 194
Leach, Bernard 197
Leeming, Major 37, 42
Leipzig 90, 91, 106
Lemchen, Barbara 200
Lemchen, Georg 179, 199–203, *202, 203*
Lemchen, Hannah 200
Lemchen, Ruth 200, 201, *202*
Lemchen, Susi 200
Lemmer, Julius 135
Lenz, Eva Maria 100
Lenz, Siegfried 82, 272
Levuka 39
Liebermann, Max 200
Liegnitz 137
Liesing 193
Lilburn, Douglas 91, 116
Lindsay, Alex 116, 121, 225
Lintz, Chris 251
Lochore, Reuel 29, *240*, 241
Lockwood, Annea 93
Logan, Colonel Robert 40
Lorenz, Almuth 251, 252
Lovelock, Jack 78
Lower Hutt 45, 113, 117, 201
Luckner, Count Felix von 3, 8, 37–49, *37, 39, 43, 44, 45*, 68, 218, 219, 220, 221, 223
Luckner, Count Nikolaus von 37
Luckner, Countess Ingeborg von 37, *43, 44, 44, 45*, 46, 220, 221

Ludwig Ferdinand, Prince of Bavaria 218, 219
Lyttelton 8, 161
Lyttelton Harbour 8, 42, *43*

Macarthur, Ian 230
Macdonald, Colonel C. R. 41
Mackay, Yvonne 100
Maconie, Robin 91, 92–3, *92*
Maddock, Shirley 46
Maderna, Bruno 91
Magdeburg 204, 273
Mahler, Gustav 90, 93, 192
Mai, Uli 200, 201
Main River 156
Main, Stewart 103
Mainz 147, 148, 149, 150, 252
Major, John 256
Manapouri, Lake *see* Lake Manapouri
Mangakino 194
Mann, Thomas 79, 106, 107, 145
Mannheim 95
Mansfield, Katherine 77, 78–9, *79*, 84, 85
Manuherikia 181
Marc, Franz 150
Mareikura, Matiu 102
Marlborough 251, 252
Marshall, Owen 228
Marshall, Sir John 230
Martinborough 251
Martínez Sierra, Gregorio 115
Marton 23
Marx, Karl 157, 160
Mason, H.R.G. 214
Mason, R.A.K. 82, 109, 116, 143
Massey, William 21, 41, 140, 141
Masterton 45
Maynard, John 100
McCahon, Colin 65, 125, 126
McClelland, Sarah 228
McGechan, Robert 230
McKay, Mr 23
McKenzie, Don 144
McLeod, Jenny 91, 92, *92*
McNeish, James 77–8
McPherson 39
McQueen, Cilla 77, 78
Meliskey, Redmond Kirp 182
Messerschmidt, Ute 245, 247
Messiaen, Olivier 92
Methven 169
Meyer, Werner 103
Milton, John 143
Mita, Merata 97

Mitford family 120
Moholy–Nagy, László 66
Moog, Christa 84, 85
Moore, Colin 221
Mopelia Atoll 8, 38, 43, 220
Mörike, Eduard 79
Morrison, Bruce 95
Morwitz, Ernst 143
Motuihe Island 3, 8, 21, 37, 37, 39, *39*,
    40, *40*, 41, 42, 45, *45*, 177
Mount Eden 108, *108*
Mount Roskill 194, *195*
Moutere 251
Mozart, Wolfgang Amadeus 201
Mühsam, Helmut 163, *163*
Muldoon, Robert 166, 241, *269*
Mulgan, John 99
Mülheim 12
Müller, Karl *43*, 220
Müllers 68
Munich 66, 71, 73, 97, 106, 218, 219
Munz, Anne (née Vickerman) 170
Munz, Carlotta 169
Munz, Eva 169
Munz, Leo 169
Munz, Peter 136, 144, 158, 169–74, *170*,
    172
Muroroa Atoll 248, 256
Murphy, Geoff 100
Murphy, Walter 15
Murry, John Middleton 79, 85
Muschg, Adolf 82
Musil, Robert 145

Nadolny, Sten 248
Naenae 194
Napier 66, 181
Napier (electorate) 261
Narbey, Leon 97
Nash, Walter 25
Neckar River 156
Nelson 251, 258, 259, 264
Nelson area 19
Nerger, Captain Karl August 8
Neuhaus 186
Neumann, Professor 148
Neurath, Otto 157
Neustadt an der Weinstrasse 253, 254
New Guinea 7
New Plymouth 24
Newman, Frederick 177
Ngauranga 215
Nidden 229
Nieschmidt, Hans-Werner 266
Nietzsche, Friedrich 79, 145

Nikisch, Arthur 114
Ninety Mile Beach 247
Nippert brothers 24
Niue 38
Nono, Luigi 91
Norsewood 182, 183
North Cape 8
North Shore (electorate) 261
Northcote 223
Northland 126
Nuremberg 94, 118, 120, 124, 148, 200

Oberhausen 97
Obermayer, August 271
O'Connor, D.D. (Dan) 116
Oesterreich, Hans Günther 220
Onegin, Sigrid 114
Opawa 196
Opononi 84
Opua 129
Orage, A.R. 79
Orakei 193
Orbanz, Eva 101
Orff, Carl 90, 93
Oriental Bay 115
Ormondville 180, 182, 183, *183*
O'Shea, John 95, 96, 97–8, 101
Ost, Frederick 65
Ostrava 65
Otago 180, 187, 188, 190
Otahuhu 180, 184, 221
Otaki (electorate) 261

Paderborn 186
Page, Frederick 91, *91*, 92
Pahiatua 9, 164
Palmer, Geoffrey 256
Palmerston North 45, 180, 181, 184,
    266, 268
Panzer, Professor 148
Paparoa 155
Parton, Hugh 158
Paul, Blackwood 195
Paul, Janet 124
Pearl, Ruth 122
Penrose 221
Petrarch 150
Philips, Julius 123, *123*
Philips, Kurt *123*, 124
Philips, Margot 59, 65, 123–7, *123*, *125*
Philips, Selma 123, *123*
Picton 72
Pillsbury, Sam 96
Piranesi, Giovanni 70
Plato 160

Plischke, Anna (formerly Lang-Schwizer) 69, 192, 197
Plischke, Ernst 35, 69, 177, 192–8, *192*
Pohlmann, Gerd 97
Pomerania 78
Popper, Sir Karl 35, 109, 136, 157–61, *159*, 170, 171
Porsolt, Imre 177
Porter, George 194, 196
Posen 199
Pound, Ezra 143
Pousseur, Henri 91
Poverty Bay 252
Prague 66, 147, 148, 150
Prideaux, Editha Greville 154
Prussia 137, 224
Puhoi 21, 154

Rainbow, Stephen 258
Randow, Ilse von 70
Ranov, Theo 214, 215
Rare, Vanessa 102
Rarotonga 97
Rauch, Professor 148
Raumati 197
Reagan, Ronald 256
Red Mercury Island 41
Reed, Alan 158
Reger, Max 90
Reid, Nicholas 98
Reinhardt, Max 114
Remuera 118
Renger-Patzsch, Albert 68
Rheinhessen 252
Rhine 147
Rhineland 147
Rhodes, H. Winston 165
Richards, Pia 110
Richardson, Sir George 45
Ridley-Smith, Roger 211
Rie, Lucie 197
Riethmaier, Elsie 223
Riethmaier, Gregory *43*, 68–9, 178, 218–23, *218*, *220*
Rihm, Wolfgang 94
Rilke, Rainer Maria 79, 80, 106, 114
Ripapa Island 37, 42, *43*, 45
Robb, Douglas 107
Roberts, 'Tiki' 221
Robinson, Sir Dove Myer 71
Rodchenko, Aleksandr 66
Rodin, Auguste 150
Rodney (electorate) 261
Rommel, General Erwin 5, 14, *15*, 16
Rongotea 23

Rosenberg, Ann (née Eichelbaum) 164
Rosenberg, Bill 168
Rosenberg, George 166, 167
Rosenberg, Gerhard 162
Rosenberg, Wolfgang 136, 162–8, *163*, *167*
Rosenfeld, Max 177
Roth, George 158
Rothmund, Sigi 97
Rotorua 222, 226
Rowling, Sir Wallace 162
Ruben, Margot 107, 108, 109, 110, *110*, 111, 143
Runciman 143, *144*
Russell, Bertrand 157, 158, 170

Salmon, Guy 260
Salmond, George 179, 210, 212, 213
Salter, Len 155
Sametz, Philip 93
Samoa 6, 7, 9, 19, 20, 39, 40, 42, 178, 220, 222
Sangl, Heribert (Harry) 71
Sargeson, Frank 82, 84, 109, 110, 143, 144, 155
Sartoris, Alberto 193
Satchell, William 77, 78, 86
Sauer, Professor 148
Savage, Deborah 103
Savage, Michael Joseph 6
Scales, Flora 66
Schat, Peter 92
Scheel, Walter 71, 237, 239, *240*, 268, 269, *269*
Schellbach, Oscar 219, 223
Schiele, Egon 128
Schiller, Friedrich 78
Schlag, Evelyn 84
Schlosser, Katrin 102
Schmidt, Armin 63
Schnabel, Artur 225
Schoenauer, Peter 71, 72–3
Schoenberg, Arnold 91, 92
Schorss, Erika *29*, 94, 121, 149
Schrödinger, Erwin 158
Schubert, Franz 208
Schulz, Dr 39, 42
Schuster, Daniel 251, 253
Schwartz, Joseph 114
Schwarzort 229
Scott, Margaret 85
Seaview 215
Seibel, Norbert 251, 252, *253*
Seifried, Hermann 251
Seresin, Harry 226

Seuffert, Anton 73
Sewald, Hugh 21
Sewell, Arthur 107, 143
Shadbolt, Maurice 83, 84, 98
Shakespeare, William 116, 143
Shand, Carol 210, 213
Shand, Tom 166, 210
Sharell, Richard 66, 67, 68
Shaw, George Bernard 114, 116
Shelton, Lindsay 96
Shorland, W.P. 230
Sierra *see* Martínez Sierra, Gregorio
Silesia 137, 204
Simkin, Colin 158
Skinner, H.D. 189
Small, Tony 244
Smalley, Denis 92
Smith, Campbell 125
Smith, Shirley 196
Smith, Sir David 164
Smits, Kathryn 272
Society Islands 8, 38
Somes Island 9, 20, *20*, 21, 39, 140, 177,
    178, 218, 222, *222*
Sorenson, Jans Christian 183, 184
Southern Alps 247
Spangenberg 50
Steidinger, Uwe 73
Steinhof, Caesar 109
Steinhof, Hanna 109
Sternberg, Alfred 199, 200, 202
Stettin 219
Stockhausen, Karlheinz 90, 91, 92, *92*,
    93, 94
Stowasser, Elsa 128
Stowasser, Friedrich *see* Hundertwasser,
    Friedensreich
Straub, Mr 39
Strauss, Alice 110, *110*
Strauss, Franz-Josef 239
Strauss, Richard 90, 94
Strauss, Wolf 110
Strewe, Chris 69
Strewe, Odo 69
Strindberg, August 114
Struck, Hermann 63
Stuckenschmidt, Hans-Heinz 90, 93
Student, General Kurt 14
Sutch, W.B. 196, 204
Sutherland, I.L.G. 158
Sutton, Martin 154
Suva 39

Tacitus 245
Tahiti *43*, 220, *220*, *245*

Taihape 22, 180, 184, 197
Taita 194
Takapuna 84
Tamahori, Lee 103
Tamaki 194
Tamaki (electorate) 259
Tapsell, Peter 131
Tarakohe 194
Tasman, Abel Janszoon 194, 245
Taupo 222
Taylor, Gary 260
Te Anau, Lake *see* Lake Te Anau
Te Kauwhata 251
Texidor, Greville 154, 155
Thames 23
Thatcher, Margaret 256
Theresienstadt 150
Thiele, Frederick *43*, 220
Thiele, Jürgen 73
Thorn, Max 22
Thorndon 230, 232
Tillich, Paul 114
Tomalin, Claire 85
Tönnies, Ferdinand 179, 204, 206
Trentham 194, *195*
Trittin, Juergen 257
Tübingen 145
Turner, Lieutenant-Colonel C.H. 40, 41
Turnovsky, Fred 62, 216, 225
Turvey, Eleanor 181
Tuwhare, Hone 77
Tyler, Linda 193

Ueberweg, Friedrich 206
Upper Hutt 179, 200, 202
Upper Moutere 23, 251

Varnham, Mary 149
Vaughan Williams, Ralph 90
Vienna 45, 64, 68, 110, 113, 114, 128,
    129, 144, 157, 188, 192, 193, 198, 208,
    214, 243, 244
Vieregg, Axel 272
Viëtor, Karl 148

Wachau district 142
Wagner, Richard 79, 90, 93, 94
Waigel, Theo 244
Waiheke Island 258, 261
Waihirere 251
Waikanae 197
Waikato region 59, 123, 124, 126, 127,
    142
Waitemata Harbour 118
Wakatipu, Lake *see* Lake Wakatipu

Wakaya Island 38, 39
Waldberg, Professor von 148
Walker, Tim 126
Walter, Bruno 114
Wanganui 23, 122, 140
Ward, Vincent 99–100, 101
Weill, Kurt 94
Weinberger, Caspar 212
Weizsäcker, Richard von 237, 239, *239*, *241*, 271
Wellington *10*, 21, 28, *28*, 32, 44, 45, 67, 68, 72, 93, 101, 102, 115, 116, 118, 121, 122, 124, 131, 138, 139, 145, 161, 163, 164, 166, 192, 193, 194, 195, 196, 197, 198, 200, 201, 202, 204, 206, 210, 214, 215, 221, 225, 226, 227, 229, 258, 269, 273
Wellington Harbour 8, 25, 39
Wells, Peter 103
West Clive 180, 182
Westbrook, Eric 70, 125
Westland 187
Westphal, Lilian 272
Weyher, Captain Kurt 8
Whangarei 129
White, Frederick 158
Wilkinson, Janet 194

Willendorf 142
Williams, Sir Oswald Michael 214
Wilson, Gordon 193
Winter, Holm *43*, 220, *220*
Wittgenstein, Ludwig 157, 158, 170, 172, 192
Wohnsiedler, Friedrich 22, 251
Wolfskehl, Hanna (née de Haan) 106, 110, 111
Wolfskehl, Karl 35, 59, 81–2, 86, 106–12, *108*, *110*, *111*, 143, 144
Wood, Fred 121, 170
Wood, Joan 121
Woollaston, Toss 66
Wootten, Mr 182

Zanussi, Krzysztov 95
Zatorski, Walther von *39*, 40
Zedlitz, Baroness Mary von (née Wolff) 138
Zedlitz, George von 9, 22, 135, 137–41, *139*, 158, 159
Zedlitz, Karl Abraham von 137
Zimmermann, Jenner 73–4
Zimmermann, Walter 92, 94
Zuckermann, Wolfgang 120
Zürich 73